This BOOK is NOT REQUIRED

THIRD EDITION

An Emotional Survival Manual for Students

INGE BELL ▮ BERNARD McGRANE
Chapman University

JOHN GUNDERSON
Chapman University

PINE FORGE PRESS
An Imprint of Sage Publications, Inc.
Thousand Oaks • London • New Delhi

For information, address:

Pine Forge Press
A Sage Publications Company
2455 Teller Road
Thousand Oaks, California 91320
(805) 499–4224
E-mail: sales@pfp.sagepub.com

Sage Publications Ltd
1 Oliver's Yard
55 City Road
London EC1Y 1SP
United Kingdom

Sage Publications India Pvt. Ltd.
B-42, Panchsheel Enclave
Post Box 4109
New Delhi 110 017 India

Printed in the United States of America

Library of Congress Cataloging-in-Publication Data

Bell, Inge.
   This book is not required : an emotional survival manual for students / by Inge Bell, Bernard McGrane, and John Gunderson.— 3rd ed.
       p. cm.
   Includes bibliographical references and index.
       ISBN 1-4129-1011-0 (pbk.)
   1. College students—United States. 2. Universities and colleges—United States. 3. College students—United States—Psychology. 4. Universities and colleges—Social aspects—United States. I. McGrane, Bernard. II. Gunderson, John. III. Title.

04   05   06   07   08   10   9   8   7   6   5   4   3   2   1

Acquiring Editor:	Jerry Westby
Associate Editor:	Ben Penner
Editorial Assistant:	Vonessa Vondera
Production Editor:	Sanford Robinson
Copy Editor:	Cheryl Duksta
Typesetter:	C&M Digitals (P) Ltd.
Indexer:	Naomi Linzer
Cover Designer:	Ravi Balasuriya

This
BOOK
is NOT
REQUIRED

THIRD EDITION

*To my dear one and my inspiration, Rupa,
and to my beloved daughter, my one and only Melanie.*

Bernard McGrane

*To my loving wife Holly and two beautiful boys,
Dan and Jack. You give my life meaning, joy and inspiration.*

John Gunderson

Contents

Preface to the First Edition   vii

Preface to the Second Edition   ix

Preface to the Third Edition   xi

1. Welcome to College   1

2. Grades: Can You Perform Without the Pressure?   39

3. Support Your Local Teacher: Or the Care and Feeding of Professors   59

4. An Academic Question   73

5. Questions of Academic Integrity   83

6. Everybody Hates to Write   91

7. Wisdom and Knowledge   103

8. Pursuing Wisdom in the Academy   115

9. Adventures in Desocialization   129

10. Media Me   145

11. Love   153

12. Trouble With Parents   179

13. The Painful Avenues of Upward Mobility   197

14. Graduation—What They Forgot to Mention   211

15. The Career: Friend or Foe?   223

16. Directing Your Own Development   235

Appendix 1. For Teachers and Students Using This Book   243

Appendix 2. Buddhist Sociology   247

References   259

Index   261

About the Author and Contributors   269

Preface to the First Edition

This is a book that invites you to look at your college education: what it could be, and what, alas, it often is. It is a book which suggests to you what you can make of this opportunity, given the resources at your disposal. If you want to become truly educated, you will have to educate yourself, and at times you will have to do it in spite of the academy. Perhaps this is good, because knowledge which comes too easily doesn't train one to be an independent thinker, and only an independent thinker is ever truly intelligent.

We will not look at these four years merely in terms of the formal world of classes and professors. We want to look at the larger experience: at your whole environment and your whole life during these four years, because some of the most important learning is always done outside the classroom.

I have tried to make this a survival manual for undergraduates: emotional survival and intellectual survival. I will even say that it speaks to the issues of spiritual survival, if by "spiritual" we mean the capacity to live in harmony with oneself and with the universe.

You will undoubtedly disagree with parts of this book. It is only one person's view. But if it connects with your life at any important point, I shall feel that it has served its purpose for you. I have tried to give you the broadest possible picture of your position as a student in the academic world and in the larger society of which you are a part. To do this, I have had to use a large brush, and I have undoubtedly made mistakes. But I have always considered this broad perspective more important than the fine attention to detail given by the academic specialists.

This is not an academic or scholarly work. It is a very critical look at academia by one who has been through it from freshman to full professor. Occasionally, I will suggest a book which I think you might like. But you will not find an *ibid.* or an *op. cit.* littering these pages.

In my years as a college teacher, I succeeded in what was ever the chief ambition of my career: to keep my students awake. Of course, there were always a comatose few who hadn't gotten to bed until four in the morning, or had mononucleosis, or were merely in love. But on the whole, I succeeded because I discovered that students always came awake when I laid aside academic sociology and talked to them about their lives as students—about the academic institutions in which they labored, and the how and why of how those institutions functioned; about the competition and anxiety created by grades; about their ambitions and their difficult choices of major and career; about the travail of those who came from minority or working-class families; yes, even about their love affairs and their loneliness. We talked about how you find out what you want to do in life and about how you can keep your integrity and your sanity in this very difficult society.

Eventually, drawing on sociology and Eastern philosophy, I developed a course devoted solely to these questions. I shall describe that to you in the chapter "Adventures in Desocialization" and give you some of the exercises and "walking meditations" which I used to help students gain insight into their own functioning.

As I discussed life in the academy with my students, I also listened, and learned a lot. It is therefore to all my former students that I dedicate this little book, because much of what I have written here I learned from them.

It is, perhaps, ironic that after writing a chapter called "Everybody Hates to Write," I found myself hugely enjoying the process of writing this book. After the writing I had done in the usual, stilted language of social science, it was a huge relief to talk good English. I always loved to write, and I think I did pretty well at it until I got to graduate school and had all the style knocked out of me by the demands of academic sociologese. I always resisted a little. I remember my dissertation chairman asking me sadly whether I had "turned against sociology" because I used too much plain English. In writing this book, I felt that I had regained my writing voice after 30 years.

Acknowledgments

I hope you will bear with me for a moment while I thank the good friends who helped me write this book. My thanks to Glenn Goodwin of Pitzer College who helped me, as he has helped so many students and colleagues through the years, by commenting on and improving the manuscript. Above all, he has given me constant inspiration and encouragement. Glenn struggled mightily with me to provide more documentation and to give credit to more of the sociologists whose insights I have used. I resisted, because I didn't want this to be a scholarly book. But I should say here that most of what I know has come to me through the great sociologists I have studied, as well as the writers of Eastern thought. Probably the only original thing about the book is its focus on undergraduate life.

My thanks equally to Ellin Ringler Henderson of Pitzer College, who made many useful suggestions and whose careful, loving red pencil brought elegance and clarity to my prose. I would also like to thank Barney McGrane for using the book in his teaching long before it was published. Barney sent me much valuable student feedback and encouraged me greatly in the writing of the book. My thanks also to Dawn Hassett, who suggested the title.

Finally, of course, my warmest thanks to Ted Hoffman, who helped with the writing. His confidence in me and my work has been my mainstay.

Needless to say, the errors and shortcomings of the book are entirely my own.

My thanks also to my former colleagues and to the staff and faculty of Pitzer College for creating an environment in which innovative teaching was not only permitted but rewarded.

—*Inge Bell*

Preface to the Second Edition

As a professor committed to the possibility of the college classroom being a space of transformative education, enlightenment, and joyous discovery, I have found that Inge Bell's *This Book Is Not Required* is, simply, indispensable. I have used it for many years in almost all my classes with extraordinary effect.

"It was not a fish that discovered water," an old saying goes. Why? For a fish, water is too deeply familiar, too ordinary—hence, invisible. Bell's book, using the wisdom of sociology, somehow helps us school-fish recognize, for the first time, the deeply familiar-yet-invisible institution of school that we have been swimming in all along.

Through the initiative of Steve Rutter, the innovative founder of Pine Forge Press—a house that I see as adventurously committed to quality education rather than merely safe, profitable textbooks—it became clear that, as classic and timeless as Bell's book is, nevertheless it was in need of revising and updating, sort of like a historic building. The task was balancing "what's new?" with "what's best?"—two ancient human concerns. At the same time it became clear that those best suited to this task would be the fish themselves: students who have most deeply been transformed, touched, and awakened by her work. Their ear is most finely tuned for intuitively distinguishing what in the book sounds dated from what is "timeless" and perpetually current—similar to noticing dated bell-bottom trousers in an otherwise timeless film. I began announcing this project in my classes and just spreading the word. Students began self-selecting themselves. We got together, named ourselves "Team Bell," and began the work according to our own ability and our own need. This was an opportunity, both as a team and as individuals, to give back and contribute to this work, this collective vision and enterprise of educational liberation founded on the dignity and basic goodness of *students* everywhere.

What's new? The language and examples have been freshly painted in current events where necessary. Whole new sections have been added to many chapters and two new chapters were added as well—"Media" and "Graduation." Our vision—using the Internet—and our invitation is that you, our readers, our student brothers and sisters, will in your turn, feel the calling to also take up this wondrous task of educational awakening.

I would especially like to thank the reviewers for *This Book Is Not Required,* First Revised Edition:

Robert E. L. Roberts, California State University, San Marcos

Monika Ardelt, University of Florida

F. Kurt Cylke, SUNY, Geneseo

Peter Espinosa, Saddleback College

Rolf Kjolseth, University of Colorado

Richard Mason, Hobart and William Smith College

Susan McWilliams, University of Southern Maine

Michael Miller, University of Texas, San Antonio

There were a number of us originally on Team Bell who through life's ever unknown twists were unable to remain and I'd like to acknowledge them here: Meredith Sanders, Lori Feldmeyer, Marco McFerren, Maria Rebecchi, Brian Pilgram, Shahib Zagari, and Melissa Giordano. I also want to thank Elisabeth Scatina for her cover idea and Kate Chilton for her superb copyediting skills. Ted Hoffman, Inge's husband, has been truly generous and supportive in keeping her work alive and Diana Dahl has been excellent and steadfast as business manager and distributor.

—*Barney McGrane*

Preface to the Third Edition

The third edition of *This Book Is Not Required* continues to mark out a new realm in college participatory education. Two new chapters, one titled "Welcome to College" and another titled "Questions of Academic Integrity," have been added as well as numerous new student essays. *This Book* was worked on and composed by college students (we continue to call ourselves "Team Bell") under the leadership of Dr. Bernard McGrane, a sociology professor at Chapman University, and Dr. John Gunderson, an education professor at Chapman and a high school teacher. McGrane was a colleague of the late Inge Bell and an heir to her vision of Buddhist sociology. We continue to view *This Book Is Not Required* as a collaborative, participatory work with you, the student readers. We would like to keep it a *living*, continuously relevant document, updated and expanded every 4 years (one college generation). We therefore extend an invitation to those of you who, as you read this book, become inspired—inspired as we were—to become coauthors of the next edition of this work. We invite you to join Team Bell. This is an opportunity for you to contribute to your own university education and to make a difference for the next generation of college students and the quality of their education.

We would like to thank the members of Team Bell for this, the third edition: Christopher Patrick King, Veronica Fematt, Andy Wang, Lawrence Lu, Kenneth Chow, Jeff Chen, Sunshine Serrano, Artin Sodaify, Shawna Wood, Andrea Crane, Jasleen Ahuja, Ann Tsueng, Jordon Kagan, Nkemdilim Nwosu, Lisa Miyake, Melissa Reggiardo, Sara Kalawi, Gagendeep Sandhu, Christine Hebling, Sheyda Bogosyan, Stavros Kavoulakis, Christie Vong, Lauren Bragg, Ann Amigable, Katherine Ho, and My Pha Ninh.

We would also like to thank the reviewers of *This Book is Not Required,* Third Edition:

Jane Penny, Eastfield College

Laura Nathan, Mills College

Gina Petonito, Western Illinois University

Ed Sbarbaro, Colorado College

Rik Scarce, Montana State University/Skidmore College

Michael Weinstein, University of Hawaii, Manoa

Alan Willis, Northern Michigan University

> *The years which a student spends in a school must leave behind in him a fragrance and delight.*
>
> Krishnamurti (1974)

In *Horse Feathers,* Groucho Marx plays Professor Wagstaff, president of Huxley College. As a money-saving move, he suggests tearing down the dormitories. "But, Professor," says the dean, "where will the students sleep?"
"Where they always sleep—in the classroom!"

Barney McGrane, John Gunderson
mcgrane@chapman. edu; gunderson@chapman. edu

CHAPTER 1

Welcome to College

elcome to . . . is a sign we are all familiar with. Most of us pass these words on signposts around our hometowns and don't pay much attention. However, when we embark on a journey, these signs take on new meanings and indicate we are entering a foreign land filled with new culture, new customs, new ideas, and new vocabulary. As most travelers know, even the most ordinary necessities can be hard to find in a new location if you don't know how to ask or look. These disconcerting situations can range from silly and embarrassing to dangerous or life threatening. Luckily, most of these traps can be avoided with a little help or guidance.

College is also a destination to which we travel. It doesn't turn out to be much different from traveling to a foreign land for most new students. The same problems that afflict most new travelers in a foreign land can be seen in the experiences of new students on campus. Unfamiliar terrain, foreign culture, unknown rules and customs can make a new student stand out on a campus like a stereotypical backpack-wearing, camera-holding tourist in a foreign city. Even the most confident educational travelers need a guidebook to help make sense of this new world they are entering.

Unfortunately, most colleges don't have a simple guidebook that explains some of the real do's and taboos of college life. Many travelers now pick up guidebooks before they head off to a foreign land to help keep them out of trouble and make their transition a little easier. New students, on the other hand, are left to fend for themselves as they are immersed into this new world. Frequently, this lack of information can get our new travelers at the college into a bit of trouble that could have been avoided with a little help. One saving grace for most new students is their numerous fellow students; they are not alone in their struggles.

The plight of the new student is not hidden from view or unknown; even the words used to describe them illuminate their situation: *freshmen, underclassmen.* These anxious new educational travelers are fresh and ripe for picking if someone wants to take advantage of them, just like a traveler in a foreign land. It is like a rite of passage for many of us who have experienced this awkward vulnerability. It is almost as if we tell ourselves that we went through it ourselves, so it can't be that bad.

The result is that there is not much help, guidance, and condolence for the educational traveler in this transition. However, a little help and guidance can go a long way in making your transition to this new land a much happier, safer, and more successful journey. Ask for help from some of the "locals," who are always good guides, and after asking don't forget to listen. Remember a description of the terrain is much different from the experience of the culture, and remember your seasoned educational travelers have already paved the way.

Listen to some of these travel guides in the pages that follow and then map a course for yourself.

Welcome to college.

To Shed the High School Self and Awaken to the College Self

A Senior's Advice

Before I graduated high school, I had this sudden realization—in a couple of short months I would be in college! What would it be like? Would I make new friends? Would the classes be too hard? I had a million questions that it just seemed that no one could answer. I had a few friends who were already in college, so I decided to ask for some advice. The best advice I got at this time came from one of my best friends who was attending UC Irvine's (UCI) undergraduate school at the time. He told me not to be afraid or intimidated by anything. He opened my eyes to the fact that each of us was in the same boat, especially as incoming freshmen. It doesn't matter if you were valedictorian or a mediocre student in your high school bubble, *when you get to college you start from square one.* Professors don't know if you were a stellar student in high school or not. Their opinions of you are entirely based on your performance from the first day of class onward.

Also, my friend told me to be aggressive and ask a lot of questions. Sometimes it can be intimidating to raise your hand in a room of one hundred students in order to clarify a point. Am I asking a dumb question? Are people going to laugh at me and think I am stupid? No way. He told me that what I had to say was important, and that most likely the people sitting next to me had the same questions on the tips of their tongues; they were just too scared to ask. I totally found this to be true as I dove headfirst into my freshman year. It was amazing. I could almost see neighboring students thanking me with their eyes as I asked the professor to reiterate a point. Plus, I built my confidence, communication skills, and ensured that I fully understood the lesson being taught.

Regarding friendships, those come with time if you embrace them. Chances are your two best buddies in high school are off to life in the real world or in college in another city. For the first time in your life you are probably removed from your comfort zone and submerged in a world of strangers. This can be scary, but before you make friends with anybody you need to make friends with yourself.

This time of independence promotes a lot of soul searching and testing of your morals. If you were an angel in high school, you can rebel at any moment and explore a whole new world of trouble (or vice versa). While not being assigned to a set track of required classes, you might find yourself spending a lot of time alone. This alone time may be a first for you, and it can be weird initially. Even if you live on campus with a roommate, it doesn't guarantee a 24-hour companion. During these times outside of a group, it is great to look inside yourself and get to know who you are as a person. All kinds of questions come up if you allow yourself to embrace these thoughts. What makes you happy? What do you look for in a friend? What kind of food do you like? What is God? You never stop learning about yourself, but college is a great place to start this healthy habit. For me, once this exploring had begun, I became much more comfortable with myself, and as a result I became more comfortable around others. It was only natural that I later made some great friendships that have brought me much happiness. I really feel that these words of advice were really what gave me the confidence to begin the journey through college that had intimidated me for so long. Now I am about to graduate, and I find that I have grown in so many ways and made so many new friends. College was a wonderful experience during which I learned a lot about people, the world, and most importantly, myself.

Sarah Kalawi

Orientation Is Required

I highly recommend going to orientations. This is where I met some of the most interesting people who are now my friends; one has become my roommate for 2 years and probably more. When I first stepped into the big university in the big city I was scared. I had no friends. I didn't know my way around. After orientation, I knew my way around this large campus almost like the town I grew up in. Next, living in the dorms is awesome. If you live near campus, you should still live in the dorm. This place helped me socially and intellectually. Everything was there! First I became friends with my roommates, then neighbors, soon the whole floor. It helps to leave the room door open, and also living in front of the elevators helps. You should also participate in floor activities organized by the floor's program assistants or residential advisors. I'm not saying it's a must to go to all of the events, but go to as many as you can at least for the first 5 weeks. Networking is very important in college, not to mention an essential for life once you're out of school. More places to meet people are found by joining clubs or fraternities or sororities. But beware—don't fall into the segregated cliques or groups. I opted to stay out of the fraternity system, but this doesn't mean I can never communicate or party with them. You just need to know one or two of the members in the Greek house to reap the benefits. This includes getting into parties with those long lines that don't seem to move because only the girls are being let in. Basically, the strategy is to start with whatever you feel comfortable with—start small. I started small and branched out; it's better that way, plus it feels good to know people almost everywhere you go.

Kenneth W. Chow Jr.

Making Decisions Alone

A tough question I had to ask myself after entering college was, Am I happy with the decisions I am making? This question took on a whole new meaning from when I asked myself this in high school. In high school, the decisions I made were affected by parents, counselors, friends, coaches, and mentors. College brought a feeling of indescribable loneliness. I don't live with my parents, counselors are hard to come by, I have a whole new set of friends who don't really know me, I don't play a sport anymore, and I have yet to find someone I can really confide in here.

The decisions I make seem to be more individualized and unguided than ever. So how do I know that I'm making the right ones? My parents have given up on their dreams of making me their little doctor. I've switched majors, picked up new hobbies, and made friends that are polar opposites from friends I had in high school. This has been the biggest handle I've had on the decision-making process of my entire life. When I was a kid, choosing which flavor ice cream I wanted from the store was hard enough. Chocolate or mint chocolate? Decisions, decisions, decisions!

These days, my decisions are much tougher than ice cream. The hardest and most conflicting decisions for me are deciding what major to choose and deciding what I want to do when I graduate from college. It's a constant battle between practicality and passion. I'm continually reversing the choices I make—one minute I'm an English major with a political science minor, the next minute I'm a political science major with an English minor. The routes continue to intertwine—I'm not exactly sure which path I'm even on anymore.

Or is a path even necessary? Often, I wonder why it is that I can't just take classes that sound interesting, whether they be psychology classes, political science classes, math classes, or English classes. Someone suggested that I become a liberal arts major, and that didn't seem like such a bad idea. Then my cell phone rings, and I get into a long discussion with my parents about "The Future." Dum, da, dum! Their new path for me, law school, looms menacingly in front of me. Perhaps law school will provide the comfortable life my parents want to ensure for me. Perhaps when it comes closer to graduation, that is the decision I will make.

For now, I've decided, college has become a place for me to partake in activities that I want to partake in because . . . it's my life. And following my heart has always brought better results than following my head or someone else's heart. I've decided to concentrate my major with creative writing, seen as a wholly impractical decision by some but a wholly inspiring decision for me. I've never felt happier and more secure in my life because in the end the decisions I've made have been decisions that have been the most fulfilling for me.

And that is the lesson I've learned since entering college. College has empowered me to be able to answer my own questions, make my own decisions, and carve my own path in life. That path, titled "Dreams," will be the path I choose to follow for the rest of my waking life.

Jasleen Ahuja

The Image High School Gives You of College

As I entered college, I could honestly say that I must have been blind, or at least tremendously naïve. My take on life was that I would graduate from high school, go on to pursue higher education in college for about four years, graduate, and then start working and have a family life. Let's just say that I was in for a rude awakening. Somewhere toward the middle of my freshman year, I was informed that it would be very difficult for me to make a "decent living" (whatever that may be) with only a bachelor's in psychology. My belief was that I would get my bachelor's and begin practicing clinical psychology. Hah! Little did I know.

I realize how foolish I was now that I look back on all this, *but the truth is that most college students enter college with a completely distorted picture of where their lives are headed.* High schools today are more or less prep schools to get you into colleges, but that's about it. They don't bother teaching students to step back from the high school and college bubbles and look at where they want to see themselves in the end. High schools paint a picture that college is the end of your education, but the truth is that it is only the beginning. It is only after you enter college that you realize you are doing this for you and nobody else (at least, if you're lucky enough).

I believe that this is the time you should actually realize the worth of your education. Everything just begins to make more sense at this point—why you were in school to begin with, why you're taking the classes you are, and how you see yourself applying it to your life in the future. I now understand that I will have to go to grad school for about another 2–4 years after I finish college, but this is not something that I dread. To be honest, I do not feel as though I would even be remotely prepared to go out and practice psychology once I graduated with my bachelor's. I actually want to go on and learn as much as I possibly can so that I may one day be the best psychologist that I am capable of being. However, when I compare the way I am thinking now with the way I was thinking 2 years ago when I was a senior in high school, my mental perception has made a 180-degree turn. Don't get me wrong—I still want to graduate fast so that I can go on with the rest of my life. But the thing is that I have now realized that this is more or less what I will be doing with my life, so there is no need to rush through it. It is better to take it all in and to actually understand what you are doing and pursue it to the end than to do it just for the sake of getting the degree and getting out.

So, basically, my advice is that you should be open to new things when you enter college. The impression that you get of life when you are in high school is not a very accurate one, so you have to be willing to be open-minded when you enter college.

Sheyda Bogosyan

Reflections on Romance and Relationships

Facing the Unknown

No one said it would be easy.

And you can never fully prepare yourself for what life sends your way.

Each day we graduate into a new stage of life. Yet only after every 4 years are we recognized with a diploma for "completing" something, for taking one more step along the educational path. In reality, we ought to receive a diploma much more often than this. Life will be filled with myriad challenges and opportunities that cannot be expected or prepared for. Yet as we "graduate" from each new turn, we learn something much more profound than any class could ever teach us. We find out about life. We take a "class" about *ourselves*.

High school graduates of the class of 2001 experienced the trauma of September 11th before they began their college educations. With the world, they learned a collective lesson about hate, fear, and uncertainty. They reevaluated life and gained deep insights about people.

We all experience change differently, yet we all experience it somehow. September 11th was but a single, vivid change that is easy to pinpoint and recognize. But often we get so caught up in preparing for the next step that we forget to fully immerse ourselves in the moment.

We earn a master's in *doing* while forgetting to master *living*.

We could compile an endless list of everything that you could experience after you graduate. You will enter summer, go on vacation, say good-bye to friends, leave family behind, shop for new clothes, buy supplies for the dorm, and hope that you will be "ready" by the time school starts. The problem is that we all too often forget the changes around us. We will make new friends, but we will leave others. Perhaps we will attend a relative's wedding over the summer, only to resume packing the next day. We are so busy "getting ready" that we miss and fail to deal with the deep, profound change that we are about to experience.

Universities will not offer classes in slowing down and being present to change. But it is the change that we undergo that will most fully impact our lives: marriage and divorce; new friends made, others to whom we bid farewell; excitement for something new; sadness over leaving the "known" of our life behind; birth and death.

Indeed, our diploma marks a completion and a stepping-stone to that which lies ahead. But our diploma in life details something more profound: We shed the high school self and awaken to the college self. The body remains static; the person subconsciously adapts to change.

Some of the changes will be wonderful. Others will be painful. You might fall in love and find a soul mate or a friend. The next day, a beloved grandfather may die. You'll party the night away in pure, unadulterated excitement that finals are over with newfound college friends, then awaken to the reality that alcohol really does cause hangovers.

All that is known is that everything will be unknown.

You cannot fully prepare for change, but you can welcome it when it comes by being fully present to it. You can learn to live and not merely to do.

After 4, 5, or maybe even 6 years, you might earn a diploma for your efforts. But you will never receive an award for the most important classes you shall take in your college career.

The classes in life, learned by waking up each day, will teach you more about yourself and about others than any novel or scientific proof ever can.

Mark Twain said, "I never let my schooling get in the way of my education."

Before graduating as a master of your discipline, graduate first with a mastery of the self.

Christopher Patrick King

Rejected From a College?

One of the hardest reality checks that I have ever had to deal with was receiving a letter of denial from the college that I had dreamed since junior high of attending. Everything that constituted my reality for such a long period of time had suddenly come crashing down, and I had no clue what to do. For all of my high school life, my hopes of getting into that one university was what gave me the drive to push harder and take one more advanced placement (AP) course. But now it seemed as though all that I had based my motivation on had been stolen from me. I had reached the end of the rainbow, and the pot of gold that I had hoped to find there was missing. This unexpected rejection that I faced at the end of my senior year of high school forced me to reevaluate my entire reality, not just for the time being and for the times to come but also for everything that I had endured in the past.

I had attended private school all of my life, and whether we liked it or not the whole class knew everything about each other since all of us, a group of about 45 students, had been together for the previous 12 years. We all had expectations for one another, and we more or less knew what each one of us would do with our lives (or at least we thought we did). Even our teachers knew us on a one-to-one basis and had certain expectations for each of us. Basically, if one of us screwed up, there were a lot of people there to let us know, starting from our parents to our teachers to our friends. For this reason, I felt that, when I got rejected from the school that I was hoping to get into, everyone was really disappointed in me. This may have been a complete distortion of reality. However, I put so much emphasis on getting into that school that I had let it define who I was, and once I got rejected I was afraid that everyone would be disappointed in me. I interpreted people's actions as negatively as possible and felt as though I didn't matter anymore. I was a failure. That one letter of rejection made me evaluate myself from head to toe. I began to wonder if I really deserved to go to that school or if I had what it takes. Maybe I really wasn't good enough for them. Was it that my grades weren't good enough? Or maybe it was my SATs? But that wouldn't make sense since I had friends from other schools that had lower scores than I but had gotten in.

So what could it be then? It must have been my personal statement essay. My experience must not have been as exciting or as dramatic as everyone else's. Maybe that would have done the trick. No matter what I said to myself though, the reality of it was that I wasn't going to be going to that school. *I had done everything that I could, and they felt as though it wasn't good enough.* As disappointed and bitter as I was, I knew that I had to pick another school to go to, so I told my backup school that I would be enrolling there in the fall. I was closing one chapter in the book of my life and opening another. All I could hope for was that this new chapter wouldn't be as disappointing as the previous one.

No matter how much I told myself that this was a whole new beginning for me, the rejection I had faced was embedded in the back of my mind. I felt as though I wasn't good enough and that everyone was much smarter than I. Also, I lost a great deal of confidence in my writing abilities since I was convinced that the main reason I hadn't gotten into my first-choice school was because of my personal statement. Regardless of all this, I gave my schoolwork my all. I took the hardest classes that I could and was determined to get A's in them, even if it meant that I had to be in my TA's office every other day. I was determined to make the school that had rejected me kick themselves later on for doing so.

A few quarters passed, and I really began getting used to my backup university. Although I had entered the school not really wanting to, it really began to grow on me. I felt as though I was in a different world when I was there. I was away from home and did not have to explain myself to anyone. This gave me a sense of responsibility that I probably would not have attained had I stayed home and gone to that other school. On the flipside of it, though, I really missed home. I have always been really attached to my family, so moving away was and still is a very difficult process for me. This had positive effects for me though because it kept me motivated to get through school faster so that I could move back home as soon as possible. I was very focused and knew exactly what I had to do to get where I wanted to be. My bitterness slowly faded, and I realized that I had come to the point where I was no longer doing all this to show the other school what a mistake they had made, but I was doing it for me. I had declared my major as psychology and really loved what I was studying. I was at a school where I actually had the opportunity to go and talk to my professors and get their opinions about certain issues or even have discussions with them. I was in a school where I could actually get the classes that I wanted to take without having to wait for my senior year to do so because there was no room. Even the little things, like being able to find parking in a matter of 15 minutes, made my life a lot easier than that of my friends, who were going to the school that I had hoped to get into. I felt as though I had my life under control and that I knew what I was doing with it. Because going to school was not as big an ordeal for me as it was for my friends who were in the other school, I even had time to get a job that was directly related to my field and that I love doing. Everything just seemed to fit together, and I felt as though I was one step ahead of everyone else even though my original plans had been forced to take a detour. *It was a great feeling for the first time in my life to know that I was doing all this for myself and not to satisfy everyone else or to meet everyone else's expectations for me.*

Who knows, maybe if I had gotten into that school I would be doing much worse than I am doing now. I highly doubt that I would be as ahead in school as I currently am, and I could guarantee that there would be no way that I could juggle working and going to school with the drive that I would have to go through every morning and evening. Now that I think about it, I would have probably had a lot of trouble getting involved in a research project with a professor so early in my college experience or even being able to contribute to this book. To sum up my point, although the rejection that I had to face after high school was a very difficult thing for me to deal with, it worked out for the best. I cannot say that I am completely over it and that it doesn't bother me at all because the truth is that I do not think I will ever forget how I felt in the months after receiving that letter, but the important thing is that now I see all these events in the context of the big picture. It's easy to sit here and tell others who may be going through this that everything will be all right and that you shouldn't let a school tell you who you are or where you deserve to be, but the truth of the matter is that if you are feeling the way I did in any form, you have to deal with it in your own way. The main answer for me was time. There was nothing that anyone could tell me at the time that would have made me feel that it wasn't my fault that I didn't get in. I had to prove that to myself.

However, some questions that I asked myself made me feel better about all this. For example, *why am I in school to begin with?* If I'm here because I am truly interested in the field that I'm pursuing, then why does it matter which school I'm in? *I could get the same education in any school as long as I make the effort and keep myself in close contact with my professors.* Also, do I plan on going to graduate school? And if I do, then isn't learning the material my first priority? The main thing to focus on is that as long as you truly have a passion for what you are doing, you will be the best at it, regardless of any obstacles that you may face in life.

It is a very difficult thing for 18-year-olds to deal with the concept of being rejected from a school that they have been working very hard to get into, but in the long run it really does make you a stronger person if you extract the right thing from that experience. You can't let one rejection hold you down from being what you want to be. If anything, let it make you a stronger person. It is a very difficult thing to work through, but do everything you can to make it work in your favor as opposed to having it work against you. *You should never let anyone or any institution tell you who you are or what you can achieve.* As long as you have the motivation and the drive to get to where you want, nothing should stand in your way. Speaking from experience, I know that it is very difficult to work through bitterness, but it's not impossible. Hang in there and consider this experience as a sign that you can prevail through any obstacles that may be thrown in your direction.

Everything happens for a reason, and as long as you're determined enough, fate will lead you in the right direction, making you the best in your field of study.

Sheyda M. Bogosyan

College *Should* Be . . .

Going to college should be about parties, playing the field, and meeting tons of new people, or at least that is what I thought it was about. Three years after entering college, I realized how much that mentality stunted my growth. I met my boyfriend the summer before entering college at orientation. He was a junior when I was a freshman, and in a way I deeply resented that he wanted to date me when it was only my first year at school. I mean, I thought, "I can't have a boyfriend. I should be dating the field. Why should I limit myself?"

Coming from an all-girl Catholic high school, I was a boy-crazy girl who just wanted to meet tons of new people and date around. I wanted the "ideal" college life—you know, the whole frat-party-getting-drunk kind of life. I honestly thought that was what college was about. I pushed my boyfriend away for a long time while I was adjusting to living away from home, trying to find a major, and finding my niche in school. I pushed him away further with my mentality that college was about dating the field. I broke up with him several times to date the field and wound up going back to him because deep down I knew that he was someone I could see a future with. *I lived by the "college should be" mentality given to me by the media and society instead of listening to myself.*

Now, I'm not saying that you should go get a boyfriend and stick with him for your entire college career. What I am saying is that *there is no standard college experience.* Everyone's college experience is different. We all experience different majors, classes, and relationships, so how can there really be a standard experience? Looking back, I regret that I pushed my boyfriend away so hard for such a dumb reason because our relationship could have been stronger and healthier had I known that there is no standard, ideal college experience. Three years into college I finally learned to just enjoy college as it is and go with the flow. I learned not to get stuck on the should's because it might stunt my growth as a person, a student, and even as a friend.

Christina Le

The Single Life

You can feel the moist sand beneath your feet as you slowly stroll the beach, hand in hand with your significant other. You gaze into each other's eyes for what seems like eternity. You sigh deeply, content with just being in the presence of your better half. You feel a gentle breeze waft through your hair and the soft glow of the setting sun radiating on your skin. You shyly smile at each other, never wanting this moment to end. Everything seems so . . . perfect.

Okay, so not all relationships are blissful like this. However, it seems as if the media and society itself have glamorized the idea of relationships to the point where someone feels lonely if he or she does not have a significant other at the present moment. Think about it logically. Do you really need a boyfriend or girlfriend to make you feel good about yourself? If so, being in a relationship may not be right for you. You need to establish your identity and understand yourself first before bringing another person into the equation.

When my friends and I talk about the things that we regret doing in the past, topics that often come up are having a boyfriend or girlfriend coming into college and entering into a relationship during freshman year. As far as the first regret is concerned, I am by no means encouraging you to dump your significant other now that you've come to college. Rather, proceed with caution because maintaining a relationship in this new stage of your life may be quite difficult, especially if both of you attend different schools. During my first year, I observed so many late-night phone calls of exhausted floor mates who still had emotional strings attached to a distant significant other. Even after a long, arduous day, my friends would make a commendable effort to catch up with their loved ones and try to find out what was going on in their lives until the wee hours of the morning. Unfortunately, despite these efforts, many of those long-distance relationships did not last. The difficulties of maintaining a healthy relationship are magnified when distance is involved, and, ultimately, continuing the relationship becomes an overwhelming task.

Now, as far as the second common regret is concerned, I understand that you may be on your own for the first time and are eager to explore various opportunities and relationships. This sudden surge of freedom that accompanies the entrance into this new and exciting environment can cause people to feel somewhat insecure and become dependent on a significant other to make them feel happy and confident. Yet it is during this first year that one should really try to make good friends, not boyfriends and girlfriends. Many people tend to cut themselves off from their close friends, or potential friends, while in a relationship. You definitely do not want to be cutting off people in your first year but rather should try to really get to know as many people as possible. *Be social. You only get one first year, so you might as well make the most of it.*

Relationships are inevitably time-consuming. It may be more important for you to take some time for yourself instead of finding a significant other at this stage of your life. Hang out with friends. Join on-campus clubs and organizations. Go out and party. Study and do well in your classes. Being single gives you many opportunities and a lot of time that you may not have in the future, once you enter into a relationship.

This may sound cliché, but carpe diem! Seize the day! Or, rather, seize the time you can enjoy as a single adult. You have plenty of time in the future to date people and find the love of your life. As for now, enjoy the time you can spend with family and friends and enjoy the freedom of single life.

Lisa Miyake

Long-Distance Relationships

When I entered college, I was involved in a long-distance relationship. My boyfriend Robert was in his senior year in high school in Michigan, and I was in college in California. Most people would think that long-distance relationships never work out, but Robert and I have proved them wrong because regardless of the physical distance between us our relationship, like any other "normal" relationship, continued to grow and develop into a very serious, committed, and healthy relationship.

I admit, however, that I did have some fears and doubts about us when I entered college. One of my fears was that one of us would feel resented or taken for granted by the other person. I didn't want Robert to feel like I was neglecting him or forgetting him, and I didn't want him to think that I felt neglected or forgotten, either. I don't know if I ever told Robert or if I'll ever tell him, but I did sacrifice many opportunities to go clubbing and many house events just to spend time talking to him over the phone or instant messaging. Essentially, I spent a great deal of the first two quarters of my freshman year just sitting around and waiting to talk to him, but I don't regret it at all.

Also, I was concerned about people talking and putting ideas and thoughts into our heads and making us doubt ourselves. Personally, many of my housemates thought I was crazy and stupid for what I was doing. One guy even told me that I was being played, but I didn't listen to him because I knew that if I started listening to what he was saying I would start to doubt my faith in Robert and our relationship. I don't deny that there was a time when I almost believed what people were saying because I would wait for Robert to call me and he'd never call, or I would call him and his mother would say he was at the movies. Moments like this made me feel like a fool for spending so much time waiting for him while he was having fun. But the last thing I wanted to do was admit to myself that there could be a possibility that what people were saying could be true. So when I got to low points like this, I just reminded myself that I should never doubt Robert because he would never doubt me.

Another fear of mine was that Robert and I would grow apart because we couldn't actually see each other or be with each other on a physical level. We had about 2,000 miles separating us. I feared that because I couldn't see Robert and spend some quality time with him that our personalities and lifestyles would drift off onto different paths. To be honest, I was always afraid of what the next e-mail would read or that the next phone call conversation we'd have would be our last because he might say something along the lines of he didn't think it was going to work out because we were different now.

In retrospect, I realize that not only did I spend a lot of time waiting my freshman year, but I also spent a lot of time stressing over my fears and doubts. I see today that all those fear and doubts were nothing but fears and doubts. The truth was that I had nothing to worry about because we never stopped loving each other, and that love kept our relationship together. Till this day, I still wonder if Robert ever questioned whether the voice on the other side of the phone, the person replying to his instant messages, or the person reading his letters was the same person he last saw, touched, hugged, and kissed. I hope that others who are themselves in long-distance relationships will see that our relationship proves that any relationship can work out regardless if it's long-distance or not because, if both people are committed and willing to be a part of the relationship, then anything is possible.

Christie Vong

Finding Balance

The Professional Juggler

When I call myself a professional juggler, what on earth am I referring to? Who and what is a professional juggler? Well, we all are. As students we are all trying to juggle school with our social lives. This issue may sound a bit trivial to address, but if we take a good look, we will find that if we don't juggle these two with care, grave consequences can result: academic probation, suspension, drop in grade point average (GPA), financial assistance revocation—all these things have rippling effects in our lives forever; therefore, it's imperative to go from a novice juggler to a professional one—and fast. The failure to do so could mean risking everything you have worked so hard for.

As we all know, college is a whole different world with new temptations awaiting us. We make friends with people from all over the United States and even around the world. Suddenly, the umbilical cord is cut, and we find ourselves independent for the first time. We finally have freedom. The problem is that some of us might go a bit freedom crazy; after all, we worked hard to get here. Why not go out and have some fun? We deserve it, right? The problem involves being able to recognize when partying becomes excessive. Most of the time we won't be able to until our alarm goes off and we're too hung over to figure out where the snooze button is—"What 8 a.m. class?" The secret is learning how to balance both worlds, academic and social.

Balance is not an easy thing to do when you have many influences around you that are pro partying. Friends play a huge part in helping you decide whether you should stay home and finish your essay or go out with the clan. As students of higher learning, we tend to see peer pressure as something that was left behind in high school; we're too smart to fall for those old tricks, aren't we? To be perfectly honest, I myself gave in to my friends' invitations plenty of times, even though I knew I had tons of work to do and even more to catch up on. What makes this worse is that I have done my fair share of partying prior to entering the University of California (UC) system, yet I found myself going out with the girls every chance I got. There were new places to go and new people to meet. I found myself justifying this excessive behavior by convincing myself that I needed to go out: "I've been working too hard" or the never-failing "I need to take a break from schoolwork." The prevailing mentality among college students is "this is what college life is all about." Hey, we've all seen the movie *Animal House*, right?

Unfortunately, being a college student also involves making decisions, and we need to make decisions about the friends we make and keep while in college. When it really comes down to it, birds of a feather do flock together. The circles of friends that we keep can really influence our decisions as far as school is concerned. I barely survived my junior year; I kept partying with my girls. I know I could have done better academically, but my best friend at the time was Procrastination—you might know my friend, too. One of my girls really knew Procrastination: I think they were in love, and Procrastination messed her up really good. She kept putting her work on hold and went out and lived it up for the majority of her junior year. When she returned the following year (her senior year) she received a letter stating that she had been dropped from the university for not maintaining a satisfactory GPA. After a letter of appeal and a lot of stress, she was allowed to take a couple of courses while on academic probation. Her financial aid has been revoked, and she's still not technically a university student. That decision is pending her grades for these courses.

The only reason I didn't meet the same fate was because eventually I wised up. I learned that if I wanted to go out, it would have to be in moderation. *I created rules for myself. I became disciplined.* I decided that I would only go out on weekends and only on the condition that I would have my homework for that week done and over with. I cannot lie; occasionally I would break this rule and go out without doing my homework. However, when this happened I would feel guilty the whole night and anxious because I knew that I had a deadline in 2 days. Believe me, this is the worst feeling to have at a club or a bar at 12 a.m. while everyone around you is having a blast. It's simply not worth it. Another tactic I found helpful was to lock my apartment door and actually study. Yes, it's true, studying actually helps with the whole school thing. When my friends would come by and knock, I pretended I wasn't home. Eventually, I actually learned how to say no. Believe it or not, it wasn't that hard. A simple "I can't go out tonight; I have a lot of homework, but maybe next time" and a smile can do the job.

The bottom line is this: We are now independent adults, and our parents are not looking over our shoulders every few seconds, so it's up to us to make wise decisions. Ultimately, every decision we make will have a negative or positive effect on our lives; we cannot blame anyone else for the choices we make. It's a simple matter of asking ourselves what is more important to us—our education or a good time. We have to remember that we can party at any time, but how often or for how long will we be enrolled at a university? Yes, we all worked very hard to get to where we are now, but we must remember that it is possible to have both worlds. It's all a matter of balance and moderation. Anything in excess can have heavy sanctions, and it's only when we realize this that we can go from novice juggler to a professional one.

Veronica Fematt

Time and Entertainment

As technologically dependent Americans, we wake up to an alarm clock and turn on our coffeepots to start the day. While we sip our espressos, we turn on the TV to catch a quick glimpse of what important news is going on before we go to class or work. We don't even have time to properly wake up and cook a decent breakfast anymore, so instead we turn to our toasters for a Pop Tart.

We as college students are in a constant rush, as if running from time itself, and this affects what we spend our time enjoying. To compensate for long, boring days in the office or in lecture halls, we seek out spectacular displays of special effects and surround sound to get what we think is the most out of our time and money, while simultaneously releasing the tensions brought on by busy schedules. We don't have the time or patience to invest our intellectual energy in figuring out the story line of *Twelfth Night* by William Shakespeare. We save that intellectual time for studying. It is much quicker and less energy consuming during our scarce leisure moments to have the story line handed to us in a format that is easy to understand so that we can concentrate on things that don't require reflection or interpretation or the ability to savor the experience. By the time we get out of class or work, we are so mentally fried that the mere thought of something intellectual gives us a headache.

We have scheduled lunches and breaks during the day, followed by planned study times. We know approximately what time we want to sleep and how much free time we give ourselves. This means that the rest of the time isn't free but burdened with things we have to do, like sitting through class and writing essays. But even our free time isn't free anymore because we schedule and plan it to optimize its potential. Because we are striving so hard to get ahead we often feel guilty if we go to a movie during the week, so we designate Friday and Saturday nights for this activity. By doing this, we are subject to the same regulations as we are during the rest of our week. We tell ourselves that on Friday we will watch a movie that will take 2 hours and then go back to studying for Tuesday's quiz. We are in essence stealing our free time away from our planners that tell us we should be doing something else.

We go to concerts to release tension by dancing, screaming, and flinging ourselves about in a mosh pit. Our spring and winter breaks are marked in our electronic organizers to be filled with this type of entertainment, which is essential to venting out college frustrations. We can act totally crazy or just stare at the screen with blank expressions to recover from the torture we put ourselves through during the week with our intricate plans scribbled meticulously in our organizers.

Although I like to read Shakespeare and have been exposed to his work through high school and college, had *Twelfth Night* not been required for a class I wouldn't have gone the first time and would have missed out on two great performances. I would rather have gone to a movie like *Shakespeare in Love* or one of its equivalents, instead of finding time to sit through a play. One of the reasons for this is that if the movie were bad, then I only would have lost a little time and energy. Also, I can leave a movie whenever I want. But if I didn't like Shakespeare's *Twelfth Night,* I would have had to sit through the thing until intermission and would have lost the time I spent booking tickets and organizing my week to accommodate it. This wouldn't optimize my time and would only make me regret the work I did to go in the first place.

Because of my lack of resources and desire to go out and try potentially risky things with my scarce free time, I turn on the TV and watch *Ebert and Roeper* to determine which movie I would like to see. I don't have time to run around testing cultural performances to see if I like them, the way I tested *Twelfth Night,* but I can easily predict what I will see on stage at a White Stripes concert. It is more convenient to squeeze popular entertainment into our lives because we don't have to reserve tickets to a movie; we go to these events with a good idea of what to expect. We can call up a friend at the last minute and make plans to see the latest blockbuster on pay per view. Our inability to make long-term plans to go see performances is made evident when we spend time after class swapping tickets with one another because our schedules changed, and we can't make it to our required concerts and plays.

Low investment, high output entertainment for a fast-paced lifestyle is what we come to expect from the lives we lead as college students. We spend so much time trying to get ahead that we neglect the brilliance that has been passed down to us through cultural entertainment such as Shakespeare and Beethoven. Maybe if we slowed down a bit and laid off TV we could sit through a 3-hour performance, but our habits show us that we would rather spend our money on current chart-topping blockbuster spectacles.

Shawna Wood

Take a Bite Out of Time

Whenever we gather the courage to embark on an "adventure in desocialization," as Bell calls it in Chapter 9, we inevitably come up against familiar brick walls—walls that we've spent our lives staying behind, toeing the line. We give ourselves the opportunity to either accept this wall as we always have or to steel our resolve and take to the wall with our desocialization sledgehammer.

Imagine a social institution: a yardstick of your everyday life that is so deeply ingrained in you as material reality that you feel disconnection from it would mean certain social death. To make sure you're always connected to this institution, you wear a small band on you at all times to keep yourself wired in.

Whenever you glance at this band, you're reminded of its persistence, and you become more anxious. The more anxious you become, the more you glance at it. The more you glance at it, the more anxious you become.

This institution, if you haven't guessed already, is time. You may balk at considering our conception of time to be a socialized idea. After all, the sun does set every night as it rises every morning. The seasons change, and the moon waxes and wanes like clockwork.

Consider first that different cultures have different conceptions of time. While the Western tradition views it as a linear path, a progression from past to present to future, Eastern philosophy has typically seen it as a cyclical affair— dynasties will rise and dynasties will fall, just as people will be born and people will die. Most would feel humbled imagining themselves as tiny parts of this ever-churning cycle.

But this is not our world. Ours is one of breakneck schedules and all-nighters, back-to-back midterms, and precariously managed social lives. When you graduate from college, you will trade all of this for personal digital assistants (PDAs), coffee breaks, 6 a.m. mornings, and casual Fridays. We're not quite living in the present but always worrying maniacally about the imminent future. Like a cat dangling from a tree branch by a single claw, we feel like we are fighting gravity itself.

Can we really help this? We are a postindustrial society whose capitalistic foundations have bought us all the dearly beloved things our greedy little hearts have ever desired. And the most basic moral of this capitalism, this consumption, is production. We must produce to consume, we must work to produce, and we must—we must—spend time to work. To whip ourselves into shape, we install clocks in every room above our heads like false idols, and every so often we will pay homage by giving them a self-effacing glance.

Our modern work culture of ever-increasing alienation has created a systemic problem that mirrors the very timepieces we worship. Quarantined in cubicles, hidden behind computer screens, perhaps stuck in one spot on a conveyor belt for an 8-hour workday, we are less humans working together than sprockets in a clock, mechanically fitted together.

Have you ever given yourself a stomachache by eating too fast or eating on the go to satisfy a schedule demand? Have you given yourself an ulcer by stressing yourself out? Surely you know someone who has. Have you ever weaved in and out of traffic hoping to get to your destination on time—only to have shaved off at most 30 seconds? Perhaps you've failed to recognize a good friend you've passed by while hurrying to class.

You're slave to a master who has bound you by your wrist. But it's your choice whether or not you want to continue living a slave's life.

Try this the next time you're hurrying to class and you feel you will most certainly be late: slow yourself to a crawling speed and toss away your feelings of anxiety. Look around you. Is the sun shining? Are the clouds fluffy today? Maybe it's raining, and you were ignoring that spectacular din of spattering raindrops and that unique smell that always comes out when it rains a little. Imagine yourself as a speck in the ever-churning cycle of life and then imagine the ultimate consequences you will face for being 2 minutes late to class today. Pales in comparison, doesn't it?

Andy Wang

Grocery Store Analogy: How Do You Know What Classes to Take?

One major and ongoing problem you will have during your time at college is deciding which classes to take—how best to relate to the advisement and registration process. I'd like to give you some suggestions and do it in terms of a grocery store analogy. Imagine the university that you have come to is a large grocery store. You walk in and since you have declared yourself a biology major—or a sociology major, or a computer engineering major, or an undeclared major—you will be somewhat guided toward Aisle 3—or 7 or 15. You wheel your cart over to that aisle, and you begin walking down it. You first notice that this item on the immediate upper right shelf is labeled "Required." You put it in your cart. Then, as you continue on, you see that you can select 1 of these 3 items, and a bit further 2 of these 12 items are necessary. Over there is a shelf of recommended electives. So you methodically go down the aisle taking all the items that you are supposed to. You get to the end of the aisle, and you stop. You stop, and you turn around, and you leave. Of course you stop at the cash register and you pay. And then you leave. You LEAVE! During this entire process, you have been subconsciously operating on the high school model of "have-to" behavior, the conveyor belt model of being educated, or, rather, schooled. Meanwhile one aisle over was a class that would have rocked your mind and changed your life—just one aisle over. Or two aisles over there was a professor who you would have profoundly connected with. But you MISSED IT! And you missed it because you didn't look! You didn't look because you thought you were just "supposed to" go down your aisle and select.

The point of this analogy is to get you to increase your freedom and awareness level regarding this university education you are about to undertake for many years. Be a smart consumer. Go down ALL THE AISLES. Look and explore. See what is in this giant intellectual supermarket.

I have often asked my classes, "How many of you have had the experience of being in a class third week, fifth week, sixth week and had the sinking feeling, 'Oh shit . . . I hate this class'?" Usually many hands go up. It is an all too common experience. Being a smart shopper in advance can almost eliminate this depressing experience. Practically speaking, this may mean first going to the bookstore and seeing which books are being used in which courses. See which ones excite and interest you. Look at the teacher evaluations that are often publicized at many universities. Above all, that first week of classes, regardless of what classes you are officially enrolled in, *go visit and sit in on as many classes as you possibly can.* Go shopping down all the aisles. During that chaotic first week of college classes, no one really knows or cares who is registered and who is shopping. (Though, of course, many professors acutely care that their classes are not under- or overenrolled.) No one is going to throw you out for not being officially registered. It is, after all, your education. You have the right—and responsibility—to shop and see which courses really appeal to you.

I've worked at approximately 12 universities in my career and every one of them was very good at processing students. As a professor—and hence part of the university system—I too have become skilled at *processing students:* cha-ching, cha-ching, cha-ching—no problem. A factory, a post office, a line of customers at the DMV—ba-boom, ba-boom, ba-boom. Unless you take some creative control at the outset of your university education—a personal, energetic, cocreative stance—*you will be processed.* That is just the nature of institutions.

Bernard McGrane

Partying and Its Implications

Partying

As a little girl, I remember watching older family friends leave for college. Although I obviously knew little about the undergraduate experience, I quickly learned that two things were always associated with the infamous college years—all-night study sessions and beer. For as many students who attend a university for the purpose of getting an education, an equal amount go to college to have a good time.

As much as your parents want you to believe that college is purely a time for academic betterment, it's not. Much of what you will learn and remember from college will not be from the classroom. Rather, you will gain knowledge and memories from the people around you and from your own unique experiences. Although it is true that a significant portion of your time during college will be devoted to scholastic pursuits, it is also true that much of your time will not be filled with such activities. How you want to spend your free time is your choice, but for many college students this is where beer comes in.

Fraternity parties, apartment parties, house parties, and clubs often times draw more crowds of college students than do the classrooms. The combination of music, dancing, socializing, and alcohol is often difficult for most 18- to 22-year-olds to resist. Not only can you meet new people while spending time with friends, but you also have the chance to grab a drink and forget about school and various other stresses that are such a large part of college life. When handled responsibly, partying can be a very rewarding and worthwhile pastime.

Yet partying has a bad rap. Parents consistently worry about their inexperienced children neglecting schoolwork because of the great party scene appeal. Poor performance in school as a result of excessive partying is a notorious contributor to the college dropout rate. Furthermore, parents, and especially local law enforcement, do not look favorably on the alcohol present at most parties—especially the underage drinking. Ever since you were old enough to understand the word *alcohol,* you were warned of its disadvantageous effects. Alcohol not only impairs judgment but also is very unhealthy when consumed on a regular basis. Alcohol is a depressant and can cause many people to become belligerent. Not to mention when consumed in excess alcohol can cause illness, incoherence, and sometimes even death. Certainly, it is difficult to deny the dangers associated with the consumption of alcohol. However, it is naive to think that college students will not continue to participate in such activities despite warnings. College is a time when young adults want to experience things never available to them before—alcohol included.

Thus, it is helpful to distinguish between responsible partying and irresponsible partying. Yes, drinking is fun. However, getting sick because you drank too much is not fun. Having a hangover is not fun. Passing out in a strange place is not fun. First of all, if you make the decision to drink, do so with good friends, who will stay with you throughout the night and take care of you if you drink too much. Also, keep track of how much alcohol you are consuming. If you are unable to tally how much you have had to drink, it might be a good idea to stop. There is a point while consuming alcohol when you are most likely enjoying yourself and you do not need more alcohol to have a good time. Attempt to recognize this point and cease drinking. Drinking more alcohol will not necessarily be more fun, but rather it will make you ill. Moreover, always open your drinks yourself or watch your drinks being poured. This tip applies mostly to young women, who (sadly enough) must make themselves aware of the threats of date rape drugs, such as roofies. Moreover, it is worth noting that if you are an inexperienced drinker, it may take some time to discover your alcohol tolerance. Thus, it is all the more important to be especially cautious when drinking. Drink slowly and be aware of your surroundings. Do not put yourself in a situation that seems dangerous; try to exercise good judgment. After all, you are an intelligent college student.

Yet, most important, you do not have to drink to party or to be social. Plenty of fun can be had without drinking. In fact, more college students than you would think actively choose to abstain from drinking because of religious, moral, or family-related reasons. And like many of their alcohol-consuming counterparts, these students successfully find activities that help make their college experiences pleasurable—whether it is going to parties or participating in various other group activities. Thus, although drinking may be prevalent in the college atmosphere, it is not necessary and therefore should never be forced on anyone. Peer pressure may be difficult to overcome, but following your personal beliefs and goals is self-empowerment that will help guide you through any tough situation.

The fact is that even the most studious of college students do not want to devote all their time to studying. Furthermore, if one did want to study for every waking hour of the day, he or she would still find the task difficult. Anyone who has studied for extensive amounts of time knows that it is very exhausting; studying can even wear on one's sanity. In fact, to be most productive when studying, it is helpful to maintain a balance between school and social activities. Spending time with friends, participating in group activities, or partying in your free time can act as a stress release and make the time allotted for school more productive and perhaps more enjoyable. Socializing also helps you build relationships among people who are similar to you, many of whom you will be friends with for years to come. However, this balance between academics and social activities is easier said then done. Creating a healthy balance for you may take some practice, but the prospect of doing well in school while also enjoying your college years is well worth the effort.

Melissa Reggiardo

First College Experience

You spend 4 years of high school trying to get into an outstanding college, and when you arrive what are you confronted with? Books? Classes? No, partying.

As a freshman coming to this university I was apprehensive about what the college experience would bring. I didn't know if I would be able to adjust to living away from home and away from my friends, in a city I wasn't familiar with. Would I be able to live with two other girls in a tiny room for a whole year? These things plagued my mind all summer before move-in week, tossing in my head until I would finally drop off to sleep. Little did I know that as soon as I got unpacked there would be a huge party waiting to greet me and other unsuspecting freshmen.

It was the first Saturday of the quarter before classes started, and I was still adjusting to living in the dorms. As I was walking down the hall I overheard some of my floor mates talking about the biggest frat party of the year. It was going to happen on Sunday. I took this into consideration but kept walking anyway. The thought of a frat party didn't particularly stir me. I didn't think it would be too much fun going someplace with a bunch of strangers and lots of alcohol. But as the day progressed, the idea seemed to get even more popular among my floor mates until everyone was talking about going. Even my room mate, a biochemistry major addicted to studying, was planning on going. So this convinced me.

With the first giant party of the year only a night away, people from my floor decided to go to a frat party on Saturday to see what it would be like. So we gathered together our new acquaintances and headed down to frat row to find a party. It wasn't very hard, and soon we were on a patio looking onto a dance floor in a room lit by a black light. Before we began dancing, my new friends headed over to the bar and were greeted with hard liquor. Apparently they had run out of beer. My roommate and I didn't get anything, but there was one in our group who seemed determined to get drunk as soon as possible. After alcohol was obtained, we danced until we became tired. Then we went out onto the patio for some fresh air, where we were greeted by a frat boy trying to give us more alcohol. We already had some and denied his request to give us more, but I couldn't help thinking how desperately they wanted us drunk.

A couple of our floor mates weren't having a good time and decided to leave, and my roommate and I followed them after a couple of hours. We danced for the remainder of the time in a pretty mellow atmosphere of glowing objects and music. We headed back up the large hill to our dorms with our drunken colleagues in hand, literally. To keep them from falling into the gutter we had to hold them. We went back up to our rooms where two drunken boys climbed up to my roommate's bed and stayed there for a couple more hours, talking with us about college and high school and general getting-to-know-you things. My roommate talked about our experience.

She liked the party and was glad we went in a group because she felt safer, even though our group was a bunch of strangers who lived on our floor. She told me she drank, and I asked her when because I had never seen her with a drink. She said she drank off of someone else's because she didn't want a whole drink to herself. I couldn't believe what I was hearing. What a dangerous decision! But she didn't know it was dangerous. She was new to the party scene and had no idea about what proper precautions to take. Luckily, her friend's drink wasn't laced with anything. I then proceeded to tell her the rules of safe partying, to make sure that I wouldn't have to worry about her on Sunday.

On the morning of the big day I was excited about what the biggest party of the year could hold, but I was a little scared at first because I had heard rumors of fraternity life, and I didn't want to get myself into a situation that I couldn't escape from. If what I just went to was only a fraction of what was to come, then I might be in trouble. Rumors were floating around about how the police would have to shut it down and fire hoses would drench spectators. Every frat would participate in the event, so there would be an overwhelming crowd, and we would have to arrive early to get in. And so we did.

Before we even reached the party, the visual we got was insane: All of the frats were filled to the brim, and long lines of students snaked through the streets with large crowds just wandering around looking for a potential frat. Frat brothers were shouting for us to leave so that they wouldn't be shut down. That didn't stop us. We had been thinking about this party for 2 days, and we weren't about to leave without a fight. So we pushed and shoved to get to the front of the line of a frat that would let our guy friends in. Apparently they aren't too strict on girls, but they don't want a lot of guys. Maybe they think they have a better chance if the male-to-female ratio is tampered with. This is rather ironic anyway because they are supposed to be recruiting for their frats.

Finally, we found a suitable party and waited in line with the rest of the freshmen to try to get in. But there was a list, and apparently we weren't on it. Still determined we pushed our way through the crowd and somehow past security into the party. Three floors of dancing and drinking! Oh joy! But the pushing didn't stop there. It was really crowded and disorienting. Loud music shook the floors as we vied past people to get to the top of the stairs. We made it, and I found myself again among strangers. I didn't feel comfortable, and after all the work we did to get in the frat, I left and went back to the dorm.

As I entered my floor, I saw people playing cards in the study lounge. One of them was a fellow partier from the night before. I regaled him with a tale of chaos from what I had just seen, and he seemed really eager to go. Being easily swayed, I went down there with him—for the second time—to see if we could get into a party. I thought maybe I could find one I liked better. A huge mass of people had accumulated in that short time, and now it was impossible to get in. So we sat ourselves down on a giant university sign, one of the ones that borders the school, and watched havoc ensue. The people were all in the middle of the street, which had to be shut down. This tightly packed group swayed back and forth as if trying to get somewhere. Pushing and bottle throwing started, and we watched from a safe distance, remarking on how crazy it all was. Tomorrow everyone would go back to normal lives, but some would end up in the hospital instead. Firefighters and police were waiting on the edge of the mass for a cue that they should exert their authority.

As midnight struck, they shut the party down. With fire hoses in hand, the firefighters threatened the crowd as loudspeakers announced the end of the party. We would all have to go home. The crowd wasn't happy, but my friend and

I didn't stick around to get hosed. We went back up to our dorm and told everyone we had been to the biggest party of the year and survived.

What happened to my roommate you may ask? She ended up freak dancing with a guy on our floor and felt guilty about it afterward. Later on, she was in a long line with him for the bathroom, and someone asked if they were together. She said they weren't, and he asked if she was drunk. She said no and asked why. The stranger said he wanted her to go in the bathroom with her freak-dancing partner to make the line go faster. Go figure. What a wonderful way to start your first year of college!

So this is what many of us face when we go to college. Books and tests will follow, but partying will always be there for us, even when we least expect it. We all hear about college parties, but not all of us expect to go to one of this magnitude as soon as we move in. We are all pulled into a world far removed from the safety of our homes and the nurturing of our parents.

Shawna Wood

Rape: What They Forget to Mention About Partying

It begins as a slight tremor that runs down the entirety of her body. It seems as if she is dreaming, for she is still sound asleep. Then within seconds, the slight tremors turn into violent shakes. Her body writhes uncontrollably, snapping her to consciousness. But even though she is now fully aware of her surroundings, the violent writhing maintains possession of her body. Tears begin to flow from her eyes.

But all this is manageable.

It is the deep moans of an intense inner agony that tear the witness apart. The moans resemble a person dying of a disease that has consumed each part of the body. The psychological pain is so intense that it captures control of her muscles, and she is reduced to a shaking, sweating body that desperately calls out for help in the form of awful wailing.

It is hard to wake up next to someone like this in the middle of the night. It is hard to see someone you love suffer from something far deeper than a physical ailment.

Indeed, survivors of molestation and rape bear worse scars than mere physical maladies. For their scars rest on the mind and on the heart. These painful marks can never be erased, never be controlled, never be medicated. They arise at random and stay at will.

If parties on college campuses were intended to be enjoyable, it would seem that each could control him- or herself, be social, and meet new people. But as we mix alcohol, drugs, and yearning hormones in a confined space, we create an ideal atmosphere for abuse. Take away our inhibitions and we undergo a massive deconstruction of our socialization in seconds.

We become true human animals. Our instincts and drives become increasingly difficult to control. And people get hurt.

If the debauchery of parties confined itself to that magical night of the event, it would be easier to rationalize negative consequences emerging from such situations. A sexual rendezvous could at least be reasoned away—I got out of control once, it's over, let's move on.

But the emotional scars last for *years,* for lifetimes.

An epidemic of heinous acts is taking control of our college campuses. As naive students leave home for the first time, the freedom that parties offer tempts normally bright students to experiment and try new things. But when 27.7% of all college women report a sexual experience that meets the legal definition of rape or attempted rape, we know it is time to reconsider the merits of parties, drinking, and drugs.

If we reflect on this number, what does it mean? When a woman shops with three of her other friends, one of them will be carrying an immense emotional burden, a horrific story of survival. In an apartment of college-aged women, one of the four will likely experience sleep disturbance, an eating disorder, decreased appetite, and sexual dysfunction from the psychological trauma of an attempted rape. Count three or four of your best female friends. At least one experienced a life-shattering event. And perhaps it was or will be you.

Parties on college campuses are not the causes of rape. But they place young people into a situation that multiplies the chances that rape will occur. The combination of alcohol; frequently dark, isolated spaces; hormones; and newfound feelings of complete freedom from parents encourages actions that have lifelong implications.

Rape survivors often feel encouraged to systematically repress the traumatic event. The sickness of rape and attempted rape lies in the fact that the "victim" tends to blame herself. Society itself blames her. We question her sexual history, as if this holds relevance to the fact that she was forced into a sexual act: She should have been more responsible, she should have resisted more, she had it coming. We create an atmosphere where we blame the victim through implication. In this social atmosphere, one of the sheer injustices of rape is that an estimated 84% go unreported to authorities. The survivor blames herself and wishes not to implicate the friend who raped her.

Tragically, *friend* is the right word: 92% of assailants are known by the victim, over 50% are friends, and 26% are intimate partners.

Partying is an important part of college life. The movement from youth to adulthood offers a wonderful chance to experiment with life and to develop one's own morality. So the abolition of social events surely is not a justifiable answer, although survivors may disagree with this. Instead, it is important for young people to realize that there is wisdom in using caution around alcohol and drugs. There is wisdom in living moderately and consuming moderately. It is important to party with friends who can watch out for each other. And no matter how cynical and horrible it sounds, it is important to remember that friends sometimes hurt friends.

We live in a world where 40% of rape victims are under 18 years of age, and of that 12% are under the age of 12 years. And, sadly, estimates suggest that the reported 27.7% of female, college-aged rape survivors is really closer to 50%.

The statistics abound, but behind each fact are thousands of faces: stories of late-night panic attacks, stories of depression 15 years after the attempted rape, stories of women not trusting men to be kind and sensitive, stories of attempted suicide, stories of survivors who experienced not just the physical rape but the more damaging psychological rape that comes as well. And so there are stories of successful suicide, too.

College students must balance idealism with awareness and fun with safety. It may be a tall order, but it is little to pay in the grand scheme.

It is a life-changing experience to wake up next to a rape survivor during her panic attack from the stored mental trauma. The inner anguish spreads beyond her pain. The rapist violates far more people than he could ever know. How dare he. How dare *we*.

No one deserves this life sentence.

Christopher Patrick King

Nontraditional Experiences

For the Nontraditional Student

College is a great place to be for anyone who wants to learn. This is a very true statement. However, *anyone* usually means the typical college student. By typical, I mean an 18- or 19-year-old girl or boy who has graduated high school and now lives on campus in dorms or lives with her or his parents and commutes to campus. Well, if that is the case, then I am not your typical college student. Yes, I may be 18, and yes I did graduate high school, but I don't live in the dorms or with my parents. Actually, I have my own home where I live with my husband, Scott, and my two-year-old son, Dominic. Pretty amazing, huh? And a lot of people would look at me and my situation with pity, but there is no need.

I am actually doing quite well despite all of the past obstacles in my life. My parents divorced when I was 7 years old, and my father died later that year, leaving my brother, sister, and me (I'm the baby) with only half a family. Then 2 or 3 years later, my mother remarried, and it was really hard on us kids. I mean, he wasn't our father, but he sure tried to be. My parents and I never really got along after that, until I was about 17.

When I turned 15, I decided to rebel against my parents. I did a lot of bad things; I drank and did a horrid array of drugs. And toward the end of my self-abusing spree, I got pregnant. My parents hated me even more than before, or that is what I thought at the time. So as I became more pregnant and the months continued to pass on, so did my boyfriend's interest in me. But I didn't let that stop me. I was determined to clean up my act and make something of myself, not for me, though, but for my unborn baby. I stopped doing anything and everything that could harm me or my son. I also began to work very hard in school and pulled my grades up. So my parents began to come around and really helped me through the pregnancy. I realize now that they were always there for me;

I just never saw it. My son's father was still around, but that was temporary. He left when Dominic was about 3 months old. What a great guy! But that was okay because I met Scott a few months later.

I continued to work hard and was able to graduate high school a semester early. But I didn't stop there: I went into college early. Kind of a jump-start for me, I guess. So I got married and moved away from my parents' for the last time. And here I am.

At first, people were a bit shy of me because I was very different. I quickly found out that there were very few people who were married or had children and still attended college. Actually, it really surprised me. It took a few weeks, but people began to come around. And now I have quite a few friends who now practically beg me to see Dominic. It's kind of nice to feel accepted. (If you have children, bring them to campus! Your classmates will soon reveal themselves as tribal aunts and uncles. It's good for your classmates, and it's good for your child. And for you.)

But not all of this just happened. I had to work really hard and clean up my life. My mother still tells me that having this baby saved my life, and I now think that she is right. As you can tell, my parents and I now get along better than ever. They don't necessarily accept my past, but they were willing to work beyond it because they love me. Oh, and my mother's husband is now Dad in my book. He is a big part of the reason that I am here today.

Scott is my son's father, and nobody can say otherwise. Who would want to? He came into this relationship with his eyes open, and he was accepting of everything. It took some trial and error to get the diaper thing down, but overall he has been amazing.

So do everyone a favor if you meet a nontraditional student: treat him or her like everyone else because they are; they just have different circumstances. We can all still go out and have fun; we just might have to find a baby-sitter first.

As you can see, I am no longer "a baby raising a baby." I am a college student with a family, just like everyone else.

Lindsay Steen

The Motivation Behind Nontraditionality

As a nontraditional student, sometimes I look around at other students on campus and wonder what it would be like to live such a carefree existence . . . I never feel like I can give anything 100% of me. That is to say, I constantly feel torn between being an attentive mom, supportive partner, a good student, a model daughter, a positive friend. I realize that I am incredibly blessed, but I worked hard to get to this point. Often, I feel like I am unable to appreciate my daily experiences in the classroom, on the playground, and in my bedroom because I am exhausted. I exist in a state of semiconsciousness, which is punctuated by jolts of caffeine. My time is limited, and sleep is a luxury.

But what would motivate me? My awareness of my reality is what fuels my mind, body, and spirit. I know that I am creating a space for future generations of bright women that must not be forgotten. In the classroom, I am the voice of all my sisters who cannot be here because they are working two jobs, raising children alone, caring for parents, and trying to survive. I have a responsibility to myself, my mother, and my daughter to fulfill my childhood dreams and reach my goals. I will not forget who I am. I will not sacrifice my dreams. The best gift I can give to my daughter is a powerful role model. The best gift I can give to my mother is a legacy. The best gift I can give to myself is a sense of purpose and pride. I may be a nontraditional student, but I come from a tradition of strong women.

Sunshine Serrano

International Student

As a freshman at Columbia College, I took the class called INCC/Introduction to Columbia College. The class helped me and the rest of the freshmen to get a good and easy start to college life. Our first assignment was to read a chapter in *This Book Is Not Required* and then write a paper about how we felt about the chosen chapter. The book deals with problems and issues a college student may have or get during his or her college career. I read a couple of chapters, and I had a hard time relating to any of them because none of them addressed my issue: being an international student. I'm a student from Denmark, and this is my first year in the States . . . I want to tell how it is to be an international student and express my personal feelings. . . . We live in the era of globalization, and more and more students move from their home country to another to study; therefore, I think that it is very relevant to write about how college life looks from an international student's point of view.

Basketball is my big passion, so I decided to try to play overseas, and I found Columbia College to be the right place for me. I arrived at Columbia College in the middle of August from my native country of Denmark. I was looking forward to spending my first year away from home, even though I knew that it was going to be hard being away from my family and friends. So now I've been here for roughly 2 months and I'm comfortable. Even though I'm at ease here, I still feel like it is just an extended vacation. I can't face the fact that I have to stay here for a couple of years! But I don't want to think too much about it because that is when I start to feel homesick and depressed. I find myself best when things are going fast, so I don't get the chance to think too much.

When you arrive, the pace of time is running fast. You receive so many new impressions that you don't have time to sit down and digest all the new things you have experienced. You find out the first couple of weeks that you are in constant need of sleep. After you have been away from home for a while, you start to miss things more than you would ever expect, and it's the weirdest things you long for. You find out how much you miss traditional home-cooked food that you only can get in your home country. Even though all the fast food is good now and then, you realize that you get tired of it in the long run. At one point you call your mom and beg her to send your favorite candy because you can't stand the candy over here. So she sends you candy for over $100 so you can taste home.

Luckily I'm from western Europe and can speak the native language, English, which is a huge benefit for me. I'm able to communicate with everybody, and the majority of the people I meet think that I'm a regular kid from Ohio. It has mostly advantages, but it also has a disadvantage. On the surface, I might look like a native, but under the surface I'm a stranger in a foreign country. I make mistakes like anyone else would do in a foreign country, but because people think that I'm a native they don't cut me any slack. What people don't realize is that, even though we look like each other on the surface, underneath we have totally different cultures and norms. So it takes some time to adapt to the lifestyle over here and you have to feel your way, but as time goes by you are able to interact like a native.

I feel at home here, but my home is not here. I left it in Denmark, and I think it's going to take a while before I feel like Columbia College is my home. But I'm enjoying every day here, and I believe that is how you have to attack the situation. My advice to international students is take one day at a time and put out your antennae and gather everything you can. Use every sense. Smell, taste, and see as much as possible. So when you come home you feel like your family and friends haven't been missed in vain.

One thing that you can be sure of is that you've come to a country with very friendly people who will stand upside down to help you with any problems. That is the spirit of America you feel as soon as you arrive . . .

Andreas Jakobsen

Some of Us Were Raised in an Asian Culture

I was raised in a culture that does not like to outright ask for or refuse another's request. For example, when I was younger, I was used to refusing second servings and then expecting the person who gave out the food to give it to me anyway. Generous gifts given were politely refused and then given anyway. Even though no one really wants to pay the bill, we all fight over it. (If you're wondering how this could work, it's usually seen in the context of the situation—e.g., if you were broke and couldn't buy a drink, you would talk about how thirsty you are and hope that someone would offer to buy you a drink.)

So when I met with others outside of my culture with a different communication style, strange problems would ensue. I would refuse the offers of friends, even if I needed their help, with the expectation that they would give it anyway. And I was always secretly surprised when my friends, after my initial rejection, did not help me.

It wasn't until I took Life Skills for Women, a class offered at my school for women, that I learned how truly strange my behavior appeared to others.

Ann Tsueng

The *Real* College Experience:
What Every Transfer Should Know

If freshman students have worries, woe to the transfer student; the minute students transfer in they already have to start thinking about leaving. One minute we are at our community college, stressing to finish our university application and revise our personal statements, when we need to repeat the same laborious task for grad school. Grad school deadlines start dropping on us like 10-ton bricks by the end of our first year in the university system. In addition, it wasn't too long ago that we decided on a major, and now we have to decide on a career! There are several obstacles and disadvantages that transfer students encounter that faculty may attempt to help with yet cannot give any solutions for. The typical response I receive from faculty is, "Yes, I know it's hard," followed by a sympathetic face. I'm left thinking, "Yes, it's hard, so what can I do about it?" Universities are not transfer friendly; transfer students must fend for themselves. Perhaps, universities don't see the obstacles that transfer students confront, or maybe we're second-class citizens in a land that doesn't care to accommodate us.

The dilemma that most would-be transfer students encounter is that all we know, all we've ever known for the past 2, maybe 3, years is that higher education up to this point has been too foggy because it was out of our reach. Community college students have one major goal: to get out of there as soon as possible. We want to transfer and move on with our lives. The problem is that in our hurried state we become too engulfed with fulfilling requirements and starting the paperwork for the next level, so we forget that there will be new priorities, requirements, and deadlines awaiting us on the other side. Making the transition from a community college student to a university student is a gradual process; it takes time to get the hang of it.

Whether this transition is a smooth one or not depends on the institution that you will be transferring into; for instance, private universities may consist of a smaller number of students, which can allow for intimate class settings and more interaction with professors. Another advantage of attending a small university is that counselors, TAs, and other personnel will not be so overwhelmed and constantly in a rush to move you along. Information also travels quicker in smaller universities, increasing awareness of up-and-coming events and deadlines that are on the horizon. Of course, not all private universities offer these advantages, so it's important that transfer students seeking such interaction investigate this matter when researching potential universities.

This is not to say that transferring into a public university is a horrific experience. It isn't. I am at UCLA, which I love. It does, however, require more tending on your part. Public universities usually have a large student body, which makes it nearly impossible to have intimate class settings. In addition, the possibility of getting to know your professors is also pretty slim, unless you make the effort to see them during office hours and try to stand out in class by frequently asking questions and sitting in the front rows. It may sound corny, but in huge lecture halls students can become faceless numbers; therefore, sitting in the front within the professors' view and asking questions can get them to eventually notice you.

As far as tending to your own education in a public university (more so than a student in a small, private university would have to), you may be wondering how this would be any different than what you have always done. As transfer students, we already have a lot of experience taking charge of our own education; we wouldn't be able to transfer if not for a lot of hard work and vigilance on our part. The reason that it's worth mentioning is because in universities the workload increases substantially within a shorter period of time. It can become difficult to keep up with papers, readings, and exams while at the same time trying to keep an eye on the road ahead.

With such a high pace, it is easy to get caught up in the moment and never notice deadlines flying right by you: "Oops, I was supposed to start applying for grad school when?" Time is a transfer student's worst enemy. The majority of community colleges go by the semester system, but once you transfer you may need to adapt, and fast, to the quarter system. At a community college procrastination doesn't have such severe consequences as in a university that runs by the quarter system. We had 4 long months in which to get things done; therefore, the workload was totally manageable. In contrast, in the 10-week quarter system we are given more work and less time. How's that fair? Where we once had to worry about reading three or four chapters, we now have to worry about three or four books, and actually I'm being kind in this example. Now, before we work ourselves into a frenzy, the situation isn't as dim as it appears. After all, everything's possible if we manage our time properly. Only by being able to manage our time better and avoiding procrastinating can we carry out our goals and fulfill the expectations that come before us.

Another way that time can work against transfer students is because, in order to finish on time, which is in 2 years since we come in as juniors, we miss out on the opportunity to take courses for the mere enjoyment of learning something outside of our major. When time is of the essence, transfer students need to hurry up and complete their majors' requirements, so there is no time for exploring other classes, especially if we're planning on grad school after graduating.

The way in which transfer students experience university life is also very different from the way traditional students do; the idea of the college experience is something that every student often fantasizes about. It is true that we all transferred from community colleges; however, most transfers don't consider this prior college experience to be the real college experience. Community college was merely the stepping-stone that was needed to get us closer to the real thing. Therefore, we have built up illusions based on preconceptions that have been forming inside our heads since high school about student life in a 4-year university. Trying to cram 4 years of experience into 2 is not an easy task. Living either on or near campus is the best bet for students who set out on this mission. Most universities guarantee housing for a year to transfers; where you choose to live is another factor that shapes your college experience. Usually, the dorms are located on campus; the dorms are where the vast majority of first- and second-year students reside. Then there is transfer housing, which are apartments located off campus. As transfer students, choosing between the two isn't too difficult; dorms are more expensive and are usually the size of a shoebox. In addition, since most transfers are older than first- and second-year students, living off campus might be the better way to go.

When I transferred to UCLA, I decided to live off campus at the university housing for transfers. Everyone in my building was a transfer student. For most of the students living there, this was their first time to move out of their parents' home and begin living with strangers. I'll be the first to say that living on your own for the first time feels liberating; we had a real sense of independence, although living in your own apartment does entail responsibility: You have to try to get along with your roommates, clean, cook, grocery shop, and pay bills. This is a small price to pay for living on cloud nine—no curfews, no one looking over our shoulder. Yes, we were on our own, but as great as this was, we all felt left out. We felt segregated. We didn't know the campus very well or what activities were going on. We had no information about anything, and worst of all we didn't have or know of anyone who could guide us.

In this situation dorms do offer some advantages as opposed to apartments; students who live there get the benefit of resident advisors/program advisors. Resident advisors are those wonderful people who also live in the dorms. Students can go seek not only information but counseling from their resident advisors. Some dorms will even provide one resident advisor per floor. Resident advisors are also responsible for maintaining the rules and regulations of the dorms: They restore order if students are getting too crazy. In other words, they are there to hold a student's hand. Well, I wanted someone to hold my hand, too. If that isn't enough assistance to students who live in the dorms, sometimes there are also program advisors who live in dorms as well. These people are even more wonderful. They coordinate special events and activities for the residents of their dorms. They put together picnics, little field trips, and so on, so not only are students being provided with entertainment, but they are also getting a chance to meet other students who live in their building. These are definitely a few things that students need to consider when the time comes to decide where to live.

Getting to know your new surroundings is also a crucial part of your college experience; when students know their campus, they get a sense of belonging. As we all know, most large universities can be very intimidating. These campuses are huge; therefore, new transfers should make an effort to explore their campus and the campus's resources. Now in my senior year, I have yet to explore the entire campus and am considering going on a tour before I graduate. It's no joke; this way I get a formal tour by a guide along with some history of the university. Besides exploring one's university, it's also a good idea to explore the neighboring cities and its establishments. Since most transfer students are also from a different area, venturing out into the new town can be fruitful when it's time to unwind (i.e., party).

Unfortunately, there are other things that transfers won't get to check off their real-college-experience list due to time restrictions. Membership in fraternities or sororities might be out of the question. Rumor has it that some sororities won't accept transfer pledges; certain fraternities might. Taking the time to research certain organizations that fit our needs or ideologies might also be too time-consuming. Being part of your school's sports department is also a hard act to juggle when you have certain deadlines to meet in your education and future career decisions. Then there's the experience that every student should have: traveling abroad. As upper division students, the classes we actually need for our major are not always offered. Therefore, if we decide to travel abroad, the classes that we would take would only count as electives and would not apply toward the requirements for our major. As transfer students, we need to get a lot done in a limited time, so traveling would mean delays, and we can't afford that. Since freshmen and sophomores are still taking their general education requirements, they have more of a selection to choose from; they could live abroad for a whole year and not worry about running out of required courses. However, if traveling abroad is a must, it can be done after graduation if you still have some leftover units lying around; speaking to an advisor early in the year can get you on the right path.

In sum, transfer students can come to feel like second-class citizens, foreigners in a new land. Oftentimes transfers, like foreigners, will arrive in a new destination and become disappointed at the realization that their expectations will never fully be met. But there is hope; it doesn't have to be this way. In retrospect, I am now able to recognize where I, among other transfers, have gone wrong. You see, it was when I first opened my acceptance letter from UCLA; at this point, I should have already started to think about life after undergraduate school. Instead, I succumbed to the overwhelming demands of being an undergrad, balancing my sanity with schoolwork, oblivious to anything else. I figured that I would gradually find things out when I needed to, but before I knew it 1 whole year was gone. Time waits for no one.

So as a word of advice for would-be transfers who are about to embark on the next journey, give yourself plenty of time to look into what lies ahead. Find out what resources your school has available for transfers. Some schools offer programs that are specifically designed for transfer students, offering workshops on how to adapt and the services of transfer counselors. The career center is also another place where a student can go to seek guidance on placement exams, graduate schools, and jobs. Ultimately, however, it's important for you to know yourself, know what it is that you want to get out of your time as an undergrad. To get the most out of this 2-year experience, transfers need to take the initiative to do their own research; at times I felt like a detective following leads to get the information I needed. Now in my second and last year, I finally feel that I have gotten the hang of undergraduate school and the quarter system.

Ideally, by providing you with my experience I am able to give you a glimpse into what obstacles may lay ahead for transfers and ways in which to ease this transition. There will be times when you will feel overwhelmed and discouraged, but you must remember that you have made it this far for a reason. You have earned this.

Veronica Fematt

When Working *Is* Required

Work and School

We go to college so that when we get out we are ready for fast-paced high-paying jobs, so where does burger flipping come in? Many students at universities are finding tuition and board a bit much for their budgets and are resorting to minimum wage work with high scheduling demands.

Coming to college I knew that I would have to get a job, the sooner the better. Never having been in college I wasn't sure what to expect, so I waited 2 weeks into the first quarter to begin the job search. I figured 2 weeks would be enough to get adjusted to dorm life and my study load. Little did I know that there were thousands of students who hadn't postponed their searches and had taken all the jobs I wanted. I applied to the different libraries on campus, but the only positions they had left were on the mornings when I had class. I applied for fast-food jobs, but they were full as well.

After 2 weeks of searching, my budget was getting low, and my patience was growing thin. By then I was willing to work anywhere. Finally, during the fourth week a cashiering position opened up, and I had my first interview. Dressed in a business outfit I headed for the interview with mixed feelings and little hope of being hired for any job on campus. I was desperate as I walked into the manager's office, and she must have sensed that because she was being really nice to me. I told her I was willing to work whenever she wanted and would alter my schedule second quarter to fit her needs. I told her I didn't care what was needed of me as long as I was hired—and I was hired on the spot.

My first college job! I was so excited—finally, a paycheck. But would the long days in class followed by hours on my feet be worth $6.75 per hour? Would staying up all night every night trying to catch up on studying be worth it? Where were all the easy jobs where I could study on the clock? I had heard about them on tours and orientation, but they seemed to be hiding. This was only my first quarter of college, and I was already feeling overwhelmed. What was I thinking? I hadn't even started the job, and I was already considering quitting in order to salvage my GPA. I couldn't work every Saturday and Sunday for the rest of the quarter! I couldn't squeeze 2 hours of work between two classes and then close at night.

My job required that I work 10 hours a week plus weekends. I also had to work a minimum of 2 hours per shift. My bosses didn't care if I had midterms or finals because all the cashiers had them and I was new. So I found myself sleeping during classes, even when I was sitting in the front row. I wasn't studying as much as I needed to get the grades I wanted, and I felt trapped. I couldn't cut back on my hours, and I was losing sleep to keep up with my reading as it was. I didn't know what to do.

Three weeks after I started cashiering, I was talking to a friend about a job she found. It paid more than mine and had a very flexible schedule. She raised funds for the university. She said it wasn't telemarketing, but it sounded like it to me. Still, the schedule was tempting. I didn't want to leave my cashiering job for one that I wasn't sure of, so I worked at both for a whole quarter. Schedules clashed, and I felt like I was being pulled in three directions. The workload from school and the time constraints of two jobs pulled and tugged until I had to choose. I chose fund-raising for the university because the schedule was better, and I have never regretted it.

Starting college presents budget restraints that may require that we get jobs. Finding one that fits your personality is key to your survival. Flexible schedules can save you during finals and make having a job seem like less of a burden.

Shawna Wood

The Curriculum of Working and Schooling

I was raised as a wealthy child. All of that changed in 1992 during the deadly Los Angeles riots, which were sparked by the infamous verdicts regarding the Rodney King beatings. After that specific point in time, I grew up real fast.

My father is an entrepreneur, as is my mother. None of my grandparents had ever had more than enough money to make ends meet. Neither of my parents possesses more than an associate's degree. However, they founded and successfully operated numerous business ventures ranging from travel agencies and flower shops to a large-scale industrial linen service and land development projects. They had worked extremely hard and had made wise business decisions for almost two decades. It was then that they launched United Food Wholesalers Inc., a wholesale food commissary that was open to the public. It was their biggest and most profitably efficient business to date. United Foods turned a net profit from the very first month of business. By the sixth month, it had exceeded projections and maintained a healthy growth rate. We were thankful and happy, as this was the peak accomplishment after decades of hard work and undying commitment to family.

So I grew up in a modern-day palace, surrounded by a loving sister, amazing mother, and frightfully assertive father who was larger than life. My father's side of the family was substantially larger and more integrated into our lives than my mother's family. They had strictly disapproved of his decision to marry a woman not of his race, a major issue in our culture, but he did not cave under their pressures. There was a short-lived period of dissonance within the families, which voluntarily surrendered itself to the happiness and prosperity that their union had bore.

The impact of the riots became very evident to my family's livelihood. It heavily damaged revenues and made it impossible to realize value from the property itself. The financial burdens became heavier as arguments between my parents became louder and more frequent. After a bankruptcy, foreclosure, legal separation, massive heart attack, and finally a divorce, my family had fallen from a great height, and I was not sure if things would ever return to how they used to be. My sister was studying chiropractic in San Jose, I was studying at UC Irvine (UCI), my mother was working in restaurants and hotels in L.A., and my father was managing a recently acquired apartment complex.

Then the phone rang.

It was my father. It was the man who had made it financially possible for me to be in college. He asked me if I would like to join him in a new business venture we would eventually decide to name TacoDeli. I finished up my spring quarter with the intention to be back by the fall of 1998. The restaurant, which is located in La Cañada, proved to be successful in record time due to the overwhelming demand for fast food of high quality, freshly prepared in an open kitchen, with a menu consisting exclusively of grilled and charbroiled foods.

I was working 14-hour days, 7 days a week, alongside my 53-year-old father who had lost everything during the last 6 years. The restaurant became my icon for hope and rebirth.

I did not make it back to Irvine for the fall quarter. By winter, my sister had graduated and came to La Cañada to work and study for her board examinations. She became intensively involved in the management, so I managed to leave La Cañada for 3 days a week. However, the requirements of being self-employed did not allow me to perform as I had been accustomed to, so, reluctantly, I withdrew. During the spring quarter, I was bouncing from La Cañada to Irvine three times a week. My things-to-do list had evolved into a things-to-do book. I became very efficient, yet somehow the time necessary to perform academically was seldom available. Discouraged, I withdrew again.

I reenrolled for the fall of 2000 with a vengeance. I was at full throttle both in La Cañada and in Irvine. However, despite all the effort I was putting forth, my energy was too diluted to achieve the level of academic performance I had proven to be capable of. I thought about withdrawing again, yet I hungered for progress, not failure.

My father began to work on other ventures, and my sister and I shouldered much of the burden. We began to prioritize my full-time enrollment in school and convinced my father to reconfigure the restaurant's infrastructure. Through an unlikely arrangement, my mother would purchase my father's share of the restaurant at a fair market price. My father and I would proceed to develop our new catering division of TacoDeli, a plan that we had been discussing for some time. This way, we could cumulatively generate more money and resolve the very issues they had been fighting over. We all felt that we were moving in the right direction. This entailed from me a full-time work commitment as well as a full-time student commitment. I resumed my stressful and hyperactive lifestyle until the ninth week of the spring semester. At that point, my schedule finally caught up with my body. The doctors diagnosed me with viral meningitis. I was ill for 3 weeks and was unable to attend any of my final examinations.

Things are better now. I'm enrolled in a full-time program at UCI, yet I also have responsibilities and research activities going on with the restaurant. Studying has become more difficult since my days as a freshman and sophomore; however, my study habits and note-taking skills have improved drastically. *I believe that my rapid entry into the real world has something to do with the way I read, write, and, most important, the way I analyze. I believe I am better off for having worked and studied simultaneously. I learned things that school does not or, rather, could not teach me.* There are always benefits and drawbacks to dividing your focus, and the decisions you make today will shape your livelihood of tomorrow.

That being said, the most important thing to identify in the process is your motivation. My motivation was my family, along with a strong interest in my parents' well-being. It worked out well for me. Not easy, but well. *The world outside of academia is not the same as it is inside, and therefore you will need skills not available in academic courses in order to realize your dreams.* Follow your heart and always bite off more than you can chew—just learn how to rise to an occasion.

Missak Michael Sarkissian

Can You Find a College Job in Your Field of Interest?

One of the hardest, yet most rewarding, aspects of college has been trying to juggle work and school at the same time. If I had to give only one piece of advice, it would definitely be to get a job related to your field of study. First of all, it gives you a chance to see the environment that you would potentially be working in the future. You may find that you love the work but despise the environment. For some individuals, like myself, aspects such as these really affect the field of work that I will go into. Also, by working in the field that you are interested in, you are already one step ahead of your peers. It is the best feeling to know that you are doing firsthand what the professor is lecturing on. The way that I see it is that the theories that are discussed in lecture are very vague and exist only in theory until you actually apply them. On the other hand, if you do not know the basics behind the work you are doing, then there is only so far that you can go with it. So by working in your field and studying the concepts in school at the same time, you're technically getting the best of both worlds.

Working while going to school also makes the material you learn seem much more interesting. It adds a dimension to your life that fills the void of wondering what you're learning all this for. Personally, before I started to work, I felt as though I was just memorizing half the things that I was for no apparent reason. I could not figure out how they would apply to anything I was doing, but now I actually see the parallels between lecture and work.

Last, but definitely not least, since most of us are starving college students, the income really does not hurt. Although most work related to your field will probably end up being an internship of some sort, the experience alone is worth it. You might not be making as much as your friend who is working at the mall, but with the experience that you are getting at such a young age in the long run you'll be the one making the big bucks (at least, that's what we tell ourselves).

Don't get me wrong—working while going to school is definitely a very difficult thing to do. There is a lot of pressure on students who are planning on going to graduate school today. Between juggling your hundreds of pages of reading, your next essay, and your research that you're doing with a professor; volunteering at different places; building up your extracurricular activities; and studying for GREs, MCATs, or LSATs, or whatever it may be it is very difficult to make time for work. If you are planning on working part-time, then already 10 or 20 hours out of your week are gone. These 10 or 20 hours may not necessarily have been spent studying, but regardless it is not fair to miss out on the social aspect, and it's hard to make time for that when there are so many other things going on. Doing all that is necessary to get into graduate school today takes a lot out of the ideal college experience and instead fills it with more pressure and stress. Everyone has his or her own road to travel. The best thing to say would be to do what works for you. You have to know yourself well enough to know your limits. No matter how important grad school may seem now, it is not worth having a mental breakdown at the age of 22.

Sheyda Bogosyan

Putting Something at Stake

I would suggest you put "something at stake" as you enroll in a course. This is a Landmark Education–derived concept. What is putting something at stake? The first time I ever heard this particular concept was in the context of what was called the SELP course—the Self-Expression and Leadership course—and the instructor's analogy has stuck with me ever since: John grew up in a relatively small town in Arizona, and as a teenager there the primary fun event was to have drag races on Friday nights. These were always fun and brought out a big crowd of teens. The races were fast and exciting and, of course, had that necessary adrenaline thrill of danger. Every once in a while, however, the two racers would race for pink slips. To race for a pink slip is to race for the ownership documents of the car: The winner gets the loser's car. Whenever two guys raced for pink slips, the quality of that particular race dramatically shifted. Everything was still the same on one level, of course, but on another everything had completely shifted. The intensity of the event, the level of participation, the degree of concentrated focus, the sheer vertical depth of reality to which the drivers and the onlookers accessed all dramatically enlarged. I would suggest you put a pink slip issue in your life "at stake" for the particular course you enroll in. For example, "In taking this course, social psychology, the pink slip issue I am putting at stake is I want to achieve mastery in influencing how my group of friends views the ecological situation of the planet" or "I want to achieve composure and effectiveness when I address large groups of people" or "I want to understand deep in my gut how the male/female world is different from my own world—in ways I am unconscious of at the present." You need to pick something specific to you and your life, something relatively significant—pink-slipish. Doing this will alter your level of participatory presence in the class. You will see, hear, and smell it differently than you would as a mere indifferent spectator.

Another useful tool or analogy that I would recommend you consider is putting yourself in the position of teaching the course you are taking. By this I mean that you might set up a situation such that you are teaching this course "in flight" to another person, even if this is merely in the form of a telephone conversation or over coffee once or twice a week. If I know that I have to personally present the material I am currently learning to someone else, I am automatically in a position of listening more powerfully. The machinery of "teaching the course" and of having something at stake is very powerful in cutting through lazy, habitual, nonattentive and distracted listening.

Imagine there are two groups of people in a class on skydiving, groups A and B, all geared up with parachutes and in a plane flying at 5,000 feet. They are all listening to the instructor give instructions on the techniques of skydiving. There is a difference between the two groups, however; namely, group A is jumping; group B is not jumping. Which group of people in this class do you think is really going to listen more powerfully, more deeply, with more precise and critical awareness?

Bernard McGrane

CHAPTER 2

Grades: Can You Perform Without the Pressure?

The only thing that will give you as much heartache in college as love are grades—the grading system with its exams, papers, and attendant complexities. I want you to understand the vital difference between operating within a set of rules and internalizing those rules. The cardinal point here is that what you don't internalize can't really hurt you, while what you do internalize can destroy you very rapidly, and this goes for the high-scoring student as much as for the lower scoring.

Let me use military service as an example. Obviously, when you're in the army, the army has got you by the ass. To survive intact you had better know the rules.[1] We all know, however, that it is a far cry from obeying the rules to actually believing that the army is a wise and just institution that will "make a man out of you."

Those who fall for this version of reality are doing what people frequently do when confronted by power: They internalize the rules. In one way this is a safe reaction because it will keep down any internal rebellion that might crop up and get us in trouble. However, we also feel, instinctively, that this path can destroy our integrity as human beings. So the healthier of us will do the minimum to survive without, for a moment, caring whether or not we are "good soldiers." This is the attitude that the Bible recommends when it says that you should be "in the world but not of it." Robert Fried (1995) explains in *The Passionate Teacher:*[2]

> A game is both a microcosm and a parody of life. It is like life: it brings forth the same energies and the same feelings, but, in the end, it is not *real.* It is a charade of something real. We may be absorbed by it and be willing to play along. But a voice within us is there to say, "Take it easy. It doesn't really matter. *It's only a game.*"
>
> The particular offense of playing the Game of School lies in the disengagement of our intellect and our feelings from tasks that deserve to be taken seriously: tasks

like writing, reading, thinking, planning, listening, researching, analyzing, performing, applying, and evaluating. We do harm when we reduce these acts of intellect, creativity, and judgment to rote exercises, perfunctory deeds, or meaningless gestures. Faced with the stresses of daily life in school, it can seem easier, at times, to pretend to believe rather than to truly believe in the value of what we are about. Despite the positive aspects of going to school that many children and adults experience, the temptation is always there to cope with school by going through the motions. (p. 95)

Regarding Grades

But what has all this to do with the seemingly more benign institutions of university education? I would like to suggest to you that the competition for grades, which you have already experienced for 12 years and will experience for at least 4 more, is a very dehumanizing and damaging system that has its roots deep in the injustices of our society. Since early childhood, it has set you against your peers and filled you with intermittent anxieties about your worth as a person. One student, Stephanie Pappas, wrote the following when she reflected back on her schooling:

> Children are programmed even as young as first grade that grades are the most important aspect of school. I clearly remember being in the third grade and having a chart with stars in our classroom, which indicated who knew their multiplication tables. As an 8-year-old child, I recall feeling humiliated that all my friends had more stars than I did. My motivation for studying my multiplication tables was no longer to learn them per se but to gain more gold stars. Learning was not my reward. It was the grade and praise I desired.

> Throughout our school years, society teaches us to believe that grades display our intelligence. Because of this, our motivation, learning, and personal growth are placed second to attaining the ultimate goal—the grade. Society first teaches us about societal norms and codes, yet it is in the school system where we are ultimately taught to imitate. We are programmed to imitate what the teacher wants. If we don't, we get a bad grade. This idea of imitation is so strong because it is reinforced through schooling for a minimum of 12 years. Imitation is the main cause for our stifled and structured society. Imitation, competition, and fear of grades hinder our discovery. Lawrence Lu, a college senior, reflects back on his school career:

> Two children scribble images that remotely resemble their names. They receive praises with perhaps chocolate rewards. The children smile, beaming at the accomplishment and relishing in the encouraging warmth of the chocolate giver. Next year, they are asked to include their name in a sentence and are given a gold star. The years continue as the praises and gold stars become fewer. Somehow, they have now mystically transformed into numbers and letters. Even more interesting is that the numbers and letters have curiously become more valuable than any chocolate treat on the planet. We speed forward another few years.

Relief was the word of the hour as my friend and I finished finals for the umpteenth time as college seniors. . . . Long gone were the kids who looked forward to school and thirsting for knowledge. Long gone were the praises, the stars, and the chocolate. In their places stood statistically skewed numbers and harsh comments about not following so-and-so format. What had happened and, more important, why hadn't anyone stopped it from happening?

We are scared of being at the tail end of a curve, of receiving lower than average marks, of expressing how we truly feel to the TA because he or she might grade us with unchecked bias, of not writing down on the test what they want us to write even though we couldn't disagree with it more, of making one wrong move that would result in a smudge on our platinum resumes, and of not getting that big job so society can feed us approval and positive reinforcements like little freakin' lab rats. We are scared to death of everything. No one cares that they don't remember what they learned last quarter because they are relieved they kept up their GPAs. They don't have time to care because they are worried again about the same thing in the present quarter. Learning? Who the hell has time for that? I'm too busy trying to pass the BAR and become a lawyer to worry about negligible trinkets like ethics. The worst part is that no one talks about it. Everyone sucks it up and accepts it as "the way it is."

In high school, the teachers did not teach for knowledge. They taught us what we had to know to pass the advanced placement tests. The notion of developing young, curious, scientific minds was a luxury that no one had time for. The SAT followed and encouraged students to spend hundreds of dollars on learning the tricks of how to best guess the correct answer. Of course, we students disregarded that the test did not reflect anything worthwhile about anyone. Why should we have cared? Every other test was like that.

Thankfully, the pain for most ended here. The average student had already been accepted by whatever college would take them, and, more important, they had adapted to working inside the system that did not care an ounce about intellectual curiosity or expansion. If you still believe that quality learning and learning for the test can occur simultaneously, then good for you. I do not. The bottom line is that I was a kid who had smiled when the magnetism lesson was the next day. I was a willing sponge to soak in anything and everything. *Then one day it wasn't about being curious. It was about the grades.* There was no room for anything else. With the grades came pressure that systematically builds. And the only emotion appropriate for describing the brief moments when we don't have to worry is relief. That is the way it just is. Period. For what grandiose treasure did we trade our souls?

Lawrence Lu

If the system has not totally destroyed your love of learning, it is only because a parent or an occasional teacher has rescued you or, perhaps, because of your own natural resilience. Almost everybody I know, including most college professors, hates and fears writing because writing is what they have always been judged on. If you have made it to college, you aren't among those who also failed to learn to read because of the anxiety school induces. Actually, the plight of nonreaders is a perfect case in point. Any child who has learned to speak can learn to read.[3] Learning to speak is really harder because it requires the child to grasp symbolism and grammatical structure. That anybody should fail to read in a society where signs and labels surround us everywhere is a profound indictment of the traumatizing effects of school. If speaking were taught in school, we would have a nation of stutterers.

Anxiety doesn't help people to learn. On the contrary, anxiety causes most people to withdraw. Research indicates that negative sanctions (punishments) are particularly destructive to motivation. Yet, year after year, schools continue to create anxiety in their students:

> Children simply do not learn better when education is transformed into a competitive struggle. To be sure, a teacher may want to turn a lesson into a competitive game to attract and hold students' attention. But the real appeal of this strategy is that it makes teaching easier, not more effective. . . . Competition does not generally promote excellence because trying to do well and trying to beat others simply are two different things. (Kohn, 1986a, p. 22)

In my classes, I have sometimes asked students to jot down the thing they remember most vividly from their elementary school education. You might just try this exercise for a moment before you read on.

Ninety-eight percent of the incidents listed were negative experiences: times when students felt humiliated, punished, harassed, and so on (remember, these were the "academic successes" I was asking for, not the "failures"). The only exceptions were students who went to private schools.

One student, Alex Hayden, wrote about his experience in a grade-free private elementary school:

> The idea of goal seeking is illustrated by the use of grades. The question is whether or not students would work as hard or learn as much if grades were eliminated. I feel that if grades were eliminated, I would learn just as much. When I was in elementary school, I attended a private school that did not have the formal grading system. I worked hard on my studies and enjoyed knowledge. However, when grades were introduced to me in junior high school, I no longer concentrated so much on the actual subjects; it became more of a game. I now had to learn how to please my professors, with their various styles, to receive a good grade. To me, school has become much more stressful since the grading system was introduced to me. I have been trying to tell myself that I am getting my grades for me, but am I really? Or, rather, am I getting the knowledge for myself and my grades for society so that I may be judged or rated for a future socially accepted activity?

Another student, Phillip Nichols, had similar insights when reflecting back on his socialization into the student role:

> If an individual has grown up in an environment where that which was desired was nurtured for its own sake, and then the same individual is placed in our educational institutions, where his or her natural desires are replaced by artificial ones, the entire process of acquiring knowledge is twisted. High marks replace

the desire to learn. . . . The traditional grading system motivates students through fear. It trains them to avoid failure at all costs, and, by whatsoever means possible, the student learns that he or she must receive high marks regardless of whether or not they are deserved. This system allows the student to prostitute his or her way through the halls of higher education, and, ironically, even the honest students contribute to the perpetuation of this blatant disregard of humanity.

My experience as a teacher has been that *high achievement is closely related to self-confidence.* Think about it. If you are afraid of failure in a certain class, don't you find yourself procrastinating and cutting class more often—in short, avoiding the cause of your anxiety? These behaviors will, of course, cause you to do even more poorly. Sometimes, in the case of a student who was doing poorly for such reasons, I have simply slipped him or her a high grade to see what would happen. Usually, by the end of the term the student was earning those higher grades. *Our expectations become self-fulfilling prophecies.* Yet the anxiety approach to education continues right through college, and even though the teachers will no longer keep you after school, they will seem to find other ways to make you feel like a fool.

We are so used to the system that it seems inevitable. Most people have to admit to themselves that, if grades were to disappear tomorrow, they might never learn another set of irregular verbs and might, indeed, just lie down and not move for a very long time. Naturally! This is a *result* of the system, not a *reason* for it. Having been bullied all your life into learning things you didn't much want to know, you would, indeed, quit if you could and so, perhaps, would most of your professors. I suspect, though, that in a few months you would get up, look around, and begin to take an altogether different sort of interest in altogether different kinds of knowledge.

Why do our schools function in this way? Why is intellectual curiosity regularly killed in order to teach discipline? Why do our schools give even 7-year-old children failing grades? Whenever sociologists see a system continually operating in "dysfunctional" ways, they suggest that perhaps we have not discovered the "real" function of the system. A hint is given us here in that the only schools that don't beat up their students emotionally are a few private and public schools that serve the rich. The real purpose of school is to make people obedient to authority. The mindlessness of school is meant to prepare people for unquestioning acceptance of the mindlessness of most jobs. Perhaps most important, it is the job of schools to convince those who will have lousy jobs and low wages that their fate is their own fault, that they just weren't smart enough (translate, deserving enough) to do any better.

Our system hugely exaggerates differences of basic intelligence in people because the concept of IQ is used to justify wide disparities in income and, in general, chances for a satisfying life. This is why intelligence and academic performance are measured, not in the spirit of helping children to grow but in the spirit of instilling in certain children basic doubts about their self-worth as human beings.

Why are small children made to stand in line and at attention in school? So they will stand in line and at attention in the army! Schools are quite open about their aim of producing "good citizens." In an old cowboy movie, there was a scene in which a small-town bank had just been robbed, and the banker was out on the street exhorting the young men of the town to join the posse to go after the robbers. One young man next to him asked coolly, "Why? I didn't have any money in the bank." It is just such "poor citizenship" that the school system is dedicated to expunging.

College is a little different. Here, you are now among the prospective winners and at least the middle-range future leaders. (If you are at an Ivy League school, you are among the high-range future leaders.) These folk will not function right if they are simply browbeaten. Because they have to carry independent responsibilities, it is necessary that they have the confidence to act independently; therefore, the intimidation becomes much more subtle, and the inducement to internalize the system becomes subtle, self-deceptive and more insidious. Of course, the sorting machine of the system is still in high gear. Only some will become leaders; others still have to be convinced of at least their relative worthlessness. Otherwise, could we count on teachers to obey principals and junior accountants to obey senior executives? In particular, could we count on everybody down the line to carry out orders that are often nonsensical, self-serving, and not infrequently catastrophic? Would social workers, for example, agree to hound their clients off the welfare rolls because they had a man living with them? During wartime, would college professors forward failing grades to draft boards? Would nurses continue to tolerate gross underpayment while doctors get rich?

I have gone on at some length about the grading system because I think it is only by getting a broader perspective on it that you can put this system in its proper place—which is not inside your gut. One undergraduate wrote perceptively about this "internalization":

> My mother raised me to be the best that I could. She always told me that as long as I tried my hardest, I could be proud of myself. This may seem like great advice, but it has cost me years of self-torment. I have never tried my hardest, and I beat myself up over it. Even if I spent 60 hours doing research for a 10-page paper that my professor loves and gives me an A for, I am not satisfied. I know I could have tried harder. I know that I could have gone to bed a little later on a few nights and done 70 or 80 hours of research. I could have written a better paper, more concise with more insight, if I had not gone out with my friends that Thursday night. I would have impressed the professor more if I had actually found that perfect quotation that I spent 3 hours looking for before giving up. I could have tried harder. I chose not to. Does this mean I shouldn't be proud of myself? I don't think that my mother intended to instill such pressure with her standard. I took her too literally. What she meant was that if I set aside a certain amount of time to work on a paper or project, and I stick to it, and if I put in some thought and effort, then I did what was expected, and I should be content with the result. She wasn't trying to tell me that I had to go above and beyond the call of duty and push myself to the limit and beyond on every occasion. I created that demand myself. I wasn't content with doing what was expected and being "just average." I wanted more. For years I sacrificed time with friends and family so that I could be not just above average but excellent. I learned, though, that it's no fun to be the best if you're all alone when you get

there. I've finally learned the benefits of being average. I've learned that I can do well in school and still have healthy relationships with others. I learned to balance academia and friendship, stress and frivolity; I'm at peace because I made that decision myself. I am finally trying my hardest to do something . . . to be happy and enjoy my life. I am proud of that decision.

Kristin Rydberg

Another student compares how this internalization/socialization takes place in countries outside the United States:

I completed 7th through 11th grade in Australia, and returning to American high school in South Orange County, California, was a little more than a culture shock. I went from a public school in St. Ives with a uniform code and an emphasis on discipline to a public school in "the O.C." with a "fashion code" and an emphasis on social hierarchy. Nothing could have prepared me for entry into such a foreign institution.

St. Ives High School ran from 7th grade to 12th grade, and I had a mere 100 students in my class. The atmosphere of the school was one of discipline until students hit the ninth grade—after a seasoned 2 years many had learned their way around all the rules, regulations, and faculty. There is no GPA in Australia or any A's, B's, or C's—only excellent, good, satisfactory, unsatisfactory, and failing. Your report card would consist of checkmarks in these areas regarding behavior, assignments, and so on as well as a percentage for your overall grade in the class and the number you rank among your peers. The latter score is the most interesting because to get first in the year held great social significance. In fact, this little number caused intense emotions between my best friend and me, both perfectionists striving to be the best. Yet to be ranked high in the year also held the stigma of being a nerd, dork, or something similar. At the same time, being ranked against one's peers created a sense of unity among the mature students—many held the perception that this ranking system was a necessary evil that the faculty and administration insisted on, and, therefore, students paid little attention to this number as they got older, and slowly its significance faded.

While the Australian grading system seems as if it would pit students against one another, I feel that the American system, by far, is worse. Students attach so much worth to their GPA, and the fact that they are not flat-out ranked among their peers makes students inquisitive as to where they stand. In Australian high school, it is a loaded question to inquire about another's grades. An example would be when an assignment is returned, and a general murmur invades the classroom: "What did you get?" Students who pretty much failed the assignment, as well as students who excelled in it, are stigmatized. It appears that the "proper" grades to achieve in high school are C's and B's. One might think that ranking students would create a lot of competition, but, when these numbers aren't presented obviously, students compare themselves anyway in a much more vicious atmosphere.

Another interesting aspect regarding grades is how American college students continue to internalize the grading system and how Australian students seem to abandon this mindset. I ventured back to Sydney to study abroad and attend university for one semester. The way Australian universities grade is with High Distinction, Distinction, Credit, Pass, and No Pass. According to my fellow Australian students, a Pass was satisfactory and a Credit deserved congratulations. A Pass translates into a C and a Credit translates into a B. Getting a High Distinction was not of much importance and was definitely not worth tailoring your life to achieve. As you can imagine, none of my Aussie friends could understand why I was stressing about getting top grades—to them passing was enough. Once I tried explaining to them that my grades made up my GPA, that my scholarship funds relied on me keeping a high GPA, and that I needed high scores to get into a good graduate school. They just looked at me and said point-blank, "You Americans are crazy."

School worldwide is a socialization tool, a place for youth to learn the do's and don'ts, the have's and have nots, as well as the role they are assigned in this miniversion of the overall social hierarchy. Yet even though this is a common denominator for all education, I believe that American schools are the most brutal in this socialization process.

At St. Ives High School, the socialization that took place was very subtle. Perhaps this was due to a combination of grade size and culture. As a result of having about 100 students per grade (and having the majority of these kids attend elementary school together), students interacted with the group as a whole, even if there were little cliques defined at recess and lunch. These cliques were loosely formed and permitted people to network between groups rather than be shut out by firm boundaries. Consequently, students knew the majority of their peers and had at least acknowledged acquaintances within the entire grade. Even those students who were not popular at all were acknowledged and fit into the social framework. Culturally, high school was not considered the stepping-stone to the rest of your life. Australian students have so many avenues that can lead to careers that the possibilities are nearly overwhelming. First of all, students can opt to drop out at 10th grade with their Lower School Certificate. From here they can either apprentice in a field of their choice or attend TAFE (which is a type of junior college that allows students to tailor their classes to fit a certain profession). Or students can choose to remain in school for 11th and 12th grade and complete their HSC (Higher School Certificate). This is a series of assessments throughout the 2 years, culminating in exams in subjects of their own choice—these scores are then weighted and combined, giving the student one overall score. This educational path is by far the most stressful and demanding because that single score determines which programs of study and universities you are eligible for.

In fact, it should be noted that several students have actually committed suicide during this time in their life from the pressure of having the scores published in the *Sydney Morning Herald* for all to see. However, not all students take it that seriously, and once high school is complete, it is culturally encouraged for students to take a year off to travel around the world. If you have ever traveled, it might make sense now that you always seem to meet Australians. Travel is considered to be essential, and many students save money throughout high school if their parents haven't already started a fund for them. Or students can begin a university course, and then at any point during their education they can defer their program for 6 months to travel. Looking at the array of paths one can take in this culture shows that high school is not a crucial element in the path to one's success in life, as they make it out to be in our culture.

For me, transitioning from the situation described earlier into an institution known among students in the district as the "snobbiest" school was an experience to say the least. At this school, there were approximately 600 kids in my class, and since I was entering at 11th grade it goes without saying that everyone had already established their own niche within the social hierarchy. I soon learned that I would be judged, acknowledged, and discarded solely due to my appearance and material possessions. Students were ruthless, and I never fit in to any clique. So I became a wanderer, an observer, and early on I decided I hated my school. Apart from feeling isolated, I rapidly began to see the system for what it was—an institution for learning the social boundaries by being thrown together and forced to survive daily. Any type of education in this system to me seemed a joke, and I was even in the honors program, a place for the accelerated students! Yet I soon realized that to work the system all I had to do was exercise by rote memory (I can confidently tell you that I remember nothing from my history class) and finesse my assignments to suit each professor's style to ensure I got that A.

Our society leads its youth to believe that a successful life will be obtained by 110% effort to be the very best of the best. Not only do we have to be on the ball and driven to succeed at every venture, but also we must know exactly where we are heading from the ripe old age of 17. Every day, high school seniors walk into their career counselor's office and are asked to decide what they want to do for a career. We expect these kids to have given proper thought to their future and to commit to it by applying to colleges that have a good program for the major that they will need for their future careers. How are kids that age supposed to know what is really out there and available to them if they have spent the last 4 years memorizing information that they suspect they really aren't going to need? College graduates often still don't know what they want to do into their second or third year of school, let alone graduating high school students.

This push for our youth to decide now, now, now is what I like to call the Inevitable Inertia of our lives—we live in a culture that is obsessed with preparing for the future. A common question asked of children in our society is "What do you want to be when you grow up?" I am sure every one of us has been asked this at some point (if not repeatedly) during our childhood. As soon as a child can articulate a sentence, we put thoughts of the future into her or his head. Then it merely escalates; in junior high, we work hard to get into the honors program at high school. In high school, we strive for the GPA (let alone extracurricular activities) to gain entry into a good undergraduate college. In college, we push ourselves to get into a good graduate school. In graduate school, we go the extra mile to ensure a good career and a high income, and in our career we work overtime so that we can retire comfortably. Therefore, we are 60 years of age (if we are lucky) when we finally stop, breathe, and enjoy our days. Our society shapes our minds so that we are continuously living for tomorrow—a tomorrow that may arrive too late.

Andrea Crane

Andrea's concluding remarks about how we are conditioned to keep our eyes on the ever-receding future brings to mind similar thoughts by a great translator and explorer of the Eastern paths of liberation, Alan Watts. In his classic work, *The Book: On the Taboo Against Knowing Who You Are* (1966), he states

> We are thus breeding a type of human being incapable of living in the present— that is, or really living. For unless one is able to live fully in the present, the future is a hoax. There is no point whatever in making plans for a future you will never be able to enjoy. When your plans mature, you will still be living for some other future beyond. You will never, never be able to sit back with full content- ment and say, "Now, I've arrived!" Your entire education has deprived you of this capacity because it was preparing you for the future, instead of showing you how to be alive now. In other words, you have been hypnotized or conditioned by an educational processing system arranged in grades or steps, supposedly leading to some ultimate Success. (p. 80)

Whether you are an excellent, poor, or average grade earner is beside the point and may not even be relevant to whether you are a good student—that is, one who really questions and perhaps even enjoys the material. You must, in any case, be absolutely clear within yourself that *the grading system is not a measure of your worth as a human being.* This is hardest for those who do well because there is usually a temp- tation to believe in a system that ranks you highly. For those who feel this way, notice the good feeling is never there permanently. Every time you are tested, you are on the line again. Internalizing leads to addiction. Indeed, John Holt (1982), in his clas- sic work *How Children Fail*, said that school makes some people into failures and others into "praise junkies." The latter can get pretty wretched if they don't get their regular "fix" of A's. Alfie Kohn's (1993) work *Punished by Rewards, The Trouble with Gold Stars, Incentive Plans, A's, Praise, and Other Bribes* also perceptively addresses this issue.

The type of intelligence measured in college is a very narrow range of the total spec- trum of abilities that determines your success and happiness in life. Practical knowl- edge is not tested in university courses because it is not taught. There is precious little relationship between people's grades and how successful they actually are at future jobs. Many skills, particularly skills in human interaction, go into one's suc- cess. Unfortunately, professors will seldom admit this. To illustrate an extreme case we have the sad spectacle of graduate schools in clinical psychology choosing appli- cants on the basis of grade point alone, when all the evidence on the success of ther- apists points to emotional traits as key elements. Remember that your professors exaggerate the importance of academic learning because that is where they were able to make their mark.

As for your chances of happiness in your human relationships, academic excel- lence will help you here not at all. As a matter of fact, it will probably stand in your way, particularly if you have taken seriously the idea that you are better than other people because you can outshine them on an exam. If this has happened to you, school has made you a foolish person, which is not at all unusual.

If you want to see whether you have internalized the grading system, just observe how you feel when you are waiting to get back an exam or a paper. Are you perfectly at ease, secure in the knowledge that you are sitting in a comfortable room, safe from any physical danger? If so, you're all right. But to the extent that you feel discomfort at these moments you have internalized the system.

Understanding Versus Internalizing the Rules

Let us now go back to the distinction between *understanding* the rules and *internalizing* them. If you want to stay in college and perhaps go on to graduate school, you will have to perform according to the rules. You must know what they are and not kid yourself about them. But you will work more easily and competently if you refuse to let grades become a comment on who you are. If you have fears about who you are—and most young people do—these fears must be dealt with on an altogether different level. You must simply make direct contact with yourself, not the indirect contact and indirect self-approval given in the grading system. If you wish to check who you are directly at this moment, sit still for 10 minutes with your eyes closed and just pay attention to what the different parts of your body are telling you. Is your stomach feeling jumpy? Then that is who you are at the moment. Is there tension in your neck and shoulders? Make friends with the tension. Don't evaluate or pass judgment on yourself. Just feel yourself directly. This is the beginning of becoming your own friend. It is absolutely direct, and you can do it for yourself without anybody else's approval. When you have become friends with your body and your emotions, you will begin to know who you are. It isn't easy, and it isn't quick, but it beats basing your sense of self on grades.

You may now be tempted to say, "But if I don't aim for certain grades, how will I control my efforts sufficiently to keep from flunking out?" The answer is that you must learn to organize your life so as to give a reasonable and steady amount of time to your studies. Do this sensibly and then accept whatever grade result it produces.

Students develop a particular lifestyle, and, as a student, you will get caught up in it to some degree. It will be more intense if you live in a dormitory than if you live at home. With regard to schoolwork, the student lifestyle is a hysterical alternation between feast and famine, indolence and cramming. About 3 weeks before the end of every semester, the college atmosphere becomes noticeably more harried. Eyes become bloodshot, and dark circles appear under them. Hands get shaky. People begin gulping down caffeine and other artificial stimulants as they stay up all night typing papers that they have put off for the whole semester and studying material that they should have read weeks ago. By the last week, many are in the campus clinic suffering from exhaustion and a variety of physical ills stemming from the same causes.

Yet this pattern of squeezing everything into a few weeks at the end of the term does not make the average undergraduate carefree and elated during the first

13 weeks of the semester. On the contrary, students are feeling guilty all along about their indolence. In one class where I ask people to make a list of their favorite self-accusations, laziness is on everybody's list. One undergraduate wrote the following:

> In college, laziness is like a disease, one that I am deathly afraid of. While some people wallow in laziness, I spend every waking moment trying to avoid it. I finish class readings weeks before I have to, and I write papers long before they're due. I get so worried that I won't get it all done that I do a semester's worth of work in the first 3 months. I fear laziness so much that I literally breed stress within myself. That's not the worst of it, though. I don't relax once the work is done. I keep pushing. If I relaxed, that would be lazy. I feel that, since I have so much free time, I should be using it wisely. I should be rewriting all of my papers and rereading the assignments. I should do more research and maybe some fieldwork. If I don't, I'm just being lazy. I fear laziness so much that I won't even enjoy the free time that I've earned.
>
> *Kristin Rydberg*

The student who does not suspect him- or herself of laziness doesn't exist. A pattern of nervous procrastination has nearly everybody in its grip. Indeed, if we look at the college culture as a structure of time, we can see that it breeds procrastination almost like certain yeasts breed yogurt culture.

But if you are perceptive and look around, you will notice that there are always a few people who don't fall into this deadly cycle of indolence, guilt, and harried labor. They are not noticeably worse off during the last 3 weeks than during any others. If you investigate these folks, you will probably discover that they also do pretty successful work. They have discovered what I am about to tell you.

It is perfectly possible to do well in school without having to get hysterical at any point if you set aside approximately 15 to 30 hours a week, as best you can, of study time, in addition to your class meetings. A reasonable schedule, for example, might be 3 to 4 hours a day, Monday through Saturday. If you put these hours in early in the day, your evenings, Saturday afternoons, and Sundays should be totally free. If you are a night worker, you might wish to plan a very different schedule. The important thing is—like an athlete with training—*to keep your schedule pretty much without fail from the very first week of the semester.* The schedule will be tougher if you also work, as most students do, but in that case it is even more essential. Barring emergencies, just put in the time. Just sit at your desk or in the library as a daily practice. Don't make any elaborate demands on yourself. Just put in your hours. Beyond this, be satisfied regardless of your grade.

If you are worried by some piece of work you have to do, do that first. Don't procrastinate to avoid it. *Procrastination inevitably increases the anxiety,* whereas tackling it will get you past the chore and leave you feeling better for the rest of the day. What I am suggesting here is that you replace self-laceration with self-discipline. It is so much easier.

If your schedule seems to demand a much heavier investment of time, then take a close look at how you are choosing classes. Always diversify. Take some easy courses along with the hard ones. Try to work in a "fun" course every time—something like music or dance, which doesn't require much homework. Unfortunately, many professors seem to think that it is reasonable to expect students to put in 50 or 60 hours a week—a figure vastly in excess of anything required of the workforce. You have the right of self-protection here.

Of course, nervous procrastination and unreasonable professors are not the only reasons students run into disaster with their schedules. Another common reason is overinvestment in college activities. Every college prides itself on having lots of organizations and events. For students, this means that the college world is often aglitter with things to become involved in, to delight in, and to learn from. We are a greedy society, so it is not surprising that we are greedy individuals. Perhaps you thought that greed only meant desiring material possessions. But it is much more subtle than that. We are also greedy for learning, for experience, for participation, sometimes just for things to list on our future job applications. We forget that we have only a finite amount of time and energy to expend. So we have to face this greed and recognize it for what it is. The question is, would you rather try to grab it all and have a harried schedule, or would you prefer to be more modest and have a serene and reasonable schedule?

The quality of your learning and maturing during these 4 or more years means infinitely more than the mere quantity of what you learn and do.

Having read this far, some students have objected, "Your attitude toward grades is all very well and good, but what if you have to make grades to get into medical school or law school or some other graduate training?" My answer to that is this: If you have put in steady time and are getting poor results, you should see whether your basic study and writing skills can be improved. Talk to your advisor and other professors and ask if they can recommend writing courses or other ways to improve study skills. Check into any tutoring programs your college provides. This is especially important if your high school background is weak.

If you have done all this and you are still not making the grades for graduate school, you must accept the results—because they indicate that you are heading for the wrong profession. *Reevaluate your goals.* I say this because, if you have to stay up all night and wear yourself to a frazzle to get grades for graduate school, imagine how difficult it will be for you once you get there—and perhaps also how difficult and burdensome the profession will be once you get into it.

Usually there are alternatives you can explore in the same general field to which you were heading. If your grades suggest that you cannot become a physician, how about opting for physical therapy or dentistry? Or perhaps you are heading for the wrong field altogether. This is a time to go to the career counseling center and widen your horizons on the great variety of careers that are available. If your school doesn't have good career counseling, try a professor in the general field in which you might be interested. Career possibilities in most fields are quite complex. In the field of primary and secondary teaching, for example, there are many specialties for which one can train: Besides classroom teachers, there are reading teachers, speech therapists, special education teachers (for disabilities of various kinds), school counselors, and educational administrators. Each specialty requires a different kind of graduate training. The complexity is so great that you really need to become rather familiar with a field before you can see where it might lead you. Therefore, don't make up your mind and close off all options. Proceed one step at a time, being guided by which subjects you like and feel good at (plus, if possible, some direct looks at the jobs themselves). That your father wants you to be a lawyer or one of your childhood heroes was a wonderful doctor should not dictate your own outcomes prematurely.

Another word of advice about choosing a career: If you have any very strong preferences about where you want to live, you would do well to research the situation to see whether you can find employment in your chosen location. College teaching, for example, offers very little choice of location because the job openings are so specialized. On the other hand, a skill such as nursing can take you almost anywhere. If you long to live in the country, you shouldn't aspire to become a television executive. Some types of specialties are in great oversupply in certain desirable urban areas. Research these questions through your campus job counseling service or by contacting practitioners and institutions in the area in which you are interested.

Experimenting

When we were kids and had bicycles, we used to love to coast down hills with our hands dangling nonchalantly at our sides. If you would like to get some of that "Look Ma! No Hands!" feeling about the grading system, try doing some work without grades. If your campus permits it, you might take some courses on a pass/fail basis. Or you might ask the professor to give you comments, but no grades, during the semester. When it is time to pick up your final grades, ask a friend to remove the "ungraded" course grade, so you won't see it. Or if you want to take a real flyer, take a whole quarter or semester this way. See if you experience a change in the educational process. Students who have tried this report very encouraging results, and some excellent books to help you develop your skills are John Gardner and Jerome Jewler's (1992) *College Is Only the Beginning* and David B. Ellis's (1984) *Becoming a Master Student.*

Pass/No Pass Experimentation

"Should I take it pass/no pass?" This familiar question is normally reserved for those killer classes that you have no hope of getting a shining A in. However, the true benefit of gradeless classes—and the reason they were first installed in the 1960s—is to allow for freedom within a pressurized academic environment. By taking a "normal" class without being graded, it is possible to escape (partially, at least), from the stress and paranoia surrounding the dreaded grade. If you commit to taking a class pass/no pass, you must decide also to commit to the work. Professors don't like lazy students who opt out of being responsible by avoiding a grade, but they do tend to favor those students who proclaim that they do not wish to be graded but will be doing the work, taking the tests, and showing up to class. One wonderful anthropology professor at the University of

California at Irvine (UCI), who actually dared to fill his lecture time by asking his students to discuss topics he introduced to them, spoke individually to students who wished to take his class without the grading hierarchy to make sure that they would be involved and would put the same amount of energy and effort into his class as they would if they were being graded.

Now, certainly the first class you ever take pass/no pass will instill some aspect of laziness (due to the freedom), but if you take yourself and your education seriously, you will come to the realization that classes are indeed much more interesting and provocative when you include yourself in them.

According to many people, grades are the motivation behind success. Another perspective, however, is that such assessments of your worth restrict your actual growth by confining you to worrying over five little letters. Should you be concerned with grades? The answer is, of course, yes. Should you let this concern consume most of your waking moments? This is harder to answer. You have to decide early on whether the grading system ought to have the right to run your life, determine your schedule, and support (or more likely deflate) your ego.

The point of taking classes on pass/no pass basis is not to avoid learning or to avoid grades. Rather, the purpose is just the opposite: *By realizing how strong of a grip the grading system has over you, you will be able to loosen the grip and enjoy your courses more.* Most schools have a limit to the number of such classes you can take, so it's not to your benefit to load up on them. Still, an entire term (quarter or semester) without grades could make a big difference in the way you view school.

Now, you may be stuck in a field that presents academic competition as a prerequisite to success. For instance, most premed programs don't allow for pass/no pass and, worse, tend to weed out those who can't study all day or won't sabotage their classmates (tales of flag switching on anatomy specimens are quite common). Obviously, if you choose this line of curricula, you won't be able to envision the changes I've mentioned. However, you are not at a total loss, either. You can still take nonmajor classes without the pressure of grades to offset your major classes that thrive on competition and one-upmanship.

Tatian Greenleaf

If You Just Can't Stand It Anymore

In the remainder of this book, I realize that I have been fairly easy on the academy. I have not dwelled on the teachers who humiliate students in class or the ones who spring a paper on you just before vacation. I have not mentioned the frustrating difficulty of getting into required courses in certain fields. I have not really said anything about the pitfalls of dealing with the administration in many of our huge institutions.[4] Paulo Freire (1970) in his *Pedagogy of the Oppressed* boldly stated the following:

Education must begin with the solution of the teacher-student contradiction, by reconciling the poles of the contradiction so that both are simultaneously teachers *and* students. This solution is not (nor can it be) found in the banking concept. On the contrary, banking education maintains and even stimulates the contradiction through the following attitudes and practices, which mirror oppressive society as a whole:

a. the teacher teaches and the students are taught;
b. the teacher knows everything and the students know nothing;
c. the teacher thinks and the students are thought about;
d. the teacher talks and the students listen—meekly;
e. the teacher disciplines and the students are disciplined;
f. the teacher chooses and enforces his choice, and the students comply;
g. the teacher acts and the students have the illusion of acting through the action of the teacher;
h. the teacher chooses the program content, and the students (who were not consulted) adapt to it;
i. the teacher confuses the authority of knowledge with his own professional authority, which he sets in opposition to the students;
j. the teacher is the subject of the learning process, while the pupils are mere objects. (p. 59)[5]

If there has been little bitterness in my tone, it is probably because it has been many years since I was a student. I would like, therefore, to quote at some length from a paper sent to me by a University of California at Los Angeles student. What she has to say is very incisive.

Confessions of a Student Slave

To a large extent we are graded in school on our ability to memorize trivial things and, even more, on our endurance at memorizing. The more items a student gets right on an exam, the more he or she is credited with knowing. From years of this kind of reinforcement, it is not unnatural for students to develop the conviction that knowledge consists of the accumulation of hard facts by hard work. Unfortunately, students are being conditioned to falsely associate persistence and a good memory that can readily recall information for exams with being a bright and knowledgeable person. It is not *what* students are taught that does the harm but *how* they are taught. Teachers think providing substance to students is force-feeding their minds with a goodly store of general ideas, available on demand. Students are robbed of their will and sense of power and made into apathetic slaves of authority. Teachers encourage students to spend a considerable amount of time memorizing facts, theories, and definitions to do well on exams. They reinforce this activity with good grades and praise, which are of utmost importance to students. At first, this process seems very useless and demeaning, but as time goes by and it is continually reinforced, it becomes very appealing to most students. They adopt and identify with the system and thereby become a slave to it. What this system does to students is where the real danger lies.

This system traps us and stifles our minds by reinforcing us to NOT think. Our own ideas and thoughts are suppressed, while the regurgitation of other people's ideas and thoughts is reinforced. The consequence of this is put very succinctly by Schopenhauer, who says, "The safest way of having no thoughts of one's own is to take up a book every moment one has nothing else to do. It is this practice which explains why erudition makes most men more stupid and silly than they are by nature." This system discourages thinking and learning to the point where we actually choose to pass up learning experiences and seek to suppress our own ideas and thoughts. The students' view of what knowledge is is distorted by how teachers go about measuring it. It is much harder to develop one's own ideas than it is to memorize and regurgitate those of others. The system reinforces the latter, which is not only much easier but also highly unproductive. Students' desire to suppress their own ideas is clearly shown in their choice of classes: Mickey Mouse courses and classes that have multiple-choice exams and no papers are highly relished. Students have an overwhelming dislike for writing papers, especially those that require some individual expression. They dread expressing their own ideas and strongly prefer to work with other people's because this activity has been reinforced to such a great degree in the past.

One of the most damaging effects of this system is that we are conditioned to seek reinforcement from others rather than from ourselves. We tend to avoid learning experiences and opportunities for creative thinking that do not lead to external rewards (i.e., grades) because these kinds of thought processes have not been reinforced in the past. Internal rewards are seen as foreign and are not recognized as being important. A pathetic condition exists where we learn for others and not for ourselves. This is illustrated in students' reluctance to put forth any extra effort that is not required for a course. If it is not on the test or we are not going to be graded on it, "forget it" is the prevalent attitude. Extra nongraded assignments for learning purposes (i.e., experiments) and voluntary readings are quickly dismissed. What makes this effect even more damaging is that it does not stop once one graduates; it tends to prevail throughout one's life. Knowledge for its own sake is not seen as a valid and valuable goal.

Another detrimental effect of the system is that we get used to NOT thinking and become afraid of it. The thought or act of thinking and developing our own ideas becomes very frightening. Thinking is an activity that is not reinforced in the system, and therefore we have little practice at it. Thinking is an ability that does need training; it is extremely difficult to develop and impart ideas. Initially, we are all lousy at it, but this is a shock to most people. It is not until one has to think that he or she realizes to what a great extent they have relied on other people's thoughts. Blinded by the fact that thinking does require training, it is hard for us to face the fact that thinking is a very difficult process, at least initially. The most common response is avoidance because we are afraid of failure. "What if I can't think?" is a prevalent fear that haunts us. But fortunately for us we are saved by the system that does not reinforce thinking, only regurgitation of other people's thoughts. As a result, we don't think, and we don't learn.

Lorraine Feldman

If college has brought you to the point where you just can't stand it anymore, you should at least know that you have some alternatives to just continuing to drag yourself through. Many students interrupt their schooling at some point to work for a while or to travel or even to spend a semester or year at another institution. I have always encouraged students to take these bypaths because I know how much it can enrich their education. Any professor who has taught older, returning students will tell you that it is a special joy to teach people who have been out in the world for a while because they bring so much sense of purpose to their education. They have a much clearer idea of what they are looking for, and their experience of the world greatly augments the book learning of college courses. *It is, in fact, a grave mistake to process people through college directly from high school. It would be better if everyone had to spend at least a year or two working between high school and college.* Time off in the middle of college can serve the same purpose. Ideally, you will come back to college refreshed by your "time off."

Parents often oppose such a move because they are afraid you might get lost and never finish and thus doom yourself to a low income. I think that these fears, though genuine and heartfelt, are misplaced. Often, they arise from the parent's own sense of inadequacy in dealing with the world. It may be necessary for you to oppose your parents on this score.

There is yet another possibility: You may decide that you just do not want a college degree or the type of career to which it normally leads. There are alternative ways of life out there. I have known quite a few craftsmen and craftswomen who like what they do and are perfectly happy without a college degree. You can become a carpenter or even a master cabinetmaker, an electrician, gardener, plumber, tile setter, or auto mechanic. Not all trades are manual in nature. Some combine manual and intellectual skills, and some are purely intellectual. A look at a community college catalogue tells me that they give 2-year degrees in animal science, ornamental horticulture, business information systems, commercial art, photography, marketing, drafting, electronics, musical instrument repair, aviation service, welding, and preschool administration, to take only a small sample.

You will not get rich in these occupations, but you may find satisfying work and make enough to survive quite well. Many of these skills have the added advantage of giving you some freedom to locate where you please. It is sometimes cheaper and more pleasant to live in rural areas than in cities. Of course, you should check out whether opportunities for a given trade exist in the location of your choice.

In northern California, where I live, as in rural areas throughout the United States, there are even a lot of people who are surviving on the land by raising their own food and taking occasional jobs in town. Many worked for a number of years before they were able to put together a down payment on a plot of land. These folks are not prosperous by the usual standards. They face many hardships, but they are some of the happiest and most satisfied young people I have met.

If you are considering such a drastically different lifestyle, you should proceed with some caution. When you have decided on an area in which you would like to settle, spend at least a year there, picking up whatever jobs you can and getting to know people who are working the land. Such a way of life involves very serious sacrifices and changes and you should not commit yourself without investigating these thoroughly.

Unfortunately, society uses the invidious phrase *dropping out* for people who take up a rural way of life. I can assure you, though, that most people who do it feel neither "dropped" or "out." I don't know any who would trade their situation for an urban lifestyle. Not getting a bachelor's degree does not automatically mean failure and unhappiness any more than a bachelor's degree ensures success and satisfaction.

Throughout your educational journey, keep in mind that certain subjects generally, and academics broadly, may not play to your personal strengths. A parable by George H. Reeves highlights this crucial idea:

Once upon a time, the animals decided that their lives and their society would be improved by setting up a school. The basics identified as necessary for survival in the animal world were swimming, running, climbing, jumping, and flying. Instructors were hired to teach these activities, and it was agreed that all the animals would take all the courses. This worked out well for the administrators, but it caused some problems for the students.

The squirrel, for example, was an A student in running, jumping, and climbing but had trouble in flying class, not because of an inability to fly, for she could sail from the top of one tree to another with ease, but because the flying curriculum called for taking off from the ground. The squirrel was drilled in ground-to-air take-offs until she was exhausted and developed charley horses from overexertion. This caused her to perform poorly in her other classes, and her grades dropped to D's.

The duck was outstanding in swimming class—even better than the teacher. But she did so poorly in running that she was transferred to remedial class. There she practiced running until her webbed feet were so badly damaged that she was only an average swimmer. But since average was acceptable, nobody saw this as a problem—except the duck.

In contrast, the rabbit was excellent in running, but, being terrified of water, he was an extremely poor swimmer. Despite a lot of makeup work in swimming class, he never could stay afloat. He soon became frustrated and uncooperative and was eventually expelled because of behavior problems.

The eagle naturally enough was a brilliant student in flying class and even did well in running and jumping. He had to be severely disciplined in climbing class, however, because he insisted that his way of getting to the top of the tree was faster and easier.

It should be noted that the parents of the groundhog pulled him out of school because the administration would not add classes in digging and burrowing. The groundhogs, along with the gophers and badgers, got a prairie dog to start a private school. They all have become strong opponents of school taxes and proponents of voucher systems.

By graduation time, the student with the best grades in the animal school was a compulsive ostrich who could run superbly and also swim, fly, and climb a little. She, of course, was made class valedictorian and received scholarship offers from all the best universities.

Notes

1. I don't mean, by using this example, to imply that everybody should lie down in front of an unjust system. Some very wise and brave people will take the system on. But they had better understand clearly what to expect.

2. I'd like to recommend *The Passionate Teacher (1995)* and *The Passionate Learner* (2001) for anyone interested in looking at teaching and learning from a uray human perspective.

3. I'd like to recommend a very interesting book to you here. Joe Salzman's (1993) *If You Can Talk, You Can Write.*

4. For a scathing (but not undeserverd) criticism of the American professoriat, read Charles Sykes's (1989) *PROFSCAM: Professors and the Demise of Higher Education.*

5. Copyright 1970 by Continuum. Reprinted with permission.

CHAPTER 3

Support Your Local Teacher

Or the Care and Feeding of Professors

The central figure in your formal college education will be the professor. If you are attending a small liberal arts college or community college, you may get to know a few of these worthies quite well. If you are at a large university, they may remain figures on the podium, and your immediate contacts will be with young aspiring professors called teaching assistants. The latter are usually in some advanced phase of study for a doctorate and, therefore, will share the general orientations and values of the professors. It is important for you to know what professors are all about, not only so you can choose them and approach them wisely but also to understand why a college education is structured in the peculiar way that it is.

As you might expect, most professors are people who were outstanding in the academic competition from childhood. Most were the stars of their respective classrooms from kindergarten on. For many, this intellectual superiority became the basis of what might otherwise have been a shaky self-image. Hence, it is hardly surprising that they consider the academic intellect to be the highest form of human expression. They are also people who succeeded in the academic game, which makes them highly competitive. Luckily, their competition is mainly directed against each other rather than at you. You are an element in that competition only in the sense that, in some liberal arts colleges and community colleges, popularity as a teacher may win faculty some points in the competitive game, though it is more likely that having a few very bright students who go on to graduate schools will win them more points. In large universities, however, it is a mark of status to do as little teaching as possible. In these institutions, professors specialize in getting research grants, which can free them from contaminating contact with undergraduates. In many of these research and publication institutes thinly disguised as universities, undergraduates are seen as a necessary evil. Even graduate students may be treated with some contempt and condescension in these settings. From this angle, we can see that educational suppression is committed by the institution itself—the very system that seeks to educate.

The arena of important competition for most professors is the nationwide network of fellow professors in their particular discipline, rather than the local campus where they happen to teach. In this network, often referred to simply as "the discipline" or "the profession" or "the field," teaching does not count.[1] In fact, the professor's skill as a teacher is not part of his or her reputation at all. Here it is publication of research that counts, and quantity of publication often counts for more than quality.

Once when I was teaching at a campus of a major university, my colleagues and I were to consider hiring a rather well-known professor for our department. A couple of us, who were greenhorns, did the unusual and actually read some of the books and articles on this man's lengthy list of publications. They were terrible. But when we brought this fact up at the department meeting, the chairman regarded us with some annoyance and said, "But look at the length of his list." We were silenced.

The academic professional associations in the various disciplines have a variety of annual meetings at which exceedingly dull papers are usually read, and very important personal contacts are made. Personal contacts are the name of the game. Without them, no academic could land a job, and few would get their work published.

What all this means to you is that you must realize that you are a side issue in your professor's career. At Pitzer College, where I taught for many years, this tendency was counteracted by our procedure for promotion and job tenure. For these reviews, we actually interviewed large numbers of our undergraduate students about a professor's teaching, and this evidence was weighed quite heavily, though there was a continuing battle between those who wanted to emphasize teaching and those who wished to emphasize publishing. However, even in a small college that values teaching, professors know that, should they find themselves back on the job market, their publications would be their major selling point. At the other end of the scale, on large university campuses popularity as a teacher may even be somewhat suspect, like spending too much time on your golf game.

Why Has Teaching Been Relegated to This Position of Unimportance?

Teaching has been relegated to unimportance, for one, because professors are elitists in an elitist profession. They are much better informed than most people, and the degree of their expertise is partly measured by the sophistication of their students. As college education has become available to larger and larger numbers of people, professors have felt their status threatened by the requirement that they teach "run-of-the-mill" students. Many sociologists, for example, really want to teach students who are going to get doctorates in sociology. They would rather ignore the obvious fact that most of their undergraduate students will go into middle-rung occupations, such as teaching in public schools or doing social work. They do not really want to be bothered with such students.

Another reason teaching is devalued is that too much good teaching might encourage freely questioning, heretical minds. Sacred cows such as "free enterprise," "the free world," or the "happy consumer society" might then be called into question. Should such questions lead to action, universities stand to lose their federal grants, while trustees and their political friends bring unpleasant pressures to bear. The intellect is always a danger to those in power. Hence, it is necessary to curb a too free and stimulating exchange of ideas. Professors are cordoned off by the requirement that they publish exclusively for their fellow professionals and generally in a secret language, which is unintelligible to the layman.

Professors who write best-sellers are looked down on as "popularizers." Good teachers are also frequently suspected of this sin. As long as professors only talk to each other, the general public will not be the wiser.

One of the things that happened on campuses during the 1960s that mightily alarmed trustees and university presidents was that students and some professors started communicating in class and elsewhere about the state of the university and the world. This turned out to be extremely "disruptive." Even though some reforms were pushed through during the 1960s to make teaching more rewarding and relevant, few of these innovations survived the 1970s, and now professors are safely back in their own corrals.

During the last 10 years, at a time when there has been an oversupply of professors, academic institutions have taken advantage of the weak bargaining position of young faculty by setting up a two-class system within the professoriat. Young scholars are hired on as visiting lecturers (titles may vary) who are never eligible for advancement or tenure and who are generally kept on for only 2 or 3 years, so tenure can be avoided. Persons hired into such positions cannot advance into the regular faculty no matter how well they perform. Their pay is usually dramatically lower than that received by the tenured faculty, whose salaries may run more than twice as high. The worst aspect of this new system is that young professors are forced to tear up their roots, disrupt their personal lives, and move every few years. Increasingly, this army of migrant professors is generally used to cover a large proportion of the teaching load.

I would like to quote from a memorandum by Bernard McGrane and J. William Gibson, two tremendously popular University of California, Los Angeles, instructors, whose temporary contracts were not renewed despite considerable protest by students:

> We believe the "Visiting Lecturer" position (as primarily teaching load coverage) has the exploitation and devaluation of teaching structurally built into it. It seems to be somewhat of a migrant farm worker position to be filled with disposable, throwaway lecturers. If you go quarter by quarter for the last 2 years, Bill and Barney have taught 22%, 23%, 24%, 13%, and 29% of the total undergraduate sociology student enrollment. Hence, 5% of the sociology faculty (using 40 as a base) has taught 23% of the undergraduate students. (These figures would probably be more "dramatic" if we asked, "What percentage of the sociology student body is taught by all of the Visiting Lecturers? How much of

the overall UCLA student body is taught by Visiting Lecturers?") As migrant workers we receive lower wages (Barney, $21,000 1st year, $23,000 2nd year; Bill, $18,000 1st year, $22,500 3rd year) for higher teaching work, thereby embodying an implicit institutional devaluation of teaching. If we do well as teachers we get larger and larger student enrollments . . . without ever getting any proportionate increase in resources (e.g., always just one Teaching Assistant), thereby the department institutionally penalizes good teaching. We "process" more and more students, inspire more and more students to become sociology majors; we produce the body count that enables the department to get more resources and more tenure track positions. As migrant lecturers, we're subsidizing other people's research in the department. In turn, our own research becomes more difficult.

That social scientists should take part in the creation of such a class system within the academy or that they are powerless in the face of it is evidence, I often feel, that they have learned nothing from their own disciplines. *If there is one clear phenomenon in the comparison of societies, it is that wider class differences invariably produce greater social pathology. Such differences inflict great pain on the oppressed, while destroying the integrity of those at the top.*

As students, you have a real stake in such developments. Very simply, you must speak out to retain good teachers. In so doing, you should be aware of your power as students. Even the threat of boycott (taking either the form of students transferring out of the affected department or transferring to other schools) will make senior faculty and administrators sit up and take notice. Their budgets are based on the number of students they serve, and nobody is ever indifferent to budget questions.

Understanding the institutional structure governing the professor's career situation will explain to you the widespread phenomenon of poor teaching and indifference to your needs as a student. The major way you have of dealing with this is judicious selection of classes. Whenever your requirements allow some choice, you should choose your classes by finding the best teachers, rather than choosing them by subject matter. The most fascinating subject can be made dull by an indifferent teacher, whereas the most obscure material may, in the hands of a gifted teacher, become a vehicle for teaching the art of disciplined thinking. Your academic advisor will not usually clue you in to which teachers are good or bad, since they are your advisor's colleagues. You must pick this information up from more experienced students on your campus. Some campuses even publish student ratings of professors, but this is rare.

Try the occasional campus radical—indeed, anyone with an unusual perspective. Because such folks are generally interested in persuading people, they are motivated to teach well. Luckily, you will find, on almost any faculty, a few wonderful characters who are original people and well worth knowing. This is because the academy has always been a haven for nonconformists. Despite the real pressures toward conformity, teaching college still remains one of the very few jobs where no one can tell you to wear a tie to work.

When you find a professor with a good reputation for teaching, remember that you are this person's main incentive for teaching. Such deviants in the academic scene must get their emotional rewards from their interaction with students. Here is where you can become a rewarding person for your professors. Giving emotional support is also important in the case of poor teachers, because, despite the irrelevance of student opinions to career, it is still pretty unpleasant to get up 12 hours a week in front of a patently uninterested audience. Even the poor teacher is grateful for a supportive student. It goes without saying that the supportive student will be rewarded with personal attention and even, perhaps, friendship and will often get a better deal when grading time comes around.

Support your professors during class. All of you know how hard it is to get up in front of a class and give an oral report, yet most of you quite wrongly assume that professors do not suffer the same anxieties. Not so! Professors have egos as sensitive as anybody's. The student who dozes off during class is a very depressing sight indeed to the hapless lecturer. In one of the first classes I ever taught, a large young man regularly sat in the front row and dozed off. At times he would lurch forward so dangerously in his seat that I would nearly reach out to catch him. Yet he always woke up just in time to pull himself back into his chair. He was not my favorite student. But, oh, for that rare individual who actually makes eye contact with me during class and whose expression tells me that I have occasionally brought home a point! That is the student whose name I will remember. In line with this, it stands to reason that the professor will never notice you if you sit in the last row nearest the door. Strut right up to the front of the class.

Ask questions whenever the size and format of the class permit it. Nothing is more discouraging than a mute audience. Don't worry about whether your questions are sophisticated. Don't worry whether your questions will make you look ignorant to your fellow students. It is the professor you are trying to contact, and for the professor any question indicates the stirrings of the intellectual fire he or she is hoping to kindle. The only type of question to avoid is one that is too directly utilitarian. Never ask, "Will that be required on the exam?" This is an oft-repeated question that professors disparage noisily among themselves. In this process of questioning, you must, of course, use reasonable restraint. Remember that others also want to ask questions or hear the instructor.

Ask questions during class, after class, and in the professor's office during office hours. What professors love is genuine curiosity about their subject matter. You cannot fake genuine curiosity nor should you try. It is easy to become a fake, even a successful fake, but fakery will make you a poor human being. What I am suggesting is, rather, that you allow yourself some genuine intellectual curiosity. Ask yourself how what you are studying relates to your own life or to other subjects you have taken. If the Greeks believed in the golden mean, how did they justify slavery, which is rather an extreme institution? Or what would they have thought of our tendency to put all our efforts into succeeding competitively? As you read your assignments, jot down a question or two for the next class. It will stimulate you to approach your reading actively rather than passively. An added bonus of asking questions is that you will learn more. You will get specific information that is of more interest to you than the general material. You may even experience an occasional "aha!" And remember that your "aha!" is your professor's "ahhhh!" Good teachers live for those "aha!" moments in their students. Again, don't fake this but remain always open to it.

Everybody knows that most classes are boring. We have experienced this since kindergarten. As children, we screamed with undisguised delight whenever we were released from the boredom of the classroom. When I was in grammar school, on that last day of class in early summer, we would wait expectantly for the final moment when we were directed to place our chairs on our desks for the last time of the year. At that moment, a wild, collective shriek of joy went up and rang from room to room.

By the time we reach college, the shriek of delight has been internalized. We are running from class to make a date rather than to climb trees, but the general feeling remains. Class is something to be suffered through. This is not inevitable or even normal. Private schools exist in which children are given enough freedom and offered enough truly relevant, interesting subject matter to make learning a delightful experience. But, unfortunately, 99% of our education institutions from kindergarten to graduate school are pretty dull and really designed to discipline you rather than to stimulate and delight your intellect. The very format of school works to ensure boredom. At 9:00 a.m. three times a week, you are supposed to become engrossed by medieval history. Never mind that you broke up with your boyfriend last night or that your parents are on your back for not majoring in business administration; at 9:00 a.m., it's medieval history. Our education has, all along, been answering questions we never asked. When we were in high school, we needed to know why we weren't popular or why our parent came home drunk, but these subjects could not be brought up in class. At the same time, we were expected to show genuine interest in the causes of the Civil War.

All this is merely to say that, yes, classes are often boring. How can you cope with this while being a supportive student? Believe it or not, *the best way to deal with this situation when it is unavoidable is to concentrate on the material being offered.* The time will actually go faster than if you were dreaming of last night's party or doodling elaborately in your margins. I have always been immensely bored by meetings (and, believe me, there are lots of meetings one has to attend as a professor). I used to enrage my fellow academics by doing needlepoint during meetings in an attempt to escape the boredom. But I made an interesting discovery. The time went faster if I concentrated on the business at hand. Since then I have always volunteered to be recording secretary. For this job, one must keep one's mind intensely focused on the discussion, so the time passes much more easily. Try this tactic in your classes, and I think you will see that it works. It is also a cardinal lesson in attaining the wisdom talked about in Buddhist philosophy. The Buddhist masters always tell us to be alert, alert, alert. In short, don't drift off or daydream.

The following is a beautiful story recounted in *The Little Zen Companion* (Schiller, 1994):

> One day a man approached Ikkyu and asked:
> "Master, will you please write for me some maxims of the highest wisdom?"
> Ikkyu took his brush and wrote: "Attention."
> "Is that all?" asked the man.
> Ikkyu then wrote: "Attention. Attention."
> "Well," said the man, "I really don't see much depth in what you have written."

Then Ikkyu wrote the same word three times: "Attention. Attention. Attention."

Half-angered, the man demanded: "What does that word 'Attention' mean anyway?"

Ikkyu gently responded, "Attention means attention." (p. 17)[2]

The Care and Feeding of Professors

The care and feeding of professors extends beyond the classroom. Pay a visit to your professors or teaching assistants during office hours. Go with questions, maybe questions having to do with mastery of the material. If you are at all worried about a coming exam or paper, always go and discuss it. Professors, being human, will generally be more tolerant of the student who cares enough to come in and get help. If the material gives you no trouble, think about the larger questions it raises in your mind and go in for a more general talk. If you can possibly resist it, don't ask about your grade. Don't monopolize the professor's time. Very few professors will make you feel absolutely unwanted. Most will generally clue you in to how much time they have available for you. Be sensitive to this.

Pitzer College in California is admittedly atypical in its concern for students, but some of the things that delighted me with students there can be tried in other environments. I always enjoyed the student who would bring an occasional relevant newspaper clipping or magazine article to class or to me for my own perusal. I also enjoyed suggestions for things the class might do, such as inviting guest speakers or having a film or going on a field trip. I taught several classes solely at the request of a student or a small group of students. Of course, your suggestions should not imply that the course is lacking in interest. It may even be good to preface suggestions with a good word about the class, but only the most neurotic professor will resent a show of interest or initiative.

Always remember that professors who care about teaching are going counter to the official system of career rewards and punishments. They need the student feedback to keep them going. It is in your interest to provide some of that feedback. Everybody will be better off for it.

How personal should your relationship with professors be? In this regard, you must proceed with hope and caution. It is distinctly unwise to discuss your personal emotional problems with most of your professors, even though these problems may sometimes greatly affect your academic performance. Most professors consider it unprofessional to deal with students as emotional creatures. Indeed, those who are willing to do so are frequently accused by their peers of coddling students. In fact, of course, professionalism is a convenient way to hide from the acute fear many professors have of their own and other people's emotions. Intellectuality is often used to keep threatening emotions at a distance. Young women who cry in professors' offices are particularly dreaded. Those profs who are open to emotional issues are usually known by reputation or will communicate where they stand during your intellectual conversations with them.

However, any professor whose ideas interest you may be cultivated as an intellectual friend on that level. If the general setting of your school allows for informal interactions with professors, you would be wise to nurture a few such contacts. Professors, as I have said before, may often turn out to be very interesting people. It is also the case that they are generally a whole lot nicer off the job than on. Unfortunately, the social role of professors brings out the worst in people. I have often been pleasantly surprised by the way particularly stiff-necked colleagues change into warm human beings around their children or while doing their hobbies.

Let me also say a word about social class background and personal contact. Professors are, by definition, upper middle-class people, regardless of their social origins. Hence, children of similarly placed parents will feel much easier making friends with professors than those of you whose parents were not so long educated or highly placed. Such class-based cultural differences are very real barriers to human contact. It will help you to be aware of them, so you can make a little extra effort to overcome them. Most professors are not consciously snobbish about their class position and will bend over backwards for an interested student from any background. In encountering class and ethnic barriers within the academy, it may help you to remember that it is only ethnocentrism that causes us to look on some people's cultures as more valuable or of higher status than other people's. (More about this can be found in the chapter titled "The Painful Avenues of Upward Mobility.")

A word should be said about the opposite sort of problem: the professor who wants to know you more personally than you wish to be known. This applies mainly to male professors who pursue their young female students, though, increasingly, female professors are also guilty. If the professor is young, attractive, and unmarried, this may not seem like a problem. But you would be well advised to postpone the relationship until you have finished the class. Imagine the consequences of a broken affair while class is still going.

When the professor is older or just not attractive to you, it can put you in a very delicate situation. High-status males in our society generally assume that they deserve physical access to the young and sexually appealing, and society is much more accepting of older man–younger woman combinations than their reverse. Secretaries, flight attendants, waitresses, and similar folk have long had to deal with this problem, and female students are in the same boat. Sometimes the approach is so oblique and indirect that you really don't know how to cope with it. The professor may come on fatherly, for example, or assure you that his only concern is to free you from psychological inhibitions. If any of this begins happening, you should promptly withdraw from the class and, if appropriate, report it. If there are grading problems or other academic issues at stake, talk to your advisor or someone you trust in the culprit's own discipline. Faculty members usually know each other's reputations on this score. Remember that you have an absolute right to protect yourself from sexual exploitation. Indeed, we increasingly have laws that forbid sexual harassment on the job or in schools. Female faculty will probably help you in these difficulties and so will any feminist groups on your campus.

Finding Your Local Professor

The key to succeeding in college is to take a personal stance on your education. Too many students follow the requirements and never stray to find their passion. Students need to realize that they have the right to change their education. In high school, I rejected teachers I didn't believe had my best interest at heart by switching classes. The administration was set against this, so I had to put a little muscle behind my wishes. I complained of poor teachers, but I also did something to rectify the situation. The gym teacher lecturing on history wasn't going to cut it for me.

Every school has teachers who are decidedly better than others. The beauty of college is that there are many more teachers available in a medley of styles and personalities. Find teachers who inspire you and light a fire beneath you. And once you do, hold on tight. I began to realize that it wasn't so much the course titles that mattered but rather the instructors who did. A course on artificial intelligence could be as dry as sand, whereas a lecture on sand could be as exciting as artificial intelligence should be, if delivered by a dynamic professor.

Getting to know your professors is another step in personalizing your education. Many students feel intimidated by these landlords of academia and rightly so since professors are likely to exude an atmosphere of intellectual superiority.

As a student, your education is in your possession. Instead of sopping up the good with the bad, in an attempt to be a productive sponge why not demand a worthy response from your teachers? Involve yourself.

One common misunderstanding that students have about professors is that *faculty* is synonymous with *administration*. Although their union does exist at some level (otherwise, how would the university function?), it is rarely the case that professors agree with administrators' disregard for students.

Keep on the lookout for visiting professors and guest lecturers so that you may take advantage of their predisposition as good teachers. Most new (non-tenured) professors are there to teach, especially if they have been to several schools before yours. These are often the people to search out and take classes with. They may be the few people at the university who have not drowned in the publish-or-perish sea and are there because of their desire to help you learn.

Tatian Greenleaf

Support Your Local Teaching Assistant

In the search for good professors, the teaching assistant (TA) is often overlooked. These are folks you do not choose, and they can either make or break a class. A positive, creative, dynamic TA can bring out the best in his or her students, while a slumbering, patronizing one can stomp on students' interest to learn. Teaching assistants are the workhorses of the academy. They are enrolled full-time in graduate school, and, on top of that academic load, they are part-time teachers. Some large schools even use TAs to teach small lectures, thereby increasing the strain on them. In spite of their heavy time commitment, teaching assistants are a wonderful resource for undergrads who have even the slightest glimmer of curiosity about graduate school or, better yet, about the educational system they are currently swimming in. Graduate students, if picked when ripe, can make wonderful mentors and often are more giving of their advice than professors.

One of the most empowering experiences I ever had at college was student teaching. If you are lucky enough to get to know a professor well enough to find out what he or she is up to around the campus and to have taken a few classes with him or her, find out whether the professor will allow you to become an undergraduate teaching assistant or at least to facilitate discussions among classmates. The key is that you become both a student and a teacher at the same time. This in-between state is a wonderful place to be.

Tatian Greenleaf

The In-Between State of the Undergraduate PC

As a professor committed to undergraduate learning yet responsible for huge lecture courses that frequently occur in the University of California system, I coparticipated with students in creating what we called an undergraduate participation coordinator (PC) program. I'd like to quote from a formal description of it (which I include in letters of recommendation) with the hope that it may provide an inspirational tool for you in your current undergraduate situation:

A PC (participation coordinator) is something like an undergraduate TA (teaching assistant). A PC is an undergraduate student of high academic excellence who, after already having taken one of my large (150–350 students) undergraduate lecture courses, voluntarily returns when it is offered again. They return to independently run a small 8 to 10 member group of students currently enrolled in a weekly seminar. The PC student does this under the auspices of a four-credit independent study project. The Participatory Education Program, of which the PC is an integral part, was begun in 1986 under student stimulus at UC Irvine.

PCs take on a very large responsibility as undergraduates in that they not only lead the weekly seminar discussions, keep attendance, create group exercises tailored around deepening the students' understanding of the course's central concepts, read and comment on weekly student journals, reattend the course lectures, work on an extensive term paper, and attend weekly community meetings with the instructor and graduate TAs, but they also feel and experience the responsibility of a new and unknown "teaching role" that few undergraduates have ever encountered. As former PC Melissa Rose put it,

It seems as if we all live within a world of walls. We're brought up to believe that we have to stay within these walls to fit into society. . . . One of the most profound walls I've ever encountered was that surrounding education. We are roped into a role as "student" or "teacher," both of which are mutually exclusive, and never allowed to venture beyond it for fear of crumbling the entire educational system. . . . Becoming a PC I, a student in my own right, became a teacher and at the same time learned more than I ever have in any classroom as a student.[3] It's almost as if I was playing an unrole as a PC because it was my responsibility to undo traditional roles of "teacher" and "student." In any case, what eventually happened was that I learned how to learn from the world at large, not just from the entity behind the desk.

A PC then is one of a small number of students here at UC Irvine who has independently initiated and collaborated in an experimental program in participatory education. Instead of just conventionally and passively receiving an education at this institution, as thousands of their peers do, the PCs have voluntarily undertaken the responsibility of coforming, cocreating, and actively participating in their own education and that of their peers.

Bernard McGrane

One former undergraduate student contributed a powerful reflection on this unusual role of suddenly becoming a teacher:

I would like to think I am not mentally ill or have any disorders that could be classified by the *DSM-IV.* However, every time I walked into the role of being a PC, I felt dissociated from myself, as if another person emerged from within me and took over my body. This exhilaratingly scary feeling of seeing the behind-the-scenes show made me feel afraid, as if I were breaking the rules. I became anxiety ridden, and all my insecurities and uncertainties attacked my mind as I thought of undoing the role of being a student.

I can recall my first section when, before class started, I sat in the room as a student. I was a student, lost in the crowd, listening to everyone murmur and wonder if they were in the right room. But, as soon as the clock struck 3 p.m. and it was time to begin the section, I slowly got up and walked to the front of the room. I looked up, and silence fell in the room. Thirty-two eyes were looking at me. Me! In that moment, I was not a student anymore. I could not understand the feeling that was rushing through my body. I felt naked, as if someone stripped me of the identity that I had held for 21 years. Still, they continued to look at me. Me! They were waiting for me to define their reality for the next 10 weeks. They had implicitly put their fate in my hands. I could not understand how I was given this power. Me . . . a student!

This feeling of undoing the role of being a student was phenomenal. It gives one a powerful rush as well as an incredible amount of responsibility. I do not know how to be something other than a student. I have forgotten how to be just a person, without an identity that defines my role in society. It is amazing how we internalize the roles that are assigned to us. It is almost as if we are not who we are but rather what our role is. Our role labels us and allows society to make its judgments of us. It is our label that defines our status in society. One can be a professor, a doctor, a student, a prostitute, a garbage man, or even a homeless person. Society's view of us is based on the label that has been given to us.

Students have yet another sublabeling system that defines their status. This is the label of grades. Grades define their reality. Grading, this process of placing a letter on our knowledge, has reduced each of us to a mere letter. Our GPA determines our status. The honored elite few who have received A's are equivalent to the upper class of society. They both have one thing in common: They have learned to chase the grade (or the dollar) by allowing the system to degrade them. It degrades them because they are not being evaluated on who they are but rather on what they have become following the selfish mode of society.

Students have internalized the grading system to such a point that their health is dependent on the grades. It was not until recently that I realized how I allowed grades to control my life. I had these two midterms back to back, and I literally became ill from stressing over the grade I might receive on the midterms. *I put the grade before my health.* I was blown away at that realization. A mere letter of the alphabet became more important than my health. *I cannot understand where I stopped being the individual that I thought I was and started becoming the robot trained to chase the grade. At that moment, I realized that I had given someone else control of my life.*

Someone else holds the key to my life. This person decides whether my future will be one of joy or pain. This person decides whether I am competent or not, whether my parents will be proud of me or lecture me on the importance of receiving that A. I have no control over my life as long as I am a student and grades continue to exist. Now, I understand that grades are supposed to be simple feedback on our work and a way for us to learn. However, we have been trained to value grades more than the knowledge itself. In all my courses, it does not matter that I learned an intense amount of knowledge but that I receive an A in that course. That is so sad. The knowledge means nothing; the chosen letters of the alphabet are what define our reality. The worst part is that I am a prisoner to this system, and I do not know how to free myself. It is almost as if I would cease to exist if grades stopped defining my reality. This is the world I know, and I cannot get away from it.

The funny thing is that I have become so dependent on grades that I actually receive some psychotic pleasure from having grades structure my life. They keep me from having to decide for myself. There would be utter chaos if grades were eliminated from our educational system. Students would have mental break-downs; their entire identity would disappear. They would lose their status and their label and their role. They might as well not exist.

Somewhat like the magic pill in the film *The Matrix,* being a PC helped me see how the grading system works. Being a PC gives me a chance to see the other side, the side that is the forbidden fruit for the rest of the student body. I get the opportunity to see the grading system that is controlling my life. I am so dependent on this system, yet I know nothing about how it truly works. Sure, I know the difference between the different letters that are used to control me, and I had always held this image that the person who grades my paper is some unapproachable sacred symbol, until I became that person.

I remember walking into my sections for the first time and telling my students that I was just like them, a student and a friend. However, I was not *their* friend. One cannot grade someone and be a friend at the same time . . .

Being a PC gave me the chance to grade my peers and feel the power that my TAs hold over me. I think this is the scariest part. The mere idea of someone else in control of my life and me doing the same to another scares me. It's a vicious circle. I know that I need to take a step back from this viewpoint because grades are not supposed to be a life-altering thing, but I cannot help but feel this. I just cannot understand when grades became so important to me that I would jeopardize my health over a simple letter. Now, from being a PC I have learned that grades are not supposed to be life altering, and I can preach this to everyone and feel quite passionately about eliminating the grading system, but at some unconscious level I know that I would be lying.

I am learning though. I have erased the concept of TAs being unapproachable and being these all-knowing, powerful beings. I have learned that they are people, too, and so are professors. I used to be deathly afraid of talking in class until I became a PC. Here, I was forced to speak. I learned to be more confident, and surprisingly enough I could lead a section of students staring at me and listening to me and following my every move. I do not think that I ever gave up the role of being a student when I stepped over to the other side, but rather I used this to my advantage. I became a friend and used the classroom as a family room where we could all share our thoughts and feel comfortable. I allotted students the freedom to speak their minds without worrying about being criticized.

I have learned that knowledge is supposed to be the key to our freedom, but I think that knowledge is what enslaves us. It taunts the mind because it shows us what we could have but does not show us how to meet the desired end. We attain knowledge through our education, so we can become a commodity in the free market after we ultimately get flushed out of the university. We learn how to sell ourselves to chase the dollar to meet our ultimate goals of life, yet we learn nothing on how to decondition ourselves of this time-honored tradition. However, from being a PC, I learned how grades have affected my life, and, most important, I learned that it is much easier to learn when one is not going to be tested on the material. Nevertheless, I am still searching for the answer to how to alter my ways of thinking and freeing myself from this grading prison that I am trapped in.

Gagendeep Sandhu

Notes

1. There are minority movements in some disciplines to strengthen teaching, but these forces are still very small voices in the wilderness of "publish or perish."

2. Excerpted from David Schiller's *The Little Zen Companion*. Copyright 1994 by David Schiller. Used by permission of Workman Publishing Co., Inc., New York. All rights reserved.

3. As the reknowned educator William Glasser once said, "We learn . . .

   10% of what we read.

   20% of what we hear.

   30% of what we see.

   50% of what we see and hear.

   70% of what we discuss with others.

   80% of what we experience.

   95% of what we teach to someone else.

CHAPTER 4

An Academic Question

"We call it 'academic freedom,'" said the queen, "because everybody is free to be completely academic."

(Lewis Carroll, 1865/1960)

An *academic question,* as we all know, is a question about such an obscure fine point that only an academician would bother with it. Thus, our very language informs us that there is something a little bit weird about the kind of knowledge offered up at the academy. In this section, I would like to talk primarily about the "social" or "behavioral sciences" because it is from these fields that we would normally expect a lucid explanation of how our society works. Further, it is these fields that have, in large part, sold out the goal of seeing social reality clearly.

The first thing that strikes anyone entering the province of social science is that there are several different secret languages. Sociologists cannot really speak psychologese, psychologists cannot decipher articles in the *American Anthropologist,* and economists are stumped by sociologese. The ordinary layperson encounters a deafening babble of tongues. Looking down the table of contents of a few prestigious social science journals, we encounter such puzzling titles as the following:

"A Spatial Autocorrelation Model of the Effects of Population Density on Fertility"

"A Quantitative Analysis of Temporal Symmetry in Microsocial Relations"

"Paradoxical Consequences of Excess in Structural Complexity: A Study of a State Children's Psychiatric Hospital"

"Analyzing the Instrumental Use of Relations in the Context of Social Structure"

"Additive Clusterings: Representation of Similarities as Combinations of Discrete Overlapping Properties"

This is enough to send most people running for cover. However, earnest students, who applied themselves to making sense of the contents of these articles, would discover that after reading, let us say, *The American Sociological Review* for a whole year, still would not have the faintest idea that the United States has the most severe poverty problem of any industrialized country, that we have a greater percentage of our population in prison than any country except South Africa and China, that big money controls the nomination processes of both major parties, or that the leadership of this country is perfectly willing to trade in total annihilation to gain its ends in the world—in short, reading the *The American Sociological Review* tells you almost nothing about the important things going on in our society.

In the 1950s, there was a radical sociologist named C. Wright Mills, who wanted to use social science knowledge to change society. He wrote in plain English to persuade as many people as possible. He also had the temerity to attack the secret language of sociology, particularly as it was written by an eminent Harvard sociologist named Talcott Parsons. No one, to my knowledge, has ever unmasked the secret language more dramatically than Mills does in *The Sociological Imagination* (1959), where he offers the following "translation" of a passage from Parsons (1951). To get the full benefit, really try hard to understand Parsons in this passage before you go on to the translation by Mills:

Talcott Parsons: An element of a shared symbolic system which serves as a criterion or standard for selection among the alternatives of orientation which are intrinsically open in a situation may be called a value. . . . But from this motivational orientation aspect of the totality of action it is, in view of the role of symbolic systems, necessary to distinguish a "value orientation" aspect. This aspect concerns, not the meaning of the expected state of affairs to the actor in terms of his gratification-deprivation balance, but the content of the selective standards themselves. The concept of value orientations in this sense is thus the logical device for formulating one central aspect of the articulation of cultural traditions into the action system.

It follows from the derivation of normative orientation and the role of values in action as stated above, that all values involve what may be called a social reference. . . . It is inherent in an action system that action is, to use one phrase, "normatively orientated." This follows, as was shown, from the concept of expectations and its place in action theory, especially in the "active" phase in which the actor pursues goals. Expectations then, in combination with the "double contingency" of the process of interaction as it has been called, create a crucially imperative problem of order. Two aspects of this problem of order may in turn be distinguished, order in the symbolic systems which make communication possible, and order in the mutuality of motivational orientation to the normative aspect of expectations, the "Hobbesian" problem of order.

The problem of order, and thus of the nature of the integration of stable systems of social interaction, that is, of social structure, thus focuses on the integration of the motivation of actors with the normative cultural standards which integrate the action system, in our context interpersonally. These standards are, in the terms used in the preceding chapter, patterns of value-orientation, and as such are a particularly crucial part of the cultural tradition of social systems. (Parsons, 1951, pp. 12, 36–37)[1]

Mills's translation: People often share standards and expect one another to stick to them. Insofar as they do, their society may be orderly. (Mills, 1959, pp. 25–27)[2]

Interestingly, Talcott Parsons was the leading theorist in sociology,[3] whereas Mills was, in his lifetime, considered "unsound" by most establishment sociologists. The 1960s generation rediscovered Mills, and he briefly attained the wide audience he always deserved.

I do not mean to say that nobody should ever make up a new word. In studying any subject, we come across phenomena for which the language has no word readily available. We cannot use our discovery unless we give it a name, so any field will necessarily require you to learn a certain amount of vocabulary. In learning new words, you are really discovering and pinpointing new phenomena. But obviously, the secret language of the social sciences has gone far beyond these modest necessities. The secret language is obscure, nothing more. It is meant to block communication with the outside world.

Now, we have to ask ourselves, why would scholars do this? What purpose does it serve? Secretive writing is not novel in our century. Many medieval writers wrote for a very limited audience in a cryptic style that only the very dedicated and intelligent could decipher. They did so because they feared offending the Catholic Church, which occasionally burned unwanted scholars at the stake. Do our scholars also fear reprisal? Not only is this the case, but also the pressure to become obscure is so great that it is completely internalized by most social scientists. That is, they are not just hiding the real picture from the public—they actually manage to become so confused about reality that they no longer know what it is themselves.

This is the situation that threatens them: We live in a society whose official ideology is so utterly different from its actual practice that people who look around and plainly state what they see are bound to stir up the most profound doubts about the legitimacy of the group in power and the reasonableness, and even the sanity, of the policies they pursue. The danger lies not in that there is poverty, racial discrimination, costly but poor medical service, and a deteriorating environment for all but the well-to-do. Societies have existed for centuries with inequality, injustice, and neglect of citizens. But most societies of the past had an official ideology that supported this state of affairs. In the Middle Ages, people believed that nobles and peasants were two separate species, destined by God to their respective positions. It is only when you juxtapose an egalitarian, humanistic philosophy with conditions of inequality that you are in peril. "All men are created equal" is tough to live up to. But we were all forced to memorize it in grammar school.

Surprisingly, we shared this dilemma with Communist pre-Gorbachev Russia (USSR). They also had an official policy of human equality and, in reality, a class system not too different from our own. They also had to keep their social scientists from speaking clearly about reality. Many of the devices they used to curb their scholars are identical to those used in the United States. Let us look at these devices in our own society to see how it is possible for people to spend their entire lives studying society without ever telling the truth loudly or lucidly enough to be heard. This is actually quite a difficult trick.

One method used in both countries is extreme specialization. To be a proper scholar one has to become highly specialized. I recall a job applicant for a position in sociology whose entire career had been spent on the phenomenon of adolescent fighting gangs. He had written a dozen articles on the subject, and he clearly intended to teach nothing else, regardless of the names he gave to his courses.

Now, why should this specialization be a block to learning—especially when it seems to work so well in the natural sciences? The problem is that when social scientists confine themselves to such narrow phenomena, they will probably overlook important influences from outside their field of vision. This social scientist may become very good at telling us what delinquency rates are for rich and poor teenagers, but if he lacks knowledge of societies other than ours, he may miss the crucial fact that most western European countries have very little resembling our violent gang activity. He thus misses the vital point that different national economic policies might solve our gang problem.

If our scholar is not familiar with the sociology of political radicalism, he might miss that, during the urban insurrections of the late 1960s and early 1970s, gang fighting in the ghettos diminished dramatically. Whole gangs suddenly became highly politicized and turned their aggression against the system, rather than fighting one another. Clearly, the authorities prefer gang fighting and the conditions that make for it. This can be seen by the absolute ruthlessness with which police murdered members of a newly formed, grassroots, political party that dramatically advocated Black power: the Black Panther Party. This community-based, social-movement organization took on Marxist beliefs and instituted public service in their communities and commonly opposed police brutality. The police response to them was almost one of annihilation.

Highly specialized scholars usually buy the idea that they should never say anything outside their field of expertise. Hence, they are in no danger of seeing an overall view of society, with its glaring contradictions between ideal and reality. Highly specialized scholars are also hampered in their teaching. I have said that our specialist clearly intended to teach his own subject in all his classes. This is a very common phenomenon. Feeling that teaching is less important than research anyway, scholars make little effort to help their students get an overall picture of the world and their place in it. A dozen courses in such highly specialized subjects as adolescent suicide or the culture of the Northwest Native Americans are likely to leave the student with a smattering of isolated details that he or she cannot forge together into any comprehensible view of society.

Another theme taken from natural science and misused in social science is the rule of scholarly objectivity. According to this rule, scholars should never express their value judgments (this rule itself is a value judgment and one that favors the status quo). Thus, for example, scholars may study the systematic degradation of minority races in our society, but they may not express their feeling that this is evil. Indeed, the very term would bring down criticism on their head from calmer, wiser souls. Anything that cries out against cruelty or madness in our society is considered "shrill."[4]

Objectivity has enormous value, and we can train ourselves to be systematic and careful and to follow certain methods that help us to see clearly. But the most important method for overcoming egoistic prejudice is seldom recommended or assigned to students—or scholars for that matter. This would be to leave your own niche in society for a while and go to live with people of a different social class. (This is not the same as study abroad.)

The glaring failure of the objectivity practiced by most scholars can be seen in the overwhelming extent to which our knowledge is upper middle-class knowledge. Scholars and, of course, writers, journalists, and publishers are by definition holders of upper middle-class income and status. Almost everything we know of the world through the written word and through film, television, and the Internet has been written by upper middle-class minds and sifted, edited, and judged by other upper middle-class minds, generally working in institutions that are ultimately controlled by upper class money. (The complex division of labor, which made industrial society possible, would never have had half so good a press had not the commentators been the folks who ended up talking for a living.)

The occasional exception to this is the writer or scholar who stems from a different group in society and who has managed to retain his or her loyalties and insights through the whole difficult process of socialization into the intelligentsia. Thus, the Black writer, James Baldwin, predicted the Black urban uprisings of the 1960s and 1970s long before most White sociologists had the slightest idea they were coming, simply because he remained in touch with poor, urban Blacks. Those of you who stem from groups other than the White middle class may have long suspected this. (We will talk more about this in the chapter titled "The Painful Avenues of Upward Mobility.")

Scholars are also controlled through the large foundations that, together with the federal government, provide most of the prestigious fellowships for which they compete. A sociologist who is on retainer from the U.S. Department of Defense will hardly tell us the truth about the military. The Rockefeller-funded Social Science Research Council is very unlikely to fund an investigation into the political power of the Rockefellers; the Ford Foundation is unlikely to fund someone who wishes to study the alienation and exploitation of workers in auto factories. However, a work on the evils of communism, almost anywhere in the world, is quickly funded. Ambitious scholars (and, you can be sure, they will be socialized to be very ambitious) are thus lured in certain directions and blocked from others.

Another difficulty in understanding society is simply access: While it is easy to invade the haunts of the poor to study their problems, it is quite impossible to get access to the doings of the rich and powerful. In a society in which power is exercised in secrecy, social scientists really need spies more than they need researchers.[5] Spying, however, is a dangerous business, so scholars confine themselves to what is easily accessible. There have been innumerable studies of voting behavior, but very little good has been done on the real power trading at the higher levels. Meanwhile, the social scientist's emphasis on voting behavior really becomes a piece of propaganda because it implies that voting is terribly crucial to political outcomes. By their silence about the real power centers, scholars help to make these shadowy realms disappear altogether.

Scholars also want to get jobs and keep them. So we have to look at who ultimately controls their job situations: Colleges and universities are controlled by boards (boards of trustees in the case of private colleges; boards of regents in the case of public colleges and universities), which are composed largely of wealthy businessmen. The regents of the University of California (UC) are typical of the nationwide pattern: An early study[6] showed that, of the 20 regents, 10 were millionaires, and all were extremely well off. The 20 regents sat on 60 different corporate boards. There were two women, one who was appointed after her husband's death. The median age was 60 years. The only non-White regent was Wilson Riles, who was an ex-officio member of the board because he was state superintendent of instruction. He was the first minority person on the board. Over the years the regents have refused to include representatives of the faculty or students. Most of the regents were politically conservative. Several were listed in the Social Register. The majority were Protestants. Like most such boards, the UC regents represent the interests of the top 10th of 1% of the American income distribution—that is, they represent the corporate upper class. Such businesspeople frequently have little sympathy for values such as academic freedom. In another national survey of college trustees, 33% expressed disapproval of full academic freedom in political matters.

These boards remain in the background much of the time, but they have very definite veto power. At the Claremont Colleges, during the 1970s, we hired Angela Davis to teach one course on our campus. Dr. Davis had a PhD in philosophy, but she was a Marxist scholar and had also spent the 1960s working closely with the Black Panthers. This political activism put her beyond the academic pale. When our trustees discovered that she had been hired, there was such a fuss that, under the guise of protecting Dr. Davis, the class was limited in number, closed to auditors, and was held in a location that was only announced to the enrolled few just before the class actually began. Seeing this, it was clear that we could never have offered her a job as a full-time faculty member. I would like to stress that the Claremont Colleges is one of the freer institutions around. At the University of California, Dr. Davis was fired by the board of regents, despite the support of faculty, students, and administration. It only takes one Angela Davis to convince most scholars that they cannot stick their necks out very far in any controversial direction. Unfortunately, hers is by no means an isolated case.

While I am on the subject of upper class control, I must go off on a short historical tangent. It may surprise you to realize that the very shape of your college education was the work of industrial magnates. Before the Civil War, there were a great variety of colleges, largely denominational, which emphasized the classical disciplines and theology. After the war, businesspeople began giving to colleges to create programs in science and business administration. But it was not until John D. Rockefeller and Andrew Carnegie took American higher education in hand during the first three decades of the 20th century that the modern college and university emerged.

These two tycoons, followed by numerous other corporate heads, set out to standardize higher education. They picked a small number of the best schools and gave them enormous grants, thus making them into elite institutions. They demanded secularization of the schools to which they gave money, and most gave up their denominational ties. They brought about the standardized 4-year curriculum, with its grading and unit system and its departmentalization. *Standardization is a great thing for industry; it is a terrible thing for education.* Not all human beings fit easily into the lockstep of requirements and grading methods that are now nearly universal. Needless to say, Rockefeller and Carnegie used their influence to oust scholars who were critical of the way they wielded power.

Since the beginning of World War II, the government, particularly the U.S. Department of Defense, has taken the place of wealthy donors as the primary source of funds for higher education. From two thirds to three quarters of all money spent on academic research comes from the government. Government influence has been the main push for the emphasis on research and graduate study, which has left so many undergraduates orphaned in our big universities. Like the earlier captains of industry, government has used its power position to ensure that untenured professors whose ideas do not mesh with those of the corporate-state establishment have great difficulty in maintaining academic jobs.

Scholars are rewarded to the degree that they write only for a small in-group. As I mentioned earlier, those who write books that attract a large audience are quickly denigrated as popularizers. (A *popularizer* is somebody who makes knowledge available to the populace.) A scholar who acts as consultant to the management of a corporation or police department gets career credits for doing so, but a scholar who helps a poor community fight for better housing is very unlikely to list that fact in his vita.

Finally, scholars are kept so busy by outrageous publication requirements that they have very little time to speak truth to their students and their communities. Most of them are running very scared in a tight job market. The fastest way to publish a lot is to be highly specialized. It is also interesting to look at the form in which work must be cast for publication. Scholarly journals insist on a highly stylized format without which it is extremely difficult to be published but within which it is impossible to be heard.

First of all, a research article on any subject must begin with a "review of the literature," which shows that you have read everything ever published on the subject you have chosen. Since everyone is publishing for dear life, there is an overwhelming and usually repetitive amount to digest, and even the specialists can barely keep up with it. This makes it nearly impossible for a generalist to write on most topics. It also ensures us that we won't hear anything terribly new since the process of digesting the existing verbiage is so exhausting that it will drive any wayward originality out.

It is extremely difficult to pronounce a new idea in a scholarly journal. If you do not cast it in the form of an existing idea, the editors will ask, "On whose authority are you speaking?" I had the droll experience of writing an article on human relations within academic sociology departments. I noted that these relations were very poor and fraught with hostility. The editors simply refused to print this until I put it into the words of another writer, whom I quoted at length. Then it was accepted.

Establishment professors act as gatekeepers to the world of knowledge. Most journals send a submitted article to several academic editors, and the article must pass muster with all of them. It is extremely difficult to please four or five such august persons when you are putting forth a controversial idea. In short, there is a very subtle, complex, but powerful process of censorship by which the academic establishment protects itself against what it deems heresy.

But things are not totally hopeless. In contrast with the situation of scholars in the Middle Ages, we have both greater access to heresy and greater physical safety for heretics. Just about everything you need to know has been published in a book somewhere. This freedom is threatened by publishing houses being gobbled up by multinational corporations. But at present the freedom still exists. There are still dissident publishing houses. This much freedom of information on the level of scholarly books is perfectly safe for the establishment since only 1 person in 10,000 ever reads such books, and he or she can hardly hold out against the 9,999 who only know what they hear on the evening news. So there is no political consequence to allowing such books to be published. In Russia, too, specialized scholars were allowed access to forbidden books, but the process was much more tightly guarded.

Luckily for you, the dissident books that talk about what is going on are written in plain English. This is because their writers want to reach a large public. Thus, we have two kinds of material in social science: the scholarly stuff, which is indecipherable, and the popular stuff, which is worth reading. Some of your professors will favor one style, some the other. Before you sign up for a course, get a booklist from the professor; then go to the bookstore or library and peruse the assignments. Are these books or articles that speak to you and tell you something new? If they are, take the course. If not, avoid it.

What I am saying in this chapter is that the scholars have been silenced. They have been bought. There are exceptions to this rule, but you will have to look for them. You may be surprised to hear me say this because at times colleges and universities seem to be the most radical institutions in our society. Opposition to the Vietnam War, for example, came largely from academic institutions. The situation is simply this: Yes, colleges and universities are among the very few institutions in our society that ever criticize the policies of the powerful. The great majority of scholars, however, never take part in such criticism. As with the Iraq war today, during Vietnam, only a small minority of professors spoke out. Because opposition is so rare, colleges seem very visible in their critical role, despite the fact that this role is played only intermittently and by a small minority.

Notes

1. Reprinted with permission of The Free Press, a division of Simon & Schuster, from *The Social System* by Talcott Parsons. Copyright 1951, copyright renewed 1979 by Talcott Parsons.

2. Copyright 1959 by Oxford University Press. Reprinted by permission.

3. A postscript about Talcott Parsons: In the winter of 1989 Charles O'Connell, a graduate student at the University of California at Los Angeles studying the history of the Harvard Russian Research Center, discovered something interesting. After World War II, Parsons had worked with Army Intelligence, the CIA, and the State Department in an operation to smuggle Nazi collaborators into the United States as Soviet studies experts. The

most important of these "experts" was Nicholas Poppe, a Russian academician who went over to the Germans and helped the Nazis search out the Jewish communities in Russia for extermination. Although Poppe was wanted for war crimes by the Russians, Parsons was instrumental in having him appointed to the faculty of the University of Washington. Other of Parsons's Nazi protégés also joined the Russian Research Center at Harvard.

In view of Parsons's long-standing association with the CIA, it is interesting to note that his brand of "value free" sociology undercut sociology's function of critical assessment of American society for a whole generation.

4. A few scholars have attacked the myth of objectivity. If you are interested in pursuing this issue further, you might begin with Volume 9 of *Social Problems* (1962).

5. For a case where spying paid off, see William Domhoff's (1975) *The Bohemian Grove and Other Retreats.* All of his books are worth reading. Begin with the most recent and work back.

6. Data given in this chapter from the study, as well as information about the history of business's documentation of higher education, are from David N. Smith's (1974) *Who Rules the Universities?*

CHAPTER 5

Questions Of Academic Integrity

Johnny, Janey, and the Little Search Engine That Could: A Childish Story

As the story goes, Janey and Johnny were having fun being best friends at college. They were in classes, sure, but they much preferred the games and toys the other boys and girls had to play with, so they spent too much time playing in the other kids' rooms, even when they knew they needed to write their reports for class.

One evening, Janey and Johnny looked at their homework and realized everything was due the following day. Imagine how surprised they were! Johnny sat down and cried and cried. He certainly wished his mother were here now—she'd know just what to do. Janey, on the other hand, handed Johnny a clean handkerchief. Janey knew just what to do because friends of hers told her how to beat homework deadlines when they crept up on you. She told Johnny "I think I can . . . I think I can . . . I think I can get us out of this mess."

Janey sat at the computer. She called up the Little Search Engine That Could—Yahoo! It went all over, looking for other people's writing. Then it stopped to show Janey what it found.

Janey needed one page for her literature class. Because she had so many other things to get done, she didn't think anyone would notice when she downloaded some text to use. But Johnny needed much more than one page, so he began to cry all over again. Janey sent the Little Search Engine off once again, this time for Johnny. She told him to stop crying and reassured him that his homework would be done in a flash.

Yahoo! went the Little Search Engine! It found something especially for Johnny. Neither Janey nor Johnny wanted to think they had done anything wrong. After all, they didn't copy from a book or a magazine! Instead, they had simply plucked some text right out of the virtual world so that they could use it in the real world to meet a really important deadline.

Here is a sample of Johnny's report:

"Rulings on ADA related cases made by the Supreme Court have reduced the ADA from civil rights law to entitlement policy. Case law demonstrates that the bulk of decisions have been concerned with who qualifies for ADA protections, rather than offering support and guidance toward its enforcement."

Johnny and Janey were both happy. Janey told Johnny that the report made him sound much smarter than he really was, too!

Paula Apodaca

Please Plagiarize

Plagiarism has become an enormous issue of concern in academia over the last 5 or so years. Many professors feel it is like a cavity, a corruption eating away at the integrity of academic, intellectual life itself, and I would tend to agree. I think it worthwhile to present the issue of plagiarism at the beginning of each class as an exercise in critical awareness. I try to address my concerns with plagiarism as a political rather than a moral issue. That is to say I avoid bringing it up moralistically as in "I am suspicious of you; I don't trust you; I am paranoid that you are going to try to get away with plagiarism." That approach runs the risk of poisoning the atmosphere of the classroom, of poisoning the teacher-student relationship. As we point out in so many of the chapters of this book, we *already* are embedded in the dialectics of suspicion by virtue of the very fact of being in a classroom and a part of the institution of school. To approach plagiarism in any way that further reinforces that distrust and suspicion between students and teachers really does not serve any real educational purpose. Hence, I think it more effective and valuable to raise the issue of plagiarism in a political and educational context: "I and my university colleagues across the country are engaged in fighting for the integrity of academic and intellectual work. The issue of plagiarism is a vital threat to that integrity." One of my lectures begins as follows:

> Most of you, if you walked by a very pretty red sports car that happened to have the keys in it, would not simply jump in and steal it. You are already aware of all the rules and regulations regarding ownership and stealing. If you did decide to steal it, you would *know* that there *are consequences* for this act. The issue of plagiarism is not this clear. Words, sentences, and ideas are not as clear and concrete as automobiles in this context.

One of the exercises that I have found very useful regarding heightened awareness of plagiarism is to have students *consciously* engage in *doing* a piece of plagiarism. The situation in higher education today with reference to plagiarism is overwhelmingly one of ignorance, confusion, and the fog of the Internet. It has been my direct experience that many students today are not clear about plagiarism. Downloading from the Internet has been such a fundamental and ordinary part of their education for so long that there is deep confusion whether this is a normal part of composing school papers or not. Against this background context of school papers and the Internet, I have students, as a formal homework assignment, define in one sentence what plagiarism is (in their own words—they're not allowed to plagiarize the definition) and then go out and do a piece of plagiarism, preferably using the Internet. I do this so that at the end of the assignment *I am clear that they are clear* about precisely what plagiarism is. After completing the assignment and bringing it to class, we have an in-depth discussion clarifying what we know about plagiarism. I also request that, if they are comfortable with doing it, they formally write on their homework paper, in their own handwriting, "I promise not to plagiarize in this class" (or any variation of this statement that they are willing to consciously commit to).

Bernard McGrane

Plagiarism

Plagiarism is the presentation of another's words or ideas as your own. It is a *bad* thing.

Don't do it.

Turning in a paper actually written by your roommate and saying "I wrote this" would be a flagrant example of plagiarism. The same would be true if you were to buy a term paper from a "paper mill." The lightest punishment for plagiarism of this sort would be a grade of zero for the paper. Other common punishments are failing the course or even expulsion from school. As you can see, plagiarism is a very serious offense in academia.

Plagiarism is wrong for several reasons. First, it is *lying*. If you have been asked to write something as evidence that you have grasped the materials of the course you are taking, offering someone else's work as evidence is a lie. It is no different from having someone else take an examination in your name.

Second, it is an *insult* to your fellow students. When you plagiarize, just as when you cheat on an exam, you treat unfairly those who play by the rules. You seek an unfair advantage over them, and, inevitably, you will find yourself looking down on those who devote their time and energy to the task that you have cheated on.

Third, when you use other people's words and ideas without their permission, it is *stealing*. It would be wrong to sneak into a factory and steal the products manufactured there during the day, and in the academy words, ideas, paintings, compositions, sculpture, inventions, and other creations are what we produce. It is wrong to steal them and claim them as your own.

Plagiarism is a big deal in the academy.

There are many forms of plagiarism, some less flagrant than the examples I began with. However, you need to understand and avoid all forms of plagiarism. Presenting someone else's words or ideas as your own—in any form—constitutes plagiarism. Some forms of plagiarism are probably not obvious to you, so I want to spell them out in detail. I think much plagiarism is inadvertent and unknowing. I want to help you avoid that potential embarrassment.

Let's suppose you were assigned to write a book review of Theodore M. Porter's book, *Trust in Numbers: The Pursuit of Objectivity in Science and Public Life* (Princeton, NJ: Princeton University Press, 1995). In preparing to write your paper, you come across a book review by Lisa R. Staffen, published in *Contemporary Sociology* (March, 1996, Vol. 25, No., 2, pp. 154–156).

Staffen's review begins as follows: "It has become fashionable to reject the notion of absolute objectivity on the grounds that objectivity is simply unattainable or, even if attainable, is undesirable."

Staffen's opening is good, active prose. Let's suppose you like it. More important, you imagine that your instructor would like it *a lot*. You decide to start your paper as follows: "I feel it has become fashionable to reject the notion of absolute objectivity on the grounds that objectivity is simply unattainable."

This would be a clear case of plagiarism and therefore unacceptable. Adding "I feel" at the beginning is a nice, personal touch, but it doesn't change anything. Let's tell the truth: You have probably not spent a lot of your waking hours agonizing over "the notion of absolute objectivity," much less worrying about whether others would reject the notion or embrace it with passion.

Plagiarism: "I feel it has become stylish to reject the idea of absolute objectivity on the grounds that objectivity cannot be achieved."

Even this edited passage constitutes plagiarism. While you have changed some of the words—*stylish* for *fashionable, idea* for *notion*—the idea being expressed, along with many of the phrases, have been taken from someone else, without acknowledgment.

Leaving off "I feel," by the way, wouldn't absolve the sin. Anything you write in a term paper, unless you indicate otherwise, is assumed to be your own, original thought. It's fine to have original thoughts, incidentally. In fact, we encourage it. We're happiest when your thoughts and opinions are based in evidence and reasoning rather than rumor and belief, but don't feel that your professors are somehow perversely thrilled by the mindless parroting of ideas they already know about. (I know it sometimes seems like that.)

Plagiarism: "Many people today have rejected the idea that there is such a thing as absolute objectivity since they do not believe that it can be achieved."

Even though few of the original words remain in the passage, the thought expressed has been taken from another writer and offered as your own. Even if you found a way to express Staffen's idea without using *any* of her original words, that would still constitute plagiarism. Sorry. If you're going to use someone else's words or ideas, you have to give them due credit.

Use someone else's words and ideas, go to jail. Well, it's not quite that bad, but academics don't have much sense of humor about cheating. I'll admit, I kind of enjoyed the student who turned in a paper his friend had written for the same course the preceding semester. He just used white out to cover his friend's name and typed his own over it, and you could read the original name from the back of the page. He took the course again.

There is nothing wrong with presenting someone else's words and ideas in a term paper or in a published, scholarly work. In fact, any field of thought evolves as people read each other's ideas, learn from, and build on those ideas. The key to doing this properly lies in *acknowledgment* and *citation.*

When we borrow words and ideas from others, we acknowledge that we are doing so, and we give our readers a full bibliographic reference, so they will be able to locate and read the original.

It might be useful for you to leaf through some academic journal articles. It will be clear that academics think it's fine to use other people's words and ideas. It's just important to use them appropriately. Use them as resources for building your own unique contribution to the ongoing conversation of ideas.

You might want to create a sculpture of an elephant. No problem. Get a block of granite and chip away everything that doesn't look like an elephant. Just don't pretend that you created the granite. (Unless you did, in which case I *really* apologize.)

Here's an example of how you might properly include Staffen's comment in your term paper, with a bibliographic entry at the end of the paper:

Proper use: Lisa Staffen (1996) begins her review of Porter's book by suggesting "it has become fashionable to reject the notion of absolute objectivity on the grounds that objectivity is simply unattainable or, even if attainable, is undesirable." (p. 154)

This gets the information out for the reader, and it would be accompanied by an appropriate bibliographic citation at the end of your paper:

Staffen, L. R. (1996). Featured essays. *Contemporary Sociology, 25*(2), 154–156.

Here are some other acceptable ways to use Staffen's passage. Each would be accompanied with a bibliographic entry at the end of the paper.

Proper use: In her review of Porter's book, Lisa Staffen (1996) says the idea of absolute objectivity is now commonly rejected as "simply unattainable or, even if attainable, [as] undesirable." (p. 154)

Proper use: According to Lisa Staffen (1996), it has become fashionable to reject the idea of absolute objectivity altogether. (p. 154)

In summary, it is quite acceptable—even desirable—to include the ideas of others in your term paper. This can be a sign of good scholarship, as well as assuring your instructor that you've done some of the reading for the course. (We like to think you read some of it.)

However, it's important that you *acknowledge and cite materials properly.* The key is that your readers know what you are borrowing and how to look up the original materials.

By the way, if your instructor asks you to write a report on plagiarism, don't copy what you've just read here unless you cite it properly.[1]

Earl Babbie

What's the Big Deal About Cheating?

What's the big deal about cheating? Isn't it an accepted part of school, even though every student has been told that cheating is not permitted? Schools and instructors have rules and punishments that explain the consequences of breaking these standards. But when researchers ask students if they engage in serious cheating, the results are always a bit surprising to some. (Serious cheating is defined as copying another's work, using a cheat sheet, plagiarizing, turning in another's work as your own, helping someone cheat on a test, cheating on a test.) In a recent poll, 80% of high school students, according to *Who's Who Among American High School Students,* admit to cheating.

These statistics immediately sound alarming to most instructors and administrators—little do they suspect. I share these statistics with the classes I teach and ask them honestly if they are accurate. The response is always a resounding, "No!" They reply with a smile that the other 20% lied. Is it possible that *everyone* cheats?

While discussing this moral dilemma with my classes, I'm surprised at the answers they give as to why cheating is so rampant. First came the easy justifications of too much homework or irrelevant assignments. The deeply entrenched belief of the classes I have talked with is that *cheating isn't wrong.* When pushed, students usually crack and say blatant copying of a test or plagiarism is not right, but copying homework or comparing your answer on a test is just part of being a good student. In the background, what I think is happening here is that the pressure to succeed is more important than the implications of cheating.

In an era of downloading music and information, fudging on personal taxes, and corporate malfeasance, should we be surprised that students think cheating is a normal way to act? Whatever your answer to this question, the important fact is that cheating is moving from a moral and character choice to one of opportunity and success. This is something that needs to be examined more closely by us all.

So what's the big deal? Few things in our lives are truly our own. When you get right down to it, besides your thoughts and ideas, not much is uniquely personal. I know we can argue about appearance and style, but usually even these are take-offs of others' designs that we adapt to how we want to be perceived or how we want to fit in. Our thoughts, however, although also influenced, are the inner core of our selves.

We have to ask, then, what are homework, tests, and projects in a classroom? Are they arbitrary institutional checkpoints, meritocracy markers, measurement of learning, or wastes of time? Again, the answer to these questions will vary by one's experiences, but the important thing to look at is no matter what the answer, if you turn in someone else's work, you give away the only thing that you really own—yourself. Claiming another's work as your own or copying someone's work is *giving away your voice and self for a few points in a class,* that is the *big deal.* It's a form of educational prostitution.

It might sound like I'm making too much of a small thing in your life, but think of the consequences. In college, there are few things to get kicked out of school for, but one is academic dishonesty. Students are removed from school for grades and other incidences all the time and get second chances. However, if your academic integrity has been called into question, why should any institution believe that you are now honest and brimming with integrity? Plus, your whole academic record is now in question because, if you cheated once, you probably cheated in the past. This isn't much different than when an individual's integrity has been brought under scrutiny in any situation; it is hard to gain back the integrity and trust that were once given freely.

Are our thoughts and integrity worth a few points on a test or an assignment? Do we value ourselves so little now that presenting others' work as our own doesn't even make us think twice? The one thing in life that we can be assured of besides taxes and death is that we are unique and have our own thoughts. So why give away so cheaply the one thing that makes us distinctive? Stealing others' property on the Internet is a different moral choice; selling others' thoughts as your own is SELF-destructive. Internally it will affect how you view yourself, and externally, institutionally, it won't be just a slap on the hand when you get caught; it might also be a devaluing of your character.

I think we need to look at cheating as a question of character and integrity and not just as a way to achieve a prize in a competitive situation. Schools are competitive, and the pressure and consequences of success in them can be very high. However, do these pressures outweigh the costs of devaluing your character? I hope not. I believe a better choice is to accept what you know or turn in and relish that no matter what happens in terms of outcome at least it is your ideas and thoughts being evaluated. Of course grades matter, so study. Can a grade that isn't a representation of your work be more important than your integrity? So what's the big deal? You still have to look at your *self* in the mirror and take ownership for your actions. So think about it before you start that next assignment or take that next test. (Of course that won't be until you finish downloading a pirated new song or movie off the Internet.)

John Gunderson

Note

1. This text is excerpted from Earl Babbie's (1998) article, located at www.csubak.edu/ssric/Modules/Other/plagiarism.htm.

CHAPTER 6

Everybody Hates to Write

I would like to begin this chapter's discussion on writing by quoting from one of my students' papers.

Challenge the System

After 4 years of high school and 3 semesters of college, I was sick of writing boring term papers. There are only so many ways that you can regurgitate the same dry facts. I decided I wasn't going to do it anymore. I was going to enjoy writing papers, even if it meant being uncouth in the eyes of my professors. I wrote one paper as a purely fictional past life regression that included diary entries of the life of an historical person. Through fiction I was able to present my research clearly, while actually enjoying the writing process. Another time I opted to do field research rather than book research. The assignment was to explore the origin of a cultural symbol or practice and learn what it meant to different people. I went around to local tattoo and body piercing parlors conducting interviews and taking pictures of people who indulged in body art. It was the most amazing and enlightening project I had ever done. Another time I was assigned to explore the differences between men and women as presented through the media. I decided to do a video presentation. I took clips from movies, commercials, and television shows from the past and present and arranged them on two 1-hour videos. The videos depicted stereotypical and progressive roles of men and women in the media. My editing method was crude: I hooked up two VCRs in my bedroom and copied from tape to tape. Sometimes two clips overlapped, and sometimes there was a 2-minute break between clips, but I did what I could with my lack of film editing knowledge. And I got an A. My professor loved my ingenuity and creativity. In college, you don't always have to stick to the rules. Professors like it when you break the mold. When I tackle an assignment, I make sure that I am doing something that will entertain me and that I will grow from. That's why I came to college, to challenge myself and to grow. I won't settle for less.

Kristin Rydberg

Nearly everybody I know, including professors, hates and fears the process of writing, and small wonder. Since we were in grammar school, we have been forced to commit our precious thoughts onto paper, where a red pencil might, at any moment, attack them. When we tried to develop intelligent ideas, we were regularly hassled about spelling and commas and semicolons. Our labors were usually returned to us crawling with corrections and a few well-chosen insulting remarks. When we did really well, however, we usually just got back a terse "good" and nothing more. When I first began teaching, I fell into the same thoughtless habit of giving more negative than positive feedback on papers. I had a feeling that if I gave a good grade, I didn't need to defend my position, whereas a low grade had to be accompanied by a lot of explanation.

Then I had a very salutary experience. I taught a section of remedial writing. Here I discovered how utterly crushing and traumatizing our practices were, particularly for students who came to school speaking an ethnic or class-based dialect slightly different from the "King's English" (an interesting term, indicating the class snobbery involved in our notions of "proper" language). If you are Black, for instance, you probably grew up hearing a somewhat different language from academic English. Yours is a beautiful language full of imagery and rhyme and poetry. One has only to listen to the words of gospel music to see how vividly and with what wit Black poets illumined the King James version of the Bible. Yet most English teachers see it as their duty to expunge all traces of this native tongue in their Black students.

What I discovered from my remedial writing students was that they so much hated writing that the old avoidance mechanism always set in. They resisted working on papers. When they did finally write them, they dashed them off quickly and never edited them. What really hurt these students was that they weren't properly enamored of their own creations. They weren't willing to read their papers to friends and relatives, to read them over and over, embellishing and correcting (and even looking up an occasional spelling) as they went. In our class, we began to take one person's paper each week, editing it as a group. We made it a habit to give praise to every piece, as well as correction. We tried to show each person the strong points of his or her writing. From this experience, I learned to give positive feedback. If I marked one paragraph "confusing," I would mark a better one "clearly written. Do you see the difference?" Gradually, the students warmed to the task until, by the end of the semester, I had at least induced most of them to exchange editing services with a friend. Somebody else can always see your errors more clearly than you can yourself. Reading your work out loud to yourself also helps you to catch clumsy phrasing.

In an interesting article on writing problems, one professor makes the essential point that time pressures in school force students to write only one draft. This runs counter to all good writing practices. Famous writers generally write many revisions of their original drafts. Not only do the drafts improve, but also rewriting is perhaps the best way of increasing writing skills. Be advised, then, to knock out a first draft (it should not be perfect at this point) in time to revise, preferably with the help of a friend.

There are several common problems in student writing. By remembering the kinds of comments you have received on your writing, you may be able to diagnose your own ills and take the advice that applies. Some students get lost in the earliest phase of the paper by beginning work before they thoroughly understand the professor's assignment. If the topic is unclear, you must talk to the professor. If you have a choice of topics, pick carefully to find a topic you like and one that offers the chance to use material with which you are already familiar from personal experience or from other courses. If your topic is simply given as, say, "juvenile delinquency in urban areas," try to develop a hypothesis or a theme. For example, your hypothesis might be that low-income youngsters have higher rates of delinquency than higher income youths. Your title might then be "The Correlation Between Income and Juvenile Delinquency." Or, if you would rather use a theme, it might be "the influence of mass media on juvenile violence." Developing a hypothesis or theme helps you to narrow down the topic and give direction to your research.

The most frequent and grade-lowering problem with writing is lack of clarity. This is really not a writing problem but results from a failure to think the issues you are writing about through to the point where they are clear to you. Sometimes it may require you to ingest more information than you now have; sometimes you may need to discuss your confusion with a sympathetic friend. When I am in deep water, I may just drop the work for a few days, but if the going continues to be boggy when I return to it, I generally talk it out with someone. An outsider can frequently see the forest when you are lost in the trees.

Rewriting is also crucial here. First drafts generally contain some confusion, but *the act of writing the confusion down is a major step in clarification. Often, you do not even know you are confused until you try to submit your thoughts to paper.* What is most troubling to me is that *many students don't seem to know when they are confused.* I think this is because they have been confused so often at school that they have come to accept this mental state as natural. Because we teach people in batches of 30 to 40 with widely varying experience and ability, only the quickest and best prepared can insist on clarity (i.e., keep questioning the teacher until they really understand). Everybody else is going along pretending to understand until, finally, the line between understanding and confusion begins to blur and the student has lost the ability to practice self-correction. If this rings a bell with you, begin to make it a regular practice to insist on clarity in class. *Keep asking questions until you understand.* If you have to let something go, mark it clearly in the margin of your notes as "confusing." When you edit your writing, mark suspect sections in a similar way and then work them over with the professor or friends, if you can corner them. In other words, either refuse to settle for confusion or at least mark off your confusions, so you can keep them from contaminating your whole thought process. Remember that something that is perfectly clear to you will come out clearly on paper. One of the reasons why writing is hard is that it is really thinking. Improving your writing is also a way of improving your thinking, which is why it is well worth laboring over.

A related but slightly different problem concerns students who have fallen whole-hog for one of the many "secret languages" used in the academy. These students usually don't think much of their own abilities and hope to rescue themselves by learning to write in the jargon of a discipline before the jargon is at all clear to them. These unfortunate folk are catching a disease that is so rampant in academia that many professors will even reward this type of behavior. I have discussed the function of the secret languages in an earlier section. Here, I can only say stay away from any jargon you don't feel completely at home with. Don't use long, complicated words and sentences where simpler ones will do. Good writing is simple writing. Academic writing is often lousy writing.

Another writing disease directly fostered in school is padding. Anyone who really knows literature will tell you that brevity is the very soul of poetry and prose. Yet we continue to demand certain quantities of writing ("Write a 10-page paper," etc.). Of course, this is an invitation to pad. I tell my students, "Write as if you were wording a telegram, as if each and every word cost you money." When you edit your first draft, edit for brevity. If that results in too short a paper, according to your professor's lights, maybe you need to develop some additional ideas. If you just can't, take your chances with the shorter paper. Don't become a poor writer just to please your professors.

I want to tell you how not to write a lengthy term paper—from years of personal experience. I used to go at this type of assignment by proceeding to do all the research first. I would take voluminous notes just right: on an 8-inch by 5-inch card or half sheets of paper with the citation and subject at the top for easier sorting— one main item to a half sheet. This was fine, but I would invariably find myself nearing the end of the semester with a huge pile of unorganized notes, a loose collection of ideas, and a lot of anxiety about how the thing was ever going to come together. Before I could overcome my mounting fears and actually sit down to organize a paper, I would practice a ritual of self-torture. This took the form of a 3- or 4-day vigil in the college coffee shop, where I would sit from morning till late afternoon consuming coffee and cigarettes while commiserating with my fellows in the same predicament until I was quite physically ill. Only then, when my discomfort became patent and physical, would I overcome my avoidance mechanism and sit down to the dreaded task. Such rituals of self-torture are, I discovered, quite common among students before they undertake a heavy assignment. You may have your own variation. Suddenly, we enlightened, modern folk find ourselves practicing a primitive rite to appease the angry academic gods. It is really hard for us to see that the ritual adds nothing whatsoever to our efforts. The only way I know to cure yourself of these rituals is just to dare it—just once—without the ritual. It's worth it, even if you chance a low grade. What will happen, of course, is that you will come out about as usual. It may take several such leaps of daring to overcome the ritual entirely, but it can be done. (It might be fun to do a study of such rituals, exploring the great variety of forms they take in different students.)

You can develop positive as well as negative rituals. In one of my writing courses, I had a student who told us that, before she sat down to write a paper, she always imagined herself to be a great expert on the subject under consideration. She imagined the many people who were waiting for enlightenment from her pen. In this way, she jollied herself into a positive rather than a fearful frame of mind. She was, in fact, a very successful student, although she had to come from behind in terms of her earlier education. Perhaps you can develop your own variant of this fantasy. Imagining yourself to be a teacher may help. In fact, an interesting and subtle process sets in when one changes from the role of student to that of teacher. It is still the same process of mastering material, but now you are no longer the judged but are among the judges. You feel very responsible to your class to give them a straight and clear rendition. But you are working from a position of power, and this adds wings to your typewriter. Another type of positive ritual would be anything you can do to loosen up and relax your body and mind. Perhaps some exercise and meditation would work well for you. It may be easier to replace rituals of self-torture with positive rituals than just to give them up altogether. It's worth trying.

When doing library research for a paper, avoid the experience of going into the library cold. Most college and university libraries have huge collections in which you can easily lose your way. If at all possible, get some recommendations for sources from your professor. Sometimes you may have a topic on which your professor is not too knowledgeable. In that case, try to find another professor who knows the area. It is quite usual for students to ask for help from someone other than the professor teaching the course. Two sources of advice are always better than one. In some cases, librarians will also be helpful. Another valuable source of reference is the Internet. It is a modern luxury abounding with information, allowing you access to virtually any information, all with the ease of a simple finger click. Here you may also find the most recent publications and updates on all subjects.

If none of these methods has yielded a list of sources, you can sometimes use one or two current textbooks in the subject and begin by reading the relevant section and then following the footnotes. With all these methods you are getting the benefit of advice from people who have already sifted through the mass of writing on the given subject, thus saving yourself hours of frustration.

I also learned some other ways of easing the burden of a research paper. One thing I would strongly recommend to you is that you write little bits of your paper while you are in the research phase. Even if you don't yet know where—or even whether—the little section will eventually land, write it down as it occurs to you. By the time you finish your research and turn to your collection of little sections, you may find that you have your paper nearly half written. It is also the case that the process of writing forces you to clarify your ideas. You may discover, for example, that you are lacking a piece of information without which you cannot really make your point. Thus, your ongoing writing will add direction and precision to your research.

Finally, I would like to give you some advice about writing social science papers. (I cannot speak with authority in other areas.) Good social science writing has a lot in common with good fiction: It is the telling, concrete detail or example that makes a theory or generalization come to life. Never nurture, much less put down, a generalization that you don't understand well enough to translate into a specific case. Make it a mental practice to approach every theory with the question "How would this work in one individual's experience?" For example, voting studies show that husbands and wives who have opposite voting choices fail to vote more frequently than couples who agree. How would this actually look if you were peering into their living room? Perhaps you can imagine that, having just had some heated words with his spouse about the comparative venality of two candidates, Mr. A decides, "This isn't worth quarreling about; the less said about it, the better." Henceforth, he avoids listening to the evening news and eventually conveniently forgets Election Day.

Or let us say that you have just made the assertion that poor people have higher rates of mental illness than richer people. Here you want to throw in a few nice, startling statistics on rates of schizophrenia found in the latest study. There you have the illuminating fact. Now, can you see exactly why the poor might become ill more frequently and stay ill longer? You can see from your source material that the richer and better educated people are, the more likely they are to rush to a psychiatrist with the first symptoms, whereas poorer, less educated people might not know what was wrong or whom to go to until the symptoms became so severe that they came to the attention of some public agency, such as the schools or the police. Now, you can see the process in a little more detail.

Or, again, poor children who attend predominantly middle-class schools are more likely to go to college than similar poor children who go to schools where everybody is poor. Just what is the mechanism involved here? One is that the intellectually successful poor child may be excluded from his or her peer group, which wishes to punish the child for being more successful: *Teacher's pet* might be the colloquial expression of this sentiment. In a school where everybody is poor, the friendless child will usually respond to this exclusion by giving up the intellectual success to regain the acceptance of his or her peers, whereas in a more mixed school, the child may begin to attach him- or herself to a higher class, higher scoring peer group, take on their aspiration level, and make it to college. Once you can picture this youngster in the halls and at lunchtime, you have understood the mechanism behind the generalization. Now you have the picture.

At times, a telling quotation or anecdote will illuminate the point. On this particular subject, I sometimes tell my students about a friend I had who had come from a very poor background to become a professor. When he was a young teenager and unusually studious for his group, his worried mother once placed a newspaper article on his bed that discussed that homosexuals hang out in libraries. Wow! Now you really sense what it means to break with the accepted working-class role for males. If I were writing this up, I would make a direct quotation—have my friend tell it in his own words. While you never want to let a paper become a collection of quotes, you do want to collect some nice, juicy ones as you research your subject, like ripe, plump raisins you can put in the final pudding. Don't hesitate to use examples from your own experience. Only a very pedantic professor will fail to appreciate this. Thus, *your exposition in social science should always be brightened and sharpened with a concrete example* (or even a hypothetical example); a nice, crisp fact; and a telling quotation. If you have trouble doing this for a particular generalization, then you don't yet understand it.

If your college offers writing courses, it will be worth your time to see whether they have a good reputation and take one early in your college career. In most nonscientific fields, writing is crucial to successful work. Writing courses are definitely not just for the weak student. If the course is at all well taught, even the A student can learn a great deal from it.[1]

Writing *Is* Required

As some of you might have already noticed, writing is an essential part of life. Whether you like writing or not, you have already realized that writing at one point in your life is required. For many people, writing can be a dreadful experience; for me, writing went from a frightful encounter to one that became gratifying and, ultimately, my career path.

In high school, writing papers was nowhere near a satisfying experience. When it came to writing, my goal was to just get through it. In-class writing exams (as well in-class assignments) were the worst. The pressure emitted while writing during a certain period of time resulted in my worst writing. Although I would study hard for my exams, the pressure of writing four to five short answers and essays would always take me to my breaking point. For some reason, I could never portray the knowledge that I had in my head through my writing. All of my thoughts were cluttered and unorganized. Instead of using my writing to exhibit my knowledge on the exam, I would do the opposite and hand over a muddled piece of work. As a result, I tried to avoid the act of writing during my high school career. However, this soon changed when I went to college.

In my first year at a university, I did not have many writing assignments because I took mostly general education (GE) courses. However, in my second year I faced the task of having to write five to eight papers in one quarter. During that year someone suggested that I take an upper division English course— English 100W. I hesitated at first but decided to take it since it satisfied one of my writing requirements. My goal for the course was just to get through it, but somehow the class served as a life-changing experience for me. My feelings toward writing went from hesitation to that of welcome.

One may wonder how a change like that can occur. Well, it all began with the arrangement of the course. The class was set up in a format that allowed the students to work on one research paper throughout the whole quarter. In addition, all the required reading assignments were not novels; rather, they were reading assignments that dealt with the art of writing and how to break through its difficulties. As a result, I essentially spent 10 weeks working on improving my writing. Since I was working on only one 15-page research paper, I was able to constantly revise my work and identify my key writing faults. The class structure also allowed me to consult with my professor on a weekly basis about any difficulties I was having. During this process, my skills soared, and by the end of the quarter I was able to identify my writing weakness and strengthen them.

In addition to the English 100W course, I also acquired a writing mentor that same quarter. She assisted me by reading my papers, and she influenced me to become an even better writer. Thus, she helped me with gaining not only more confidence in my writing but also more insight into it.

I really did not notice that my writing had improved so dramatically until I began to take writing exams in other courses, excelling in them without feeling the pressure I felt in the past. Somehow, my thoughts became clearer, and it was exhibited through my writing. Or, rather, my writing became cleaner, and that echoed back and made my thoughts clearer. I was no longer scrambling through random ideas or trying to endure a scattered exam. Writing became a battle that I conquered. During my studying, I was able to develop various techniques and strategies for myself that would improve my performance on in-class exams as well as take-home writing assignments. These strategies include the following:

- For in-class writing exams, make sure you find out the number of questions you are going to be given as well as the time allotted for the exam in advance. This is important because it allows you to calculate the amount of time you have for each question before the exam. In addition, always make sure you allow more time for long essays and less time for short answer questions. Set aside time for yourself to think about what you want to write about, and don't hesitate to jot down any of your ideas on the side or back of your paper. Most important, bring your own watch to keep track of time; do not rely on your professor to update you on the time remaining.

- Start early on papers. If a paper is assigned 2 weeks before its due date, make sure you start as soon as possible. One of the worst habits to practice is procrastination because in most cases it ends up causing your worst writing. You do not have to write your entire paper the first day you are given the assignment, but developing an outline of some sort can be one of the best things you could do. An outline allows you to plan what you want to write in advance and the topics you would like to discuss. More important, it allocates time for you to develop a well-formulated thesis, giving you ample time to consult your professor with any difficulties you are having early in the process.

- Once you have written your paper, do not make the mistake of only reading it on the computer. Print out a hard copy and read it aloud to yourself. Both methods will allow you to catch mistakes you could have missed by reading it straight from the computer. Also by reading your paper aloud, you are able to hear the flow of your paper.

- After reading your own paper, make sure you give it to someone else to read. This is an important aspect of writing because in most cases you cannot discover all of your mistakes on your own. By letting someone else critically analyze your paper, you can get more insight in your writing style and further improve it.

- Last, make sure you give yourself enough time to REVISE because more often than not you can always develop a much better draft than your first.

After using these various techniques, I always guarantee clarity in my writing and avoid costly mistakes. As an experienced news magazine editor and script-writer, I know writing can sometimes be stressful. However, by developing certain strategies and techniques for yourself, you can learn to transform that anxiety into encouragement while steadily developing your writing.

Nkemdilim Nwosu

The Oral Report as a Chinese Opera

Almost everybody hates to give an oral report. I believe this is because students fear each other's opinions even more than they fear the teacher's. You do not want to make an ass of yourself in front of your peers. In fact, many students never speak up in class for the same reason. It may help you a bit if you realize that everybody in the class probably shares your fears. Occasionally, I ask students to jot down on a piece of paper what people will think of them if they take part in the class discussion. Everybody fears disapproval from their fellows. Perhaps the most damning thing about education by coercion is the way it sets you against your peers. When we were younger and less socialized, we used to all gang up on the teacher—remember? But as some of us began to see that we could rise in the system by pleasing teachers, we also had to cut ourselves off from the body of our peers and begin competing with them instead. This is a fundamental betrayal that our fiercely competitive society exacts from each of us: We must break faith, must sell out our friends. From the day this process begins, fear of retribution grows in us. I used to try dealing with this by kidding around a little bit in class about oral reports and by letting everybody give immediate pro and con feedback on a report. This helped, but unfortunately most professors will not go this far. What they want from you is a coolly executed, highly professional performance.

It will help you to see the oral report for what it really is: as highly stylized a performance as a Chinese opera. It doesn't follow the usual rules of daily communication, and your ability to execute it properly may have very little to do with your ability in ordinary conversation. A judgment on your report is in no way a judgment on your personality and mind.

A small, positive ritual is recommended here. Before you start, you need to spend about 10 minutes slowing down your physical and mental processes and lowering your tension level. This will help in every way but is particularly good for the most common of mistakes: overly fast presentation. If you are inclined to be very nervous, the best thing you can do is just to sit quietly with your eyes closed and get in complete touch with the physical sensations of nervousness. This is not at all a pleasant process, but you may be surprised at what can develop from it. If your anxieties are rather vague, you may wish to do some slow, deep breathing and some good physical stretching. Again, as you are about to begin your report in the classroom, allow yourself 30 seconds of quiet to collect your scattered self before you begin. Perhaps you can imagine yourself to be a famous professor, about to give the word to a collection of grateful, alert students (pure fantasy, under any circumstances).

Never read an oral report verbatim. You will lose your audience instantly. Rather, prepare a fairly detailed outline. I find that, for a 50-minute lecture, I need anywhere from 4 to 10 pages of detailed outline. The outline has a cue phrase for each major idea; it is marked off so that I can see at a glance whether I am in Part 1 or Part 3. If I plan to use quotes, I type them out verbatim. Nothing creates more anxiety than having to shuffle around in a huge sheaf of papers and books looking for a quotation or a statistic, while your listeners are waiting for you to continue.

A very effective way to break up the pace of your report and make a good impression all around is to have some handouts. Sometimes an outline of your report may be in order, though more usually a set of statistics or some graphs or diagrams or maps may be better. Occasionally a dull subject may be made more lively by bringing in some illustrations. If you are working on some aspect of parent-child relations, for instance, it may be interesting to bring in some examples of the way these relationships are treated in advertising: "Have your mommy buy you a box of Super Sugar Bombs." Rare is the professor who doesn't appreciate these signs of extra effort.

If possible, practice your report formally before an audience of your friends, and always practice your report once or twice, timing yourself in the process. Students almost universally overestimate what can be said in a given space of time. Nothing is so exasperating as having two students scheduled for a given date and having the first one take up three quarters of the allotted time. This situation can be easily avoided, and you will have the added boon of discovering that you don't need as much material as you thought.

Now, let us assume that you have prepared your outline well, given out your handouts, and gone through your preparatory ritual. You have given yourself a few seconds to become centered and are about to begin. Here, precisely, is where most people blow half a grade. They begin with a little self-deprecating giggle, pull at their hair and say, "Well . . . I don't really know too much about this, but. . . . "

That is not the way this particular Chinese opera is played. You don't have to apologize or appease anybody. Instead, you look for a moment at your audience and then dive in crisply and clearly: "My topic today is the influence of foundations on the direction of medical research." Does it sound too daring? Do you fear that you can't deliver on the promise of such an opening? Be assured! The opening itself is worth half a grade. Your opener could be more original. I remember with particular pleasure the student who began his report on the Krupp family (the powerful owners of Germany's steel industry) with a picture of the kaiser's whole family, which included a Krupp placed strategically just at the kaiser's right hand. It was a beautiful opener and the picture was worth a lot of words.

If your professor permits it, tell the class at the beginning of your presentation that you will welcome questions during your report. This helps vary the pace and keeps your audience involved and awake. Don't be terrified by the prospect of questions you can't answer. A simple "I'm sorry; I don't know that" is always permissible. Delivered in an unruffled, calm way, it can even raise your stock with the audience and the professor. People who calmly admit they don't know seem, somehow, to be in special command of themselves and their subject matter. (Look for professors who are not afraid to say "I don't know.") If you do wish to allow questions, allocate space for them when you time your presentation.

Bluebooks and Other Sadistic Measures

Unfortunately, most of you will spend more time taking short-answer tests and writing 3-hour bluebook exams than you will spend on writing term papers or giving oral reports. The latter at least have the virtue that they prepare you for much of the writing and speaking that you will probably have to do in the course of your professional work. Short-answer tests and 3-hour writing marathons, on the other hand, find no parallel in life outside the academy. In real situations, you will always have more flexible time schedules, a typewriter, and access to books and notes.

It is difficult for me to write on these subjects because I discontinued these methods very early in my teaching career. I quit using short-answer tests after I allowed students to defend their answers in writing and discovered that half the right answers were for entirely wrong reasons. Three-hour bluebooks disappeared as soon as I found that most students' handwriting undergoes drastic collapse after 2 hours of writing. I could never figure out the last third of the effort. Since then, I have used only term papers and take-home exams.

Anyone who has suffered through a 3-hour writing marathon must have suspected that there is a definite sadistic-harassment factor in most education. It really goes to extremes when you hit graduate school. In the sociology department at Berkeley, where I did my graduate work, we had at one time an examination program that required 5 hours of writing per day for 5 consecutive days. It was truly dreadful to run into a friend in the middle of this exam week and see the stubble of beard, the red-rimmed eyes with their wild look, and the general demeanor of exhaustion and suffering. Perhaps such measures are meant to ensure that only the physically toughest survive. More probably, our professors were merely repeating the treatment they themselves had received. *Adults have an awful way of believing that, whatever their youthful sufferings, surely the next generation must benefit from their repetition.*

If ever I write a final chapter to this book, titled "Academic Chickenshit," the 3-hour bluebook exam will surely be granted center stage. I cannot really offer you a way out. You can but know that, in this instance, you are victims of collective idiocy.

The only positive advice I can give you is slight. Some professors very much like bluebooks, which have an outline at the beginning. If you go in for this idea, leave the first page of your bluebook blank and put the outline in at the end of writing—when you know what, in fact, you have said. It helps to write from an outline—but keep this one on the side to be thrown away.

When taking a bluebook exam, read the question very carefully and make sure your paper speaks directly to each part of the question. Take time to read through the entire exam and plan your answering schedule. Try to stick to your schedule. In general, the same advice applies as for term papers. Use as many facts and examples as you can, but don't pad.

The other advice is tongue-in-cheek, though it may be suggestive. Very early in my undergraduate career I discovered *Weltanschauung*. This German word—one of those "untranslatables"—means "worldview" or "ideology." I took to throwing one *Weltanschauung* (correctly spelled) into nearly every bluebook I ever wrote. I don't know for sure, but I always suspected that it raised me by half a grade.

Note

1. For an unusual, creative way to enhance your writing skills, see Gabriele Lusser Rico's *Writing the Natural Way* (1983) and Natalie Goldberg's *Writing Down the Bones* (1986).

CHAPTER 7

Wisdom and Knowledge

In college, when you are in the world of your professors and their classes, you are awash in a sea of knowledge. Occasionally, you are drowning in it—so much knowledge, so many facts and names and dates and theories, so many books and articles and handouts. Research indicates that the average college graduate, interviewed several years from graduation, remembers very little of all this. Few can even remember the names of any of the courses they took.

Just exactly what is useful in all this? What is expendable? I want to invite you to sit back for a long moment, away from the things you "must know" by next Tuesday, and consider what kinds of learning you really want and need so that you can choose and absorb and forget with a little sense of direction, rather than merely reacting to each new deadline.

First, *we must differentiate between the knowledge you will actually need in your future profession and the knowledge that is served up to broaden you as a human being.* This latter part of the curriculum is usually referred to as *distribution requirements* or, in reverent tones, as a *liberal arts education.* How much of your chosen major contributes directly to your future occupation differs greatly according to your concentration. In the natural sciences, much of what you learn will be directly usable. In the social sciences, arts, and humanities it may be very little. A Bachelor of Arts in these subjects seldom leads to a specialized job. Students with degrees in sociology or English or economics may end up waiting tables, doing secretarial work, working for the phone company, or processing unemployment insurance applications. A few luckier ones may squeeze in on the bottom rung of a publishing house or land a good job organizing recreation for the city parks system. Those who go on to graduate schools usually find that it doesn't matter very much exactly what they majored in as undergraduates. There is a kind of pretense that this is not so. But when push comes to shove, the only job for which these majors directly train you is a job teaching somebody else social science, humanities, or art.

The claims of higher education are not limited to preparing you for a job. In small liberal arts colleges, there is a point of pride involved in the idea that these 4 years are not primarily directed toward utilitarian pursuits. These schools still wear the mantle of preparing the children of the rich. It is assumed that these folks have 4 years to spend on broadening themselves before they go on to some more definitely focused graduate education. Even though big universities and state and junior colleges proclaim less about the liberal arts, their undergraduate curriculum is largely indistinguishable from that of the small college.

In this section, I am not concerned with the occupational part of your training. What interests me here is the liberal arts portion of your studies: that portion of your education that is supposed to give you breadth and depth, to make you an "educated person," to acquaint you with the body of knowledge this culture has at its disposal so that you will not wander as a lost stranger in your culture but will be able to direct your future development with some discernment.

The first thing we must consider is that we live in a society whose store of specialized knowledge is so staggering that, confronted by it, any single individual, no matter how educated, is like a person wandering into the United Nations and trying to understand all the languages being spoken. On this score, we differ dramatically from earlier societies. One hundred fifty years ago, a college education could acquaint you with most of the general knowledge available in science, history, philosophy . . . in all fields. Today, 4 years of higher education cannot even acquaint you thoroughly with a single discipline. Obviously, then, we must be sophisticated in our approach to this huge forest of knowledge. What do we really need to become successful human beings? And, on the other hand, what can we leave aside, knowing that we can always dig it out of a book if we really need it?

I would like to suggest to you that what is essential is not knowledge at all but something else—something that has become almost unmentionable in the modern college or university: *wisdom*. We all know roughly what knowledge consists of. But what is wisdom? What I mean by this word is the ability to keep your emotional and mental balance in life, to understand yourself well enough to live comfortably with yourself. Thus, *wisdom is essentially self-knowledge*. But it also involves understanding the world you live in well enough to get where you want to go or to see danger coming before it hits you. Wisdom cannot be wholly self-centered, however. It must always include making contributions to other people and the natural world around you. There is wisdom in the old Jewish saying, "If I am not for myself, who will be for me? But if I am only for myself, what am I?" Self-knowledge is one aspect of wisdom; another is the emphasis on direct, experiential knowledge, for books are the tools of knowledge but experience is the tool of wisdom.

The academic version of knowledge involves a strict separation between pure, disembodied intellect on the one hand and the emotional/experiential life of the scholar on the other. These are two very different kinds of knowing. Let me illustrate the difference with an example. I taught a course in race relations during the stormy era of the early 1960s when the civil rights movement was at its height and the Black urban uprisings were just around the corner. I had assigned my students some very angry writings by the Black author James Baldwin. But White students seemed unable to take Baldwin's message in and respond to it. Then I invited a local Black activist to come and speak to the class. He turned out to be a young man who was so angry that it was difficult for him to express the extent of his emotion in words. But one could feel it in the tone of his voice and the look on his face. After his talk, several students came up to me and said, "Hey, they are really mad, aren't they?" and "Now I suddenly understand what Baldwin was trying to say." The experience of the human contact broke through where the written word could not. Intellect alone could not fathom the phenomenon of Black anger. *The word is not the thing.*

Students seem, for the most part, to accept the separation between life and scholarship, which is considered good form by most of the faculty. This was often very frustrating to me as a teacher. For example, I used to teach the sociology of social movements. Each student studied a living movement and presented his or her findings in class. Throughout, I emphasized the ideological side of movements. The establishment has its own crazy ideology, of course, but movements show the craziness of belief systems more because they are likely to run counter to the established beliefs and are therefore more easily perceived as bizarre. Here is a group that preaches the advent of the savior in South Korea; here is another in which members speak in tongues to attain salvation; here is a little group clinging to the teachings of Leon Trotsky, one of the leaders of the Russian Revolution of 1918, later exiled and killed by Stalin. Over here are people who believe they can be cured of all the symptoms of aging through an all-vegetable diet; here is another group that believes that communists have taken over the United States. What we learn, of course, is that there is no belief so fantastic that some group of people will not adopt it if doing so makes them feel better. The mind is endlessly inventive, and the mind is the servant of our emotional needs and wishes.

I did not suspect that I was throwing a curveball when I asked my students to comment on what the course had suggested to them about their own personal ideologies. To my great surprise, nobody had made that vital link; the students hadn't asked themselves, "If this is how other people's minds operate, what might this imply about my own beliefs?" This kind of separation in learning produces learned fools— people who can rattle off the ideologies of countless groups but still naively trust that their own version of truth is immutable and not to be questioned. I have said that wisdom is an unmentionable in the academy. Anyone claiming to offer it would be considered arrogant, opinionated, and unprofessional. Worst of all, such a one would be branded unscientific. Yet there is always the unspoken assumption that a lot of history will give you something called perspective, that literature will provide "insight," that social science will enliven you as a citizen, or that psychology will make you a little saner. The academy has not altogether given up on wisdom but has left it glimmering vaguely on the horizon without daring to approach it too closely.

To understand this state of affairs, it helps to take a look at the history of the modern academy to see how it got this way. The earliest Western universities were schools of theology designed to train priests. The Bible and Catholic theology were medieval Europe's version of wisdom. At the same time, it was their cosmology and included all the knowledge considered important. When modern science began, it developed in the shadow of this body of belief (though not entirely within the universities). Gradually, over several centuries, the various scientific disciplines developed and gained a foothold in the academy. At first, they were squeezed in under the general heading of "philosophy." Only in the 19th century were they given a separate status.

As the astounding power of science developed, the new fields broke off great chunks of the subject matter previously included in theology and philosophy. By the beginning of the 20th century, they already towered above all other subjects. Science was the goose that laid the golden eggs of medicine, industrial technology, and weaponry. In our century, all other subjects have existed only in the shadow of natural science. Theology was kicked out and permitted only a limited existence in graduate schools designed to train priests and ministers. To survive at all, social science, literature, and philosophy took on at least the outer trappings of the scientific method. To appear scientific (and, as I have suggested, to avoid conflicts with power), these subjects abandoned the claim to wisdom and gave themselves over wholeheartedly to the gathering and ordering of knowledge. Philosophy increasingly abandoned "value-laden" subjects like ethics for the more mathematical and scientific, and hence more respectable, areas of symbolic logic and philosophy of science. *Objectivity* became the watchword. Scholars were told to completely separate themselves as human beings and citizens from their role as social scientists and to drop forever the questions that have always haunted the human race: questions of justice and injustice, avarice and generosity, enlightenment and stupidity.

Of course, there were always those who fought a rear guard action against these tendencies. The humanities, particularly, became the preserve of those who still wished to investigate values, yet even they were heavily contaminated. In every field, scholars had to become specialists to be respectable. Specialization had worked so well in science that now the historian had to be an expert on a single century; the professor of English had to lay claim to a single writer or period. Quantification invaded even fields like literature. Computers were drawn into service to analyze the use of adverbs and conjunctions in Shakespeare. Since highly specialized research was adding up to enormous breakthroughs in science, it was also posited that all the specialized, well-ordered research of social scientists and professors of the humanities would somehow, somewhere add up to a kind of knowledge that would serve us in the same dramatic way that science has served us. Students of these subjects were to benefit by becoming acquainted with the scientific methods applicable to their chosen fields and by studying examples of the many specialized fragments of knowledge that were becoming available. They were permitted to stand by and watch the research process, which might eventually lay another golden egg. As part of this process, students, like their teachers, were to separate themselves as human beings from their role as apprentices of research.

It is, of course, a tall order to evaluate the outcome of some 50 to 80 years of development in the social sciences and humanities, but we cannot wait forever. So far, the golden egg has not hatched. We have lots of psychologists but continue to run enormously high rates of mental illness. We have sociologists galore, but the social fabric continues to disintegrate at an alarming rate. We do not lack for historians, yet our national policies do not even take the next generation into consideration.

Social science has not achieved any real amelioration of our serious social problems. This is not because leaders do not know ways of lessening these problems. They know! The problem is that the necessary changes require a commitment of resources and a willingness to break with established ways of doing things. Our leaders are unwilling to do either. This leaves social scientists exactly where the astronomers and engineers would be if there were no commitment to the space program. In light of this situation, it would behoove the social scientists to go over the leaders' heads and educate the public. Unfortunately, most do not even try to educate the public nearest them—that is, the students who pass through their classes.

More damning than this is that these disciplines do not even seem to enlighten the very people who specialize in them. It is an old joke that the psychologists are the craziest people on campus. This is perhaps untrue, but they are certainly not noticeably saner than their colleagues in math or physics. Sociologists, who specialize in forms of human organization and who have studied the inner workings of every major academic discipline, organize themselves exactly as badly as every other discipline. Nor are they known for their superior human relationships. Historians do not seem to have more perspective than other people, specialists in marriage get divorced at the same rate as other people, economists seldom get rich, and political scientists are as subservient to power as anybody. In fact, sad to say, academicians live no more wisely than other people. They are every bit as arrogant, competitive, and quarrelsome as corporation executives.

We would be suspicious of a physician who could not cure his or her own ill health, and we would think twice about depending on a safety engineer who burned his or her own house down. But we accept without much thought the overwhelming evidence that "physician, heal thyself" does not seem to apply to the experts who study human beings and their cultural creations. We cannot believe that all this expertise doesn't work. That is partly because in one way it certainly does work: It provides a good living for the experts. It may even provide you with a job someday. But if you wish to become wise, you must demand a little more than this.

Perhaps what I have said so far leaves you with the feeling that the situation is hopeless—that college will speak to your real human needs no more than high school did—even, perhaps, that wisdom is unattainable or must fall on a lucky few from out of the sky. Things are not entirely this bleak. The academy offers greater diversity and greater freedom of choice than high school. *If you know what you are looking for, quite a lot can be found.*

* * *

Before we look for sources of wisdom in the academy, we better zero in more closely on wisdom in its pure, concentrated form. It would not have surprised your grandparents, but it might surprise you, that wisdom is essentially to be found in the great religious traditions of the human race. We must discuss Christianity because we live in a culture that is heir to this religious tradition. But our modern culture has so twisted and obscured the real import of the New Testament that most of us have stopped looking in this direction for guidance in living our own lives. It is, indeed, a little difficult to imagine the average suburban church as a vehicle of wisdom. This is not to say that there aren't some wise people among the clergy, but you have to look hard for them, just as you have to look hard among your professors.

In their pure and original form, all religions, including Christianity, are really operating in the area we now call psychology. That is, *they are a body of practices and teachings that enable followers to be happy, effective people.* They teach us how to meet life's difficulties with equanimity. They provide us with practices that teach us how to handle our mind and our emotions. Most of modern Christianity, however, has lost the psychological insights and has become a historical belief—for example, believing that about 2000 years ago a certain person was born. This is history, not psychology.

Christian doctrine also contained a critique of established society, including the established church of that time. These are referred to as "the world," whose values we must shun if we are to have a happy life. But Christianity has long since made its peace with the world. To the extent that it survives, it generally sells out to the values of this world.

The supposed Christianity of our civilization has not kept us, as a nation, from stockpiling weapons to fry our enemies wholesale. Indeed, it is not an exaggeration to say that the modern consumer-oriented culture in which we live is, in many ways, the very antithesis of a religion that once advised us not to lay up treasures on earth. Under capitalism, the meek don't inherit the earth but end up tilling it at wretchedly low wages while the landowners ride around in luxury cars. In short, we have lost the wisdom of our religious tradition. It isn't at all difficult to imagine that perhaps, in a few decades, everybody will look upon December 25th as a commercial festival, quite forgetting that it ever had anything to do with a person named Jesus.

This is not at all unusual. Belief systems are seldom discarded by societies, but rather they are frequently reworked into their opposites—so that the very words that originally carried the kernels of wisdom become opaque and incomprehensible, even while they are dutifully repeated once a week. Indeed, there is a sense in which the core of religious teachings brought to us by some saint or prophet is already corrupted the moment it becomes institutionalized into the almost inevitable hierarchy and respectability of a church.

The Christian religion is, of course, only one among several great religious traditions in the world. In each of these, there is a body of teachings that purport to guide human beings in living their lives. The people who brought these teachings were what our society calls mystics. We have chosen to designate them with a word that indicates mystery because from the standpoint of our modern culture these people are, indeed, a mystery to us. What can Madison Avenue or Main Street make of a Buddha who spent years sitting quietly under a tree, not even thinking? We have a pretty good idea where they would put a modern Jesus who tried to drive the moneychangers out of Wall Street. Mystics are, to us, impractical people who don't know how to make a buck and might even end up on food stamps.

Let us look a little more closely at mystics and mysticism. Perhaps we shall find that they dispel mystery. Mystics are people who have their own direct experience of enlightenment. They are not theologians; indeed, they may advise their followers to throw away written tradition: "It is written, but I say unto you . . . " They usually also make short work of religious institutions and their hierarchies. They are those rare souls who have broken free of inherited belief systems. In the realm of life, they are the explorers, the spiritual adventurers, the experimenters. They are closely akin to poets and revolutionaries, vagrants and saints. People hang around them because just being in their presence is joyful. (There are always more false mystics than real ones. And, since both kinds attract a following, much of what is taken for enlightenment is really just a group high.)

In every religious tradition, there are small groups of people who keep the essential wisdom alive. Unfortunately, they are difficult to locate in our society. In the Catholic Church, some of the religious orders perform this function. In Protestantism, the Quakers are notable for preserving the tradition. In Judaism, the Hasidic sects are close to the spirit of things. If you have access to any such groups, you are fortunate. But it will be difficult for you to judge when you are getting the "right stuff." Put it to the test and ask yourself, do the teachings provide you with joy and balance? Are the teachers themselves joyful, balanced, alert, and effective?

Strangely enough, the most powerful and pure modern representatives of religious mysticism among us are the Buddhists. This is not to say that Buddhism cannot also become institutionalized and go sour: It has done so in many of its home countries. Yet for a variety of reasons, we currently have, in the United States, a fairly large number of genuine interpreters and teachers of Buddhism. I would like to tell you how I came to study them.

Fifteen years ago I found myself utterly dissatisfied with the knowledge I had accumulated during many years of studying the most sophisticated modern behavioral sciences. I had ranged widely, over all the main fields of social science, and still I felt I had no real answers for myself or for my students. True, sociology enabled me to point out those features of society that make people unhappy. I could suggest changes in social organization that would ameliorate mental illness and crime. I could probably design a school that would make children creative rather than anxious. But the society in which I lived had no intention of permitting these changes to be made.

In the meantime, I and my students were stuck with the problem of how to live successfully in the world as it is. I looked around me at the college where I taught and saw that students were up to their ears in every kind of knowledge, yet most were feeling very lost. They couldn't handle their parents. They didn't know how to discover what work they were suited for. Every love affair sent them into paroxysms first of joy and then of bitter anxiety. They lacked for friends among their peers and for role models among the adults around them. In short, their lives were out of balance. We were all, students and faculty, caught in harried schedules and making ourselves physically and mentally ill trying to keep up with each other. In classes, students feared the judgment of their peers and professors. Professors, on the other hand, labored in fear of their peers on the faculty and faced their students with various combinations of fear and contempt. True, we were making a living and getting our students certified to make a living, but the enterprise just didn't seem to be going anywhere. The more words we read and wrote and corrected, the further we seemed to be from peace of mind.

I had been acquainted with Protestant Christianity in adolescence but never really understood it. Most of our earnest discussions seemed to be about trying not to swear. Later, I read Western philosophy and decided to become an atheist because I couldn't imagine a God who actually assented to the injustice and brutality of life. When life became unmanageable for me, I frequented psychotherapists who helped me get over some of my more obvious madness. But, still, I felt that perhaps the problem of the meaning of life was just too deep. Nobody had the answer. I studied sociology in the vague hope of getting a larger perspective. It never seemed to come. Instead, sociology always circled back on itself with this theorist commenting on that theorist, who was trying to make sense of yet somebody else's theories: footnotes upon footnotes.

In the course of my studies and political activities, I came across mysticism. The Quakers appealed to me first because of their energetic and highly successful social programs. Yet I also found that I liked their form of worship, which was, essentially, just sitting in silence. Silence made more sense to me than all the words swirling endlessly in my head. At least it had a healing quality and dignity. *People are frequently charlatans with words, but it is hard to be a charlatan with silence.*

I also became interested in the writings of Mahatma Gandhi, who led the Indian independence movement against the British, armed only with his philosophy of nonviolence. Gandhi, too, I found, valued silence. In fact, he shocked my scholarly soul by suggesting that "the great principle of nonpossession" extended to the possession of ideas as well as worldly goods. My God! My whole life consisted of collecting ideas. I was paid for my collection of ideas. I put his view down as anti-intellectual and stored it away in the "useless" cubbyhole of my brain. And yet it haunted me. Gandhi advised his followers to avoid needless talk because that would help them avoid needless thought. Could one really be better off without thought? It ran counter to my whole mode of life.

There was another direction from which my respect for systems of thought was being undermined even as I mastered more of them. Within sociology there is a field that is seldom taught and even considered somewhat obscure—the field called sociology of knowledge. It is the study of how one's social position influences what one thinks. Karl Marx was the modern founder of this field. He pointed out that every social class has its own particular idea system (he called these systems ideologies). He showed that the ideology of a class always functions to buttress its own power position. If you were rich, you would believe in a whole philosophy that justified the survival of the fittest and proclaimed the ultimate good that comes to the community from the competition of rich people. If you were poor, you would believe that the rich are all corrupt and only the working class could govern in a just way if it took power. I was very intrigued by this type of analysis. As I studied the ideologies of various social movements, it did indeed seem to me that the human mind can believe anything that justifies its own ambitions and desires. The subtlety of this mind and its power of justification and invention are phenomenal. People can believe that the world is coming to an end next Thursday or that aliens have taken over the world banking system. People can believe that they should never see themselves in the mirror naked or that only in becoming nudists can they attain mental health.

But, still, I was a scholar. Didn't scholars have some kind of inside track on interpreting reality? About that time, I studied a book called *Ideology and Utopia* (1936) by a very famous German sociologist named Karl Mannheim. In it he took off from Marx and showed how even the time sense of human beings was tied to their social position. If you were oppressed, you saw the past and present as leading to an inevitable future revolution followed by paradise. If you were powerful, the present seemed immutable to you. If you were in a group whose power was declining, you saw everything in terms of how the present had degenerated from an idyllic past. There it was again, the treacherous, self-serving human mind. And then Mannheim pulled a whopper. He said that the only people who could make sense out of the world were the scholars because scholars didn't really have their roots in any of the economic classes. He called them the floating intelligentsia and proclaimed them the only source of wisdom. But wait a minute: Isn't this just the ideology one would predict for scholars? Hadn't he done just exactly what he accused all the other groups of doing by erecting a philosophy that made his own group out to be the best and only one to lead society? Mannheim was swallowing his own tail. At that moment I stood on the brink and looked over the edge to oblivion. We were all going round in circles.

But I was a professor, earning my living by teaching ideas. Although my discovery shook me, I locked it away somewhere where it wouldn't bother me in my day-to-day work.

Fifteen years ago, I took some of these threads out of the closet and looked at them again. I perhaps was impelled by something that had happened to me in my personal life. (I never could keep my personal search separate from my scholarship as I was supposed to. I always had my grocery list on the back of my lecture notes.) For the first time, at the age of 40, I had found a happy love relationship. It profoundly changed my life and made me keenly aware that inner peace, joy, and all those unreachable items were indeed on the menu if one knew how to order them. Other experiences had also given me the confidence to break with my scholarly tradition. Over the years, working in different universities and colleges, I had discovered that my learned colleagues were frequently very cowardly and untruthful. To my enormous surprise, I found that I had a little more courage than most of them. Here, too, was something my students were asking about—not just "How can you be happy?" but also "How do you retain your honor?"

It was at this point that I decided to take a few years off, if need be, to see whether religious mysticism might not hold the keys to what I was searching for. I began reading Eastern philosophy. The first thing I learned was that the Buddhist and Hindu philosophers insist that you really can't understand them on an intellectual level alone, that you have to do a thing called practice: You have to meditate, to seek the realm beyond words and beyond even thought. So I began to practice. It was all very undramatic. Not much happened at first. Yet the deeper I went into this new area, the clearer it became to me that *I had discovered a thought system about human life that was far more sophisticated and far more practical than anything I had learned so far.* As I studied the Eastern masters, *I began to remember and understand portions of the Christian Bible for the first time.* They began to make sense, and it became evident that there was much in common between these seemingly disparate religious traditions.

I was particularly struck by one characteristic of the traditions I was now exploring, that the teachings insisted that "physician, heal thyself" had to be the real test. Those who called themselves masters of this mystical art were indeed people with very special personalities. True masters are very rare, but I was able to hear and take classes with a few who were obviously real. It made me feel better just to be in their presence. They seemed to radiate something we might call love, yet they were also fierce and direct, seeing into the lives of their students with a startling clarity. What they seemed to be saying was, "Who you are is important, not what you know." Knowledge might be a trap. Krishnamurti (1969), one of these true masters, has even given us a book called *Freedom from the Known*.

In sociology, we studied a process called socialization, the process by which the human child learns the rules and definitions of his or her culture. We looked on this process as a benign one, without which the human being would remain an animal, unable to live in society. But the Eastern philosophers looked at this socialization process through different eyes. In *Zen Mind, Beginner's Mind*, Suzuki (1970) says, "If your mind is empty, it is always ready for anything; it is open to everything. In the beginner's mind there are many possibilities; in the expert's mind there are few" (p. 21). To become enlightened one had to unlearn one's culture and reconnect with the beginner's mind. *Eastern philosophy reminded us that, as little children, we enjoyed a much more vivid experience of the world.* Christianity, too, had advised us to become like little children again. The healing power of inner silence was a key to this unlearning—a break in the inward chatter that keeps our definitions alive. It did not mean that we would forget which fork to eat with at a formal dinner. *You could know the rules and conform to them outwardly when you chose to do so, but it did speak of being inwardly free from the rules.*

They told us that we never see the world as it really is. A gray veil of definition and admonition has been drawn between us and reality. We do not see a dance; we see sin. We do not see the human being; we see a Jew or a Black or a Republican. We react, not directly but through categories. When we make love, we do not just make love; we worry about whether it will improve or hinder our social status. We choose a life's work from similar considerations, never noticing until it is too late that we do not actually like the day-to-day routine it involves. Our marriages go sour because we never see our partner directly but only through a distorting prism of wishful thinking. We are caught inside our minds in repetitive circles that go round and round but never offer a way out. We are, in short, caught in illusion, and this illusion is learned from our culture. It can become so great that people commit suicide because they have lost their social position or march obediently into fire because they are loyal to an idea—the idea of their nation.

Even the very words we use to understand reality can obscure that reality. If you want to investigate the power of words over your thinking try, for a month, to substitute the word *massacre* for the word *war* whenever you come across it in spoken or written communication. Now we have "World Massacre I" and "World Massacre II" and "The Civil Massacre"; we buy our children massacre toys. Changing this one word can alter your whole understanding of the phenomenon we call war.

While society trains us in its particular set of ideas, it also teaches us that without these ideas we would be monsters of immorality. Yet if one thinks over the list of atrocities committed in our century, *they all seem to stem directly from belief-systems, not from any absence of such systems.*

If liberation lies in the direction of unlearning one's culture, then how can we get anywhere with this in college? College is, after all, a continuation of our indoctrination. If we don't watch it, it will not only fill our heads with a surfeit of ideas, but it will also teach us that we are better than other people who didn't go to college, part of a privileged elite. It is so tempting to become arrogant about your knowledge. *It is so simple to become an expert.* How can we pick our way among these boulders and find something liberating in this wilderness?

The very first admonition I would lay on you is that you never separate yourself, who you are and how you experience life, from your studies. The key question to ask of any subject matter is, "What can it teach me about myself?" A related question is, "How does this apply to the way life is structured on this campus?"

CHAPTER 8

Pursuing Wisdom in the Academy

Having said that the academy offers a great deal of knowledge, but little wisdom, I will nevertheless point out to you ways in which you can use your undergraduate years to enhance that very experiential form of knowledge we call wisdom. In college, you have two great advantages. First, most of you aren't working the full time 40- to 60-hour week, which means that you have more time at your disposal than you may ever have again. The problem here is simply *to make your search for wisdom count as part of your course load.* I suggest ways in which you can do this. Second, you have at your disposal more cultural resources than you may ever have again. In this chapter, I talk about how you can use these to the maximum.

Using the College Ambience

Just as the best way to learn about your country is to travel to a different one, so the best way to learn about yourself is to make contact frequently with selves different from your own. This is why I have suggested that you seek out the nonconformist professors. Even more important is to seek contact with fellow students who differ from you in some important regard. *Students always learn more from each other than from their professors.* If you come from a White, middle-class home, hang around a bit with minority students, foreign students, students with disabilities, gay students, radical students, or any other group that is present on your campus. If these groups are organized, join one that holds a point of view different from your own. You can tell them you are just exploring. Groups are generally glad to attract new members on any terms.

The transition from high school into college forcefully introduces you to a much larger sphere of personalities, cultures, and sexualities. To hold strictly to your preconceived notions of personality types ("jocks," "nerds," "druggies") from high school is to do yourself an injustice by clouding your view and disallowing any social learning. While you will still find people who fit these isolated types if you focus narrowly enough, the truth is that most college students are rounded out by the experience of going through college with so many varied people. Allow yourself some freedom from judgment and view people as they are, not as you expect them to be. You may not even be sure where you fit in, so allow yourself some freedom in your own roles as well.

I am suggesting that you throw your net for friendship and acquaintance wider than just the cozy few with whom you feel most comfortable. Of course, you want these folks around, too, but they will only reinforce your own view of the world. You see, *you cannot even know that you have a peculiar view of the world until you come in contact with differing views.* (This is also, by the way, the classical liberal arts justification for requiring you to take a foreign language—a route for you to discover that you have, all along, been speaking your own peculiar language.) Without this, you will just assume that your version is the only possible one, or you may know that yours is only one point of view in a very general sense but without the specific little insights that create usable knowledge. Hence, your map of reality will necessarily remain narrow, and you will be blocked from many moves that you could make. Personal contact here is worth dozens of books or courses for stretching your mind and soul.

To make the most of your human contacts, *make it your practice to become a listener.* Ours is a society in which everyone is desperately struggling for attention. This was nicely addressed in an analysis of conversation behavior titled *The Pursuit of Attention* (Derber, 1983). In it, the author describes all the ploys and gambits people habitually use to bring the subject of the conversation back to themselves and to grab and hold the floor as long as possible. I believe the constant media romancing of "celebrities" is largely responsible for this sad state. But in such an environment, the occasional listener can benefit in many different ways.

First, listening is a wonderful spiritual discipline.[1] Listening forces you to lay the demanding "me me me" aside for a while. Thus, you deflate that overblown attention-craving ego that gives you so much grief. At the same time, you attract people to yourself because everybody loves a sympathetic audience.

Most important, listening will enable you to learn a great deal. *The talkers only repeat their tired old ideas over and over again to any audience. But the listener is constantly picking up new perspectives.* Perhaps you will discover that other people's grief, fears, and embarrassments are very similar to your own. Perhaps you will be surprised to discover that some people operate very differently from yourself. In this arena, it is not the generalizations that matter but the vivid detail. It is the detail that catches you unaware and makes you say, "Aha! Maybe I don't need to be sexually jealous of my girlfriend—here is someone who isn't that way at all" or "Aha! Here is someone who is just as anxious about talking in class as I am, but she has found a way to nerve herself up to it."

So that you can make the most of listening, let me pass on a few techniques learned in doing sociological fieldwork. First, shift your own preconceptions and categories into neutral. You can always pick them up again when the experience is over, but, for the moment, listen to the categories your acquaintance is using—try to "feel" along with this person when he or she is angry, hurt, and so forth. In short, listen so attentively that you can, for the moment, stand in the other person's shoes and know how the world looks and feels to this person. To check on the accuracy of your understanding, play back what you think you heard: "You mean that you have never felt comfortable on this campus because it is a White outfit?"

In doing research, I also found that, to keep people talking, I did need to offer an occasional experience or view of my own. This is because, as people reveal themselves to you, they become uncomfortable if they don't also know something about you. Therefore, you must occasionally respond with an "I had that experience too once," or "I know just how you feel. I felt that way myself." Only a little reassurance will keep the conversation going. Let every contact become an opportunity to voyage beyond the narrow self.

To forget the self, it is sometimes necessary to first explore the troublesome aspects of ourselves. We need to know ourselves, our weaknesses, and our confusions. Most colleges and universities offer psychiatric services to students. Take advantage of this. In later years, the same help will cost you a great deal. If you are troubled or perplexed about yourself, see a therapist. Most clinics permit you to change therapists if the first one doesn't suit you. They usually have a variety of people available. Getting a good, objective outsider's perspective on your problems can only help. Never feel that by going to the clinic you are admitting that you are flaky or weird. A very high percentage of students use these services, and it is by no means the sickest who seek the service out. Not only does it take a little confidence and energy to make an appointment, but it also takes a little sense of humor about yourself. We are all a little crazy—it is just a matter of degree. Someone once said, "Normal is what people are until you get to know them."

If you don't feel you need individual help, consider joining a therapy group run by the clinic or perhaps a consciousness-raising group run by the women's center or some similar campus group or agency. Therapy groups (or encounter groups—they go by many different names) are absolutely wonderful because they enable you to observe other people with their masks off. Even though we know that we ourselves wear masks, we somehow believe the masks of others. Thus, we often think we are the only ones afraid or nervous—even though everyone in the room feels that way. We misperceive the world because we experience our own insides, but we only see other people's outsides. A group enables you to look behind the scenes, and this experience can greatly extend your capacity for sympathy with your fellow human beings. Ultimately, this will turn into sympathy for yourself—something almost everybody could use more of. Of course, you can also use the group as a sounding board for your own feelings, but be assured you can almost always avoid doing so if you don't want to. In most groups, there is a lot of competition for the floor. You can usually lie low as long as it suits you.

So go over to your counseling center and see which groups or workshops are offered. Jump into a few. Psychodrama is a particularly good method. Again, as with professors, try to find out the reputation of the various group and workshop leaders. The usefulness of groups depends heavily on having a good leader, though I have been in some very good groups that operated completely without professional leadership.

Wisdom in the Curriculum

Now, let us take a look at ways in which you can seek wisdom within the curriculum requirements of your school, remembering that wisdom consists both of self-knowledge and of a lively "feel" for the world in which this self lives and moves. Cultural anthropology is almost always conducive to developing wisdom about how your culture molds your personality. As you study and compare societies very different from your own, you will have many "Aha!" experiences: "Well, so every culture isn't as afraid of touching as ours"; "By comparison with this group, how little human solidarity we have to live with"; and so on. Cultural anthropology is usually a popular course and for good reason. Avoid it only if it has a bad reputation among students on your campus.

Psychology courses, particularly clinical psychology and social psychology, can also make you wiser to your own functioning. These courses may come under a variety of headings, like "Social Psychology," "Theories of Personality," "Abnormal Psychology," "Psychology of Small Groups," and "Self and Society." Sociology can prove a fruitful field. Sociology also offers courses in social psychology and small group behavior. (Look out! These sometimes can be highly quantitative, in which case they will not serve our purposes.) Sociology also offers classes on the structure of society: for example, "Class Stratification," "Race Relations," "Complex Organizations," "The Media," and so on. At their best, such studies can offer you a map of the society in which you must travel all your life. It helps to know where the brick walls are, so you won't run into them. They will also, it is hoped, extend your sympathy for your fellow human beings.

If you are fortunate enough to be on a campus with minority centers offering courses on Black, Hispanic, and Asian American people, women, and other minority groups, take a few of these and expose yourself to classes in which there will be a very different student group and different atmosphere from the rest of the campus. If there is no special center for such courses, they may be offered in the regular curriculum. These courses are often best when offered by professors who are themselves members of a minority group (though this aspect is, of course, no guarantee as to the quality of the course).

If you wish to explore your ethnic heritage, but find that there aren't any courses on Italian Americans or Jewish Americans or your own ethnic background, you might consider taking a course in the history, literature, or culture of the country from which your forebears came. Area studies are worth checking for this. Of course, you could zero in on the American phase of your background by designing an independent study on your group's sojourn here.

The fields of political science and economics are also fertile domains to explore though sometimes they can be more conservative than the fields of sociology and psychology. They are closer to the realms of power because they train many students to go into government or corporate service and sometimes their faculties tend to have closer ties in these quarters. Yet you may find economics departments giving a course on the economics of Marxism, giving you a glimpse of a usually "forbidden" heresy. In political science—as also in sociology, history, and economics—look for "comparative" courses, such as "Comparative Revolutionary Movements," "Comparative Analysis of Industrial Democracies," or "Comparative Socialist Societies." A comparative course is good for getting the broader picture.

Many great fiction writers were wise people, so there is real wisdom to be garnered in the area of literature. The difficulty lies in the fact that many literature professors are more interested in form than in content, that is, in the writer's skill with words rather than in his or her wisdom. My friends in literature tell me that looking at the form of a novel is looking at it as art, as a thing of beauty. They say that beauty and truth are one. Yet I must argue back that artistic talent does not necessarily go with the kind of wisdom needed to live one's life. Artistic ability occurs in people of the most diverse personality styles. There are happy painters and suicidal painters, joyful writers and psychotic writers. Certainly, *their artistry must have been the best part of some of these sad lives, but it was not enough to heal.*

To me, the most troublesome aspect of Western fiction is that by constantly describing to us the character's emotions and verbal thoughts, the authors imply that the noisy, storm-torn mind is the inevitable state of human consciousness. If you can find a literature professor who is willing to argue some of these issues with you, you might just have a lot of fun.

All of the applied arts—music, dance, drama, creative writing, painting, sculpture, glass blowing, weaving, and so on—can be fun and a welcome break from your other courses. Sports can also function this way. Try to work such a course into every semester if you can. Courses in literature or in the history of art or in music theory are likely to involve more of the usual reading and writing but may be worth taking if they are well taught. Experience with a sport or art can greatly enlarge your enjoyment of professional performances, even if you are not particularly talented yourself. If you are, they can provide you with a satisfying hobby.

Wherever you can find a natural science course (or professor) that preserves and honors science's connection to human life and inquiry, it will prove most interesting. The problem here is that most science departments design their introductory courses to serve only their own future majors rather than offering courses broad enough to be of interest to nonmajors. You are fortunate, for example, if your campus offers courses in the history of science or technology for nonmajors.

It always puzzles me that in a society that revolves so heavily around science we seem to garner so little wisdom from our scientific knowledge. To see ourselves in the perspective of evolutionary time, or geological time or, even, the immense time of the astronomers should surely help us to assess our importance in the scheme of things. Yet scientists seldom draw such connections between their specialties and the culture in which we live. If you can find such a science professor, he or she would be well worth your while.

Languages, if you enjoy them, are interesting because *they are windows into another culture.* When you travel, you will also find that it is a far more exciting experience when you know even a little of the language.

Philosophy and religion departments may offer courses such as "Individual Morality and Social Justice" or "Man, Nature, and Society in Western Literature," for example, which explore problems we confront in our own lives. A course in Marxism would be good. Courses in existentialism may also be of interest.

Existentialism has a lot in common with Eastern thought. I used to tell my students that Buddhism is just existentialism without the "oy veh!"

Courses in Eastern thought or in mysticism may be offered by philosophy or religion departments. These courses may be so academic as to be nearly useless for your purposes. Check the readings. If they stress a history-of-ideas approach with lots of dates, names, and the history of various schools of thought, you should avoid them. The useful course will offer readings that speak to you directly about your life. But we must be cautious here because Eastern thought is difficult to understand at first, even when it is the real thing. This is because such books invite you to observe the workings of your own mind, and this is difficult for the mind to grasp. The English language, with its Western cultural connotations, is also a difficult language in which to express the insights of Eastern thought. A measure of difficulty must therefore be expected.

Most large campuses will also have some organizations that teach Buddhism, yoga, or meditation. These would be worth exploring. One college professor who recently reviewed this book made the following very valuable observation:

> Meditation is understood by most of my students as a weird, freaky, bizarre activity for cultists. Something reserved for strange out-group types—definitely not for them. Therefore, it would be helpful to give an example or two of some important person who regularly uses some form of meditation for strictly practical purposes, such as better achievement in sports, greater stamina in arduous campaigns. For example the former president of Costa Rica told me that he amazed his cocampaigners with his stamina, which was sustained by recurrent 10- to 15-minute moments of meditation—a technique he learned in India on a trip with his friend Vincent Hardin (who was one of Dr. Martin Luther King's close advisors). It's like the "siesta" that students think is for the lazy when in fact a half hour siesta is what allows many of the world's inhabitants to get through 17-hour workdays. I dwell on this topic because simple, practical forms of meditation are one of the most concrete and valuable things students can take away with them and use to their advantage throughout the rest of their lives.

To line up your courses, curl up with your institution's catalog one evening and really explore the offerings. When looking for courses to take, remember my advice in a previous chapter and choose by the professor's reputation rather than by the subject. Go to a lecture by the professor you are considering the semester before you would sign up for the course. This will give you a little feel for the professor's teaching. If you can, strike up a conversation with a student in the class and see what he or she says about the professor's teaching methods.

Ask the professor to give you a booklist and spend a few hours in the bookstore or the library looking at the material to see if it interests you.

Watch also for interdisciplinary courses or courses that are different, new, or experimental. Professors and students alike are usually up for such courses just because they are out of the ordinary. If your school offers semesters abroad or exchanges with other American schools, take advantage of these if at all possible. Travel to new environments is invariably enlightening.

Seeking Direct Experience of the World

Now, let us turn our attention to ways in which you can garner wisdom outside of the ready-made courses we have been discussing. Because direct experience and human contacts are so crucial to the development of wisdom, choose fieldwork over library research whenever that option is offered in any course. Even if the option is not specifically offered, professors may give you special permission to do fieldwork in place of library research if you go to them with a convincing project. Fieldwork projects will also ease the heavy reading requirements you always face in college.

Let us say, for example, that you are taking "America Since 1900." A fieldwork project here might be to interview older people about the changes they have lived through. Your town's senior center or a minister could probably provide you with names of respondents. This is oral history, a perfectly legitimate aspect of the historian's craft. Or for a trip to the library that is a little more fun than the usual, take an event that interests you—perhaps the freedom rides of 1961 or the Cuban missile crisis—and look up the contemporary coverage of the event in old newspapers and magazines. You must take a very specific situation because there is so much coverage available. Old newspapers are a bit more difficult to explore because they are usually on microfilm, but old magazines are in the original and can give you a real feeling for the look and texture of another historical period.

Let us say you are taking a course in social stratification. Here you have many fieldwork possibilities. You could take two churches or two elementary schools in different income neighborhoods and visit each. In the case of churches, visit services and smaller meetings and interview the minister. In the case of schools, ask to watch several classes and observe playground behavior. A session of sitting in the teachers' coffee room can also be very enlightening. In each case, contact the principal or minister ahead of time, preferably with a letter from your professor on school stationery vouching for your earnest purpose. It is a good move to offer the institution a copy of your final paper in the hope that your findings may be of some use.

If you are interested in city planning, do a survey of recreational facilities and parks available in different income areas. Students of mine have investigated hospital emergency rooms, massage parlors, clothing stores, restaurants, and many other neighborhood features in this way.

With a little imagination, you can think up unusual projects for many classes. When you approach the professor, you should be able to present a good reason for wishing to engage in your project: "I would like to work with older people when I become a social worker" or "I am planning to be an elementary school teacher, so I would like to observe class differences in schools."

Perhaps you can mention that you have become interested in this particular phenomenon through personal experience or through some previous course work. If you are going to do interviews, have a first draft of a questionnaire ready to show the professor. If you are going to observe, have a well-considered list of things you plan to watch for and make notes of. Ask your professor to suggest a relevant existing study or two.

Your very best opportunity to design your own education lies in independent study courses. Most campuses offer these, but relatively few students take advantage of them. All it takes is a professor who will sponsor you. Let us say, for example, that you are planning to be a teacher and have gotten yourself a job helping part-time in a school; it may be a volunteer job or it may pay a little. Let us also suppose that you are working in a predominantly minority school. Find yourself a professor of sociology—whoever teaches sociology of education would be a good bet—and tell him or her about your job. Suggest that you enlarge your understanding of the things you will be encountering in your job by interviewing teachers, principals, and board of education members about the problems of the district. (You may be mainly interested in minority children, but it is wiser not to announce this specifically to school authorities, as they may be particularly touchy in this area. Of course, let the professor in on your true interest.)

Gather together a few books pertinent to the subject and ask the professor to suggest others to you. When approaching a professor about fieldwork independent study, it is wise to include some reading in your plan. Since professors generally believe it is their duty to get the maximum of reading and writing out of the student, you don't want to give the impression that you are trying to get out of this requirement. You will, of course, usually have to write a paper about your findings.

You may have found yourself a paying or volunteer job with your local senior center. You will learn a great deal in this setting, but you can enhance your learning and garner academic credits by arranging an independent study in which you can write up your experiences, together with doing some reading in the field of gerontology. A sociologist who gives classes on aging, the life cycle, or urban problems would be a good bet for this project.

These two projects can provide excellent support on your applications for graduate school or for jobs in teaching or working with older people, especially if your independent study director gives you a good letter of reference. Both the experience in the field and your initiative in designing such an independent study will make your application stand out.

A student of mine who had a very ordinary summer job at Big Sur did an excellent independent study analyzing the social groups making up that resort area and their interactions with and opinions about the tourists with whom they dealt. Another student, who was wrestling with his homosexual feelings and trying to explore the gay world at a local gay bar did a brilliant analysis of the various types of gayness, which gays themselves recognize and distinguish. Another student turned a trip to Scandinavia into an independent study by visiting elementary schools in Sweden and the United States and doing a comparison of the two school systems. The project enriched her experience in Scandinavia and looked very good on her application to a graduate school of education. Another student who was planning to go into architecture did a study of the way campus space was used by formal and informal groups. He focused on where people hung out, where they studied, made love, or even did drugs. His report took the form of a large map with several overlays depicting various types of use.

Perhaps you are wondering whether you would become a conscientious objector and refuse to be drafted. Although you have been taught the dates and names of all our wars over and over again during your schooling, none of it has given you the slightest idea of what actual combat is like. All media falsify this subject, and combat veterans usually keep silent because the experience is so utterly alien to everyday life that they fear people wouldn't understand. Yet you may find that, if you begin to talk with relatives and friends who have been in combat, they will begin to tell you the truth. Such an interview study would also fit into classes in history and sociology.

There are many ways to explore different future occupations that interest you. A very good one is to do an interview study of people who have been successful in a particular occupation: successful lawyers, teachers, legal secretaries, and so forth. You can get a good feel for what the job is like, what people love or hate about it. There will usually also be some published research available on such occupations. Some institutions may permit you to become an intern or just to sit by as an observer of the work environment. This type of experience can develop easily into an independent study and can greatly help you in deciding on a future occupation.

Let us say that you have been elected to chair your local feminist group, and you would like to get some credits for the time you will put in. Here you might plan an independent study in which you will prepare, for your written report, a handbook for future chairwomen of the group, recording everything that will be of use to them. Is your group having trouble getting enough members? Do an interview study of a sample of women students to see whether they are aware of your group, why they do not join, and what would draw them in.

Perhaps you would like to make an independent study project out of an attempt to bring about actual social change in a nearby community. One of the most dramatic ways I know of for changing the whole atmosphere of a retirement home, reform school, prison, or children's group in an inner city neighborhood is to get people gardening: vegetables mainly, but also some flowers. There is a nationwide organization, the National Gardening Association (write to National Gardening Association, 180 Flynn Avenue, Burlington, VT 95401), that sponsors such projects with support money and gardening supplies. In many areas, they also teach gardening and how to develop community gardens. Nothing is more therapeutic than gardening. Of course, you could start a community garden on your campus, too. If your independent study is in sociology, part of your project would consist of assessing the changes in individual behavior and group morale brought about by the garden.

On some campuses, professors are only willing to take a small number of independent study students each semester. Therefore, you must set your course up during the preceding semester. This will also give you time to pursue several teachers until you find one who is willing to take you. If, after making a timely and well-prepared effort, you cannot get anyone to take you on, you have a complaint coming. If your school doesn't offer independent study, you also have good cause to complain. Sometimes such a complaint may get you some action.

Independent studies are excellent ways of getting at least one or two professors to know you well enough to write an informed recommendation when you need it. Once you have set up such a study, you should put forth your very best effort. *Remember that the trick lies not in getting out of as much work as possible but in designing work that really interests you and then doing it well.* Students sometimes fall down on independent studies because their other courses seem more immediately pressing. It is best, therefore, to schedule a number of meetings with your professor and to set up a schedule of the work you will complete for each meeting.

The key to a good field research paper is keeping notes regularly, day by day. After each interview session, sit right down and type out your notes. After each visit to the school or church, write out your impressions. You will lose 50% of the important details if you wait 2 days and 80% if you wait until the end of the semester. Take notes whenever the situation allows you to do so without disrupting what is going on or destroying the rapport with the people you study. These notes will necessarily be brief. This is why you have to fill them out right after the contact is over. It is best to type them onto half sheets or cards with one respondent and one subject per card. These may later be easily sorted.[2]

One final word about fieldwork: Unfortunately, our government's economic policies have created abject poverty in most of our inner cities. These areas have become the scene of much violent crime. You must, therefore, enter these areas with caution. I hope you will enter them because our ignorance of this disaster is catastrophic for our society, but you must also be realistic. Before you undertake a project in such areas, talk to people on the faculty who know them. You might also approach the area through a church or social agency. They will know the ropes well enough to clue you in. Never go alone at night. If at all possible, it is better to work in such areas in twos.

Finally, if your campus permits you to design your own major, this is an excellent opportunity for you to think through exactly what you would like to get out of your college education. It also allows you to combine two or more fields that interest you, sometimes enabling you to omit required courses you wish to avoid in any one field.

A good reason for designing your own major is that major requirements and the curriculum generally have not really been designed with undergraduates in mind. Rather, they directly reflect what your professors had to study in their graduate PhD programs. They are therefore directly applicable only to students who plan to get PhDs—a tiny minority.[3] For example, if you are planning to be a social worker, it makes little sense for you to take all the requirements for the major in sociology or in psychology. The "History of Sociological Theory" will not help you much, neither will courses in learning theory in the psychology department. What you need is a combination of courses chosen from both fields, with courses at any available minority studies centers thrown in.

Many campuses offer joint majors, which allow the student to combine and revise the requirements of two related disciplines. If your college doesn't let you design your own major, a joint major may offer some of the same advantages.

In this section, I tried to start you thinking of ways in which you can make your education more directly experiential and thus more conducive to wisdom. In doing so, you will be counteracting what I call the maximum learning blockage of higher education. By this I mean the recent historical arrangement by which 18-year-olds with little knowledge of the world are locked away for 4 years with others similarly inexperienced and usually from the same background: the White suburban middle class. Where possible, all these folks are put together in dormitories. Then, they are assigned so much reading and writing that they can rarely leave the campus. Though this arrangement has been shifting in the last decade, it still remains the primary structure of college. If one were to design a method for making the future professionals and business leaders ignorant of the world, one could hardly come up with a better trick. It is unfortunate enough to do this with science or art students, but to do so with students of social science appears to be quite lunatic. Add to this the fact that field and laboratory experience is always offered in science but only rarely offered in social sciences. No geology department would dream of teaching only out of books. Society really wants good geologists; it doesn't want good sociologists.

Where one sees a lunatic pattern applied almost universally, one must perforce ask the question, "Is this done intentionally?" Such a suspicion gains force when one considers the hostility with which the academic establishment met the demands for the admission of more minority students and students from low-income groups during the struggles of the 1960s. It was felt that such students would harm "academic standards" and could easily become " disruptive." Education, it seems, should be a matter for the elite, and one certainly does build in-group loyalties with that elite by these methods.

Indeed, many within the academy would say that any de-emphasis on reading and writing is anti-intellectual. On this score, I would like to say that attaining the wisdom to lead one's life is no more an anti-intellectual undertaking than learning to play the flute. You cannot learn to play by reading and writing about it, though you may wish to study some written texts on the instrument. To play the flute you must educate the ear, the hands, and the mouth, in addition to developing certain aspects of the intellect. Attaining wisdom is very similar. It requires the education of the body, the senses, and what we sometimes call the heart. An overemphasis on reading and writing—as in the case of the flute—can get in the way.

Thus far, we have talked mainly about observing the world. You will, of course, also gather self-knowledge in these encounters. In the next chapter, I would like to introduce you to some of the ways in which you can zero in more directly on the problem of the self by sharing with you some of the ways in which I tried to combine Buddhist philosophy with behavioral science to help students explore their inner landscape.

Traveling Abroad

Traveling abroad, whether it is for leisure, business, or for academic purposes, can truly be an enlightening experience. It will not only allow you to develop new perspectives on foreign cultures and lifestyles, but it can also influence your existing domestic views.

You must not, however, merely *travel* abroad but instead allow for immersion in the different culture(s). This can be achieved by living in the chosen society for a substantial amount of time. *Living abroad* (if your budget permits), rather than being a tourist, is the most effective method for this life-enriching, unforgettable experience.

Being a tourist means that you are giving yourself a label that says to others that you are foreign or different. The purpose of living abroad is to allow yourself the opportunity to incorporate yourself as much as possible with the locals, to truly give yourself a sense of the cultural and societal similarities and differences, and to ultimately give you a better understanding of yourself.

Living abroad will definitely enhance your life. However, if you can only be a tourist, you can still enrich yourself historically and socially by visiting the sites and interacting with people as much as possible—it is imperative that you have conversations with "the natives" and always leave your familiar home group as much as possible. It is truly amazing to be able to see firsthand the places you once read and learned about in your history books. The interaction will allow you to delve into the culture more deeply, and it helps to alleviate or destroy possible cultural barriers.

Most colleges have programs with various foreign colleges throughout the world. If a particular country or program is not available through your particular campus, other local colleges may offer them, and arrangements can usually be made through your academic counselors to have classes and credits transferred. These programs also vary in function, ranging from academic classes to internships and work opportunities. Independent studies in one's related field can also be organized. Almost any kind of program is available, including a semester at sea. In addition to the vast choices in countries and types of programs available, the choice of the length of the program also varies. Depending on your preference, a summer, quarter, semester, or even a year or more can be spent on your adventure abroad.

For most college students, going abroad is very appealing, but only a small number take full advantage of such an opportunity. One of the major setbacks and concerns for people is money. What many people do not know is that financial aid and scholarships are available. One's college years are the prime time for such an opportunity, and some people have even taken loans to help finance the trip. I will not tell you that it is not expensive, but I will tell you that it is *well* worth it.

Yet another concern of people who are interested in going abroad, especially to a foreign country, is that they may feel awkward and uncomfortable in an environment where the people, languages, food, customs, and places are all different. We all have felt awkward entering a new school, starting a new job, or moving into a new neighborhood, but as time passed, we became accustomed to our surroundings and eventually found our own comfort zone. Traveling abroad is similar. One of the most important and necessary things for one to truly benefit from living abroad is to consistently practice an open mind and cultivate an attitude of inquiry. Naturally things will be different. That is one of the main reasons for going!

One of the greatest advantages of going abroad is freedom. Studying abroad will of course not completely free you academically, but it will allow you to be free in other unexpected and unforeseeable ways. It frees you from parents, siblings, roommates, bosses, and other constraints or obligations, even if it is temporary. If you have never lived away from home, it will teach you in a very accelerated way to become independent and a more self-sufficient person. If it is not your first time away from home, it will undoubtedly give you time to grow as a person and gain a better understanding of yourself.

It allows you free time to reflect, where you can both directly experience and analyze views of the world and where you and others fit in it. It opens your eyes to what you have accomplished and what you have yet to accomplish. It opens avenues for future opportunities—not to mention it looks great on resumes!

Since I am from the UC (University of California) system, let me discuss how that is set up: There are a number of different programs that are available and that work quite conveniently with the regular course curriculum. This type of program is called EAP or Education Abroad Program. The way in which this arrangement functions is that the UC system works through and with different schools intra- and internationally to allow students the opportunity to enhance their college careers. It is convenient in the sense that the student generally has a wide selection of classes from which to choose, and those classes transfer directly as credit toward their intended degree.

For the most part, these programs give the student the opportunity to interact with other students from the host country and to experience the culture firsthand. Also, because these programs encompass the entire UC system, it allows the students a bit of security, in cases where they might start feeling homesick. In my own experience, I got the chance to meet other students from my own school and even my own hometown.

It really felt great being able to come back to school knowing and seeing a few extra familiar faces. I sometimes would stop and think how, without going on the program, these people would be just some more of the faces in the crowd whom I would not know and just walk by. There are a few other people who live a bit farther away and whom I cannot see on a regular basis, yet still I stay in touch and network with them either on the phone or through e-mail.

The other types of programs that include working, volunteering or interning are generally considered nonacademic and fall (under the UC system) as IOP or International Opportunities Program. The countries that have EAP opportunities generally also have programs through which IOP opportunities can also be arranged. One negative about this type of nonacademic program is that financial aid is not applicable in the same way as it is for EAP programs. Because IOP is nonacademic, grants and other regular sources available as financial aid for the school year are not applicable as they are for EAP programs. There are, however, special scholarships and loans specifically for the participants of these programs.

One of the things going abroad opened my eyes to is that there is such an infinite wealth of knowledge in the world. I remembered a statement that I once read, "The more I know, the more I realize how much I do not know." So for me, the more I learn, the more I realize how much I want to learn. The program I went on was in Cambridge, England. It was an EAP summer program at Pembroke College. I took two classes, "The World Economy Today," which fell under my economics major, and "The Glories of Venetian Art and Painting." The contents of both classes interested me, but I was fascinated by the professors' stories and knowledge.

Part of the reason for my fascination was the more intimate size of the class, whereby the professors knew everyone's name. (This was something I was not accustomed to at the University of California, Irvine, where my classes were mainly in large lecture halls.) Also, the professors were multifaceted, very personable, and they ate lunch with the students almost every day, addressing any concerns that became evident during the duration of the program. Some of the other factors in my personal experience that made it memorable was seeing and being around buildings with amazing architecture that housed numerous scholars.

I cannot stress enough the value of such an opportunity. The fear of missing family, friends, a boyfriend/girlfriend, or other activities while you will be gone should not hinder you. Upon returning, you will usually find that really not much has changed since you left, of course except yourself. Also, modern technology allows for easier forms of communication, and absence does make the heart grow fonder.

I hope that I have stirred up thoughts of going abroad. I encourage you to explore further the vast number of opportunities available. Of course, use the Web, but the best resource for this would be at your school department or office that handles international academic affairs. There will be interesting pictures of places and information about programs abroad as well as scholarship and financial aid information. There are many catalogs about the programs, schools, and the host countries. There are even lists of participant students who can be contacted as references (and probably recommendors) of their respective programs. You will also generally find enthusiastic people working there who have probably gone abroad themselves and will be happy to address any questions or concerns that you may have. You can also pick up a few interesting and informative brochures to read and to show your parents. Once you have run out of excuses, you can start making arrangements for your trip. It requires some paperwork, and, whenever it is that you are reading this, deadlines are fast approaching!

Lynette Albovias

Notes

1. I must explain how I use the term *spiritual*. Christian doctrine separates the human being into flesh and spirit, and Western psychology and medicine adopted this division, calling it body and mind. This distinction is purely imaginary and conceptual. In the real world, we have only the human being, in whom what we call body and mind are inextricably intertwined. There is, in fact, no separation. I use the term *spiritual* to mean the whole person: body and mind and perhaps something that goes beyond the concepts of psychology and posits that there is, in the human being, a capacity to rise beyond the external circumstances—to live triumphantly, rather than merely being "well-adjusted."

2. For more advice on fieldwork and more ideas for projects, see my book *Involvement in Society Today* (1972).

3. Often what gets included in an academic discipline is the result of historical accident. The social science and humanities fields are not governed by the strict internal necessities that govern more natural science fields.

CHAPTER 9

Adventures in Desocialization

When I was teaching, I tried to find a way of using sociology to make students aware of the ways in which society has trained them to look at the world and at themselves. The object was to free people from the influence of society, that is, to begin to undo the indoctrination each of us has undergone growing up in this particular society. I believed that as we became conscious of the many specific ways in which our inner experience of reality had been conditioned, we might throw off this conditioning and create greater inner freedom for ourselves. In line with this, I developed a course called "Adventures in Desocialization."

Socialization is the name sociologists give to the process by which children are inculcated with the beliefs of their culture. Sociologists study this process in great detail, demonstrating how we are, completely, creatures of our culture. However, they never seem to step beyond this stage and actually try to free us from social conditioning, nor do they point out that this freedom is even possible.[1] Yet their studies of resocialization during adulthood—when someone goes into prison or into the army, for example—demonstrate that we are capable of changing enormously if our environment changes. We know that it is possible to resocialize people, but is it possible to desocialize without taking on any new set of beliefs and pressures? The Buddhists say yes, that this, in fact, is the path to enlightenment.

In this section, I offer you a series of exercises that were successful in helping students to begin to free themselves from conditioning. Of course, the exercises are only a first step, but they can introduce you to new ways of observing the world and yourself. They are the initial wedge entering between you and your internalized beliefs and habits. I suggest that you do each exercise before reading about the way my students responded so that you will have your own experience first, before you see what you have in common with, or how you differ from, others.

The Self: Reality or Illusion?

I have said that *wisdom consists of self-knowledge*. We have to look at this in greater detail. None of us is very fond of people who constantly think about themselves, analyze themselves, and talk about themselves. All of us like somebody whose "self" doesn't intrude very much, in the sense that such a person has plenty of attention and energy available for people and things outside. These people probably engage in relatively little self-criticism and self-laceration. We sense that, somehow or other, their self is not a problem. So perhaps what we wish to eliminate is something we might call the problematic self, the one that gives us problems.

It may help us to look at the way *self* has been conceptualized in more than one culture. We can compare our view of self with that of a radically different cultural system, that of Zen Buddhism. The New Testament strongly advised people not to take the self seriously. Are you worried about how you are dressed? The New Testament tells us to be like the lilies, which never worry about how they look but are nevertheless beautiful. It warns us not to inflate the self through the possession of wealth, power, or fame. It even advises us to "lose ourselves" to attain salvation: not in the hereafter but in the sense that we may find refuge from all worry right here in this life. These messages accord closely with Zen Buddhism, which goes so far as to call the self an illusion that has been implanted in us by society: a sort of bogeyman who scares us but, when we look, is not there at all. Unfortunately, over the centuries, European Christianity perverted the meaning of the Scriptures. *Selflessness* came to mean self-condemnation. We were supposed to despise the flesh as sinful and to engage in all sorts of self-laceration to drive the devil out of ourselves. Thus, subtly perverted, the message became one of paying constant and fearful attention to ourselves, lest we fall from grace through a wrongful feeling or thought. The self, far from being dropped as an illusion, became the center stage on which the drama of salvation and damnation was played out. In addition to our troublesome earthly self, we now had an eternal self to worry about, and since the afterlife was fraught with terrible hells, our anxieties have increased accordingly.

A reaction to a bad system is all too frequently another bad system, which really is the mirror image of the first. During the 19th century, American mainstream culture began to throw off the idea of sin and hell, salvation and damnation. Yet we were not to become lighthearted, as the Scriptures suggested; self remained the central concern, only now salvation meant the worldly success of the self, and damnation meant poverty and failure. These changes in the culture paralleled the dissolution of family and communal bonds, which actually left the individual very much alone. For the first time in history, most of us human beings must now reckon with the fact that no group will accompany us from birth through death. We will move through many groups, even several nuclear families. Essentially, we will be alone on our journey. This socially isolated self became psychologically isolated because, as the old bonds dissolved, competition came to take their place.

Today we even have a magazine titled *Self.* We are constantly bombarded with images of celebrities whose lives consist of nothing but self-adornment, self-glorification, and self-seeking competition. Such folk are our heroes and role models.

As in the perverted version of Christianity, the self remains at the center of the stage, and we all have stage fright.

Now let us return to the Buddhist idea of the self as illusion. Actually, this idea accords rather closely with the sociologist's view of self because both regard the self as a socially learned construct, even though sociology does not go as far as Buddhism in asserting that we might get rid of the illusion. At first, this may seem preposterous. Our own self seems to be the one most solid, unavoidable thing with which we are in direct touch. In what sense can it be illusion? To approach this question, I would like you to do a little exercise I do with my students. Take a piece of paper and list on it all of the aspects of the self you can think of, beginning with such obvious items as "my reputation," "my clothes," "my grades," and so on. When you finish your list, come back to the book and see how it corresponds with one I have compiled from various student lists.

Exercise: Components of the Self

MY:	MY:	MY:
reputation	*hobbies*	*physical space*
clothes	*future*	*youth*
grades	*past*	*writing*
body	*life story*	*hates*
sex appeal	*family*	*dislikes*
friends	*ethnicity*	*spiritual development*
lovers	*status*	*peak experiences*
acquaintances	*prestige*	*security*
opinions	*neuroses*	*religion*
tastes	*career*	*competitive position*
image	*style*	*grudges*
ideal self	*sense of humor*	*regrets*
real self	*dreams*	*self-accusations*
talents	*daydreams*	*desires*
virtues	*role models*	*credentials*
vices	*ideals*	*personality*
habits	*knowledge*	*titles*
accomplishments	*skills*	*privileges*
fears	*beliefs*	*uniqueness*
wishes	*credit*	*honor*
ambition	*ancestors*	*name*
goals	*looks*	*sins*
IQ	*life*	*bank balance*
memory	*moods*	

As you look over this list, you will notice that it is very long. No wonder the self is problematic. It is a huge, overblown contraption. You will also notice that the items on the list are, indeed, items we have learned from our culture. Even "my body," which would seem to be a given, existing prior to culture, is socially learned in the sense that how we regard it (too fat, beautiful, clumsy, etc.) is learned from our culture. Even the way we relate to our body, for example, whether or not we are sensitive to its aches, depends on cultural conditioning.

But surely some of the items on this list are worth collecting. "Knowledge" and "opinions," for instance, are in very high repute in the academy. You are here to gather these, and your professors are paid for having lots and lots of them. Buddhism speaks to us very clearly on this point. The scholar's type of knowledge is considered one of the greatest hindrances to enlightenment. The great spiritual teacher Krishnamurti defined *expert* as "somebody who knows so much that he can't learn anything more." Buddhism tells us that, if we wish to attain wisdom, we must come with beginner's mind—we must come with an empty cup, otherwise nothing new can be poured into it.

Even the habit of intellectual speculation gets in the way. Krishnamurti tells a delightful story about a drive he took in the country with two scholars who had come to learn from him. Unfortunately, the driver of the car wasn't looking and ran over a goat. The two scholars in the backseat didn't notice it because they were so busy discussing awareness.

In studying people's ideologies, it is easy to see how our assumptions blind us utterly to the reality we are living through. Two men can go into combat in war, and one will come out a convinced pacifist, while the man next to him will come out a confirmed and aggressive patriot who believes we must be constantly ready for war. They lived through the same experience, but it was only the same outwardly. Just so, you can take a group of students to see a terribly poor inner city neighborhood. The left-wingers will see pure evidence of economic oppression, while the right-wingers will see confirmation of their belief that poor people are just lazy, dirty, and vicious.

To keep reality from intruding and upsetting our ideas, our brains keep up a constant babble. Above all, this babble is designed to keep the illusion of self alive. We are constantly rehearsing something we need to do next week or going over an argument we had yesterday, trying to improve on the line we took. We daydream about improving ourselves or adding luster to our name. This stream of ideas not only keeps the illusion of self ever alive, but it also comes between us and our bodies so that people can strain themselves until their heart or their stomach lining gives way without ever having heard the warning signals of impending disaster. *They are too busy thinking to listen to their bodies or to see the world around them. They are self-absorbed in the sense that they are constantly working on the illusory self.*

Surely we cannot just throw all knowledge out the window. How could we live? Krishnamurti again comes to our aid in differentiating *psychological thinking* from *technical thinking*. The latter is the knowledge we need to lead our lives, from knowing our address to knowing how to cook. The knowledge you need to carry out your job also falls into this category, although this can become complex when your job seems to require opinions. It is clear, however, that most of the daily thinking we do, the thinking that makes us uncomfortable, is just the sort of rehearsing and rehashing described previously. Thinking about the self is psychological thinking, and it is this that takes up most of our time and emotional energy.

Exercise: Self/No-Self

Now, let us do two exercises on the self/no-self. First, we will do a meditation on the self. Allow about 15 minutes. Sit up straight in a comfortable position and close your eyes. Now, review as many of the aspects of the self as come to your mind—concentrating on those especially troublesome to you. As you bring up each item, imagine it turning into a heavy weight that you must hold and carry. Each time, tense the muscles holding the items. You may pile these up in your arms, pile some on your head, lay some on your lap and on your feet, and so on. Gradually increase the tensions in every part of your body that must bear the weights. Then, when you have built up maximum tension, imagine all of the weights lifting away from you and simply floating off. Relax all muscular tension and stay in the sitting position, eyes closed for several more minutes, enjoying the feeling of lightness and relaxation that comes from letting go of the self.

For the second exercise, find a friend to join you. Both of you write down four items you regard as important aspects of your "ideal self" and four that you believe describe your "real self." Make these lists separately. Now, compare notes. Do you think your friend's version of his or her "real self" is correct? Does your friend think your list is realistic? After discussing this, go over the list for the real self and see if you can remember how each item was inculcated into you by the adults around you when you were growing up.

If no friend is handy, at least jot down four items for your real and ideal self before reading on.

Ideal Self, Real Self: Both Illusions

Most people show a disastrous gap between their real and ideal selves. The ideal is usually something like confident, successful, energetic, friendly, and the real is often fat, lazy, shy, incompetent. Right away we see why such a self is highly troublesome. Most students assume that their ideal self is a kind of daydream but that their real self is just a straight report of the facts. Actually, both versions are pure fantasy without the slightest substance. If you had a tough parent, for example, you may think that your real self is pretty awful. The same biological you, having had loving, self-confident parents would feel much more self-approval even though this second person had the same looks, brains, or energy level. It all depends on who held up the mirror to us as we were growing up.

Buddhism tells us that to get rid of the problematic self we need not change any aspect of it. We only need to accept what is there. Of course, to truly accept, we need to know what is there. A person who cannot admit that he or she is afraid cannot accept fear; hence, this person will be constantly wrestling with it and will remain tense and anxious. The suppression of laziness is a good example of this. Our culture demands much difficult effort from us from early childhood. It disapproves most strongly of laziness. In school lazy and stupid are about the worst things you can be. Vicious and cruel would be mild condemnations by comparison. This means that to get approval we had to deny all our urges to rest. As we deny them, they collect and grow bigger. It takes constant effort to keep this huge pile of laziness under cover. Simply everybody suspects themselves of laziness. Had we grown up in a different culture, the accusation might never have entered our minds.

A note of caution: Don't interpret letting go of the self to mean that you should ignore your feelings. On the contrary, as we sweep away concern with the problematic self, it leaves the mind more available to stay in touch with our body, its physical sensations and feeling states or emotions. Mind should look after body/feelings the way a good parent looks after a child. There is a saying in Buddhism, "When you are tired, lie down." I often think this should be engraved over the entrance of all college dormitories.

Exercise: The Critical Voice

Here is an exercise designed to make you more aware of how your insides function. Take paper and pencil and begin by giving your particular inner critical voice a name. Students come up with a wonderful variety of such names: the clobberer (a mean one), the nag (slightly less mean), the cold-eyed commentator, the nudge, the judge, the accuser, the perfectionist, the mother, the father, the quibbler, and so on. Freud called it the superego; some call it conscience. Most people have to cope with some form of critic; only a small number of lucky people don't.

Now, write out a list of the most frequent criticisms you hear from this voice. It is important to get your inner workings out on paper where you can get a different perspective on them than if you only go over them in your head. One tricky aspect of this task is that, in many people, the criticisms are not consciously heard. All that is conscious is the self-justification and self-defense about something: "I do spend my money wisely. I saved by not buying that dress last week" or "I do well in many of my classes; the ones that are important—I never mess those up." The unheard or subconscious part is "You are a spendthrift" or "You mess up in all your classes." Whenever you defend yourself like this, you know there is a silent accusation afoot. For your list, you may infer these accusations.

Now, go over your list and rate the correctness of each criticism. Then, give an overall assessment to the critical voice: right 50% of the time, 90%, 10%, and so forth. If you have a friend who will join you in this exercise, put your heads together over each list and see what your friend thinks about the accuracy of your critical voice. In the next step of the exercise, let the critical voice (always address yours by the name you've given it) justify itself: Make a list of justifications. Let the voice claim various benefits it brings you—perhaps it will claim that you couldn't function without it. Now assess the believability of the defense: very believable, barely believable, not too believable, or utterly wrong.

Although there is a wide variety of forms taken by the voice in different individuals, the accusations are usually rather similar: too lazy, too fat, not nice enough to parents, procrastinator on schoolwork, and so on. You can easily see that the content of the accusation is learned from the attitudes of the people around you as you grew up. Had you been born a Trobriand Islander, for example, you might have criticized yourself severely for any playful or slightly intimate interaction with your brother or sister.

The severity or even the presence of such an element of personality depends on culture, specifically on the severity with which children are treated during their upbringing. In a study of Polynesian culture (Malinowski, 1985), the author tells us that, when he asked people whether there was anything the individual wanted to change about himself, he usually found that the respondent couldn't think of anything at all.

How people rate their critical voice on believability seems to vary greatly, but the rating appears to have no correlation to the individual's talents or personality. Some really wonderful people believe the worst accusations about themselves. This, again, is related to childhood experiences.

You have to see the critical voice as a saboteur who constantly undermines and rattles you, while claiming to be your friend. The voice makes you dread failure, and fear of failure is one of the most common causes for failure. In many years of teaching, I learned that very few low-scoring students were failing because of lack of intelligence. Rather, self-confidence is the major ingredient in success. When you are confident, you procrastinate less. We all hate to spend time at something that makes us feel bad. The confident student talks more in class and learns more by asking questions. He or she is likely to be more adventurous and creative. In short, whatever destroys your faith in yourself undercuts your performance. Learn to see the critical voice for the enemy that it is.

This doesn't mean that you are unable to see and correct errors in your work. You have to be able to see, matter of factly, where you are wrong—that is a necessary part of the process of learning. But that is quite different from the voice. You can see your error in a flash—your understanding is that quick. The nagging and inner backbiting of the voice comes on top of this quick knowing. It drags the whole affair out and makes you a culprit for having been wrong. If you knew everything already, why should you get an education?

Next time you have a severe attack of self-criticism (it may also feel like depression), take it as a perfect occasion for catching the critic. Sit right down and make a list of the accusations—get them out into the daylight. Read them to yourself out loud. Share them with a friend.

When working on the critical voice, notice that this part of your brain is very agile. When it sees you coming after it, it may quickly switch sides and join in the new game by criticizing you for being self-critical. It is perfectly capable of such treachery. What you have to learn to recognize is not so much what it says but the tone of the criticism and the way that tone makes you feel.

The critical voice is tremendously subjective. It is, in fact, incapable of objective, fair judgment. For example, it will blame you for things it would never criticize in another person. In fact, if you criticized your friends so severely, you probably wouldn't have any friends. To strengthen your capacity for cool, unbiased self-judgment, try the following exercise: At various moments during the day, whenever you think to do it, just observe what you are doing—not what you are thinking or feeling—briefly and quite unemotionally and without judgment: "I am walking to my math class," "I am watching a movie," "I am reading an assignment," "I am having coffee and a chat with a friend." This exercise should be done over a period of at least 3 weeks— catching yourself about once or twice a day—don't overdo. If you forget easily, wear something unusual to remind yourself occasionally of the exercise. Everyone will obtain his or her own result from this exercise, and I won't spell out what your result might be. Try it and see. After 3 weeks, go back and look at your list of accusations and your assessment of their correctness. See if your feelings toward the critical voice have changed.

Exercise: Roots

Before you can let go of this troublesome self of yours, you will have to explore it and study it and understand it. (Don't use what I am saying to think about yourself incessantly. Watch instead. The understanding I am talking about comes as a flash of insight, not as the result of endless rumination.)

To a much larger extent than our culture lets on, we are still the products of quite distinct subcultures. In my course, my students researched their ancestry as far back as they could go. They interviewed relatives and wrote letters to all the older members of their families whom they could find. Then we had a come-as-you-were party: come as your grandfather or great-grandfather or one of your parents. As we exchanged family histories, we began to get a strange sensation of how much of a melting pot this society really is.

Here is a third generation German Jewish immigrant whose grandparents fled from Hitler in the 1930s. Here is a Chicano student whose family has lived in a Chicano neighborhood near the Mexican border for generations. They were former landowners, pushed out when the Anglos grabbed California and reduced the family to the poverty of farm laborers. Here is a Black student, whose grandparents made it out to California from Arkansas to work in the shipyards during World War II and whose parents made it up to the level of skilled blue-collar workers. Here is an individual whose family of Presbyterian New England farmers has been in America for many generations. Here is a young woman who was born in Taiwan and whose own parents had an arranged marriage. She tells us that it seemed to work about as well as most marriages she sees around her in the United States. Here is a young man whose ancestors were queens of Hawaii. Had we gone back two generations we would have spoken in a babble of tongues; we would have come from rags and riches. We would have exchanged passionate enmities; in no sense would we have been members of a common enough culture so that we could easily understand one another.

We tend to be fooled by externals. All of these disparate people now look pretty much alike. Not only do we dress the same, but also *we organize our faces similarly.* We wear the same expressions; our body language signals the same reserved friendliness, the same underlying disapproval of our bodies. On the surface, we are indeed alike, but it is amazing how the old ethnicity hangs on. If we look at any trait, from people's politics to the way they discipline their children, we will always find that differences in ethnic and social class origins still show up.

I put ethnicity and class position into the same bag because they come combined in patterns that reflect the historical circumstances under which each group came to be part of the United States. Black people came in chains, and Black ethnicity is still correlated with lower than average class position. The Italian immigrants came without money or urban skills primarily during the years 1880 to 1920. They began at the bottom but were only partially blocked by racism and hence managed to get into better paid working-class positions and into the lower middle class. The wave of Jewish immigrants who came in the 1930s were mostly middle class and came into our economy at that level, and thus it goes. The patterns vary from family to family. Some families moved up fast; others remained in the same economic position for generations.

There are so many subtle aspects to this heritage of ours. I was the first generation child of Austrian Jewish parents who fled from Hitler. By a fluke my family moved to Southern California, away from the other immigrants who stayed on the East Coast. Luckily, there wasn't much anti-Semitism among my young schoolmates in Claremont, California, and I grew up feeling myself to be totally "American." Yet one day I found myself majoring in sociology in graduate school at the University of California at Berkeley. I looked around me in seminar and realized that 80% of my classmates and professors were Jewish. "Isn't it strange that I ended up in this group?" I thought, and then I began to put it together. My father had been a socialist and had raised me as one. Many of the sociologists at Berkeley at that time were socialists or ex-socialists of some stripe or persuasion. They had gravitated naturally to sociology because it was the newest and most militant social science, and it counted Karl Marx as one of its most influential intellectual parents. Jews have historically often been political radicals because they lived for so many centuries as outcasts within the Christian nation-states of Europe.

I married twice, both men with backgrounds completely different from my own. Neither marriage lasted. And then I found Ted and a kind of immediate understanding, as though, for the first 40 years of our lives we had thought roughly the same thoughts and found the same comedians funny. There was something even more subtle afoot. The way he played with me and teased me reminded me very much of my father. Ted's mother was thoroughly American, but he is a throwback to two Russian-Jewish grandfathers with whom he lived during his childhood and who teased him and played with him in the same way my Austrian Jewish father had played with me. One of them was a labor organizer and a radical.

Another thing we discovered at our come-as-you-were party was that some people had large, cohesive, happy families with lots of positive ties and common sociability, while other people came from tiny fragments of once extended families in which bad feelings had eaten like acid into the old kinship ties. Happiness seems to run through generations and so does unhappiness. Don't take this as an edict from fate; human beings can remake their family situations during their lifetime, at least up to a point. You cannot will a warm, extended family into being, but you can create a small happy family on the strength of your own wisdom. In fact, it is quite possible to learn as much from bad examples as from good ones so long as you are clear about which is bad and good.

Many of the interviews and letters from relatives turned out to be wonderful. Perhaps it was just a chance for young folks to talk with the old folks and find out about old times. That used to happen naturally because people lived near each other and weren't segregated so sharply by generations. I once read a study in which it was found that children who have close ties with grandparents feel more optimistic about life and about getting old than children who are cut off from those ties. The Roots exercise was a way to bring a little of this contact about.

Do your own roots. Perhaps you could do it as a half-credit independent study or in connection with a course. In that case, there are many interesting books, fiction and nonfiction, which you could read on just about any ethnic group. A sociologist should be able to help you find resources. Or organize a come-as-you-were party among a group of friends who are willing to put a little time into it. You will find clues to your own identity and broaden your sympathies toward others from different origins.

Exercise: Slowing Down

Time is our modern nemesis. We are slaves of our wristwatches in a social system in which 5 minutes is considered a significant interval (i.e., the difference between being on time or late to class). Imagine living in a society whose smallest unit of discussible time is the time it takes to boil rice—and not instant rice, either. It is ironic that, while previous cultures had far fewer labor-saving mechanisms, they possessed a feeling of plenty of time; whereas we, with all our labor-saving devices, feel chronically time poor.

Evans-Pritchard (1940) describes an African herding people, the Nuer, as follows:

[T]he Nuer have no expression equivalent to time in our language, and they cannot, therefore, as we can, speak of time as though it were something actual, which passes, can be wasted, can be saved, and so forth. I do not think that they ever experience the same feeling of fighting against time or of having to coordinate activities with an abstract passage of time, because their points of reference are mainly the activities themselves, which are generally of a leisurely character. Events follow a logical order, but they are not controlled by an abstract system, there being no autonomous points of reference to which activities have to conform with precision. Nuer are fortunate. (p. 47)

One of the reasons we have to time everything so carefully is that we must coordinate our actions with a highly complex system of activities, and we must do this alone. You don't move from class to class to luncheon date with any single group. You are generally entirely on your own, and the structure sets up unyielding demands. Another reason our machines don't make life leisurely is that our society is so competitive. Having your own jet doesn't put you safely ahead of other executives who also have private airplanes. Having a calculator in math class doesn't put you ahead of other students similarly equipped. As soon as everybody has a labor-saving device, nobody is benefited by it. Twenty years ago, social scientists were predicting that the coming of the computer would shorten everybody's workweek. We got unemployment instead, and there hasn't been a decrease in the workweek since World War II.

The sense of urgency that fills our days has been turned into a virtue by the folks who lead our institutions. A number of years ago, I decided to try enlightening my faculty colleagues at Pitzer College by sending out a brief questionnaire that simply asked whether the individual felt he or she had *plenty of time, just enough time,* or *short of time,* in connection with work at the college. As I expected, most people checked *short of time.* I had planned to make this situation known to the faculty to see what we might do about it. I was stopped short by the marginal comments that graced at least half of the questionnaires. Next to the box *short of time,* people had penciled, "I am glad about this; it keeps me going," "Short of time—of course—what professional is not?" and so on. In other words, they celebrated the shortage. This is not really surprising in a society where the answer to "How are you?" is frequently "Keeping busy," which means the same as "Well, thank you."

Yet there is probably no single cause of tension greater than this chronic feeling of time nipping at our heels. As one surveys this scene, there is a feeling that we are caught in a social structure much larger than ourselves—a structure whose wheels just revolve too fast for our comfort. But we can change these feelings for ourselves as individuals and do so without becoming incompetent. You may begin to see this for yourself by trying the following daylong exercise.

Get up 20 minutes early tomorrow and do 20 minutes of the "slow walk"[2] before starting your day—that is, for 20 minutes walk around your room as slowly as you possibly can without losing your balance. It may take you 10 minutes to cross the room. Just concentrate on the body feelings of walking slowly. Don't do anything special with your mind—let it relax and go along for the ride.

Now, for the rest of the day, do all your accustomed tasks at about 50% of your normal speed—even less when it seems possible. Walk to class slowly, take notes slowly, eat your lunch slowly, do your assignments slowly, go out on your date slowly, and so forth. Another way of getting into the feel of this exercise is to think of each separate activity as a time frame. Our usual habit is to lean forward into the next time frame—that is, as we walk to class we are already thinking about class; as we shower, we are already dreaming about seeing our date. This time, try leaning back into your present time frame. Say to yourself, "How nice, I have a 5-minute walk now. I hope it lasts a long time, so I can settle into it comfortably." With practice, you can even learn to lean back into quite short time frames.

At the end of the day, for your own records, jot down your impressions. Try to see what you have learned about yourself, other people, institutions, and so on. Do this before reading on.

Students generally come back from this exercise astounded about something. Perhaps they sense for the first time how much they habitually rush. "I don't usually taste my food I eat so fast," says one student; "I never realized how fast everybody dashes around," says another. But the greatest surprise is, "I got everything done just about as well as usual" or "I actually got more done than usual because I felt so sane" and "I wish I could do that every day." Well, why not? It is possible to change one's inner experience of time. Nobody need be the wiser. You won't look that different from the outside. Experiment has shown that runners actually make better time when instructed to run at just 80% of their normal speed. *When tension decreases, we actually become more efficient.*

Of course, this exercise, like all consciousness-changing exercises, requires much practice. You spent 20 years learning to feel hurried. It will take time and practice to undo that. A problem with such practice is that you forget to do it once the novelty wears off. One way to help yourself is to wear or carry something unusual, which will remind you to do the practice. You may wear an unaccustomed bracelet, or change the arm on which you wear your watch, or carry a bright notebook cover, and so on. The slow walk, by the way, is a very nice meditation you can use at any time to calm down. I would recommend you look at Thic Nhat Hanh's *A Guide to Walking Meditation* (1985). The activity of the mind is tied to the physical body. *When you slow the body down, the mind also slows down.*

Desocializing doesn't have to be as severe as it sounds. Although escaping reality can be a form of removing yourself from socialization (and society in the process), desocialization may be much softer. Desocialization is more like drifting to the edge of the fish bowl we're all in rather than jumping out. Once you are at the edge, it is possible to view everyone in the middle with less biased lenses. Try this: At some point during the day when you have a break between classes that's more than 10 minutes, go to a quiet spot of the campus. It may be the park in the center of the school or just a quiet block along the main street. Put your stuff down and sit quietly or walk slowly. Allow your mind to wander away from the stresses of school. Do this until a feeling of calmness comes over you. If you can achieve this peacefulness, you will be able to, at least temporarily, remove yourself from the routine pressures of school. Do this every so often and you should start to see these pressures in a different light.

Maximizing and Minimizing

One of the basic, underlying styles of our culture is the tendency to maximize and minimize everything: to push everything as far as possible in a given direction—to always expand to the limits of endurance. We have seen how we do this with time. We are always making the best use of our time; we can never allow ourselves to waste time. If we get an extra piece of time thrown our way, we immediately find something to fill it—something that had not been pressing before suddenly becomes pressing. Thus, we seldom allow ourselves a leisurely sense of time.

We see this tendency at work most dramatically in our attitudes toward spending money. Average Americans spend to the limits of their capacity. When we get a raise, we immediately increase our purchases accordingly. Thus, we are always financially uncomfortable no matter how much we make. We could feel rich if we simply stayed at our present spending level when we get a raise, but we just cannot do this because we are surrounded by appeals to spend.

Just as surely as we maximize our spending of time and money or our attainment of sexual satisfaction, we minimize in other directions. Many of us are constantly on a diet, minimizing our food intake; at home we minimize our housework; at school we must minimize our errors. Not for us the golden mean of the ancient Greeks or the middle way of the Buddhists. The inevitable accompaniment of this style is strain. Ask anybody on campus whether they feel strained by time, by finances, by sexual needs, and you will usually find a strainer. At the same time, the culture demands that we maximize "happiness." To be less than happy is to be somehow in disgrace. Yet happiness just cannot be found in this basic mode. The demand is a cruel contradiction in terms.

I know of no way to break through this pervasive pattern except by pulling yourself up short when you are about to maximize or minimize some situation and asking yourself, "Would it not be better to find the golden mean, the middle way? Suppose I don't try to write the longest paper for glory or the shortest paper to minimize the discomfort of research? Suppose I write a paper of middle length? Suppose I hit for the medium price range in my purchases? Suppose I settle for being slightly overweight? Suppose I don't change my spending patterns when I get the raise? Suppose I don't rush through every country in Europe so I won't miss anything?" It will perhaps seem inglorious to you, but it is certainly more comfortable. You may still choose to maximize some area of activity, but don't let the culture rush you into doing so every time. *Be aware of this tendency and use your awareness to increase your freedom.*

Daydreams and Great Expectations

Zen Buddhism has a very simple recipe for enlightenment: attention to the present moment. At first, it may seem to us that, of course, we pay attention to the moment. We don't, after all, fall downstairs or run into trees very often. We couldn't survive if we paid no attention. As we begin to observe the workings of our mind, we find that the attention we pay is usually minimal. Most of the time we are relying on habit and an occasional glance to get us through the environment. As we dress, brush our teeth, walk to class, or drive into town, our heads are usually filled with thoughts about ourselves. We see ourselves as heroes and heroines of many a dramatic fantasy. In short, we daydream.

If you want to see for yourself what happens to your attention during habitual tasks, try this simple experiment. Next time you are washing and getting dressed, try keeping your mind firmly glued to the present moment by describing each little action to yourself: "I am walking into the bathroom," "I am washing my face," "I am drying my face," "I am putting the towel back," and so on. You may be surprised by what you find.

Over the years, I have been impressed by the stubbornness with which students defend their right to daydream. "But I don't want to stop daydreaming" is a frequent response to the stricture of Buddhism to remain in the present moment. Daydreaming is enjoyable; it seems to fulfill some great inner need, and, anyway, the ordinary world seems repetitive and boring much of the time. In view of this resistance by my students, I had to ask myself, "What is wrong with daydreaming? What is the price we pay for daydreaming?"

One clear price we pay is that daydreaming stirs up our emotions when we could be perfectly calm. Even though we are only walking down a quiet street, our body chemistry is responding to our thoughts of adventure, danger, revenge, triumph, and so on. Hence, we are seldom as serene and inwardly quiet as we could be if we were only responding to our environment. Thus, we tend to be either "up" or "down." We do not find our inner center and hence cannot respond to the happenings of the day from this center. Rather, the day's problems flow into the daydreaming, and we really cannot separate and deal with the real problems realistically. There is a kind of clean simplicity and innocence in our experience during those rare times when we are "just" in the physical environment.

Our daydreams are very frequently dreams of fulfilling our every wish. Our thoughts run so far ahead of our real acquisitions that we feel forever in need of more goodies about which we have fantasized. The daydreams make us dissatisfied with what we really have.

Daydreams can also deprive the real happenings in our life of the luster they would have if we came upon them innocent of expectation. Indeed, expectation is the great enemy of satisfaction. When we begin a flirtation with someone, our mind immediately rushes ahead to what it could be like to make love to this person—to travel with them—to be wonderfully flattered and complimented by them. By the time a real relationship develops, we are primed for disappointment. It will never be anything like our daydream. Perhaps we will never see the potentialities for new experience with this other person because we are looking through the old stuff of our daydreams.

In reality, it is our daydreams that are old and repetitive and hackneyed. It is reality that is ever new and continually amazing and challenging, but we live so little in this reality that it doesn't penetrate to us. We blunt its impact. One day in class I remarked on the beautiful and fragrant citrus tree by our classroom door. I discovered that most students had not seen or smelled it. Daydreamers are like people who spend nearly all their time watching movies. Perhaps they are really in a splendid natural scene and surrounded by interesting people, but they only take out a few minutes between movies. During those few minutes, the last movie is still so much in their mind that nothing in the real scene penetrates their emotions. Immersion in the media is a good analogy to immersion in daydreams. The media are the stuff that feeds our dreams, and our constant exposure to media helps to make daydreamers of us.

In *Great Expectations,* Dickens (1982) relates the story of a woman who was jilted on her wedding day. Refusing utterly to face the reality of this, she spends the rest of her life dressed in her wedding gown, sitting at the banquet table that was to have been her wedding feast. When she is very old, she upsets a candelabra and sets her finery, herself, and the whole house on fire. Her great expectation consumed her entire life.

Ted and I had some interesting experiences with expectations as we began to plan for our early retirement. Ted's dream since childhood had always been to go to the South Seas. He thought that, perhaps, he might even want to live there. So we set out on a 6-month tour of the South Sea Islands. Having always centered my travel interests on Europe, I had never even thought about going to the South Pacific.

During our tour, we had our good and bad times, as one always does when traveling. The worst thing was that it rained much more than usual and spoiled a lot of our planned outdoor activities. An unexpected delight, on the other hand, was the marvelous diversity and beauty of the art, music, and dance of the peoples of Melanesia and Polynesia.

Our responses to the trip were very different. I experienced the journey as a great pleasure. Every new, unexpected facet of the area surprised and delighted me. At the same time, I took the bad weather rather philosophically. Ted, on the other hand, found the trip unexpectedly depressing. It did not meet his lifelong expectations, and, whenever it fell short, he suffered a real sense of loss.

Some years later, when we decided to settle in Northern California, we bought 3 acres that had been a once-beautiful garden but was long neglected. Gardening had always been my passion. I had always been land hungry on my little city lots. During all the years in which lack of space constrained me, I avidly read garden books and magazines and seed catalogues. *The media are specialists in promoting unrealistic daydreams.* Just as the houses shown in home magazines are generally only affordable by millionaires, so the garden magazines contained doctored photographs of perennial borders made beautiful by the last-minute addition of hidden pots of flowers grown in greenhouses. How many such perennial borders had I planted in my mind (while skipping the chapters called "Pests" and "Diseases"?) Ted, on the other hand, had no expectations of the garden. He didn't even know whether he would enjoy gardening. He just sort of went along with me in picking this particular acreage.

Of course, the results were predictable. As I began to face the real difficulties of getting 3 acres under control, I suffered a good deal. While I had pictured myself working 6 or 7 hours a day in my dream garden, I discovered that, at 53 years of age, working even 4 hours is very likely to land you a tennis elbow. All in all, the garden quickly became my nemesis. In the meanwhile, Ted innocently began to prune the trees and found that he hugely enjoyed the activity. He was able to take pleasure in the garden just as it was at any given moment, while I always saw weeds and other errors crying out for correction. We both learned about the influence of expectations the hard way. Luckily, reality is always there to wake us up. As I bow to the realities of my garden, I find that the garden is reshaping me quite as much as the other way around.

Often, our daydreams seem to function as rehearsals and we have convinced ourselves that rehearsals are useful. Without them we might not be prepared to meet various situations. That this is an error you can substantiate for yourself. Observe whether or not an encounter for which you have rehearsed ever comes off the way you expected. In my experience, real encounters are always grossly different from rehearsals. In fact, if we didn't quickly drop the rehearsed material, we would be incapable of dealing with the real situation. The very best way to meet any difficult encounter—whether an oral examination or a painful dialogue with a friend—is to go into it with a calm, quiet mind, primed to be totally alert and open to the situation as it develops.

If you want to get a handle on your own daydreaming, carry paper and pencil around with you for 1 day and make a tally for every time you catch yourself daydreaming. You can also make a quick note of the subject of each daydream. At the end of the day, you can take a look at what goes on in your mind.

That is Exercise 1. For Exercise 2, wait until some event is coming up from which you expect either pleasure or pain. When such an event appears on your horizon, make it your practice to forego absolutely any kind of daydreaming about that particular occasion. Of course, you may do some necessary preparation for the occasion. But this is different from daydreaming. Pick just one event at a time because this is difficult and will take energy to carry out. Be absolutely ruthless about this one event. Whenever you catch your mind wandering even near it, strike at the roots swiftly, as if you were wielding a very sharp sword. If you discover that you are in the middle of such thoughts, drop them immediately. (Don't prolong it by berating yourself.) Then, when the real event happens, see if there is any difference in your experience of it.

Desocialization Course Resources

This is a list of books I used in the desocialization course. Most of these books are available at www.amazon.com.

Cohen, S., & Taylor, L. (1976). *Escape attempts*. Middlesex, UK: Penguin.

Fischer, L. (1963). *The essential Gandhi*. New York: Random House.

Fromm, E., Suzuki, D. T., & De Martino, R. (1960). *Zen Buddhism and psycho-analysis*. New York: Harper & Row.

Herrigel, E. (1971). *Zen in the art of archery*. New York: Vintage, Random House.

Krishnamurti, J. (1969). *Freedom from the known*. New York: Harper & Row.

Maslow, A. (1962). *Toward a psychology of being*. Princeton, NJ: Van Nostrand.

Matthiesen, P. (1978). *The snow leopard*. New York: Bantam.

Powell, R. (1961). *Zen and reality*. Middlesex, UK: Penguin.

Putney, S., & Putney, G. (1964). *The adjusted American: Normal neuroses in the individual and society*. New York: Harper & Row.

Stevens, B. (1970). *Don't push the river*. Moab, UT: Real People.

Suzuki, S. (1970). *Zen mind, beginner's mind*. New York: Weatherhill.

Trungpa, C. (1969). *Meditation in action*. Berkeley, CA: Shambhala.

Watts, A. W. (1961). *Psychotherapy East and West*. New York: Ballantine.

Notes

1.   For an exception, see Dennis Wrong's classic chapter "The Oversocialized Conception of Man in Modern Sociology" in *The Study of Society: An Integrated Anthology*.

2.   I learned the "slow walk" at the Nyingma Institute in Berkeley, California. This is a Tibetan Buddhist institute founded by Tarthan Tulku Rinpoche. Although the founder is in retreat, the teachers he trained are running the institute, which offers many workshops, classes, and an academically accredited program in certain subject areas.

CHAPTER 10

Media Me

We are socialized throughout our lives by the mass media. This agency of indoctrination is even more powerful than the school system because it comes in the form of entertainment and hence doesn't arouse the inner opposition which school, thank heaven, always arouses in the hapless pupil. The folks who do media spend many dollars and hire many experts to find out exactly what forms of entertainment will grab you. Their object is to get your absolute attention when the ads come on. That is why there is so much violence in media. It is part of our animal heritage that we become wide awake when there is any physical danger around us. Research shows that when incidents of violence are pictured on the screen, a milder form of this instinctive reaction goes into effect: We pay attention.

Getting Behind the Media Curtain

Media culture is a culture that has been invented to sell soap. There is precious little wisdom in it. Yet we are all deeply influenced by media versions of reality. Indeed, we depend on media and on schools for nearly all the knowledge we have of the world that lies beyond what we can immediately see and experience. Ask yourself, for a moment, how you "know" what China is like, how you "know" what sort of people politicians are, or how you "know" what your hometown was like a hundred years ago. If you are honest, you will see that, conceivably, you could have been lied to about all these things.[1]

Who controls what comes to you in TV, films, or newspapers? Almost without exception these forms of the mass media are owned by giant, multinational conglomerates that are interrelated in many different ways with the whole network of huge corporations that dominate the American economy. What do rich people want you to know about Cuba? South American revolutionaries have a nasty habit of nationalizing American corporate property in their countries. The United Fruit

Company stands to lose every time a Castro appears on the scene. Will they tell you that, under Castro, Cuba has developed the best medical care system in Latin America? What will they tell you about the nature and reality of war, when it may be necessary for you to be drafted to fight a war for rubber in Asia or for oil in Iraq or Venezuela? These are questions you must learn to ask yourself. In fact, you should become suspicious of all information you do not get firsthand. The source and the bias of the source must always be considered when getting information at second-hand. You must also consider whether your source had access to good information. During Vietnam, for example, very few Americans in Vietnam spoke the language. This meant they could only speak with Western-educated Vietnamese in the cities. No wonder they didn't know what was going on in the much larger countryside.

On those rare occasions when the media cover something we know about first-hand, we are usually amazed to see how distorted the picture is. But we seldom generalize from these occasions because it is pretty difficult to admit that we don't know as much as we thought we did. It may help you to keep in mind that realizing how little one knows is the inevitable beginning of wisdom.

Media work on us in much more subtle ways than just misinforming us. Media inculcate general attitudes toward life, love, pleasure, and pain. What do the media want you to know about the real nature of love, if their object is to sell you hairspray? What do they want you to know about contentment, if the object is to sell you linoleum? How do they want you to feel about yourself, if they are softening you up to rush out and buy the latest designer jeans? Advertisers are well aware that it isn't effective to break into an honest story about human life with an ad that tries to tell you that happiness lies in the right choice of shampoo, so the programming must be brought down to the simplest level that serves this manipulative advertising.

Media mediate not only between us and events beyond our immediate world but also between us and events in our immediate world by influencing us to define and see that world in a certain way. In the final analysis, media get right inside your personality and mediate between you and yourself. Take the critical voice, which says "too fat," for example. Isn't your ideal of the proper body form taken mainly from media? Look around next time you are at the swimming pool. See what the real range of human shapes looks like.

Exercise: Developing Specific Insight

Generalized suspicion of media information is not enough. Rather, we need to develop very specific insights. I would like to suggest to you an exercise to start you on your way in this direction.

Sample 4 hours of television programming, picking a variety of media forms: soap operas, evening weeklies, old movies, talk shows, and so on. Pick programs that present types of human beings. For this purpose, skip sports, news, and documentaries. Concentrate on media fiction or on programs that present those media creatures we call celebrities. Take detailed notes as you watch. List the major characters and describe them in some detail: How are the characters dressed? What sort of bodies and faces do they have? What sort of posture? What do they do for a living? Are they rich, poor, or middle class? What is their ethnicity? How do they talk to each other? How old are they?

After the first 2 hours of observation, take 2 hours for real-life observation. Pick two spots in quite different neighborhoods. Choose places where you can watch people easily. Self-service laundries are very good for this, as are public parks, bus terminals, airports, and so on. Pick several people to watch and make the same observations that you made for your media characters.

Now, go back for 2 more hours of media watching. You may add new categories for observation if they occur to you during your first set of observations. Follow this with 2 more hours of real-people watching. Then, just for your own information, look over your notes and start drawing some major comparisons between media people and real people. Can you see the direction in which media is distorting? Can you assess the effect of these distortions on your own attitudes toward other people—toward yourself? If you do this exercise thoroughly, I believe it will forever change the way you perceive both media and real people. I won't tell you any results on this one. I will let you find out for yourself.

If you happen to have a class or independent study in which you could use these observations for a project, one good way to present your findings is by making a visual presentation for the class. If you don't have a camera, you might try comparing people in magazine advertisements to magazine pictures of real people. (You will find real people rather hard to find in most magazines. This itself is an eye-opener.) In preparing such visual programs, I found that it was nearly impossible to find pictures of real blue-collar workers in magazines. I also discovered that my pictures of real people were mainly in black and white, while the advertisement people were mainly in color. How subtly such a difference acts on our intelligence, making the advertisement pictures somehow more vivid and real than actual people.

If you have a camera and don't mind taking pictures of people or can do so inconspicuously, you can prepare slides of real people and compare them with slides made from magazine advertising. There are many possible variations on this theme. For example, you might compare just people over 65 years of age in media and reality—or you might do teenagers or non-Whites. Take any aspect particularly interesting to you.

I hope that in this chapter I have given you the idea that knowledge can be acquired playfully. It is when we play that we are most imaginative and also the most open to new ideas. Perhaps you can design some exercises of your own to explore some dimension of experience that fascinates or frustrates you.

Mind, Self, and Media

The media has become so all pervasive in our society that it is no longer easy to determine whether the media is an extension of our culture or whether our culture has become merely an extension of the media. While there is certainly enough in this issue alone to write a very lengthy (and probably very dry) book, I would just like you to consider for a moment that this is not an issue that should be of concern only to bespectacled professors and social philosophers.

This is an issue that strikes at the very root of your experience of college and, indeed, may strike at the very root of what it means to live in this society.

To start with, I would like you to consider the idea that we are not born knowing what it means to be human. We are not born with an instinctual framework or the hard wiring that allows us to unerringly relate to others. We do not come into the world with some ingrained, prescribed set of roles and rules for interactions between ourselves and with ourselves. Unlike a bee or an ant, which seems to be born already capable of acting perfectly within the role given to it, we are born with a largely undetermined way of being. Instead, we are born into a culture, and this culture, in large part, determines what it means to be human and how we are to express this humanity in and through ourselves. Our culture, in large part, determines who we are, determines our identity.

Considering the role that mass media plays in our culture, and the role that culture plays in shaping our identity, it is imperative that we begin to look critically at our own personal relationship to the media and, probably more important, how this relationship affects our experience of the world.

If we stop for a second to consider where we get most of our information about the world outside of our direct experience, it becomes obvious that most information is delivered and filtered through one of two sources, either the media or educational institutions. Fortunately, our educational institutions are structured in such a way that there is some involvement in the process; it is possible to engage in healthy questioning and dialogue concerning what we are being told. Information from the media, on the other hand, is presented in such a way that we are passive, usually sitting in our living rooms or dorms while the images and words are played in front of us. The result is that we are given a view of the world that is exactly what someone else wishes us to see. This should raise some concern when we think about what the possible motivations are for presenting exactly what we are shown. Rather than listing what some of these motives might be, I think it would be helpful to let you engage in this questioning exercise yourself.

It is not only through news programs that the media shape our perceptions of the world. On a much broader and more insidious level, media shape our experience of the world through television, radio programs, and advertisements. Media culture depends on selling products for its survival, and most of its vast machinery is geared with this end in mind.

There is something that is required for the realization of this end, however. It is impossible to sell an endless line of products to people who are basically content with who they are. The survival of media culture depends first on us seeing ourselves as always lacking in some fundamental aspect. This is why the images of people given to us through most television programs and magazines are nothing like representative samples of the public. Quite simply, the media culture could not survive if it allowed itself to show us images that are closely related to what we really are. Instead, we are given an image of humanity that is very narrow, to say the least. We tend to take these images as what we are supposed to be, internalizing those images as some sort of true picture of reality. But, of course, most of us are nothing like these images.

Media culture creates, for us, an identity based not on who we actually are but rather on what we are not. We are not inherently attractive, so we need makeup and hairspray to closer approximate the image of feminine beauty given in the latest prime-time sitcom. Our bodies are not shaped properly, so we need the latest fad food supplement. And then, when it seems that we are actually catching up and have the latest fashions and the fastest computers, corporations come out with a new line that makes what we presently have obsolete.

Think for a moment about why there are new high-fashion lines presented at least yearly or why car manufacturers come out with new product changes every few years. We are told that it is to bring the consumer the latest, greatest achievements of the industry. The real reason is very different. The simple fact is that our consumer-driven media culture cannot ever allow us to think that what we have is enough. Nothing ever will be enough, so long as we internalize that critical voice of the media, which says "not thin enough" when we look into the mirror. We are never whole and complete exactly as we are.

There is a very subtle philosophical principle that the media understand and use very well. The principle is that human beings tend to use the world as a mirror of themselves. We tend to define ourselves by our experience of the world. What is cruel in the media culture's manipulation of this is that the media ensure that we are constantly inundated with images that are literally impossible to attain. The actual models in magazine advertisements can't even meet the images given of themselves! After hours of makeup and uncomfortable posing sessions, the photographs are airbrushed and, these days, enhanced by computer imaging.

This all leaves you in a position that would seem comical, if it weren't so deadly serious in its effects. We look to the world to see what it means to be a human and are given images of humanity that are complete fabrications. We tend to take the images given in the media as some sort of ideal humanity, a model of ourselves that is somehow a perfection to be attained. We are put into a position of seeing who we really are as someone who is lacking. What is tragic, and at the same time comic if you can free yourself from it, is that these images are not only not authentically ideal, but also they are not even human. We are left trying to attain some grotesque characterization of humanness while ignoring that to be human means to be exactly what we are, right now.

In short, media not only mediate between ourselves and the outside world, but they also make immediate experience of who we are very difficult. Look at your own criticisms of yourself and especially your body. Whose voice is it that is really doing the criticizing? Look at your relationship to where you live and the material things that surround you. Do you spend much time really appreciating any of it, or are you always looking for something more, something better? Look at the career you might be presently considering. Are you considering it because you really think you will find some self-expression in it, or are you looking for the power to buy more material things? When those are gained, will they be enough, or is something different needed for true contentment?

I would like you to consider one last thing in this section: the idea that real contentment is not a matter of having or owning certain things but is rather about freedom. I would like you to consider the possibility that there is a sense of the word *freedom* that we have very little acquaintance with and that we should get much closer to. Freedom, in this sense, is not the outside freedom that we usually talk about when we use the word. It is not freedom of speech or expression or anything along those lines, no matter how noble these ideas of freedom are. It is certainly not the sense of freedom that media culture gives us, freedom to get more and more, to merely own whatever it is we want at this moment.

This other type of freedom is much more radical. It is an inner freedom that isn't about how we act or what we do. This freedom is concerned with who we are. In this view, freedom isn't about being able to do, or own, what we want when we want. Instead, this freedom is about being something beyond what we have been told we are and what we tell ourselves we are. It is about being something beyond our culturally conditioned identity. It is a sort of radical self-determination, a freedom to not be limited by what you think you are or are not.

We are sort of conditioned to view freedom as the ability to do what we want, yet we rarely consider that what we want is often determined by others. In our media-driven culture, this is especially true. This sense of freedom is actually a very confined space. The radical sense of freedom, however, is very different. It is the freedom to allow ourselves not to want, to allow ourselves to simply be what we are, a freedom to be complete. Most of us don't see ourselves as simply what we are. Instead, we see ourselves as not-yet-thin-enough, rich-enough, kind-enough, you-name-it enough. A large part of this is a direct result of growing up in the sea of media. Another part of this freedom is the freedom to let the world, and especially other people, be exactly what they are in our experience of them. All too often, we experience the world through the filter of the media. Instead of experiencing our apartment as what it is, we experience it as not big enough. Our families may not be loving enough; that stranger is not attractive enough or not as approachable as we want him or her to be. This freedom is also about giving freedom to others to be exactly what they are.

But this freedom is not something that can really be sensed by talking about it. It must be experienced, so there are listed here a couple of experiments to help give you a taste of that freedom. It is my hope that you will experience a little bit of breathing space through these exercises. I always find these little tastes of freedom to be satisfying in the same manner that a good afternoon nap is satisfying. You may find yourself returning to these exercises again and again.

First, look at yourself nude in the mirror, briefly, and write down the judgments that you make about the image in the mirror.

Now, as in the previous exercise, sample 2 hours of television programming, taking detailed notes on how characters are dressed, what sort of bodies they have, their posture, and the manner in which they relate to each other. Do this on a fresh sheet of paper. Are they rich, poor, or middle class? What do they do for a living? What is their ethnicity? How old are they? For this exercise, skip news programs, sports, and documentaries. Focus instead on media fictions and especially on any programs that highlight media celebrities.

After doing this, take 2 hours and observe people in real life. Try doing an hour each at two spots in quite different neighborhoods, both in places where it is easy to observe a large number of people, such as self-service laundries, shopping malls, airports, and so on. Take the same type of notes that you did in the first part, but this time add another category. This time, *list also the judgments that you make about the people you see.* Do you see them as attractive, unattractive, fat, thin, rich, poor, and so on?

Then go back and do another hour of media watching and another hour of real-life observation and look back over your notes. Draw major comparisons between the images given in media and the people seen in real life. In what direction does the media distort images of people? Pay particular attention to the judgments you wrote down.

Now, compare those judgments to the judgments you wrote down about yourself. To make those judgments what are you comparing yourself and others to? Do the judgments about yourself make sense when compared with observation of people in real life? Do those judgments arise from a comparison to the real world or to something else? Are the judgments even valid in comparison to the real world? Finally, is that critical, judging voice even you, or can you identify that voice with how the media would like you to see the world?

As a final step, go back to the mirror, nude, and listen carefully to that judging voice and, as far as possible, do not do anything about it. Don't try to squelch it or identify yourself with it or change it. Stand in front of the mirror for at least 15 minutes and simply observe your image and the judging voice. What happens to both?

Rick Hartman

Note

1.   If you would like to see whether your schooling thus far has misrepresented American history, read Howard Zinn's (1980) *A People's History of the United States* and James Loewen's (1996) *Lies My Teacher Told Me: Everything Your American History Textbook Got Wrong.*

CHAPTER 11

Love

I did not yet love and I wanted to love so I sought what I might love, in love with loving.

—St. Augustine, *Confessions*

Love is like a faucet, it turns off and on.

—Billie Holiday

Music comes close to being the religion of your generation, and one only has to look at the titles of a few popular songs to see what is getting you down:

"Love Me Tender"

"When a Man Loves a Woman"

"I Need Someone to Hold Me When I Cry"

"Heartbreak Here I Come"

"Your Cheatin' Heart"

"The Power of Love"

"Whatcha' Doing to Me?"

"Can't Get You Off My Mind"

"Somebody's Gonna Get Hurt Before We're Through"

"Everything I Do, I Do It for You"

"Chained to Your Love"

"Can't Let Go"

"After the Love Is Gone"

"Help Me Get Her Out of My Heart"

"I Can't Help Falling in Love with You"

"You're Gonna Get What's Comin'"

"Ever Since You've Gone"

"Love" has you wallowing in a sop-sorry miasma of negative emotion. Go down any dormitory hall and you will find most people in varying stages of the ancient American saga of boy-meets-girl, girl-meets-boy, boy-loses-girl, and the oh-God-I'm-alone-again blues. Tune in to any soap opera, go to any movie, put on any record, and there it is: good love, bad love, repetitive love, heartbreaking love, unrequited love, glorious love, and so on. In our media mythology, hardly anything else is going on. *Because you are a creature of this culture, your life reflects the great obsession.* In this chapter, I want to look more closely at this phenomenon to see whether it is possible to live without the pains of romantic love.

Love in Our Culture

When we are overcome by the various emotions of romantic love—longing, jealousy, desire, exuberant joy, horrible blues—we generally attribute these to the working of the powerful sexual instinct, and it seems to us that we are just putty in its hands. Actually, pure sexuality has relatively little to do with this flood of emotion. We must look at what is really going on.

Every culture embroiders the simple fabric of human sexuality in its own way. A look at other cultures quickly shows us how enormously malleable this emotion is. There are African cultures in which many men take more than one wife. Not only do women feel no jealousy whatsoever in this situation, but also women count themselves unfortunate if their husbands can afford only one wife: "If there is only one wife, who will help me with the housework and take care of me when I give birth?" In the Trobriand Island culture, brother-sister incest is considered so likely and its attraction so overpowering that a rigidly formal code governs the interaction of even very young siblings. In Western culture, during Victorian times, it was considered perfectly possible to die of love, and people actually did. In yet another culture, it is recognized that husbands and wives very occasionally develop a deep feeling of love, but this is regarded as uncommon, and people do not count on it happening to them any more than most Americans count on becoming millionaires.

For every person love has a different meaning, but for most the first thought that comes to mind is romance. Romantic love is the one thing that everyone in our culture dreams of and hopes to someday find. The idea of romance to most of us is a mystery. We think we have an idea what romance is, but it seems all we have is fantasies, and it is fantasy that keeps us anxiously aroused. When will it happen, and how will it feel? The fact is we all have love or at least most of us have love in our lives. The problem, is when we are not romantically involved with someone, we think of ourselves as alone and unloved. *We take for granted all other aspects of love in our lives.* From the first day on this earth, we have all been loved by parents and family. Then, as we grow older, we soon learn the love for friends and friendships. As we grow older, we soon learn the love for material possessions. We love our animals or pets. For some, there is the love of knowledge, for others, the love for their calling or career.

The emotions "love" arouses in us are complex and varied. *Most Americans cannot tell the difference between love and anxiety.* This situation was parodied in an old film called *High Anxiety,* in which the hero sings that he knows that he is in love again because he once again has that old feeling of high anxiety. We also frequently take hostility to be love. In fact, some biologists have sagely assured us that the physical reactions accompanying anger are similar to those accompanying sexual arousal. Probably any physical arousal works similarly on some of our glands, but only a deep-seated cultural confusion leads us to confuse anger and love. Watch any John Wayne movie and you will see the taciturn macho man—who would really rather be in a good fistfight than make love—as he becomes the object of some "weak" woman's desire. As they move into the final clinch, you are never quite sure until the last minute whether it will be a fight, a rape, or mutual attraction.

Competitiveness is another powerful emotion we confuse with sexual attraction. The ideal romance of song and story is the Cinderella myth in which physical love is joined with a sharp rise in social status. Most of us have at some time "fallen in love" with the most popular boy or girl in the class. Our sexual longings are really indistinguishable from our longing for popularity and wealth. On the other hand, most of the time when we are pining away for a lost love, what we really have is a bruised ego, a sense that we've lost the game.

When all of these powerful emotions, which our culture fosters, are conjoined with sexuality, we do, indeed, feel ourselves in the grip of something so overwhelming that it is tempting to look at it as an instinct that has physical power over us to such an extent that it can raise us to heights of joy or fling us into the abyss of gloom.

Our Orientation Toward Love

He was a gritty man, a man who would have made Ernest Hemingway proud. He coached football, taught math, and lifted weights. His biceps bulged at 20 inches, and it seemed as though his heart were guarded by 20 more inches of muscle or rock or ice. He showed no emotion.

But for the first time in his life as a father, tears began rolling down his cheeks. His baby girl was leaving for college. And it was time to let go.

His love for her was as real and intense as the secret he held within. He had just shared with his daughter that his roommate was really his lover: His homosexuality was now known by one more of a precious few people.

People may never have the nerve to call him faggot, just as they never would think of questioning his love for his daughters.

All humans, and especially all children, deserve to be raised in loving environments. *And love is not contingent upon one's sexual orientation.*

In today's society, gays and lesbians represent the untouchables. Fundamentalist religions tend to reject them as perverts of nature, and even more moderate groups tend to accept homosexuals only if they remain celibate. In other words, it is acceptable for married couples to engage in acts of lovemaking, yet if gays and lesbians make love, religious groups consider them sinful. In fact, many social groups in general find it difficult to accept any type of public displays of affection among gays and lesbians—this trend exists on television sitcoms as well.

Even American society—predicated on theories of freedom and justice—tends to abhor the idea of gay and lesbian marriage. Even the most accepting people often find it strange to witness two males holding hands or kissing. But when such feelings arise, it is important for us to deconstruct our feelings and investigate their roots.

We are socialized from birth to believe that mommy and daddy kiss and hold hands. Later, in late grade school and junior high, children develop hormones and begin feeling attractions toward each other. Most often the attraction is to someone of the opposite sex. So follows the process of imitating parents, and youth begin holding hands and kissing.

But what about young people who find themselves falling in love with members of the same sex? It is often at this point that parents step in, and if parents fail in their attempts at socialization, society steps in. As sociologist Ernest Becker (1973) finds, a child's sexuality is checked for his or her own good by parents in early adolescence (Becker, 1973). Later, when faced with their attraction to members of the same sex, young lesbian women and gay men will systematically repress their own yearnings in order to fit in with the current social norms and thereby maintain a functional life within society. In this sense, we can define *functional* as meaning free from persecution, overt hatred, and misconceptions.

Social norms teach us not only what love is, but, worse, they also teach which love is acceptable. Thus, feelings of discomfort at the sight of gay men or lesbian women engaging in public displays of affection arise from a long history of socialization into the model that love and attraction are for men to enjoy with women.

Humorist David Sedaris (2000) tells a moving story in his book *Me Talk Pretty One Day*. While growing up, David knew he was "different." He did not like football and remembers that "There were names for boys who didn't like sports" (p. 5). David began learning the acceptable role of males in society. The sickness of this societal response to those who are "other" than we is such that we attempt to coerce, mold, and change people. Indeed, David spoke with a slight lisp and could not pronounce the letter *s*. He faced ridicule from peers when he would lisp, and he gained the label of "faggot" for having such an obvious deformity (vs. conformity). In fact, the school hired a speech therapist to "cure" David, to force him to conform to that which is normal and acceptable. Instead of conforming to something that was beyond his control, David learned to reformulate his speech.

"Me talk pretty one day" is an example of how far David went. He spoke in sentences that never contained the letter *s*. His vocabulary grew while his freedom shrank. The negative sanctions for being different, for being gay, forced David to re-create himself. He altered his speech and gave up his autonomy.

Most colleges offer us a chance to break through this deeply ingrained socialization. We can see and interact with people of all backgrounds. We study with Black, Asian, Hispanic, and White students. We work with people with mild mental disorders. We may even find ourselves as roommates with a gay man or lesbian woman. And it is at such moments of egalitarian interaction that we discover a fascinating truth: We all are *human* beings.

The story of the Good Samaritan reminds us to open our hearts even to those we fear. A Jewish man walked along a path and suddenly was accosted by robbers. They took his money, beat him, and left him on the street. A rabbi eventually came along the path and saw the man, a fellow Jew. But the man was too bloody and too ragged: The rabbi walked on. The man's friends then came along, but, not recognizing their friend, they labeled him a beggar and told him to get out of their way.

Finally, a non-Jew, a Samaritan, came along the road. Seeing the helpless man, the Samaritan knelt, washed his wounds, and walked him into town. Although Jews and Samaritans believed each other to be enemies, deeper *human* truths united the men. Love for one's neighbor mattered more than religion. The Samaritan saw a person in need, a neighbor.

The question to us is, do we see "fags" or do we see people?

When we step outside of our comfort zone and explore new relationships with new people, we find common truths about individuals. The love a gay college student shares with his partner likely sounds much like that of a heterosexual college couple. The struggles with identity and life challenges are difficult enough for college students to handle. Throw into the equation the implanted need to repress a huge part of one's nature—sexuality—and the individual's struggles multiply by a thousand.

By creating an atmosphere of open, nonjudgmental exchange, we encourage discovery in the university. The hope is that, as young leaders, we can bring this atmosphere to the rest of society. Falling in love is a wonderful, painful, and essential experience in our lives. Feelings between two women or two men ought not be degraded because they share the characteristic that all long-lasting relationships seek: mutual love.

The most "sound" argument against gays and lesbians rests on the grounds that they are somehow "perverted" by nature: They could never form a truly loving union because they are not capable of experiencing love, a result of some defect of character or some genetic flaw.

As one, if not the greatest, of the world's prophets urges us, "Stop judging and you will not be judged. . . . Love your neighbor as you love yourself. Do this and you will live" (Luke 6:37, 10:27). A greater perversion exists, then, than being homosexual. This perversion is missing the point of the commandment to love all people without bounds.

Today, the media displays images of gay men—seldom do we see lesbian women, though—on shows such as *Will and Grace* and *Queer Eye for the Straight Guy.* Although these shows create and perpetuate stereotypes of gays as effeminate, asexual (the "best friend you always wanted"), and carefree, they are an initial step toward acceptance. *The crusade for homosexual rights mirrors the civil rights movement.* Indeed, minorities sought some relatively positive exposure to at least bring attention to their crusade. Minorities must fight to tell their real story and not the metaphorical one. The homosexual community hopes for a similar process. Ideally, such shows will at least show people that gays and lesbians are not "evil" and "perverted," always seeking sex in strange places. Rather, they show a *human* side of another oppressed group. Though images of gays as decorators may tend to pigeonhole homosexuals, for now at least we are seeing some nondefamatory exposure of a historically shunned group.

As we enter college, it is important to consider that love cuts across the sexual orientation divide. Perverted love may more correctly apply to the parents who psychologically hinder their children through addictive behavior or through teachings that promote hate. The gay and lesbian community is a loving and accepting one. It knows degradation and marginalization only too well to fall victim to the same abuses it fights. Of course we are all human, and lesbian women and gay men have flaws, too. At the end of the day, our sexual orientations may divide us, but it is our shared orientation to love that will bring us together in understanding.

Christopher Patrick King

Romantic Love

"Romantic love" as we know it came into European culture in about the 12th century. It was conceived as a relationship between an upper class woman and her admirer. The troubadours, who went about making up songs for the entertainment of the nobility, were the carriers of this devotion. They would compose songs and poems for the object of their desire. The love, though, was seen as being essentially unrequited: The two lovers never really got together. It was just a matter of rosy romance and longing, and it always took place outside the bonds of matrimony.

The spirit of this medieval version of romance is marvelously portrayed in the old Nordic myth of Tristan and Isolde. Tristan is sent by his liege, the king of Ireland, to fetch Isolde from her homeland to become the king's bride. During the voyage, Tristan and Isolde drink some love potion by mistake and fall instantly and blindly in love. They cannot help themselves despite the fact that they both owe loyalty to the king. There follows a series of adventures during which it is intimated that the two "lovers" never quite manage to consummate their desires, and the whole thing ends in death. Here we have all the elements of the modern myth of romantic love: Love is most appealing when it is illegitimate and secret. The emotion is seen as so powerful that it simply sweeps the participants away against all their better judgment. The hanky-panky never really gets good, and, in the end, a great tragedy is enjoyed by all. (If you want to read the whole brilliant analysis of the myth, look at the first section of De Rougement's (1941) *Love in the Western World.* It is a rather complex but extremely interesting piece of writing.)

During the last 200 years, the idea of romantic love trickled down to the rising middle class and, finally, to the working class. It also took a rather sharp turn from its early origins and became associated with marriage. In the modern version, romantic love leads, after much ado and complication, to marriage and "living happily ever after," a state so boring that a good story always ends at just that point. In our media, only troubled love is considered interesting.

Knowing the origins of romantic love doesn't explain why the myth persists so vigorously in our own day and plays such a vital part in the mythology that governs our present culture. I would suggest that the myth of romantic love performs several crucial ideological functions. First, it is the great equalizer. We live in a country whose official philosophy is egalitarian but whose real social structure is grossly aristocratic. This presents a problem. Inequality has to be legitimized to a populace raised with some real, if abstract, expectations of equality. Romantic love is perfectly suited to this task. According to the myth, romance is available to everyone equally—rich and poor alike. Everybody has a right to expect the romantic-love-marriage-happily-ever-after sequence in life, and it is only a few errant, mismatched souls who lose out. By putting the love experience at the center of life, the mythology deftly draws attention away from opportunities that are very unequally distributed, such as work satisfaction, a pleasant environment, and security in one's old age.

It seems to matter little that the myth is contradicted by reality. Evidence indicates that happy marriages are the exception rather than the rule. Marital bliss is also highly associated with class position: the rich scoring more frequently than the poor and working class, among whom lack of money is the major source of marital friction. However, because these facts are not openly admitted, the myth can be used to persuade people that unhappiness is their own fault, that they have only themselves, not society, to blame. Average blue-collar workers whose work is frustrating, who are not respected as successes, and whose home lives are equally unsuccessful are forced to believe that their unhappiness is the result of some deep, humiliating flaw in their own makeup. Thus they are kept from seeing that they have problems in common with millions of others and that many of these problems stem from inequalities in the class structure of society. Hope of salvation is kept alive by the persisting belief that "some day" they will find "true love" and live happily ever after. It is our modern secular version of the old "there'll be pie in the sky by and by" religion.

Love as the great equalizer can be seen most clearly in the Cinderella theme, which I mentioned before. The poor but pretty working girl can dream of marrying her boss and becoming not only happy but also rich in the happy hereafter, though in real life it is likelier that the old man will only sleep with her and go back uptown to his wife. The poor young man can dream of marrying the boss's daughter. Love is the magic arena within which we can all become princes and princesses for an hour—and, in our dreams, forever. That this dream of upward mobility through love comes true for a small number of people keeps the myth alive.

The romantic love syndrome also lends itself perfectly to the purposes of advertising and commercially driven popular music. We are all familiar with the fact that the promise of romance is used to sell everything from cigarettes to deodorant to automobiles. How convenient for the advertisers to have delivered to them a nation of frustrated romantics who are desperately looking for any gimmick that might make this love thing work for them.

Independent Woman

The mass media, including various artists of the musical pop culture, emphasize the way we ourselves should be. Looking at the most popular songs on the charts right now, we can see that the idea of women has been changing drastically. As a growing woman in today's society, what is it that I have to be to survive?

All the women I admire are all women being independent. My parents are always telling me, "You know you should learn to be independent; you should not depend on anyone but yourself to take care of yourself." So there is stress about getting the right job, being focused, and being independent. The popular song "Independent Woman" is all about women making their own money and being able to survive without the help of a man. Popular songs do not only continually emphasize the romantic view of love, but they also dictate the characteristics that shape our individual identities. They affect our relationships that we tend to have with the people around us, and the expectations we have of each other and ourselves.

But where do all these contradicting statements about having a relationship come from? Could it be from the songs themselves? "The shoes on my feet, I bought it! The clothes I'm wearing, I bought it! I depend on me!" These are lyrics from Destiny's Child "Independent Woman." Growing up in a family where my parents were divorced, I experienced separation and sometimes had an inner fear that I, too, would end up just the same. It wasn't until I had my own love relationships later on that this fear, in fact, became an inner statement within myself. The relationships I had did not work time and time again. Was I cursed in love? My mind kept circling around one convincing statement: "Relationships do not work!" And with this statement I began to notice why songs with independent-woman themes seemed so often empowering. To hide my fears and give proof to myself of my inner statements about relationships, I cling to the importance of being independent. Of course, when I hear the lyric "All the women [being] independent!" it becomes my theme song. It reminds me of what I need to do to get away from "relationships don't work" and makes my convincing statement all the more convincing. In turn, my very convincing statement in my own mind has had its good and bad effects. A good effect is giving me motivation to do things for myself. The bad effects are alienation, fear, and anxiety. When you are in a relationship, these feelings might drive you and your partner crazy. As one begins to already think something is not going to work out before it develops, it holds a certain negativity that can cause detrimental effects to a relationship. This negativity becomes present in one's self and distorts one's self-perception. A quote I remember from my social psychology class is W. I. Thomas's "If men define situations as real, they become real in their consequence." If you keep telling yourself and your partner that "relationships don't work," chances are it may become a real consequence.

Katherine Ho

Falling In and Out of Love

Now that we have seen why the myth of romantic love enjoys such popularity in our media mythology, let us look at the social psychological mechanisms whereby people convince themselves that they are actually "falling in love." These are beautifully spelled out in a book I recommend to you, *The Adjusted American,* by Putney and Putney (1964). In it, the authors look at traits they regard as "normal neuroses" in our society: the foremost of which is love. Despite some of the changes brought about by the feminist movement, men and women are still taught to find different traits acceptable in themselves. Women are expected to specialize in human relationships, while men specialize in fierce job competition. In the process of teaching us how we should be, society forces us to bury our contradictory impulses. Girls quickly discover that being too smart threatens potential boyfriends. Boys discover that being too emotional makes them the butt of ridicule. *Girls begin to repress their ambitions, while boys repress their emotionality and sociability.* Through such repression we alienate a piece of ourselves, that is, push the unacceptable trait so far out of consciousness that we begin to believe we actually don't have the censored capacity anymore. At the same time, though, we also feel maimed because a piece of us is missing. When we find a member of the opposite sex who likes us, we are prone to project onto that person our own alienated capacities. The woman feels that she has found a man who is ambitious, aggressive, and bold, someone who will protect and shelter her poor, helpless self. The male, on the other hand, feels that he has found a woman who is sociable, affectionate, and emotionally responsive—qualities he longs for in himself but cannot enjoy directly as part of his own personality. Add to these projections all of the little fears by which we live. Are we lonely for friends? Here is a person who will meet all our needs for sociability. Do we regard ourselves as physically unattractive? Here is someone who finds us attractive, and suddenly we feel beautiful. Thus is generated that first "rush" we take to be "falling in love."

The very suddenness of this rush should warn us. Even a person we have only known for 24 hours can induce this high in us. Some even experience "love at first sight." It is obvious that we are not responding to another human being whom we really know—in fact, any number of people will do interchangeably and with equal suddenness. Two years down the road we may look at our former love and wonder what we ever "saw" in the person. What is really happening is something inside ourselves. Temporarily, we have put in abeyance all the self-criticism that usually saddens us. Temporarily, we have granted ourselves the freedom to feel new feelings that we usually deny ourselves. We love ourselves because some member of the opposite sex seems to accept us. The more we have deprived ourselves of self-acceptance, the more helpless we are in the grip of this temporary alleviation, and the more desperately we feel we need this new partner.

The problem is that what we see in our partner is not the real person but all of our own projections. We are just using the other as a screen. Since, in the first stages of a romance, everybody is on their best behavior, these projections are allowed to stand. Neither party wants to interfere with this process. As a relationship wears on, the real people begin to emerge. Now we begin to see that the girl we thought was so wonderfully sociable is really just an obsessive talker, or the boy who seemed so strong and ambitious is really just selfish. Our old fears about ourselves also reassert themselves. They had no intention of disappearing; they only took time off. As we include the new partner in our category of "self," we also begin to project onto our partner the qualities we dislike in ourselves.

At the same time that the illusions are wearing away, we are usually beset by another problem. We aren't terribly good at being honest with other people. We have been taught to be "polite." We are also afraid to alienate the precious new find, so we swallow our anger as it arises. We begin to lie about how the other's love-making really affects us. We pretend satisfaction where actually there is physical discomfort or feelings of embarrassment. We persuade ourselves that it is just our own fault that we find some new habit of the other terribly annoying. We begin to carry a heavier and heavier sack of unvoiced grievances.

As the relationship becomes shaky, a new monster rears its ugly head: possessiveness. Nearly everybody confuses possessiveness with love, and there is a good dose of it in most American relationships. I remember one class discussion of this in which one young woman told us with complete sincerity that she felt nothing negative whatsoever when her boyfriend made love to somebody else. We were all fascinated and astounded by her. Despite her very commonplace physical appearance, her personality made her a completely appealing person. We all envied her obvious inner freedom, but alas this is very rare. Our culture teaches us to be possessive about everything. It does this by making us feel needy at the very bottom of our souls because it destroys our childhood's innocent acceptance of the world and the self. To be needy is to be greedy. So we clutch onto our romantic partners and strangle them in the process.

Somewhere in the process of growing up, we get confused about the boundaries that separate us from other people. In some areas of life, we exaggerate our own separateness: for example, in the cultural belief that we have to hide our inner fears from others because these fears are so private and peculiar. In other areas, we make the opposite error by ignoring the real separateness that limits our power over others and their power over us. Possessiveness in love relationships is just one instance of this kind of mistake. If we look further in this direction, we find a very important guideline I wish you would paste up on your mirror where you will see it every day: "YOU *CANNOT* CONTROL ANOTHER PERSON; YOU *CAN* TAKE CARE OF YOURSELF."

Two ways in which we try to control other people—especially love objects—is to try to rescue and to try to reform them. Let us look at each of these in turn. The rescuer is somebody who is made so uncomfortable—indeed, is so threatened—by another's misfortune or misery that there is a compelling urge to rescue the other person from discomfort. In extreme cases, this is the kind of person who helps old ladies across the street even when they don't want to go. Rescuers all too frequently "fall in love" with deeply troubled persons whom they want to rescue. It never works. First, deeply troubled people are incapable of forming good relationships. Second, to the extent that the target person has some inner strength, he or she will resent being rescued because it is belittling. You can have compassion for others, but at the same time respect them by remembering that people's troubles are also their opportunities to grow. You have no business taking such opportunities away from other people.

The desire to rescue may stem from a fear that the troubled person will attack you if you don't get him or her out of trouble. This fear usually has its roots in childhood experience with a troubled parent who took troubles out on you. As a young child, you were thus forced into the impossible task of rescuing your own parents in an effort to deflect the rage they might inflict on you. It is a defensive maneuver that is functional in the childhood situation but unnecessary when you are an adult, and it will get pretty tiresome if the pattern is repeated continually during adult life.

Another root of the need to rescue others is your refusal to rescue yourself—that is, to take good care of yourself. In this case, what threatens you about another person's trouble is that you have similar troubles you haven't addressed. Learn to recognize the urge to rescue. When you feel it, ask yourself immediately, "Do I need rescuing in this area myself?" If the answer is "yes," then be good to yourself; rescue yourself and, with compassion, leave others to rescue themselves. Above all, never let rescuing get mixed up with falling in love. It is a sure recipe for failure.

Akin to the rescuer is the reformer. This is somebody who develops a love relationship with someone whom they really don't completely like in the anticipation that the unpleasant aspects of the other person's behavior can be reformed. Of course, nobody is going to be perfect in your eyes, but if you find a great deal to love in another person, you are naturally willing to adjust to the few aspects that displease you. You can live with them. If this is not the case, you have no business forming a relationship with the person. Wanting to reform someone is sort of like having a hidden agenda. It will be resented as it begins to surface, and it will be opposed by anybody with any self-respect. Therefore, it will poison the relationship and will not work.

The other side of the coin of "invading" your lover's legitimate turf by rescuing and reforming is that you lose a clear sense of the boundaries that protect you from what others can do to you. You really want to be rescued, reformed, and so on. When your lover doesn't respond the way you want him or her to, you feel that you cannot take care of yourself inside your own legitimate boundaries. "Don't hurt me like this; I cannot stand it" is then what you throw out to your lover. Now you make your lover responsible for your peace of mind, which isn't cricket and will be resented.

You cannot control another person; you can take care of yourself.

Walking In Love

Sometimes I look at the word *"falling"* in the context of "falling in love" and its meaning. Let's say that a person is literally "falling" as in the physical sense. Wouldn't that be considered negative? Sometimes it hurts when you fall. In fact, sometimes you experience such a sudden impact that you fall hard. Similarly, this is the way we have been conditioned in society to be when "falling in love." We experience the sudden impact of romantic love and all its tragedy and anxiety. It hits us! Is this really love?

At times, I think that the word *"falling"* in the context of love can add to the sometimes misleading ideals of romantic love. A healthy relationship does not always maintain the immediate rush that is associated with "falling" in love. The danger in falling is that most times when you fall hard it is difficult to get yourself up from the process of falling. Thinking of my childhood, mother always told me to "walk" because, if I didn't, I might trip and "fall." What about in the context of love? "Walking" in love? I know that perhaps the wording does not sound as appealing as the intensity and immediacy of "falling." Walking in its physical context demonstrates a casual pace, not as immediate as falling, and, hey, if there is danger lurking ahead, you have the capacity to look, listen, and make decisions according to your surroundings.

Sometimes, I think that this is a better word to keep in mind in the context of relationships. *When you are "walking" in love instead of "falling," you might remember to take your relationship at a much slower pace,* therefore reducing the chance of sudden trips and falls along the way. It is a much easier process than the struggle of getting up every time you fall. And of course there has to be a balance. If one person "walks" in love and the other chooses to "fall," there can be an imbalance because one person is pulling or dragging the other to get up, which can lead to emotional fatigue. I think if you keep the idea of choosing to walk in your love relationships, then if there are some forks in the road ahead, and two people cannot agree on which fork to take, it is alright to walk separate ways instead of staying in an imprisoned emotional state.

Katherine Ho

The "Alone Again" Blues

Beset by these problems, our new love relationship begins to suffer. It loses its vitality. It becomes commonplace. The process is somewhat similar to what happens when you buy a new outfit. For a month or two, the new garment makes you feel attractive; then the effect wears off.

It doesn't matter very much whether the two lovers are married or just living together. Sooner or later, one or the other will discover somebody new who holds out the promise of a fresh "falling in love." When this happens, the person who is left behind suffers a very bruised ego, which the person confuses with unrequited love. All the other self-doubts come flooding back. We are "alone again" and feel terribly sorry for ourselves until somebody else shows up and we can begin another round. We can't see the process in this light. The mythology lends enormous legitimacy to our belief that we are suffering from love and that such suffering is perfectly sensible, inevitable, and even biological. That we can suffer to music adds glamour to our plight. We sink into a quicksand of sentimentality.

Let us look at this "alone again" realistically for just a few minutes. It may help to sober us up. First, there probably are only two people in a hundred who will end up for life (happily or unhappily) with the very first person with whom they ever fell in love. This is a very good thing because the younger we are, the less experienced we are in human relationships, and the less we understand ourselves. Thus, when you are 18 or 20 years old, you are in a very poor position to make a sensible choice or to develop a mature relationship. At this point, you have to practice, to get experience. Statistics indicate that the older people are when they marry, the better their chances for a lasting relationship. It is desirable and inevitable that you will move through numerous relationships from which you will learn. Ask older people if they wish they had spent their life with their first love, and you will get a lot of resounding "no's." Most of us who have been around a while know that we could never have grown and developed if we had been stuck with our first choice for a lifetime.

It is also the case that we learn more from "losing" than from gaining relationships. In our previous scenario, in which one partner in a devitalized relationship finds somebody new, we can ask ourselves "which of these two is likely to benefit from the experience?" The answer is, most often, the one who is left behind. The pain this person can experience may teach the person to seek a different kind of partner next time or to make some changes in his or her way of relating to a lover. The one who runs off is just buying in for another round of the same game. That person hasn't learned anything.

Our fear of loneliness blinds us to the fact that what is much worse than loneliness is the lousy, lasting relationship. I have even known couples who, after living together for several years in disharmony and mutual hostility, decide to get married in the hope of improving things. Some married folks have children out of the same motives. Obviously, each of these steps just compounds the difficulties.

In a bad relationship, we have to deny reality. We freeze. We cannot deal with our inner conflicts for fear of shaking the flimsy relationship. All emotional maturation ceases. We carry such a burden of grievances that we feel ourselves to be weaker and less able to face the world alone. Let me give you a rule of thumb: If a relationship isn't fun and rewarding at least 75% of the time,[1] it is time to get out, even if it means being "alone again." The very act of making the break will give you the energy you need to survive.

If you look at your experience in this light, it may help you get a little distance from your emotions when a relationship breaks up. Not everything that causes us pain should be avoided. When you have a cavity, you grit your teeth for an hour and take yourself to the dentist. The same goes for the pain of parting. It isn't going to kill you, and if you listen to the pain intelligently, it can teach you a great deal.

When my students tell me that they are blue because a romance has broken up and they are "alone again," I always have to repress a smile. Here they are on a campus with hundreds of other single folks their own age—all looking for sexual partners—in what sense are they alone? How long can it possibly last? If we could only join into the spirit of a German song that says "Why should I be unhappy because my old boyfriend is gone? Another one is waiting on the next corner." Why does the next corner seem so far away to us at this moment? Might it not even be better to avoid the "next corner" for a while?

One of the reasons we put so much emphasis on the romantic love relationship is that, in many ways, our society makes us lonely. We have no extended family, no small community to which we safely belong. Even the nuclear family is rapidly disintegrating. Social and geographic mobility is so great that our friendships rupture every few years. On top of this, we inherit little of our social position. Each of us has to prove ourselves as an individual in a highly competitive game.

Perhaps most poignantly, our culture offers us no acceptable "touching" relationships with other adults, except the sexual relationship. There is good evidence that indicates that our needs for touching others are very great and very unmet. How far we are from earlier societies in which we could fall back on a fairly large, stable group with which we were indissolubly "in touch." Vivid in my mind is the anthropological film that shows a small tribe seeing one of its members through the ordeal of dying. The dying man is held in a bed made up of human hands. People are lined up on each side and are grasping each other's hands to make a platform on which the dying man lies. Such physical human solidarity is dramatically absent from our lives.

Even further, the meeting of our basic economic needs is organized around the ephemeral sexual bond. When a marriage breaks up, so does a household and an economic partnership. This aspect doesn't yet concern you, but it does hang over the romantic lives of your parents, and, even unconsciously, you see it coming.

There is not a lot you can do about the lack of lasting social bonds in our society. You can join a commune, but even most communes are temporary affairs. Still, *if you understand how these aspects of the social structure affect you, you can take steps to minimize their effect.* In the first place, *don't confuse your need for friendship with your desire for romantic love.* When you are in a new situation at college, make it your first order of business to forge some good friendship bonds. Nowadays these nonsexual friendships may be with members of the opposite sex almost as often as with those of your own. Put some physical touching into these friendships. Treasure them and don't just toss them aside the moment you are in that state of temporary insanity you call love. The women's movement has done us a favor by persuading women to respect their bonds with other women—not always to break a date with friends for a date with a lover. The message also goes for men. If you are in a new situation, it may take a little while to form friendships and you may suffer some loneliness. You don't have to confuse yourself about what it is that you need. Since our attitudes toward friendship are much saner than our attitudes toward romantic love, you will not have nearly so much trouble coping with the need for friends.

Love and Friendship

Valuing friendships can help you with your love relationships in yet another way. *Friendship is a much better model for what you need in a love relationship than the models paraded before you in the media mythology.* These media images are so powerful that, unless we are fortunate enough to have had parents who were happily married (a rare phenomenon), we are likely to be completely confused about love when we first start out. I was in my 30s before it finally occurred to me that, if I wanted to succeed in a romantic relationship, I would have to treat it more as I treated my nonsexual friendships. *I would have to look for the same kind of person whom I sought for a friend.* I realized that, in my life, I had frequently entered romantic relationships with people I would have rejected out of hand as friends.

Nobody pretends that genuine friendship is very close to hate, yet our media constantly pretend that sexual love can come directly out of hate. In the average romantic movie, we can quickly tell which two people are going to fall in love at the end because they are so very hostile toward each other at the beginning.

Qualities we would reject in a friend are made to seem romantic in a lover: the mysterious stranger who is from a culture totally foreign to our own is made to seem attractive, even though in a friend we would quickly see that there were just too many points of difference; the emotionally dangerous character—the Don Juan, the temptress, the wildly jealous person—are all made to look sexually intriguing, even though a friend with these attributes would be seen as pitiable. Since Alice Faye sang "He left me and pawned all my furniture, but he's my man" to a scoundrelly Tyrone Power, the movies have sold us on the charms of masochistic love. We can cut through all this bull very quickly by applying the same criteria to the selection and propagation of romantic partners that we apply to the selection and development of friends.

Using friendship as an analogy is very important because the media seldom instruct us in the actual mechanics of the happily-ever-after. Even our "great" Western literature pictures unhappy and disastrous relationships much more frequently than good ones. *There is a sort of unspoken assumption that happy relationships are at once uninteresting and self-evident.* Nothing could be further from the truth. Really good relationships require enormous intelligence, honesty, and alertness. They never stand still but constantly evolve and change. They teach us who we are in profound, unexpected ways. But, unfortunately, our myth makers have so little experience of real love themselves that their versions are either nonexistent or patently phony, such as the "family-comedies" on television. In the face of this cultural gap, our own experiences with friendship or with the love we have felt for our siblings is all we have to fall back on.[2]

Love and Sex

Why is it that the phenomenon of sex is surrounded by such a cloud of confusion? It is, very simply, *because we are heirs to a culture that has taken a totally mad view of sexuality for many, many centuries.* The sexual revolution of the 1960s only began to scratch the surface of this heritage. If we go back to the myth of Tristan and Isolde and ask, "Why did they have to suffer so long and finally die of their love?" the 12th-century answer comes back loud and clear: *because sex is a sin.* If anything can prove to us that humans are infinitely malleable by their cultures, it should be the fact that Western European Christianity (both Catholic and, later, Protestant) has persuaded generations of people that this most intensely pleasurable of human experiences is something dark and sinister and wrong. It may give you some idea if I tell you that, during the Middle Ages, the Catholic Church recommended the use of a night garment so constructed that a man and wife might have sexual intercourse without touching any part of each other's naked bodies except in the immediate area of the genitals. Sexuality was only tolerated because offspring were seen as necessary to the survival of society. The staggering degree of deeply ingrained repression that it took to turn sexuality into sin twisted human beings into strange shapes indeed. After all, Mother Nature made very sure that we would propagate the race.

Love had to be tragic because sex was wrong. Sex equaled sin and therefore also suffering. Women were especially cut out to pay for the price of sin by bearing children, legitimate or illegitimate. The persecution of prostitutes through the centuries is another aspect of this. The male customers were never prosecuted. It could also be argued that much of the present-day opposition to abortion rests on the secret desire to punish women for enjoying sexual intercourse.

The surprising amount of sadomasochistic sex that has blossomed in our society along with increasing sexual freedom also grows directly out of the sex-as-sinful attitudes. If sex is forbidden, it can only be enjoyed if one is in bondage and if one is being punished at the same moment that one is enjoying the forbidden pleasure. The reason why our pornography is artistically terrible also reflects our fear of sexuality. Pornography ranks so low with us that it only attracts the most mediocre talent.[3]

When I was a teenager, growing up in the very puritan little town of Claremont, California, a group of us once tried to vex our Girl Scout troop leader, Mrs. Lerner, by asking her a question we knew was forbidden on one level but could be asked in innocent curiosity on another. "What about sex, Mrs. Lerner?" we asked one day when that good lady was belaboring us about the sanctity of marriage. She blanched only slightly and then answered very stalwartly—I have never forgotten her phrasing—"Sex is the cement which holds the bricks of a marriage together."

For many years I went about with this image of a rigid brick wall connected in my mind with the phenomenon of sex. It was many years before I came to realize that what we needed to hear from Mrs. Lerner was that sex is more like dancing than anything else: It is very close to the sheer, playful pleasure in physical movement; there is a leading and following, giving and taking on both sides; it is more fun with a skillful partner; it is better when done to music; you can spend the whole evening doing it; and it is greatest with somebody you really like. If sex is taken lightheartedly, like dancing, you will not feel the need to possess every partner with whom you have danced, nor will you expect them to solve all your problems.

Regarding dance there are, let us say, two types of cultures: those whose dancing imitates and initiates into sex and those whose dancing is as totally asexual as dancing can possibly be. Among the former cultures are those of the Polynesians, with their wildly and beautifully hip-swinging dances, and of the Black American subculture, whose physicality influenced the dancing of White mainstream culture during the second half of the 20th century. But in Claremont, in the 1940s, we were clearly in the latter category. Our dance teacher told us with a perfectly straight face that "nice girls don't move their hips when they dance." Of course, our dancing was pathetic and so, later on, was our lovemaking.

I mention my own experiences because you are only a generation or two away from such attitudes. They still run through our culture in innumerable ways. Thus, if you have trouble with sex at first, don't be too surprised; keep trying. But there is an even deeper reason why sexuality does not usually blossom fully when one is very young. Even where sexual puritanism has been overcome, sexuality involves one's being so totally that it suffers by contagion from all of our insecurities. If we have difficulty trusting others, we cannot abandon ourselves totally in their presence. If we are too competitive, we make sex into a contest of skills. If we are unconsciously vengeful toward our partner, we may use sex as a punishment. If we are too dependent on the other person, we may be unable to enjoy sex fully because we would then have more to lose. In short, to the extent that we aren't yet at home with ourselves and in the world, we will inhibit our sexual feelings.

Because sexuality involves your most personal, intimate feelings, you should never let yourself be pushed into doing anything that feels uncomfortable to you. There is no right and wrong here; there is an endless variety of personal tastes and feelings. You must be true to your own. Don't let fads, majority opinion, or the pressure of well-meaning friends and lovers cause you to override your own feelings. I don't mean that you should be totally unadventurous. In this, as in so many things, the Golden Middle Way is usually best.

Sex in the College Environment

As a woman on a college campus, going to parties, meeting new people, and leading a sexually active life, there is nothing that I feel is more important to have control over. In an environment where it is easy to lose control—to fall behind on classes, begin drinking too much, become too wrapped up in the college scene—sex can turn into an uncontrollable, compulsive activity.

I have encountered friends forgetting to use a condom, friends allowing themselves to have sex with people they don't particularly like, friends in relationships having sex with other people—overall, friends being completely careless with this activity. What is it about the college environment that allows sex to run so rampant and be thought of as "no big deal?"

In movies, we see that sex is a huge aspect of college life—movies like *American Pie, Van Wilder, Animal House,* and *Road Trip.* However, sex is also an unspoken aspect of college life. We know that it's going on all around us, yet we often fear to talk about it openly. Sex is a big deal. Whether you're having it with multiple partners, the love of your life, or not at all, sex is an activity with numerous benefits and repercussions.

Depending on where you're from, the frequency in which you've heard this statement may vary: "No glove, no love." For those of you confused on this statement's meaning, the "glove" refers to a condom, and "love" refers to sex. This slogan should be as ingrained in our heads as the advertisements we see on television. This should be the motto of our generation—a generation plagued with the fear of a plethora of sexually transmitted diseases (STDs). AIDS is on the rise again, for various reasons. One is because our current political administration is not strong in implementing sex education programs in school. College is no exception to this—perhaps you saw a video at your orientation discussing what you should do if you are about to have sexual intercourse with someone. The video I saw at my orientation was poorly produced and laughable. It contained metaphoric scenes and barely touched on the repercussions of intercourse. There isn't enough information, even in this modern day and age.

I continue to stress the stakes of having sexual intercourse because the stakes are quite high. Sex has physical, mental, and emotional consequences because sex is a physical, mental, and emotional activity. Once you begin having sex, you are also accepting a number of responsibilities that comes with it. The most important of these responsibilities is contraceptive use. I am on birth control—I have made this decision to ensure that I won't get pregnant. On top of birth control, I still feel condoms are important since birth control does NOT protect you from STDs. I have also protected myself emotionally by abstaining from casual sex.

Sex, to me, is an activity that is meant to create a connection between people. Strangers are not people that I need to have a connection with. In addition, sex is not only a physical act but an emotional act as well, and to give my unrequited emotion to strangers is an impossible thing for me to do.

However, whatever decisions you make, as long as you are prepared for the consequences, it is up to you. Sex is something that should not be taken lightly, and, if handled correctly, it can be an enjoyable and fulfilling part of your life. When you are sound in your decisions and stable with your responsibilities, whether you choose to have sex or not, only then will you be happy with your actions and yourself.

Also, make sure you are informed—blind choices are dangerous. Educate yourself. Most college campuses have a health and wellness center where you can find out information on things that I have not touched on—the different kinds of STDs, where you can get condoms, where you can get birth control, and so on. Most colleges also have counselors who would be happy to answer all of your impending questions on issues like this. College is a place where you should be learning things that will not only benefit you mentally but physically and emotionally as well.

Jasleen Ahuja

Self-Acceptance and Love

What we come back to after all this is our old theme of self-acceptance. When you fully accept yourself, you will not put every potential sexual partner in a position to "choose" or "reject" you. Rather, you will sit back comfortably and wait to see whether you want to accept the other person. You will remain the judge until such time as you are sure the relationship is worth pursuing. Accepting yourself also means being very kind to yourself when a painful parting occurs. It means knowing how to make yourself as comfortable as possible during such a transition. Being kind to yourself doesn't always mean self-indulgence. It may also involve talking some sense to yourself, that is, "pulling yourself together" rather than wallowing in sentiment.

Above all, true self-acceptance does away with the projection mechanism we call "falling in love." A woman who accepts and develops her own strengths doesn't need a man to lean on. A man who knows his own emotions and isn't ashamed to cook himself a delicious dinner doesn't have to wait for a woman to rescue him from his cold, lonely apartment. Thus, *self-accepting people can see potential partners. They will be relating to a real other person, not to a projection of their repressed wishes.* When a parting occurs, they won't feel bad about it any longer than they really want to. *I want to stress to you that you need self-acceptance much more than you need a sexual partner.* Partners will always show up on your doorstep. Let that part of it be—flow with the stream. But make it your serious business to prepare yourself for sexual love by learning to love and take care of yourself.

Let me conclude this section by giving some first aid to those of my readers who are currently suffering the pangs of frustrated love. First, let's distinguish between purely sexual longing and the bruised-ego game. When sexual desire sweeps through you, it is stronger than, but closely akin to, what you feel when you are in a campground and suddenly the smell of coffee and bacon comes wafting over from the next camp. While there is hunger in that emotion, there is also a pleasurable thrill. Your senses awaken, and you feel keenly alive for a moment. Even if you have no coffee and bacon of your own at the time, you still do not experience that emotion as painful. You also don't try to hold on to the emotion or to manipulate it—you just let it sweep through you and then pass on.

The sharp and often excruciating pain of parting from someone you love is very real and should be handled in the same way. Let it blow through you like a storm. Offer no resistance. Like a storm it may blow a few hours or even a few days. Then it is over. These emotions, sexual desire and the pain of parting, are appropriate in certain circumstances and are, ultimately, not destructive. The short storm we can all endure.[4]

The emotion we want to become free of is the prolonged session with the bruised ego—the "alone again" era of self-pity and the internal argument over what you "could have done" or "should have done." Chronic jealousy during an ongoing relationship is in the same class of repetitive feelings that seem to hang around for months. This pain doesn't sweep through and disappear because it is not a spontaneous emotion but your mind chewing endlessly on its wounds. You have two people inside you: the accuser, who blames you for what happened and predicts further catastrophes, and the defender, answering back, "It wasn't my fault." And, frequently, even a third person can be present: "If you weren't so neurotic you wouldn't be having these feelings." This is the accuser again, catching you unaware whenever you have self-doubts and are vulnerable. Your mind is coming and going in gloomy circles.

Our first impulse is to run away from the mess inside: Perhaps we get drunk or overeat or try to sleep 24 hours a day. Or we try an internal manipulation to get rid of the pain, trying to argue ourselves out of it. All of this pain avoidance actually can make the hurt worse and cause it to hang on longer than would otherwise be the case.

When such pain hits you, go somewhere quiet by yourself and just sit with it. This does not mean thinking about the pain. In fact, it is best not even to give a name to your feeling, like calling it "jealousy" or "anxiety" or "frustration." These names all incorporate value judgments: "I shouldn't be jealous" or "Why, why am I anxious again?" All this does is carry you off into a train of self-punishing thought. So don't even give the pain a name; just feel it as a physical sensation. Notice where in your body the pain is centered. Some of my students have found it useful to write down on a piece of paper a detailed description of their physical symptoms. Being in touch with these symptoms is just like feeling a sprained ankle or a headache or like visiting a sick friend: You aren't going to argue with your friend about being sick. Maybe, if he or she is very sick, you don't even talk. You just sit there. Perhaps you hold your friend's hand. (You can hold your own hand if it helps.)

When you are aware that a train of thought has carried you off the pain, bring your mind gently back to it. Absolute concentration is beyond us, so don't become critical because thoughts carry you off. They are part of the process. Just bring the mind back to the pain whenever you become conscious of having wavered. Rather than running away from the pain, you should feel yourself moving toward it. Welcome the pain as a chance to communicate with a usually hidden part of yourself—a chance to heal an old wound, which is essentially what the pain really is. Do 30 to 60 minutes of this. Then, do half an hour of vigorous physical exercise and take a shower. Do this even if you have to force yourself. Take a firm hand.

Make it a point to use your time alone for something you really enjoy. Go to bed early with a good murder mystery and a nice snack. Go for a walk in the mountains, or look up a friend you've been wanting to see. A physical change of scene, even a short one, helps a lot.

Repeat the therapy daily as long as the pain persists.

Real Love

Having trampled as hard as I could on the popular notion of romantic love, I need, now, to talk a bit about real love. (M. Scott Peck's 1978 book *The Road Less Traveled* also addresses this issue with much wisdom.) Is love possible? How do you know when you've got it? And how do you pick a partner with whom it might work? Finally, what does it feel like?

Beginning with the last question, I would say that it feels as though you are being well taken care of, you have the comfort of a real friend, and the relationship is fostering the sanest and best part of yourself while overcoming the most neurotic parts. You have found meaning on the deepest emotional level. The lovemaking, particularly, comes up to and past your highest expectations and previous experiences. Wonderful, you say—where do we start?

I think that the first thing I want to impress on you is that, in evaluating a potential or current partner, you pay attention to deeds and not to words. Words are cheap and, frequently, are in inverse proportion to real feelings. "Romantic" men or women—those good at whispering sweet, glib nothings in your ear—should be considered suspect. Rather, look at what your partner does. Does he or she keep you waiting frequently and occasionally stand you up? Or do you have the feeling that you can rely on your partner? Is he or she a comfort in a crisis? Did your partner take care of you when you were ill? Does your love keep his or her perspective when you lose yours and help you back to sanity? In the little day-to-day things, is there thoughtfulness and consideration? Does your partner go out of his or her way to fill the car with gas when you have to make a long drive? Does your love remember your favorite flavor of ice cream when he or she goes to the store? Did your partner jump in and type that paper for you when your typist was sick and you were up against a deadline? Did he or she take pains to be good to your parents when they visited? Can you count on your partner not to embarrass you or quarrel with you in front of other people? Does your love flirt like mad with others when you are in company? In short, is there kindness?

These are the sorts of things to watch for if you are wondering whether you are loved. Turned around, they are the questions you must ask yourself if you want to know whether you are able to give real love.

It will probably occur to you that it takes a considerable period of time to discover the answer to these questions. True! That is why instant love is always partly phony. It may take a year or two before you experience a crisis with which your partner might have helped. This is a lengthy process. Because we are all on our best behavior when a relationship first begins we really have to wait until this wears off to see how our partner does then. All of this means that it takes a couple of years to know another person. Your deepest commitment should never be made early.

Which brings us to the subject of commitment. I am wary of the kind of commitment people make when they marry, not because commitment itself is bad but because in marriage we make a promise about all future time, and I am just not sure that this is possible. The danger, I think, lies in the feeling that once the marriage vows have been said, nothing more needs to be done—that the thing will take care of itself. This is never true. The best relationship requires continual readjustment. In a sense, two people who are lovers constantly negotiate their reality in what is a continual process of communication.

The basic requirement for this communication is absolute honesty. This doesn't mean that you have to discuss every little feeling. But it does mean that when you feel at all strongly about something in your relationship, you say so immediately. You don't suppress or withhold important feelings. In a very interesting study of upper middle-class marriages in the United States, *Sex and the Significant Americans* (Cuber & Harroff, 1966), the authors found, through lengthy interviews, that most marriages begin as vital relationships, but the majority of marriages become "devitalized"—dull and meaningless. *I am convinced that suppressing and withholding feelings is the first step toward such devitalization.* This is particularly true in the area of sexual love. When this is disappointing and nothing is said or done about it, the sense of deprivation will always eat into the relationship like an acid.

In addition to communicating about your relationship, you must also communicate about what is going on around you generally. Perhaps you are off on a vacation, but you just aren't having a good time. Do you suffer in silence or let your partner know? I have often thought that one of the reasons Ted and I have such a good time together is that we are always open to changes in what we are doing. We very frequently walk out on movies or workshops in Buddhist meditation or whatever else we undertake. If it isn't going well for one of us, there is always immediate communication that enables us to find out quickly when something isn't working.

Let me also give an example of renegotiating the relationship. When Ted and I started living together, we had separate incomes and kept our financial affairs separate—keeping track of what we put out for common purposes and splitting that. After some years of this, we decided to throw all our money together and stop keeping complicated records. However, we found, after a couple of years of this arrangement, that we did less communicating about how money should be spent. Sometimes a large amount was spent on a project only one of us was really interested in. This created some resentment. For example, I felt strongly about a trip to Europe to visit my aunt, whereas Ted would rather have saved the money for building a house. Yet the Europe trip just sort of developed without any explicit discussion of alternative uses for that money. As soon as we realized what was happening, we decided to go back to our previous, separate money arrangement. Things are once again going smoothly on the financial front. The neurotic part of me wanted to whisper that this was a failure in the relationship. I told it to keep quiet. As usual, that neurotic voice turned out to be dead wrong.

All of us have neurotic fears about relationships. Sometimes we are terribly afraid of losing love. At other times, we may be afraid of not being able to continue to give love ourselves. Everyone has his or her version of such fears. If *commitment* means anything, I think it means the determination to keep our sanest, best self forward and not to load our fearful neuroses on our partner. Again, I want to use an example from my own relationship since I know it best. Ted and I observed that each of us has a neurotic self. We gave them names to make it easier to communicate about them. Mine is "Little Inge, the depressive, insecure self who fears loss of love almost to the point of ruining a relationship. Ted's neurotic part is called Lionell. Lionell has a terrible temper and is mean. We discovered that we only had bad fights when we both happened to be neurotic at the same time. Lionell's temper frightens Little Inge, who starts cringing and crying. Lionell cannot stand cringing, and we are off on a fight. As long as one of us is feeling sane, we can handle the other one's neurotic side, but, when we are both crazy, Pow! We can understand all of this and communicate about it as long as we are feeling sane, but Little Inge and Lionell refuse to communicate. Over the years we have become much better about keeping the neurotic selves on the sidelines. I dislike anger and conflict, so it was hard for me to realize that, to get over Lionell, Ted needs a sane friend who will just sit by until the anger passes. For a long time I repressed a desire to laugh at Lionell for fear he would become even more infuriated. When I finally started to giggle, I discovered that laughter was the best way of banishing Lionell. Ted, on the other hand, has learned how to banish Little Inge by letting her know that he couldn't stand her for long, while at the same time encouraging the saner part of me to take command. Over the years, I have gotten so much positive feedback for being a sane person and so much negative feedback for being Little Inge that Little Inge pops up less and less. This is, of course, a great relief for me. Lionell, too, is becoming rarer.

From my own experience, I believe that a good relationship can help us overcome basic neurotic patterns. We can admit our faults in this safe setting. We can also, by being very honest about our feelings, experience a sense of being accepted. Even our most foolish feelings or secret thoughts can be expressed, and, lo and behold, we are still loved! The trouble with putting up a front is that we always suspect that if anybody looked behind the wall, they would discover us to be dreadful, icky monsters. Just let those foolish ideas and fears see the light of day, and we are reassured that we are really all right.

It is a somewhat amusing fact that when we share a deep, frightful secret about our inner selves with another person, we almost always find that our disclosure seems perfectly harmless to our friend: "So that is your most secret sexual fantasy; that's okay, as long as you're enjoying yourself" or "So that is your secret fear—well, well. I'm going to the store. Do you need anything?"

In living with another person—whether in marriage or just living together—we necessarily have to compromise to get along. Our society is so diverse that we come to such a setting with habits and expectations different from our partner's. It requires a certain openness and humor to deal with this. For example, Ted and I used to wrangle about clothes hangers. He felt that his hanger arrangements were being destroyed, while I felt he was just very picky. One day, when he was watching me put away the laundry, he began to laugh. As he watched me, he realized that we just lived in two different worlds when it came to clothes hangers.

"I see," he said, "that when you are hanging up our clothes you just reach behind you blindly into the closet for a free hanger."

"Of course," I replied. "What do you expect me to do?" It came out that, for Ted, there are three or four different types of hangers for different purposes. Wooden hangers are for coats and heavy sweaters, plastic hangers for good shirts, and wire hangers for anything else. To me, a hanger is just a hanger, and I am quite capable of hanging an old work shirt on Ted's best hanger without thinking a thing about it. We had a laugh over it when we saw it just that way. Another couple we know discovered one day, during a wrangle over cleanliness, that one of them was angry because the other never cleaned the top of the refrigerator. The culprit had never really thought about the top of the refrigerator as a place. It just didn't exist for him.

Ted and I have also found that there is a shortcut to ending fights, but you probably shouldn't try to take it if you are still having trouble expressing anger in a useful, negotiable way. The shortcut seems to lie in realizing right in the middle of some squabble how comic we are and how utterly trivial the cause of the fight is. Once, while watching ducks in a pond, we started laughing at the occasional squabbles ducks get into with each other. These usually occur when they run into each other or both go for the same morsel of food. There is a terrific moment of quacking and flapping of wings. Then, before you know it, they are off gliding along the pond again. Ted said, "Our fights are like that—just quacking ducks who have temporarily collided." Since then, we sometimes just say "quacking ducks" in the middle of a squabble and laugh it off then and there.

As you move into a relationship, try to get a feel for how the communication is going and how well you can work out differences. How to make an initially good choice is rather more difficult to say because everyone's choice is different. Luckily, no two people have the same ideal lover. I would like to make just two points. First, avoid becoming deeply involved with a partner who wants a lifestyle distinctly different from your own. You may not discover this right away and may find yourself in love in such a situation. You will have to make major and painful comprises. It is certainly better to discover this before a strong relationship develops. If your partner is very interested in a career, while you want lots of children, or if your partner wants to live in the country, while you love New York City, your relationship will be hard to sustain. Long-distance relationships often arise for students who are highly mobile. These are tough at best and should be avoided if you can see them coming.

Finally, avoid the person who is on the rebound from a previous love affair or, indeed, anyone who is in a temporary state of emotional collapse. Someone who is deeply disturbed is likely to grasp at any straw. If you are that straw, you may find yourself drawn into the disturbance. Or you may find that when the emotional disturbance of your partner wears off, so does his or her need for your support. Your best bet is to choose someone who seems to have his or her life together and is able to get along alone for a while between partners. Such folk have enough energy available for a successful relationship. Avoid romances with married people who are cheating on their partners. They are either confused or dishonest, both qualities that make for poor relationships.

Above all, there should be a sense of playfulness, lightness, and fun in a relationship. Friendship and kindness should be joined with the play of sexual ecstasy. In such a relationship, we are able to become children again in the best sense. Yet, at the same time, there is sufficient emotional maturity to support the relationship through bad times as well as good. Such a love is one of the greatest joys to be had in this life. It is worth looking for and working toward. Certainly there is always an element of luck involved in whom you meet when you are looking for a relationship. We can maximize our chances by becoming wiser people.

If the good partner is not available at the moment, spend the time learning to love yourself and your friends. That is the best foundation for loving others.

A Postscript About AIDS

Having written much of this very positive and sexually permissive chapter on love in the 1980s, before the AIDS epidemic was really upon us, I now find that I must sound a very serious, cautionary note. I didn't change the chapter because I hope that AIDS will not put our culture back where it was before the sexual revolution of the 1960s and 1970s. While I trust that we will not become puritans once again, I realize that the chapter comes out of the life experience of someone who was fortunate enough to be sexually active in that brief hiatus between Victorianism and the AIDS epidemic.

A careful study of college campuses in 1990 found that students tested positive for HIV at the rate of 2 per 1,000. I doubt whether that picture could have improved or even remained the same since that time. Yet studies found that most students continued risky sexual behavior because they felt invulnerable. That, too, has probably changed. When I asked a class of 20 students how many had changed their sexual practices because of AIDS, every hand went up, accompanied by moans and laughter.

Two per thousand looks like a very slim chance, but remember that every time you have unsafe sex, your risk of contracting the disease increases. By the time you have exposed yourself to 10 different partners, your odds are 2 per 100. The same would be true if you were with a single partner who is having sex with other people. When it comes to a fatal disease, such a risk is unacceptable. The sixth edition of

Robert Kastenbaum's (1998) *Death, Society and Human Experience* states, "The leading cause of death among young adults (ages 25–44) in the United States in cities with populations of 100,000 and over is AIDS, the outcome of HIV" (p. 10).

AIDS: The Fears of a College Student

I am a college student, and I fear the unknown: I fear the places people have been and what they have done, I fear disease, and I fear the HIV virus. I fear this virus not because I am promiscuous or lead a promiscuous lifestyle; I fear getting too close to someone who might be infected. How am I supposed to ask someone I am building a relationship of trust with if there is a possibility he could be positive? How do you know where they have been, who they have been with? Is it insulting to ask your partner to get an AIDS test? Is asking my partner to submit this information to me a signal that I don't trust this person? Each person I start a new relationship with has the potential to get serious, possibly lead to marriage, and certainly has the potential for sexual contact.

Sex is very much a part of the college atmosphere because young people are exploring. Exploring everything they had restrictions on at home. As college students, we have accepted responsibility, taken on the challenge of higher education, so we should be responsible enough to handle sex, right? Handling sex is understanding consequences, thinking about our futures, and understanding how to protect ourselves. By the time people enter college, they have been lectured to about, educated in, questioned about, and tested for HIV. Ignorance should not be the problem.

So what is the answer? AIDS is out there, but, unfortunately, it is something that is hidden. The only way to protect yourself and your partner is through safe sex, no sex, and good communication and trust. It is okay to ask your partner to use a condom. Safe sex is the responsibility of both partners and should not rest on one side or the other. It is okay to ask your partner to wait for sex, if you are scared or unsure. If your partner cannot respect your choice, then maybe you should reevaluate whether this person is someone you want to be with. Keep dating fun and exciting, don't allow AIDS to scare you away from relationships and meeting new people. Let AIDS be a reminder to be safe, to be aware and informed.

Erin Cora

Notes

1. Ninety-five percent is ideal and possible, but if you have 75%, you may have a base you can develop from.

2. Parent-child relationships are usually less useful as analogies because of the inequality inherent in most of them.

3. For a delightful exception, and a rare female perspective, see the Kensington Ladies' Erotica Society's *Ladies Home Erotica* (1984).

4. If you suffer from prolonged, chronic, or extremely intense depression, you may be suffering from an inherited biochemical imbalance. There are now medications that are extremely effective in such cases. Consult a medical practitioner who specializes in antide-pressive medication. Your college psychiatric clinic would be the place to start.

CHAPTER 12

Trouble With Parents

The last time I went home, I realized that I was visiting my parents' house—not coming home. It was a sad feeling, but also a feeling of independence and maturity. I had to say goodbye to my childhood and the familiarity of my hometown, but I realized that I have a whole adult life of my own to look forward to.

—Eve McCullah (former student)

Cut Off

I left home 2 days after my high school graduation for a job at a summer camp. It was my first real job and my first time away from home. I was going to save all my money so that I would have spending cash for the next year while I was in school. I knew that college was going to be expensive, so I didn't want to ask my parents for more money than I had to. I had it all figured out. I got home about a week before I was going to start college. I had just enough time to shop for clothes, buy a new backpack and some notebooks, and get a new haircut. I couldn't wait to go shopping with my mom. Then I got the surprise of my life. She wasn't going to pay for anything. I had earned money; that's what it was for. So much for my plan to save money. Not only that, but I was now expected to buy everything on my own, everything from toothpaste and shampoo to food to cleaning supplies and laundry soap. And I was still living at home. My parents cut me off from everything without warning. I couldn't believe that I could ever feel so unwelcome in my own home. I coped, though. I've done fairly well for myself working two jobs and going to school full-time. My mother has started to resent my independence, but really it's her own fault.

Kristin Rydberg

When I started plans for the second edition of this book, my friend and colleague Dorothy Mariner said, "You should put in something about trouble students have with their parents." As soon as she said it I thought, "Why of course! I've heard plenty about that subject over the years." In fact, next to grades and love, parents are surely the most frequent cause of vexation among students. So I took the opportunity to open up this subject with some classes that were using my book. The response was immediate. When I asked who was having difficulties with parents, most hands went up.

You Can't Go Home Again[1]

One young man says, "You come home and they think you are still the same age as when you left. I've been living at school since I was 15, and my parents still treat me like they did when I was 15."

A young woman chimes in, "When I go home, suddenly I'm back with having to be in before midnight, or my mother will lie awake and worry until I come home."

Another says, "How do I let them know that I don't need that much parenting anymore? I feel myself falling back into being-your-child-again, and at the same time I witness them go through the transformation into we-are-your-parents. They never see you in any other role—when you return home, it's this weird time warp—as if you have never been away."

Another says about going home, "I was a guest, but I was also responsible once again for all the old assignments. I had to clean up my room when they wanted me to, not when I wanted to."

"A funny thing happened between me and my mom. It was my birthday and she came to the dorm to surprise me. I really resented it. I felt she was getting on my turf. We did talk about it and sort of straightened out our feelings."

Some students found they missed their parents. There is a temptation to slip back into familiar roles. "You kind of want the child role, and they want it for you. It is such a contrast to the independence at school."

"I used to just want to get out of the house and be with my friends, now I'm with friends all the time, and I like to spend time with my parents. When I go home, it's a lot better."

"When I come home, it's strange. It's as if I'm not living there anymore. I'm like a guest. My parents took everything out of our rooms, each child as we left home. It feels so weird."

Here somebody asked, "Would anyone want to go back and live at home?" A chorus of resounding "no's" follow.

At the point of leaving home, many students find parents hanging on too hard. "They ask, 'Why don't you come home and visit this Easter, Christmas, or stay all summer?' I want to spend some of that time with my friends."

"My mother raised me. She never went to college and had it hard. Every dime went to me. She lived for me. I took skating and every kind of lesson. She lived her life for me. I could feel that even when I was 10 years old. So I went away to college, and she calls me every day, sometimes three or four times a day. She is my best friend, but I wonder if it's always going to be like this. She calls her own mother that often. When I'm married, will this go on? She does treat me like I'm 15. When I go home for summer, I have a 12 o'clock curfew."

"My parents were divorced, and at first I lived with my father. Then my mother remarried, so I went to live with her. We grew amazingly close. Now I'm out here. Last year, I was in Connecticut, and she could deal with that. She really wants me to come home. Then she brings up that my private college is too expensive. I have to look her squarely in the eye and say, 'Mom, I'm too old, 20 years old.' You've got to teach your parents that the person they raised is now a young adult."

My class discussions were with students at small private residential colleges. To balance this bias, I got some feedback from a class at a community college, where most students live at home. Surprisingly, a slight majority of these students were very well satisfied with their arrangements. In some cases, parents seem to have given the child adult status as they entered college:

"My relationship at home with my parents is good. After high school, where my grades were scrutinized by my parents, college has been totally opposite. They leave me alone about my grades. Ironically, I always end up telling them things anyway. I think our college relationship was a positive step in my maturation to adulthood."

"They basically stay out of my way. They understand that college, working, and friends can make life hard. Their main complaint is that I'm not home enough— I'm never there to talk to, to help pick up around the house, or to watch TV. I have two jobs and school, so it gets hard. All in all, I'm happy with the living arrangements at home."

In some cases, I had the impression that students who live at home are more willing to settle for a lack of autonomy because the arrangement is otherwise so useful to them. "I think my relationship with my mom is the same as it was in high school. I still have a midnight curfew, my boyfriend of 2 and a half years still can't come home when my mom is not home, and I still have to help around the house. It hasn't changed at all. It's a great relationship—we get along—almost never fight."

Another says, "I'm not saying our relationship is perfect, cause by far it isn't, but I can tell you the more I respect them, the better it gets. So maybe kids should respect their parents more; after all, they do know a lot more than us."

Those who reported not liking life at home had many of the same complaints as those voiced by students living away from home, only in the former case the conflicts have a greater impact on the student's life. "Living with my parents is difficult during college because they tie everything I do to my grades. Their control level is tremendous. Because they are paying for my education, everything in my life must not be private. They always nag at me to do my homework."

"They put a lot of pressure on me by trying to do family functions and continuing family togetherness. They don't understand that, as we get older, we want to be with friends."

"Living at home while going to school is very strained. I receive no financial or emotional support, and there is no location in the house to study for classes and exams."

The Most Hurtful of Loves

It is truly a simple equation. Adults choose to have children. They value their children, want them to be safe. They want the best for their children. Harm is the last thing in the world they would wish upon them. What could go wrong with this happily-ever-after picture?

Unfortunately, most young adults will know that the story most certainly does not end happily. Our generation's reality is that most children are estranged from their loving parents. Alienated, can't wait to get away from them, why don't they ever *get* me—thoughts like these race through the minds of countless children. They feel so helpless trying to fix such a fundamental dilemma that their only reflex is to escape and avoid it if at all possible. The parents, in all their decades of worldly wisdom, are equally as puzzled as to why they cannot connect with their own offspring. The truth, according to this author, is painfully simple.

Rarely does a single soul, in our hectic consumer-driven lives, ever take the time to stop and understand what makes each of us tick deep down inside. It is a long and tedious journey through personal issues that we tend to never give a second thought to. And, in the end, we may come to realize that no one really knows the first thing about what the hell they are doing every second of every minute of every day. My wandering words are getting at the underlying point: Kids don't get why their parents give them trouble and criticism. Parents don't understand why their kids don't listen and appreciate their "guidance and advice."

A translation is desperately needed.

A strange and clearly unfortunate phenomenon seems to happen when people "grow" from child to adult to parent. They almost completely forget what it was like to be children and become maniacally egotistical about how age somehow automatically brings wisdom. They fall into a complex where they can do or say no wrong, and they take on the crusade-like duty to point out every error that their children make. Arguably, they care a great deal about their children and do not want to see them injure themselves by behaving unwisely. However, a discrepancy appears to develop like an impregnable oil spill polluting the pure lake of care taking. They do not realize that their critical comments are destructive to the self-esteem of their developing children, far more devastating than any foolish error the children could make on their own.

The phenomenon continues and is emphasized in high-achieving immigrant families. Immigrant parents who have struggled to stand on their own feet in an alien country have no time for or comprehension of luxurious concepts such as happiness and satisfaction with one's life. They simply tell their children to be doctors, regardless if they want to or not, figuring that the stability will inevitably lead to "happiness." "What's there not to be happy about?" they think. So they yell, and the children, who have been watching their liberal American counterparts, become traumatized for life with unforeseeable consequences, without the parents ever thinking they made a single wrong move. And if you ever try to tell a parent that they are doing a poor job parenting, so help you God. This little itty bitty misconception is the root cause for centuries of potentially constructive yet tragically derailed families.

Note to parents: Listen to what you say, take a step back. Think about it. There is no rule that says you have to become an echo of your own parent.

On the flipside, we kids are not free from all responsibility. Most of it, yes. I empirically justify that by saying babies do not know how to problem solve and should not be held accountable for the ignorance of their parents. The issue of baby ignorance unfortunately endures well into adolescence, adulthood, then ultimately parenthood—circle of life. Our job, as kids of ignorantly loving parents, ought to be situational realization. The truth is that we have very few weapons in our arsenal. Learn to know that they mean well, remind yourself that they may not know what negativity they are bringing into your life, and, most important, learn from their mistakes so that your children will not have to suffer the same fate. More progressively, you might attempt explaining to your parents how you feel when they criticize you, but we know that in some of our families our voices do not carry the weight of the wind. In all likelihood, you may be blown back with a "you're too young to understand" or something to that effect. Emotional expression is truly not an option for many of us. Do not feel badly; you are most certainly not alone. Certain actions you may want to avoid, however, are yelling back aggressively, slinging insults, taking up smoking or drugs for indirect attention, and so on. In the end, be smart about it by not ruining your future. Be smarter than your parents were.

They love you. You love them. Both want harmony and warm fuzzy feelings above all else. They just kind of lose their way and forget the goal in the ho-hum of typical life. This is the dear price we pay for being so ambitious monetarily while being so careless with human fundamentals. And know that no BMW will bring your family back together. Ever.

Lawrence Lu

A Culturally Patterned Conflict

These conflicts are so common, even when relations in the family have been good, that we must look for a pervasive cultural pattern. The problem is that for 18 years, your parents protected you, felt a tremendous responsibility for you, tried to ease your path and warn you about the pitfalls of life, and now, suddenly, they have to shift gears. They have to trust the wisdom of their own child rearing, and they have to trust you to survive your own mistakes. They have to restructure the whole relationship.

At the same time, in our culture, a child is expected to leave home and become a full-fledged adult during the late teens and early 20s. Unlike the situation in many other societies, children are not supposed to remain blindly obedient to their elders. There must be a "breaking free." You all sense this and try to act accordingly. It is, indeed, difficult to go from a highly structured home situation into a very unstructured college situation.

As you meet the cultural requirements of thinking for yourself, you encounter disagreements with your parents. As one student put it, "Can you love your parents and not necessarily agree with them? If you express your disagreement, can they hear where you are coming from such that it doesn't mean that you don't love them? If I ever disagreed with my dad, it would be World War III." I asked her if she had actually tried an open disagreement. She said she had not. I urged her to try but be sure that, for her part, the disagreement wasn't part of a desire to reject him in her turn.

Often students take some issue home from a college class in the wild hope that they might succeed in driving their parents crazy. During the civil rights movement, I taught race relations and was often amused at the delight with which students latched on to this issue because it was one on which they could feel morally superior to their parents.

Breaking away is better confronted on concrete issues of parental control: for example, when they demand that you come home by midnight or insist that you have to clean your room on time. Differences of opinion work better if you are just exploring your new ideas with your parents, rather than against them.

One slightly older student told us that he had a terrible time with his conservative Jewish relatives, who became outraged when he let them know that he was no longer eating kosher. I asked him, "Who brings it up?" He said, "I guess I do." "So," I said, "why don't you just let sleeping dogs lie? They might feel much happier if they didn't have to argue the point with you. After all, on your own, you are free to cook however you like." This student seemed surprised when I told him that you don't really have to tell people everything that you think and feel. Choose your time and place and choose your battles wisely.

Issues With Immigrant Families

Much of our trouble with parents stems from an organic, generational divide. Our parents grew up with a set of experiences and values that, for the most part, differ vastly from ours. Our base assumptions about life and the rules governing it are different. For those of us who are children of immigrant parents, this barrier of communication is compounded by a problem of different cultural expectations. Our parents bring with them their cherished values to a new land of opportunity, perhaps not always explicitly hoping for instant material success but at least for the rewards afforded by an abundance of opportunities. They do this as much for themselves as for their children, but one can be certain that once children do come along, everything becomes about their children.

Children of immigrant parents grow up with the perception that their parents sacrificed everything to build better lives in a new country for them, and, indeed, they practically did. I've often wondered if I could have the inner strength and conviction to leave every childhood landmark behind and completely displace myself by moving to another country and speaking a foreign language for the rest of my days. The weight of such a sacrifice is awesome to us, and we grow up with tremendous pressure, implicit if not explicit, to succeed, in school and in a career. This kind of pressure usually prescribes a very narrow path of success, which we, as American children of individualistic freedoms, chafe under. Our parents were so careful in building a measure of material comfort; how can we take their efforts for granted and throw caution to the wind when it comes to building our own lives?

How can we possibly hope to reconcile these differences? On one hand, we owe everything to the sacrifices our parents made for us, the sacrifices they made before we were born, and the sacrifices they made for us while we were growing up. Our parents' old world values have also been instilled in us. For everything we do that makes our parents beam with pride, we also beam with pride, at first because we want to make our parents happy but then later because we realize there's a certain validity to the kinds of successes they've expected of us. At this point, we know that we are truly our parents' children—we've internalized the expectations they've always had of us, even if some of these expectations were never intended.

We then become two people in one. One sits on our left shoulder, tugging us toward emotional, intellectual, spiritual growth, while the other sits on our right shoulder, demanding practical rewards, a respectable salary, an upwardly oriented career path. When our parents chime in with their ideas on how we should plan our lives (as they're often want to do), we just as often become resentful of their interference. As others have stated, though, we often lend the advice of elders other than our parents more credibility than we do our own parents. The reality is that our resentment may stem from the fact that some part of our inner selves do agree with our parents, and we don't know how to deal with this conflict, as it is both an inner one and an outer one.

Before you can engage your parents in a mature, levelheaded discussion, you have to reconcile your own conflicting desires, or at least realize that this will be a milestone you have to reach before you can hope to move on. Remember that a perfect solution is unlikely but that what you need perhaps most of all is room to make your own mistakes. After all, as immigrants, they made a huge gamble in coming here to the United States. It can only be fair for you to be allowed the same freedom, if not so drastic.

Ultimately, your struggle between your parents' ideas and your own ideas of how your life should be lived will help you both grow toward some mutual understanding. It's important to realize that, like you, your parents are people, not unchanging monoliths imposing themselves on you. They aren't perfect, but they're full of hope for you. They only want the best for you, and there may even come a time when they come to agree with your vision for your own life, as long as you're happy.

Because what would all their sacrifice have been for, if you're not?

Andy Wang

Real Love Situations

Where there has been real love between children and parents, the difficult transition period will pass. It is always surprising to college seniors how much their parents have matured in 4 years. A few filial relationships are so good that the struggle never happens. After listening to the class discussion for some time, one young woman said, "I am really amazed to hear all this because I still live at home with my father, but we don't have any conflict. I think he has always sort of treated me as an equal. I am very comfortable in the situation."

"I live with my dad and grandfather now. It's not like living at home. I do everything now like I would if I had an apartment. We are three independent males. We come and go as we want. We do our own laundry. I don't feel like leaving home at all."

"On my 18th birthday, my father brought home some beer, and we drank it together. It was sort of a coming-of-age ceremony. He tells me dirty jokes, and we hang out together. He seems more like a friend and advisor than a parent."

"Even when you're 30, they'll still have the chicken soup ready. But I think college is the time to branch out. My parents and I are separating, but the relationship exceeds what we had in high school."

In these healthy families, parent and child may enjoy role reversal, which the child's new adulthood makes possible. An older student said, "My daughter graduated from medical school. We were going to her own home. We were her guests. She was making all the arrangements. What a feeling to have a total role reversal. My daughter worried about my son being late, and I thought, 'Oh, that's what I used to do.'"

"Since my brother and I left home, our parents, who are both teachers, are spending more money on us. They spent a lot on my brother's wedding. So now my dad wants to get a truck next year, and I'm trying to find a way to help him because they can't afford it, and I want it for him so badly. He always supported me. Now that I'm out of the house, I want to give back."

"I live with my dad but plan to move out so he can start dating by himself without my setting it up (laughter). Has anybody here got a single mom?"

Neurotic Family Situations

Unfortunately, a great many parent-child relationships are deeply neurotic and tense. Here, the struggle to break away can be traumatic for both sides. One young woman told us, "My mother tries to bribe me to quit school and move back in with her. She keeps phoning me offering me money, clothes, and other things. It makes be feel terribly guilty because I know she is living alone now and hates it."[2]

Here I had to jump in with both feet: "You have absolutely no reason to feel guilty," I told her. "In our culture, it is up to your mother to make her own life enjoyable. She may have to learn to reach out to adults her own age, to become involved in the community. You wouldn't even be doing her a favor if you gave in and went home. You would only deepen her dependency on you when she needs badly to become independent, and you would resent it so much that your relationship with your mother would become more embittered than it is now."

A student in her late 30s joined the discussion. "I'm living with my mother now. I work and go to school, and at first she kept demanding that I spend more time with her. I just couldn't. Now she has become active in a number of things and is feeling much better about herself."

Just as we can't rescue our lovers, we can't really rescue our parents, but we can sometimes push them into accepting an adult-to-adult relationship. Unfortunately, sometimes, even that is impossible.

A young man comments, "My mother says 'I'll always be your mother; I'll always worry about you.' I'm 23 and I was on the phone and we got to talking about marriage. She knows that that's not for me, at least for a while. I'll be 28 when that happens. And she says, 'Remember, when you do decide to get married, I want to have a talk with you.' And I said, 'What would you have to tell me that I don't know already?' She just said, 'I want to talk to you.' She wouldn't say what about. I cannot think, 'Did I really miss something?'" (laughter).

In dealing with neurotic relationships, the student may be up against raw fear. When we are children, parents are all powerful for us. Their nurturance is a matter of life or death. So it may be necessary to get past this fear. One way to do this is to get some *assertiveness training.*

A college counselor who teaches assertiveness training states the following:

Assertiveness training is exactly for the child-parent problem. I teach adults from 18 to 70, and I find that in every class the thing most of them want to deal with is their relationship with their parents. In assertiveness training, I teach them how to write a DESC script. Under D, people describe the problem to their parents: "You criticize everything I do." Under E, they describe how they feel: "I still feel like a child." Under S, they specify what they want: "I would like some positive feedback." Under C, they describe how it would make them feel if parents met their wishes: "If you give me positive feedback, I would feel closer to you and would be more likely to share other plans with you."

Fear is the main problem most people are up against with their parents. We deal with that through what we call cognitive restructuring—for example, the idea that we must get parents' approval or that they are always right and we are wrong. We try to get people to challenge the idea that parents still have power over them. We get them to see that they may never get parental approval, but they don't need it: "I can live without that." Changing their thinking takes away some of the emotional power parents seem to have over them (see Ellis & Bernard, 1983).

In the group, we role-play how the situation with parents should be handled. We practice until the student feels ready. We start with small assertions of power—perhaps how to ask for attention you want in a restaurant. From small beginnings, we work up to dealing with parents. (Assertiveness training may last 2 hours or a whole semester. Probably about half the college counseling centers or reentry centers offer some assertiveness training.)

Remember that parents will treat you according to the way you react. If you throw a tantrum, that is childish behavior. You should be less reactive—communicate your feelings in a direct, open way.

We really can change the kind of relationship we have with our parents by becoming the adults we need to be for ourselves. We also have to see our parents as people with their own struggles and limitations and gear our expectations accordingly. We must see that parents are no longer the gods they were when we were children.

Grades and Careers

"My parents called the school and asked for my grades. I wanted to fight with them but they won't listen to me because 'We are your parents and that's the way it is.'"

"As an only child there is so much pressure on me to do well."

"My parents bug me about grades, but I don't want to have to be an A or B student all the time. So I tell them, 'Lay off, I work at school full-time. That's all I can do. I know you're paying and all that, but there's a limit.' It just bounces off but I don't bug myself about it."

"It doesn't matter what A's I get. It's never good enough. For a time, I cut myself off completely from my parents. I didn't let them know what was going on with me. They got noncommittal answers until I learned to value myself and my own achievements. Now I'm proud of my achievements, and I pay attention to myself because no one has a right to lay their criteria on their children."

"Last summer I was so worried about grades because they're spending so much money. I landed in the hospital. My dad says, 'Don't pressure her. We have the money.' My mom won't listen. She makes me sick. Literally!"

"College isn't just learning and grades, it's about managing your time, making decisions about the future, making relationships. Grades are just one aspect. My folks know that, and they're very open about it."

"Grades are the only thing your parents can evaluate you by. You're an investment, and grades are their dipstick. Sometimes it's difficult for your parents to accept mediocrity. Every parent thinks, 'My child is so smart.' I feel like saying, 'Back off.' I'm working and going to school and earning my own way."

Sometimes parents pressure students about their choices of major, career, or even extracurricular activities. "My parents had a traditional nuclear family. They grew up in a rural area. Dad was the big football player in high school, and Mom was a cheerleader. It really gets corny. I'm the first grandchild in my family, and a load of obligations come down on me. It's never said outright, 'We want you to be on the honor roll,' but it is said indirectly. When I was a kid, we moved to Southern California. My growing up here has been so different from their lives. For years I went out for football just to please my mom. I hated every game. It took courage to quit. My dad understood, but my mom disapproved."

An older woman says, "My daughter went to medical school. Her roommate was also a medical student, but she only did it because both her parents were doctors and pressured her into it. She committed suicide."

"Why don't parents understand that—that their children have to make their own choices. I think it is because they are distant from their children. They never really see who the child is. My folks used to say, 'Whatever makes you happy.'"

Where you come up against disagreements about college majors and careers, I think you must try to prevail. You cannot let yourself be put into the position of living out your parents' hopes for themselves in your own life.

It may be that your parents didn't achieve what they wanted and now load their hopes and dreams onto their children. In other cases, parents feel they were so successful in their own careers that it would be insulting if you didn't follow suit. You cannot let yourself be pushed around that way, but you have to prepare yourself for the confrontation.

I would advise you to do some thorough research about your desired major, career plan, or summer job prospect. Go to the college placement office; get a list of the kinds of jobs your desired major will lead to. If there are graduate schools involved, research these so you can make a really informed choice. Most college campuses have an office of career planning that gives vocational and aptitude tests. Take these and show the results to your parents. Thus prepared, you will have an easier time staying calm and reasonable—always the position of strength.

Guilt About Money

The culturally patterned conflict between adult children and parents is exacerbated because often parents are still footing the bill. A student says, "I was the oldest and given lots more responsibility than my sister. I was the intellectual and got sent to a private college. But now my sister is making college decisions, and they tell her to go to a state school. We're having an uproar in the family. For my parents, I was a kind of savior, and it carried a lot of burden and guilt for me. I made my parents proud, but I feel guilty about my sister."

Sometimes students shoulder blame where none was intended. One young woman told us, "I feel so terribly guilty because my parents are spending so much to send me to this private college, while my other siblings went to state colleges. If they even mention a financial worry, it sets off this terrible guilt." I asked her, "Do you think they do resent it or was this something they really wanted to do for you?" She agreed that they were indeed pleased that she could have this experience. "So," I told her, "tell them some of the positive things that have happened to you because they did send you here. That would be much better than wallowing in secret guilt."

A young woman says, "I've been taken care of so much, I don't know what money is. I feel guilty that I've had it so easy. I feel out of control. I don't know how to get a job and save money. It's not my money. It's theirs. It's confusing. It's very hard to define it."

Guilt over money is very common. I found this out when meeting with a class. Someone asked if I was sorry that I had never had children. I said, "It has its advantages. That I didn't have to put kids through college enabled me to retire early." At this a guilty moan went up from at least half of the students present.

My suggestion is that, if you feel guilty about the money your parents are spending on you, you should begin by talking it over with them. Perhaps you will be surprised by their real feelings and circumstances. If you still come away feeling guilty, perhaps you should find a way of contributing to the cost of your education. Get a part-time job if you can. Look into loans you can pay off after you finish college.

The money situation can turn ugly, as this student relates, "Last spring, my stepdad comes up to me and says, 'You know, you're an investment. I'm paying so and so many thousand dollars a year, but I know that someday I'm going to have a claim on you and you're going to have to help me.' You know how girls say that some men make them feel like a piece of meat? That's how it felt. It made me feel like a piece of meat."

"I have so much respect for people who work and go to college. There are so many afternoons when I can go take a nap, but my roommate has to go to work."

"Independence for me now is impossible. I feel trapped by my parents' money." Another student says, "I haven't asked anybody for money. My dad, if I ask for money, he moans. I don't know how I'm doing it—I guess I'm charging it" (laughter).

Upward Mobility

One of the most intractable family conflict situations occurs when children are upwardly mobile, when going to college means moving up from the working-class or lower middle class into the upper middle class. A young woman says, "I only go home one week a year. My father and I disagree on almost everything. I don't have any rights. Sometimes I feel that he resents me for having the chance to go to college." It is very difficult for both parties in such a situation. Parents are afraid their children will end up looking down on them. In a certain sense, they are right. We all absorb class snobbery. Reassuring your parents that you love them is probably the best way to deal with this problem. It is also important that you don't shoulder a big load of guilt. You are not to blame. The class system is to blame. (For further thoughts on the problem of upwardly mobile children, see the chapter titled "The Painful Avenues of Upward Mobility.")

As you struggle with a variety of conflicts, you must see that to work through the situation with your parents *you have to make a special effort to see them as people, rather than simply as parents.* Just as they must see you as an adult, you must see them as fellow creatures. One student says, "When you are a kid, it seems like you do all the changing, while your parents are unchanging figures. I'm now watching my parents change, and it is quite a kick." Ideally, the conflict will end with both sides letting go of their stereotypes of one another and moving on to a more authentic and better relationship.

Advice From Some Wise Mothers

Never having been a parent myself, I couldn't tell you how this whole process looks from the parents' viewpoint. So I asked some wise mothers of my acquaintances for some words of wisdom. I will let them speak for themselves.[3]

I always looked on college as a maturing experience. Go, have a good time, meet people, broaden your interests. If you also happen to learn something, that's nice. If it contributes to your career, that is remarkable. Actually, my son's extracurricular activity, photography, is now his career.

I remember going up to see Doug every year over the Washington's Birthday weekend. I think it was the first part of an adult-to-adult relationship. He would show me around, line up good restaurants, take me to a movie, and introduce me to his friends, whom I would take out for a meal.

I think that college is really the last significant gift you can give your kids. Education in general. One should be generous and gracious about it and grateful that they have come this far.

Talking things over is the mature way to solve problems between adults. That is different from arguing about problems, fighting, trying to get the best of your parents. The most satisfactory way to talk is to present your feelings on the problem. Try to come from this point of view: "I am just going to tell them (calmly, quietly, without heat) how I feel about the situation. Maybe then they can tell me how they feel, how it looks from their point of view. We will understand one another better. Maybe we can begin to compromise or change or ease up on it."

If you don't ordinarily talk to your parents in this kind of way, you will need some help and rehearsing before you try it. Talk it over with a friend or two, particularly the kind of person who knows how to communicate in this way. After talking it over with someone, it can be helpful to take pen in hand and write about it. Try to state clearly what the problem is that you are trying to alleviate. If you have a lot of sore issues with your parents, pick the one that is uppermost in your mind and concentrate on it. If you can make some headway on it, you can tackle the other issues later. Write how you feel. For example, in the case of the student who is being harassed about his grades, start your sentence with "I feel hurt, angry, pressured . . . " Write about what your ideal resolution would be. Also, write what you might reasonably expect from the discussion with your parents and where you could give a little ground to reach a compromise.

Remember, the point is you are initiating an adult-to-adult discussion. You are not going to win the battle or war. Ideally, there won't be either. They will listen to you, and you will listen to them. And one thing is for sure, no matter what the upshot, you will feel better for having said how you really feel in a rational way and for having taken the initiative in a mature way.

P.S. You might ask your parents to read this chapter as a common background for discussion.

Another mother, who is also a college professor, tells us the following:

Parents do feel a deep responsibility toward their children. That does not simply end when they become college students. Often, if you don't do well, are confused or unhappy, parents wonder where they went wrong: 'What could we have done when our child was growing up to help prevent this trauma?' If parenting has been a major job, then the outcomes of their children's lives reflect on the parents' job competency.

It is also true that students both seek and take my advice, as my children do not. The respect I am accorded in my role as professor is not offered to me in my role as parent. Students seem willing, even eager, to accept professorial authority at the very same time that they resent parental authority. Are they just looking for new authority? Thus, frequently, my students receive more perceptive advice from me than my children do, and we can often have more intimate exchanges than are possible between me and my children.

Another mother says the following:

This is how we have always felt about children. Parents do not own their children. Children are very special gifts—to be loved, enjoyed, nourished, educated, guided to a recognition of moral values and to a sense of responsibility and accountability. Then follows the difficult part—a time to trust, to let go, and to hope they've done a good job. Deep inside, mothers and fathers never stop being mothers and fathers, never stop caring, but they can adjust. They can recognize maturity and can value sons and daughters as mature young men and women, capable of making good decisions. The guidelines are to listen and learn and try to understand. Anger and harsh words solve no problems. Love them, but love them with open arms, not clutching or restraining. Most important of all, believe in them—believe in their potential, their special destiny—and let them know that you believe in them, and that you trust them. Try to remember how you felt when you were young—the excitement, the challenges, the frustrations, the importance of being with your own generation. Respect them, and they will be more apt to respect you.

P.S. One of the biggest hang-ups is a mother who insists on being best friends with her daughter: the tell-each-other-everything burden. We've been watching this domineering, demanding situation for many years until it finally erupted into revolt and flight. So sad and so unnecessary.

One mother wisely observes, "I think this is inevitable: I am much more concentrated on my children than they are on me. In the same way, my mother is more concentrated on me than I am on her."

Finally, this mother states the following:

No one should be surprised that parents are trouble. Conflict between parents and children starts as early as the age of 2 years and continues right up to the day one or the other dies. It's just the nature of the relationship. How intense it is, how it is handled, how it is resolved is the big variable.

Any person who has a child invests so much emotion, so much love, so much longing, so much time into that relationship that it's impossible to step back and be totally objective about that child. The hardest part of being a parent is to let go, to say to a child, "You are your own person."

The step away from home to college is just another sort of that progression away from being parent-dependent. It's hard for both sides of the equation. Parents know a child leaving for college is making another major break on the way to being an adult individual. They hope they can say, "You're on your own" and mean it, and if both sides learn this fact in the usual 4-year process of college, they can end up being adult friends.

That, I think, is the ideal parent-child adult relationship: You are comfortable being adults together. You respect each other's adult persona, you love each other, but you know you are individuals with individual needs and differences.

Parents and children share too much to be completely detached. Conflicts are lifelong, just as they are in any human relationship, but the wise parent and the wise child learn to be patient with each other.

To conclude, I interviewed a woman whose specialty is working with older adolescents and their parents:

Separating from parents is a learning process for both sides. I find that it usually takes about 2 years, roughly from your freshman to junior years, though this differs greatly for different families, depending on how good communication has been all along. Children should realize that, for their parents, especially for mothers, the process can be extremely anxiety producing because the parents have to find new organizing principles for their lives. For the woman, the mother role has taken up more than 20 years of her life. In many cases, she came into maturity in this role, never having experienced her own adulthood before becoming a mother. Who is she, if she isn't your mother? Often she has had no adult models for taking an adult-to-adult role with her child because her own mother never made the transition and still treats her like a child.

The marriage, too, may need to be restructured. For 20 years the couple's relationship has revolved around parenting. They have both changed during those years. They need to renew their relationship as part of the process of separation from their child. These difficulties have nothing to do with you personally, but you need to be aware of them.

If there have not been good models for a friendship relationship with their children, they may fear that without the old parent-child relationship there may be no relationship at all. Here sons and daughters can help by initiating new kinds of joint activities with their parents. They can also help by not pressuring their parents to change all at once: You must bring up Mom and Dad.

This lengthy and sometimes difficult process is part of your growing into adult ways of dealing with other people. Adulthood isn't reached just by the act of going away to college. Becoming an adult involves going past egocentrism. You have to learn to step outside yourself. You have to engage your brain, instead of your emotions. If you join in a power struggle with your parents, you are stepping right back into the child role and forcing them back into the parent role. You need to study the situation your parents are in: what changes they are going through, what their fears are.

Accept your parents' right to believe as they do, however different it is from what you believe. In the same way, you have a right to what you believe. You may just disagree; it isn't a matter of right or wrong. Accepting disagreement, it is still possible to work out compromises in the area of rules.

Your parents grew up in a different time. I find that, where curfew rules are concerned, parents still feel they have to protect daughters from sexual encounters. They may even realize that society's rules with regard to sex have changed and still feel that their older values are the right ones. Perhaps they still have younger children at home and are afraid that, if they change the rules for you, they would have to change them for all the children, and they just aren't ready to do that.

I advise students to do some research. If there are older siblings, how did they handle conflict situations as they were breaking away? Seek out other adults you know who have older children and ask them how they handled things like rule changes. You may discover that your parents are, indeed, coming from left field. Or you may find that, in their concerns, they are very much like other adults. Either way, you are acquiring a broader context: getting some distance from your particular parent-child conflict. Seeing a counselor just for the purpose of sorting out these issues is also advisable. Become solution oriented rather than just emotionally reactive.

If relations with parents have been generally good, and you wish to deal with a conflict, make an appointment with the parents when you will have ample time to discuss the issue. (Sometimes it is easier to do with just one parent, choosing the one who is more reasonable toward you. One-on-one discussions give you a better chance than a two-to-one situation.) By doing this you are showing your parent that you are willing to take the initiative to deal with the problem. You don't need a yes or no right away. Just think about the problem together.

If your parents are very emotional and have difficulty communicating, I advise you to write a letter. Begin by affirming your love and by telling your parents that they have a right to their position. Then state your own position. Again, ask for an appointment.

If you are arguing about something like curfew rules, ask your parents to tell you when in the future they would relax the rule. How old would you have to be?

If you make this kind of effort, it is rare that you would make no headway with your parents. If that turns out to be the case, you have to make your own choices: Are you willing to put up with the situation? For how long do you want to put up with it? Is it desirable to make a break and accept the consequences? Now you are thinking like an adult. You can live without your parents' consent. It's nice to have it, but you can live without it.

Remember that, in negotiating the situation in these ways, you are learning the vital skills of adult relationships. In the process, you are becoming a mature adult.

All of this very good advice on communicating with your parents still leaves us with the unfortunately frequent case of a parent who is incapable of loving or honest communication. There are parents who never have and never will love you, not because there is anything wrong with you but simply because there is something wrong with them. I was well into my 30s before I was one day struck with the realization that I had done my best to love my mother, but she had not been capable of loving me or, indeed, anybody. For a few moments, I had a truly sad feeling about it. When it passed, I felt a good deal lighter. Never again would I feel guilty because I didn't do enough for her. The truth was that I had done plenty, and she had never reciprocated except to demand more.

If you find yourself in such a situation, you may simply have to do what I did after my sophomore year in college: I transferred from a private college to a state university and began to support myself completely. Yes, it slowed me down a bit. I graduated one semester late. It really didn't matter. Yes, I ran up debts. I had a serious illness and a great deal of dental work. By the time I finished my degree, I owed quite a lot of money, but it was not a great burden to pay it back.

With such a parent, there does come a time to break away and support yourself. Perhaps you can go back after some time has passed and approach him or her from a new position of strength. I continued to see my mother until her death, but she no longer had any power over me.

Notes

1. Throughout the student quotes, a new paragraph indicates a new speaker. I want, most warmly, to thank the students, colleagues, and friends whose words I have used in this chapter: Eve McCullah, Don McCullah, Theo Carrell, Barney McGrane, Ed Jamieson, Dorothy Mariner, Jane McCauley, Jim Kowalski, and Peg McBride.

2. For all those who suffer guilt in their relationship with parents, there is a cure. Read the excellent *Codependent No More* (Beattie, 1987).

3. A good book is Nancy Friday's *My Mother, My Self* (1977).

CHAPTER 13

The Painful Avenues of Upward Mobility

Our American society tells us that we live in an "open class system"—that is, one in which you must not necessarily stay in the socioeconomic class into which you were born. Such a system has various "avenues of upward mobility" through which the children of the poor and blue-collar classes may ascend into the ethereal realms of the middle and upper classes.

"Avenues of upward mobility"—it sounds so nice, so smooth and wide open— a comfortable, uncrowded highway on which the earnest and deserving may glide upward. Of course, nobody pretends that the way is without effort. Hard, competent work is required. Even a measure of competition is expected. But the person who can really perform certainly has nothing to fear on these wide, sunlit avenues. In our society, the most important avenue is the educational system. You who have made it to college have already, by definition, begun your ascent. You are the ones I want to speak to particularly in this chapter—you who belong to minority groups and you who are "upward mobiles" from the blue-collar or poverty classes, blessed ones in the lexicon of the capitalist system.

I need to speak to you because nobody in authority will admit to you that there has been a subtle misnaming here. The broad avenues should, more wisely, have been named the "painful ways of struggle" because, in fact—even for the most successful—these ways bring with them alienation, betrayal, and broken relationships. They involve a painful friction as you pick your way among the terribly innocent snobbery of those who just don't know that everybody wasn't born with a middle-class, White spoon in their mouths, past professors who imply that the vernacular you speak is aesthetically, if not morally, reprehensible. Finally, you must face the lack of unity with your fellow sufferers along the way, for this is a society that fears and, in fact, violently opposes the unity of the oppressed.[1] Society intends that you should, each of you, go this painful path all by yourself. It asks nothing less than that you betray your fellows—both those you have left behind in your old neighborhoods and those who are your companions on the avenue.

For most Americans, upward mobility involves a double change, a change from one economic class to another and a change from a racial or ethnic culture into the dominant culture of middle-class America. (Dominant, not in the sense of numbers, for most Americans are not comfortably middle class, but dominant in the sense of power. It is middle- and upper-class power that controls all the media and all the major institutions of society, including the educational institution you are now in.) Strong racial and ethnic cultures only exist below the middle class. The process of acquiring a middle-class income necessarily involves a process of learning to appear, at least outwardly, as a White American: to speak without accents or slang; to dress in generic, noncontroversial clothes; to have proper haircuts; in general, to fit a mold. Of course, these are subtle processes. Middle-class Blacks, for example, know perfectly well they are not White, but they also know that they must often appear to be culturally White. There is a painful ambivalence here. They have one foot in and one foot out—never a very comfortable position.[2]

A Model of the Upwardly Mobile[3]

On the whole, *class is a more powerful factor than race and ethnicity.* That is, minority students from middle-class backgrounds will have a somewhat easier time than nonminority Whites from poor or working class backgrounds. This may be hard to grasp because *class differences generally receive less attention than racial differences.*

First, you need to identify which of the major groups you belong to. Perhaps a simple model will help you to locate yourself in this process. Like any model, this is an oversimplification, but let's get it straight before we go on to the complications. The "normals" in college are the students from the White majority, whose parents are middle class or higher. For these folks, schooling has been a relatively simple business because the school culture has closely matched the culture they grew up in. Their parents' values, attitudes, and beliefs are similar to those of the teachers, professors, and administrators who run these institutions. They, quite literally, speak the same language as their teachers. The other groups represent different combinations of fate: the various types of upward mobiles. The following paragraphs describe examples from these groups.

	from middle class or above	*from below middle class*
from racial/ ethnic minority	PAUL	MARIA
from White/ Anglo group	COLLEGE "NORMALS"	JOE

Maria is the opposite of the normals. Her name still has an ethnic ring to it because her parents were still wedded to another language—another cultural way. Maria's parents are blue collar and borderline poor. Her father is a semiskilled worker. Her family is cohesive, perhaps giving her enough of an emotional advantage to become upwardly mobile. Maria is also a member of a minority group, whether Black or Chicano or Puerto Rican or Native American or Asian American. Perhaps Maria was one of the lucky few whose ability was recognized, even in a ghetto school. Perhaps she was tracked early into a "gifted" section, though there are other ways she might have come this far. Maria has the hardest way to go because she must readjust *both to a new class position and to a new ethnic culture.*

Paul, on the other hand, is a Black student whose father is a well-paid civil servant and whose mother went to college. Very likely, Paul went to a racially mixed school in which Whites were the majority. His background gave him the great advantage of being able to speak his teachers' language. He was always groomed and dressed according to the dominant culture's modes. Yet the world never quite let him forget his color. There was always a measure of alienation.

Joe is the son of a coal miner. He stems from early Scottish and Irish settlers who were farmers in the West Virginia mountains before that region was taken over by coal. He looks just like the Whites, but his accent isn't quite right, and his clothes never seem to sit on him with the casual assurance achieved by his peers. He isn't sure whether becoming a white-collar worker is an honorable thing to do. Back home the "pencil-pushing jackasses in the front office" weren't exactly admired, even if they were feared.[4]

Of course, the real variety of backgrounds and routes upward is much greater than this simplification. Some Marias have families who are very proud of their achievements; others have families who think she should get married and settle down and stop hanging around with a fast crowd at college "doing nothing." Some Marias attend predominantly minority schools in which they are tracked into a high section. Some make it all the way through a master's degree despite that, being Marias, they were early tracked into the "slow" section because they didn't do well on an English language test. Some had to go the hard road, taking a bus across town to a school in which they were the one and only minority student.

Paul may have grown up in a Black but middle-class neighborhood and attended a Black middle-class school. Or, again, Paul may have been the only Black or one of a handful of Blacks. The handful may have stuck together, or they may have stayed apart in mutual shame—afraid to call attention to their minority status. Paul may be a very light-skinned person whose parents disapproved if he went out with a girl of darker skin. On the other hand, his parents may have been militant civil rights fighters who went to jail in the 1960s and settled into unhappy political passivity in the 1970s. Joe, too, may have come by many different routes. He may have gotten his high school diploma in night school while contributing to the support of his family.

Group Unity and Your Morale

It is important for you to locate yourself on this complex map. Each background and each route upward has its advantages and its pains. Unfortunately, these differences may keep the group of upward mobiles in college apart because each background brings with it different reactions and different ways of handling the college situation. Some students may feel such a painful alienation from the dominant group that they want to retreat into a tight in-group of fellow sufferers. Others, feeling more confident, resent the attempt to draw them into a group that would feel limiting and isolating.

Perhaps I can illuminate the nature of the problem by contrasting the current situation with what went on in colleges during the 1960s. In that period of nationwide civil rights struggle, students from ethnic and racial minorities forcefully prevailed on colleges to give admission and financial aid to minorities and poor students. As a result, the usual small group of middle-class Blacks and Hispanics was swelled by the newcomers—the inner city kids. These students brought with them a passionate radicalism. They were enraged when they found themselves in institutions where the chandeliers could have fed a poor family for 5 years. They were aggravated beyond bearing by the middle-class pretensions in academic garb that surrounded them. They were also afraid, terrified, of failing in this strange environment that represented their only chance to get out of poverty. All these things made them outspoken. They took on their professors and their fellow students and started educating them about the bitter realities from which they came. In those days, sociology classes almost taught themselves. It was especially effective because students always learn more from each other than from teachers. There was a lot of hostility in the air, but for the first time it was out in the open and the minorities were on the attack.

In this atmosphere, it was relatively easy to forge a meaningful unity between those from middle-class backgrounds and those from the lower reaches of the class system. There was a common battle to be waged. Even many of the Whites joined in—some out of innate decency—some because, as Jerry Rubin, a highly publicized "hippie activist," put it, "It was more fun to be in the revolution than out of it."

The 1960s students volunteered for every kind of social work from tutoring inner city children to visiting and helping people in prisons and mental hospitals. There was a powerful commitment to return to the ghetto and lead one's own people up and out.

However, this stimulating situation lasted only a short time. Soon the presidents of the colleges realized that the "financial aid people" were the most radical. College administrators soon set certain sociologists to work to see what kinds of students should not be admitted because they were potential troublemakers. The sociologist's studies confirmed the college president's suspicions. Professors wanted out of this situation, too. They didn't appreciate the "insolence" of the inner city kids, and they preferred to use financial aid money to lure high school students with the highest GPAs to their schools, rather than bringing in a "disrespectful," confrontational crowd.

Very quickly the financial aid funds from state and federal governments dried up, and colleges forgot about their commitments to minorities and the poor. Soon the inner city students were a tiny minority again, and the Black and Hispanic students from middle-class backgrounds were finding it easier to wear a White mask and to succumb and assimilate to the institution. Media were busy telling them that they were now part of the 1970s generation—more conservative, more competitive and serious, and just plain good-old-American selfish. The 1980s and 1990s continued in this vein—lean and mean.

The pain of America's minorities and blue-collar poor was neatly excluded once again from the orderly halls of knowledge. Each Maria and Paul and Joe was alone again on the painful paths of struggle.

During the 1980s and 1990s, there was a decrease in the minority enrollment levels in colleges. Today, less than 28% of college-age Blacks are enrolled in college, down from 33% in 1976. Throughout the 1980s, a blatantly racist administration in Washington signaled the country that racism was okay once again. As a result, bigots on campus came out of the woodwork, and there was a considerable increase in racist incidents on campuses across the country. College administrations have reacted differently to these incidents. Throughout the 1990s and today, in the aftermath of the affirmative action debates and legislation, so-called minority enrollments are once again decreasing.

Despite the claims of media, most campuses still have groups representing minority students. All has not been lost. The best defense you can erect against feelings of isolation or unworthiness is to band together with others from your background to fight for the rights of your group. Research indicates that the most academically successful minority students are those who understand the system of racism but who also feel they can fight the system. *As the gay and lesbian movements have so dramatically taught us, those who have feelings of unity and pride toward their own background have an easier time than those who just try to lay low hoping their minority status will go unnoticed.* If you are fortunate, a group or organization of people with your background already exists on your campus. If it doesn't, it may prove rewarding to start one. A good way to do this is to undertake an independent study or class project that consists of interviewing all or a sample of the pertinent minority students on your campus about how they feel and what they want and need. This will give you contacts and good ideas about how to start and orient your group. Another good thing is to volunteer to do tutoring or social work in a nearby minority community.

Socialization Versus Education

It will help you to understand what you are up against in college if you realize that *undergoing the college-upward-mobility-assimilation trip is only in small part an intellectual matter.* Gaining intellectual skills appears to be the main game going on. But, actually, the most important part of your "training" comes in extracurricular ways—in contacts with the majority of White middle-class students, in your informal contacts with faculty, in your dormitory living arrangements, in social affairs of the college, in learning to act, speak, and dress in new ways—learning to consume in a different style. In short, college will make a majority-culture middle-class person out of you, quite apart from what it has to teach you by way of intellectual skills and specialized knowledge.

The intensity of the effect of this extracurricular training differs greatly by institution and may well determine your choice of an institution for yourself.

Community colleges and state colleges in big cities often enroll large percentages of working class and minority students. Here you will suffer the least social isolation but will also acquire less socialization toward the White middle class. Large universities are next in line. Here you will find some fellow sufferers slugging along the difficult paths of upward mobility, but the institution will make greater demands by way of changing you into a majority culture personality. Small liberal arts colleges provide the greatest "retraining." Here you necessarily live very intimately with majority students and faculty—all of whom are, almost by definition, middle class. This is the setting in which you will find the greatest personal and emotional difficulty and the greatest pressures to conform.

I will always remember a Black student I taught at Pitzer College. He was outstandingly bright and able and also a dedicated radical. In my class, he continually raised racial issues, to my delight—but much to the embarrassment of the Black students in the class who were all trying to keep a low profile. He provided an education to everyone in the class, including me. On the day before his graduation, he told me that, if he had to do it all over again, he would not choose a small college like Pitzer. "I just paid too high a price in social isolation," he said. In his case, he had been isolated, not only by his color but also by his radical politics.

As college teaches you to speak differently, dress differently, and aspire to different goals, *you may find that it is hard for you to go home again.* Your old friends may begin to resent your upward mobility, which, after all, leaves them behind. Even members of your family may resent your new "airs." One of the most painful parts of upward mobility is the feeling that you have deserted, or even betrayed, your old friends and family.

Some parents bitterly resent that the college-going child will begin to feel "better" than them. Most want their children to succeed, but it is difficult to deal with the cultural estrangement that interferes with the old, easy relationships. *How does one take one's father or mother as a positive role model, while striving so hard to supersede them in one's own life?* The strains are often just unavoidable. You may well feel yourself caught between an old environment that rejects you and a new environment in which you are also not yet at ease. Such emotional pressures can make the intellectual part of your job much harder. You are fighting a battle on at least two fronts, while most of your classmates only have to apply themselves to their studies without a worry about their social standing.

Another source of strain for children of the poverty and blue-collar classes is simply lack of money. You haven't got it to lay out for fancy clothes, DVDs, trips, designer drugs, and other accoutrements of middle-class lifestyles. It is often even hard to afford to buy all the very expensive books on the professors' class lists.

For Christmas, you go back to the ghetto or barrio or reservation to struggle with relations there, while your richer classmates are off to Utah to ski or to the Bahamas for a family holiday. Such differences also enter into your intellectual work. I well remember a very capable Latina student who felt less experienced and knowledgeable than her upper middle-class peers. When she signed up for a Latin American history class, she hoped that, at least in this subject, she would have some natural advantages. What she discovered was that half of the students in the class had visited or lived in Latin America while their fathers served in the diplomatic corps or headed up branches of American corporations. Even here, she had less to go on from her own background.

On the strictly academic side, one of your chief hurdles may be that, if you attended a high school in a poor neighborhood, you probably didn't get nearly as good an education as those who went to suburban or private schools. You may have to make up these deficiencies during your first years without getting any college credit for your efforts. If your school or ethnic studies center has a tutoring service, it would serve you well to use it. In this difficult situation, you will have to forgive yourself some temporary failures.

As those of you for whom English is a second language already know, language will be the most difficult stumbling block for upwardly mobile students. Subjects like math and science offer the least trouble in this area. In the humanities and social sciences, however, language is absolutely pivotal. The student to whom "good, academic English" comes easily will have an enormous advantage. Unfortunately, professors usually see it as their mission to inculcate academic English in their students. They may penalize you for having a different dialect and for using verbally acceptable but academically improper usages. It may actually be that your own dialect is more colorful and interesting than academic English—for example the Black dialect in the United States is far more poetic than standard English, but this will not cut any ice with your professors. The best of them realize that "a language is just a dialect with an army and a navy," but they may still feel it is their duty to instill in you the language others will expect from you in your graduate school or middle-class jobs.

Minority Pride, Majority Power

While celebrations of cultural diversity are definitely on the increase, I still feel compelled to ask, why is it so difficult for minorities to have pride in their backgrounds? It has always seemed to me that many minorities have endured heroically and survived magnificently. If I may use the example of Blacks, with whom I am most familiar, they have survived the most terrible system of slavery in human history. The slave owners tried to eradicate African culture, but Blacks brought much of that culture through. Out of their great pain, they made great music and great poetry. They reinvigorated Christianity with the bright magic of their gospel singing. They created joy and celebration in the midst of absolutely brutal oppression. Urban mural art and break dancing and rap are recent examples of this creativity in the face of overwhelming odds. Yet still it seems a constant battle to keep pride alive in the face of so much poverty—and failure is made inevitable by poverty. I believe that *the basic problem that must be confronted is the worship of power and wealth in America. If power is, indeed, the primary virtue, then the powerless can never justify themselves.* There is, however, a radically different way to look at power and wealth. As Hippolyte Taine, the 19th-century French critic, put it, "A man can achieve comfort by means of the efforts of his own labor—he can achieve wealth only by exploiting the labor of others." In fact, behind every great aggregation of power and wealth lies the destruction of human beings. Behind the Rockefeller fortune are the ruined competitors, the betrayed associates, the cheated consumers; behind the Astor fortune, the lives of poor immigrants who lived in the terrible slums of Manhattan from which that family made its fortune; behind the Ford money, the labor organizers beaten up by company goons; and behind the Du Ponts, the bodies of young men slaughtered in World War I with the weapons that made that family rich. Behind how many Southern fortunes are the lives of slaves working at backbreaking labor with barely enough recompense to survive? The truth is not that we all began the race from the same starting line. The race has always been fixed.

When we look at it this way we can easily see that the slaves were better human beings than their masters. We could even see that the poor are more decent by far than the rich. We might recover the lost insight of Christianity that the lowly are blessed, that it is harder for a camel to go through the eye of a needle than for a rich man to get into heaven. Surely one Gandhi shines brighter than a dozen Genghis Khans. If we could see it this way, we might more easily believe in the oppressed groups from which we come.

Power is in the final analysis a matter of who has the biggest guns and the greater ruthlessness in using them. Of course, once power is established, the powerful are able to prescribe standards of physical beauty, language, table manners, and personality styles. Through their hold on schooling and mass media, it becomes easy for them to make the powerless also feel worthless. I do not mean to suggest that powerless people should accept their fate. Powerlessness is a great misfortune. All I am saying is that it should not also be seen as a disgrace.

In historical perspective, the last 500 years have been a period of European domination in the entire world. But, due in part to their terrible internecine world wars, the European nations are now weakened to the point where the third world is successfully fighting back. You are a historical character in this age of the waning of European and American hegemony. In this age of the globalization of social reality, these historical forces will play themselves out in your life. To survive, you have *to see your historical position* and fashion your life accordingly. To flourish, you need to break frame and burst the paradigm, to access the unforeseen, creatively expect the unexpected, and intentionally create the never before imagined.

Becoming Bicultural

From a global perspective, college isn't doing you a great favor by acquainting you with middle-class, White language and cultural styles. The style is only worth learning because you will need it in your professional life. *You are becoming bicultural.* Imagine, for a moment, that you were suddenly sent to France to attend a university there. You would expect to have a difficult time. What you would actually find, though, is that your job would be considerably easier than what you are facing now. In learning French, everyone would realize you had to start from behind. In teaching you their social habits, the French students would not consider themselves socially superior to you. They would just be different. You would survive much more easily than in the middle-class college setting we have been talking about. Crossing countries is, in fact, much easier than crossing class lines or even crossing the street into a middle-class neighborhood. To some extent you should look on your college experience here in a similar light. You are becoming bicultural, keeping your old culture and learning the new, not because the new one is better but because you need it to get along in this different country. Becoming bicultural doesn't take an outstanding mind; normal people will become bicultural if they are exposed to a culture different from their own. If you have made it to college, you may be completely confident of your ability to become bicultural. The only blockages are emotional ones.

The analogy about becoming bicultural is a useful one, although it leaves a major issue up in the air: Different cultures breed different types of personalities—that is, they affect what we commonly think of as people's psychological characteristics. Although nearly every psychological type can be found in any culture, still different cultures favor the development of some psychological traits and discourage the development of others. In becoming bicultural, therefore, you are faced with some tough decisions about your values and your whole personality. *Upward mobility, you see, is much more than raising your class position; it creates a new "self."* Ideally, being highly conscious of what is at stake will help you to decide these issues in ways that do not damage your integrity. The following paragraphs detail some of the highly valued characteristics in middle-class America.

The model upper middle-class personality is, first of all, highly competitive. There is little sense of solidarity with others. Although such people can be polite and friendly with their fellow students or coworkers, they generally maintain a highly individualized and isolated sense of identity. This competitiveness may take the form of backstabbing and politicking against people toward whom one is outwardly friendly. Ego's own success is the main thing that matters to these people. These traits are so highly developed at all leadership levels that the coherence of the entire social fabric is ongoingly threatened and at risk.

When nobody is looking out for the common good, the entire community suffers. Out of such selfish motives corporate leaders decide on technologies that are unworkable but allow a few people to get rich or make successful careers, while everybody else suffers. This same motivation leads your professors to overlook teaching for research because the latter is more beneficial to their careers. Indeed, the entire phenomenon of career revolves around such individualistic (and selfish) motives. The only reason our society continues to function at all is because most Americans are far more cooperative and selfless than their leaders.

In contrast to our upper middle-class leaders and our strong mythology of individualism, blue-collar workers and members of ethnic minorities usually have more sense of solidarity and kinship with their fellows. Often, family ties are more highly valued in these groups—that is to say they are more actually lived rather than merely espoused and glorified. Ultimately, you have to decide how far to let yourself be pulled in the direction of selfishness. Selfishness certainly isn't the only motive for achievement. We have only to look at the lives of people like Cesar Chavez and Rosa Parks, Martin Luther King and Maya Angelou, and Malcolm X and Alice Walker, Nelson Mandela and Amy Tan to see that great deeds have sprung from loyalty and selflessness. You do have a choice here. If you need inspiration read about the lives of some of these leaders, the following books are well worth reading: *The Autobiography of Malcolm X* (Malcolm X, 1977), Martin Luther King's

Stride Toward Freedom (1958), Levy's *Cesar Chavez* (1966), and Fischer's *The Essential Gandhi* (1963).

A related personality trait is the acceptance of authority. Certainly, this is the best way to get ahead on the job. Those groups that suffer at the bottom of the economic ladder usually have some built-in resistance to authority. This is a fine trait because it keeps you from becoming a tool in the hands of others. The price may be rougher sailing—but you will be sailing under your own steam and direction.

The upper middle-class personality stresses self-control. Values like strict punctuality, attention to detail, and the capacity for hard, consistent, self-directed work are essential. You may have to strengthen yourself in these areas. You may find that you have to sacrifice an easier-going, more spontaneous personality style to achieve this. Only you can decide how far to push in this direction. Unhappily, the middle-class style creates a great many people who are highly successful but have long since forgotten how to have a good time. It is possible to lose too much in the process of becoming successful. I well remember a Chicana student I had who was in the process of deciding to go to law school and to aim for the grades that would get her in. She told me sadly one day that she was losing the capacity to "just veg around sometimes." She was becoming a tenser person.

Looking on the more positive side, the upper middle-class personality is usually highly self-confident, reaching out easily—through reading and travel—to widen its scope and understanding of the world. There is usually a sense of being able to control circumstances. Self-confidence and a feeling of effectiveness in the world have been found to be highly correlated with upward mobility. If you have gotten as far as college, you have good reason to be proud of the achievement and reason to believe yourself effective in controlling the circumstances around you.

I have suggested to you a few ways in which assimilating the new culture may affect your personality. You will be able to see more for yourself. It will help you to keep in mind that traits like those we have just discussed are not just "individual" but can often be seen as cultural or class related. The more clearly you see this, the better you will be able to pick and choose what you want for yourself.

California Proposition 209: The Death of Affirmative Action?

Well, California's Proposition 209, the anti–affirmative action measure has passed, and the Supreme Court declined to review the measure. As a minority woman (I'm Black), how do I get ahead or even in the game with two strikes against me? Will my only opportunities for secondary education be limited to expensive private universities or all minority colleges? What will the future hold for my children? Why is society taking away the little hope that I have?

Proposition 209 bars, in the state of California, all preferences in any government enterprise, including education and government contracts. California is the state to enact this type of measure, and Ward Connelly, the most outspoken proponent, is actively endorsing similar measures in other states. What is interesting about Ward Connelly is that he is full of contradictions: a Black man advocating the end of affirmative action in the name of fairness. Similarly, affirmative action is itself a study in contradictions: Initially seeking to create opportunities for those who had suffered discrimination, it has, in fact, created unintentional discrimination against other groups.

So if affirmative action is taken away, where does that leave Paul and Maria, the two examples discussed in the beginning of this chapter? While it may be true that affirmative action did cause unintentional discrimination against certain groups, nevertheless, when I honestly look around me, I can blatantly see that life's opportunities are not equal for minorities. So we have a dilemma: How do we create racial equality without causing the very thing we are seeking to rectify—discrimination.

To know what needs to be done next, it is necessary to understand the larger problem of discrimination and how affirmative action was intended to address this problem. Further, it is equally important to understand the shortcomings of affirmative action before advocating another strategy, because I believe it is only in understanding why affirmative action did not resolve racial inequality that we can devise a genuine solution.

Before affirmative action, minorities were barred from most professional and educational opportunities. Our communities usually had a lower standard of living, poor public education, and a higher crime rate. It was accepted and expected as the natural order of life. After affirmative action, minorities slowly came to be seen in every profession and to have visible access to educational institutions. Today, it does not raise much of an eyebrow for one to see a successful minority. It is now more widely accepted as, quite simply, the order of things. In this sense, affirmative action has been a great success! Affirmative action has broken the surface tension of professional and educational opportunity. Most important, it has provided a radical change in our self-image and in our estimation of our potential.

However, what are the concealed realities of affirmative action that are not often discussed? How did affirmative action fall short of its intended result?

While affirmative action created educational and professional opportunities for a few select minorities, the vast majority of our community was not benefited. In fact, the deep structural conditions of poverty, poor opportunity, substandard education, and high crime rates remain unchanged and unchallenged by affirmative action. In essence, the program would offer educational and professional opportunities to the best and the brightest in the communities, while offering little redress for everyone else. A more cynical view might point out that affirmative action allowed the mainstream White culture to redirect the push for racial equality into a direction that failed to offer substantive changes (i.e., changes that could potentially destabilize the ruling identity, ethos, feeling, and tone of mainstream White culture). And minorities, for their part, have taken a hiatus from the march toward full-blown, authentic racial equality by treating affirmative action as a panacea.

Even those who were the direct beneficiaries of affirmative action were assumed by its very precepts to be substandard, as a result of substandard education and social opportunities. But this begs the question, when would they be up to par? For society at large, affirmative action was a much cheaper solution than giving minority communities the educational resources necessary so that we might be capable to compete on a fair playing field. Also, reality has indicated that minority students still live with the stigma of being beneficiaries of affirmative action regardless. Therefore, even if we were up to par, we could not escape the lingering suspicion of being specially favored products of affirmative action.

This brings me back to Prop 209, Ward Connelly, and the purpose of creating a fair playing field called merit. It is Connelly's belief, as well as the majority of people voting in California (which is another issue), that every individual should receive a fair chance for upward mobility without concern or consideration of race or gender. What Connelly and the majority of people voting are not considering is that access to merit is something minorities have always striven to gain. Affirmative action helped prove that given the intentionally created opportunity to be there in the first place, we are, in fact, meritable of education, success, and upward mobility. What is disappointing is that Connelly, a product of affirmative action, does not relate back to that struggle anymore. Hence, with the disappearance of affirmative action and the continued absence of substantive structural changes in the educational system, minorities raised in impoverished areas are at a distinct disadvantage.

What is to be done? Rather, let me ask, what are you and I to do? You and I are pioneers breaking new ground because we will be the last to receive any assistance to move out of the ghetto. Therefore, it is incumbent on us to go back into our communities and create systems for our people to receive a better chance early on before being thrust into adulthood with nowhere to go but down. Simply, we need to be affirmative action ourselves: to be proactive and prevent our younger sisters and brothers from becoming enslaved educationally and economically.

I am not advocating that we as a group band together and exclude others because isn't that the very phenomenon of discrimination we are trying to change? What I advocate is that we, this generation, band together with the majority to show and teach them our true situation about where we come from and simultaneously continue to improve academically. I believe that the majority of people who voted for Prop 209 have not really seen or really related to the true destitution of our environments and, therefore, are controlled by fabricated ideas about "minorities taking advantage of special favors." I am encouraging you to take the responsibility and use your frustration, anger, and sadness proactively to improve the larger situation we face, our future, our status. Affirmative action brought us half circle providing a chance to a select few of us to exist in middle- and upper-class society. Therefore, we have two options: to lose what we have gained by being reactive, upset, and hostile or, better yet, to progress, drawing full circle our hopes and dreams of the plight of our people. In terms of the preciousness of our education, never forget your forefathers and mothers who fought to fund the education of Black preschool-aged children, or the "Little Rock Nine" students who first walked on to a college campus needing to be protected by the National Guard, or the 1954 Supreme Court decision in *Brown vs. The Board of Education,* which was the very first battle in the domain of education for the right to be seen as more than three fourths of a person. Thus, you and I must go forward and continue to break new ground, to be affirmative and to be in action.

Will Your Only Opportunities for Secondary Education Be Limited to Expensive Private Universities or All Minority Colleges?

First of all, considering private universities and all minority colleges is a good thing. You should consider what they have to offer you. You would learn more about yourself and the struggle out of which you come. You would gain momentum and inspiration to propel yourself to a higher level. But the reality is that mainstream society and the professional world seldom recognize a degree from those institutions as valid compared to the "normal" educational and professional way of doing business. Why? Well, what does mainstream society know about all minority colleges except that they are all minority colleges? The curriculum and degree requirements are not known and seem foreign to mainstream society. For minority colleges to be recognized as valid as, for example, USC or UCLA, the public needs to be educated. We have to actively endorse and advocate minority universities and colleges to receive the credit we need for social acceptance, acknowledgment, and upward mobility. Remember, you have to be a proponent in your cause, just like Ward Connelly is a proponent against affirmative action.

What Will the Future Hold for Our Children?

As a minority student, what I want to say to you is, simply, *do not abandon your community and your culture* but go back and inspire and give. As the former First Lady Hillary Clinton said, "It takes a village to raise a child," and for us to be able to be judged strictly on merit we must actively participate in the educational needs of our future generations. We know that public schools in our sectors do not and cannot prepare students for successful college careers. Therefore, it is our opportunity as college students to actually share our experiences and to help prepare these children. What is most amazing about doing this is that you will gain and grow more than you have in your short-lived college career, which you were doing only for yourself. We can most profoundly advance our individual educations by sharing them, by giving them away to others, by being educational affirmative action.

Why Is Society Taking Away the Little Hope That We Have?

Society at large believes that we are not earning our own way or paying our dues. The truth is that this is false. We know we are paying our dues because we know where we come from and we know that it has not gotten any better. However, our reality is that our situation is not going to get any better unless we continue to feel and to act hopeful. I do not want to sound Pollyannahish or trite, but you have to choose to look at the positives and realize that these struggles are a part of our life and our very existence.

Most important and most immediate, throughout your struggles in your college career you will often be faced with quitting and just giving up. I know because I have myself quit and given up . . . but I went back. I went back to receive and to work hard for what our forerunners set out to provide for us and to complete what I started. And, after receiving my Bachelors of Arts degree, I found that people now not only hear me, but they want me to speak and to write.

Rhonda Wofford

Notes

1. For a history of America very different from what you were taught in high school, see Frances Fox Piven and Richard A. Cloward's (1979) *Poor People's Movements.*

2. I would like to recommend Lisa Delpit's *Other People's Children: Cultural Conflicts in the Classroom* (1995) as a great resource on this phenomenon.

3. In this section, I am treating only minorities that are underrepresented in the middle class and on college campuses.

4. In a book I would recommend to you, Richard Sennett and Jonathan Cobb's (1971) *The Hidden Injuries of Class,* the authors interview a young man from an Italian American working-class background who is attending college and is assailed by doubts about his aspiration to a middle-class, white-collar job.

CHAPTER 14

Graduation—What They Forgot to Mention

Life Without Homework

Life without homework: That is how I personally describe graduating college. I am approximately 6 weeks away from receiving my degree, and I have no idea what I am going to do once I graduate. People ask me, and I have to come up with some clever answers, such as "Get a job"; "Oh yeah, I should start thinking about that"; or "I'm graduating." I avoid the question as much as I can. But I can't hide from myself when I ask that question. I went into college thinking that, when I graduate, I will be "smart." I will have skills (useful ones), I will be able to get a good job and earn money (have to pay back those loans), and, most profoundly, I will know what I want. Well, 4 years later and I am right back where I started from, still asking myself the same question and still lacking a definite answer!

Going to and graduating from a major university, or any college for that matter, gives one a false sense of security—thinking that, after graduation and the countless (and I do mean countless) hours of studying, one feels like there is something out there in the "real world" that is a perfect job. I would like to mention that I don't believe that money is the most important thing in the world; happiness, health, and love are the most important, and money will come later and without stress. But I also know that I owe about $14,000 in loans, and I do want to have money to pay for things. Money is a necessity in this world (we rarely work on the barter system—or the free system).

I want a job, and money is a nice bonus, but right now I find myself struggling. I have met with the people in the career center, and they were supposed to help me, but I came to find out that I have little "real-world" skills, no particular field of interest, and a lot of work to do—fast! I am so confused. I feel that I am a relatively intelligent person who can problem solve or figure things out rather quickly (with the exception of rocket science and some aspects of physics) and who is very personable (personality, or as my friend says, *je ne sais quoi*), and yet there is nothing for me. My 4 years of schooling have done very little for me, and I don't know why.

I have opened my mind in amazing ways over the last 4 years. The way I handle people is very different, and I have broadened my horizons incredibly. Schooling is wonderful yet very misleading (and quite profitable if your name is UC Regents). Is it something to fill the time or postpone the career decision-making process for at least 4 or 5 years?. I have decided to take education for what it really is and not for what the "supposed" outcome will be. Education is to open the mind to new ideas, cultures, people, and a myriad of things, not to provide one with a good job. The good job is just the by-product of expanding the wrinkly gray matter. Wish me luck in finding that by-product!

Lauren A. Bragg

Life After School

An interesting phenomenon occurs at the moment you graduate from college. Unless you have specific plans to attend graduate school or a set job for the future, you begin to realize that *for the first time in your life you have nowhere to go.* After preschool, there was kindergarten, then elementary school, then junior high and high school. After high school, college was the logical next step. So you skipped along, following the path of each successive school environment, until one day you looked forward and saw that there was no set path any longer. You are handed a diploma (or mailed one 3 months later) and then kicked out the door. "So long, good luck!" Now it's time to find that great job with a promising future or attend the medical school of your choice or . . . well, what exactly should you do? Is more school the answer? It worked for the last 16 years. Should you find a job? Move back home with your parents? At this point, such questions begin to overshadow your accomplishment of finishing college. Life becomes altogether more confusing. The speed of your college years of fun slows down, and you are left with decisions and the all-too-familiar "What are your plans, now?" or "What are you up to?" or "What career are you going to go into?" from family and friends. School was so much easier, it seems. Sure, there were decisions to make and studying was tedious, but at least you knew your goal was to graduate. There was no question about that. The hard part now is knowing what your goal is and how best to achieve it.

Tatian Greenleaf

College Loans—A Fine for Becoming Educated?

The thought of graduating terrifies me. I'll parade in my gown in front of friends and family and file down a neat little line to receive my hard earned piece of satin-covered cardboard with a little note inside reading, "the diploma's in the mail." And when the diploma comes, with it will be a friendly reminder: Don't forget that you only have 6 months to pick your career, a career that will last the rest of your life, a career that will make you a good citizen, a career that will help you repay your $80,000 college loan.

College loan? Oh yeah, that thing that covered just enough of my tuition to keep me scraping together money for books every year. That thing that caused so much tension between my parents and me that now we barely speak to each other. That thing that the institution has been holding over my head for 4 years. "Don't challenge our system," they said, "We're giving you money."

"Meet our standards. We're giving you money."

"Sacrifice your integrity. We're giving you money."

"Assimilate. We're giving you money."

When I chose my college, everyone told me that money wasn't important. They told me that I should choose a school that would interest me and challenge me and that the money would "work out." I was expected to choose carefully, even if I had to spend a year exploring to find just the right school.

Now, when I'm choosing a career, something that will likely be for the rest of my life, I only have a 6-month grace period before my decision is carved in stone. I'll either make it in some high-road profession, or I'll be trapped in loan-induced poverty because I couldn't choose the right career fast enough. A simple college loan soon becomes a fine we pay for being educated.

I guess it's no wonder that students are spending 5 or more years in college. Why not? By deferring graduation, you can defer your loans. But where does that leave us, the ambitious people, the people who are anxious to get into the working world but just want a little extra time to figure out the rest of our lives? We're stuck. Screwed by the system.

Well, maybe loan-induced hell is better than career hell. At least I'll have my integrity. And my peace of mind. I've got 6 months to think about it, though.

Kristin Rydberg

Graduation Day—What We Didn't Learn in School

Graduation from college is a day of celebration, of rewards, the very day that people dream about and strive to reach during their college career. For the first time, each person dressed in cap and gown is the same, regardless of race, age, and even major; for one day in our lives, we are united as college graduates. This day is a time to be selfish and to celebrate ourselves and our achievements. For myself, graduation day was about feeling a sense of successful completion. I felt proud knowing that my friends and family were present to celebrate with me, to share in my special day for what I had accomplished. It was a day of growing up, waking up on that morning as a child, and walking away, finally an adult.

This day of graduation had been built up in my mind for the past 18 years, and I was full of emotion. The entire day was absorbed and planned around the ceremony, the parties and celebrations, the time spent with family and friends. There was little time left to think. Upon my arrival at school for the ceremony that day, everywhere I looked were graduates in caps and gowns. I had feelings of anticipation and anxiousness as I checked in and had the roster searched for my name, thinking, "Please, please let it be there!" I also remember the relief felt when, after frantically searching the graduation program, I found my name, printed in black and white and spelled correctly! We lined up with excitement, as we prepared our walk, socializing with our friends, our fellow graduates, waiting as our families filled the stands. As I walked out among the procession of graduates, I felt proud; I felt excited for myself. This day was all mine.

When the day eventually came to an end, I felt exhausted both physically and emotionally. After years of anticipation, this day was over, and my future would begin tomorrow. So here I am, waking up the morning after the biggest day of my life, in my family home where I grew up as a child, sleeping in my familiar bed, thinking to myself, "What is wrong with this picture?" I look around me wondering, "What am I doing here? How do I move on now that this whole process is complete? Today, I am supposed to be an adult, so why am I here, lying in this bed, in my parents' home?" For the first day that I can remember, I thought, "What am I supposed to do today? I have nothing to do today. What am I supposed to do tomorrow, and the next day, and the rest of my life?"

For the past 18 years, my life has revolved around an educational system of one kind or another. In fact, *from the time I was 5 years old, school has been all I have known.* I can remember my first day of school, and at just 5 years old, how scary this whole experience seemed. I remember looking at all the unfamiliar faces that seemed just as confused as mine. I remember learning the importance of listening to rules, such as be quiet or stand in line, dictated by this person everyone called my "teacher." I think the most important lesson of all was when I realized that by not conforming to these rules, I would be subject to some pretty scary consequences, such as sitting in the corner for a time out or being denied recess time, punishments which, as a small child, seemed like the end of the world. From this early age, we were taught how to conform to societal structures. We learned how to fit into the mold that had been made to ensure that, if nothing else, each person would leave this system as a person acceptable to society and society's rules.

I have spent countless hours, in the past 18 years, memorizing dates from my history book, understanding formulas from my math book, reading my English books, and writing papers that would be acceptable to my teachers. I have spent most of my past agonizing about my grade point average, worrying about upcoming tests, and cramming for final exams. I now think about this time and am left wondering how much of this information, fed to me throughout the years, I have actually retained. Is it any wonder that after all of these years my life revolves around thoughts of school? There is no doubt: This system has taken over my mind. So what happens then on that fateful day of graduation? Each graduate must find a way to retrain his or her mind, to begin to steer away from the ideologies of school and academics, and to move forward to find what is ahead. This is not an easy thing to do! *Leaving school behind is not as easy as it seems.*

Looking back, I wonder how well school has prepared me for my future. After all, I thought the point of this whole process, when all was said and done, was to provide me with stability and survival for my future. All these years of attending classes, listening to lectures, studying textbooks—did it actually teach me about my future, about goals, about a self-satisfying career? I never gave much thought to what I was actually supposed to do once this whole school process came to an end. To tell you the truth, I am not sure I even realized it ever would end. It sure seemed endless. I knew that a career was to follow, but what career, and exactly how was I supposed to obtain this career? This space, this gap, between school's end and life's beginning was something I neglected to prepare myself for.

I have memories of leaving high school and feeling the high of knowing that I was now an adult and would no longer be forced to succumb to parental control. I could be myself, think for myself, and make my own decisions. Even then, when I felt as though I was finally free, finally an adult, it turned out this was really only a temporary state of illusion. This feeling of excitement came to a halt when, at the end of the summer following my high school graduation, I found myself expected by society, and my parents, to walk back into a classroom, a classroom that would ask much more of me, a college classroom. For me, college was the next step in my already prepared itinerary for life and certainly not an option. At some point in our lives, we all had to choose a college path. For some, college meant a big move, far away, to an unfamiliar place, and for others it simply meant attending a local college. I do not think many of us even knew why we were going to college. I had very few, if any, friends or acquaintances who actually had a planned course of study in mind. Personally, I had confidence in knowing that I would just enroll in the "general education" courses first, and a major would come to me later—later when the school told me it was time to choose one.

Later. Later has always been my favorite word. Everything would all be figured out later. I do not actually think I anticipated that later would ever come. After 2.5 years in a community college, where I took just about every general education course they offered, I figured out later was approaching. It was time to move on to a 4-year university, and, even more important, it was time to decide my major course of study. What?! Decide on a major?! I have no idea what I want to do with my life. How can I make such a huge decision? I am not ready. How can I decide where to continue my studies if I don't know what it is I want to study? And you expect me to decide it all now? Here I am, 21 years old and unable to decide what I want to be doing for the rest of my life. How can that be? It seems everyone has their life together by now, or so I thought. What I did not realize is that it was *okay to be confused*. I was not alone.

On my first day at a 4-year university, I entered into a classroom full of strangers, a professor I had never heard of, and, even more scary, a full schedule of courses within a major that I knew absolutely nothing about. I looked forward to graduation when this would all be said and done. I looked forward to the excitement I would feel when my days of being tested and doing homework would finally be over. The oral presentations, term papers, stress over my grade point average—it would all one day stop. I could go on knowing this happiness would come in just 2 short years. I could not wait. I saw a light at the end of this tunnel. I would graduate, and finally I would be able to do what I want to do, not what my parents expected me to do, not what my professors assigned me to do. I would finally be freed from the hassles of school.

I decided I would take a full load each semester, even take interterm and summer courses to ensure that I would graduate on time. Of course, I just knew by the time I hit graduation I would have the next step in life figured out. What career to choose, how to obtain this career, and how to accomplish my goals. Everything would finally be in order for me. I had confidence in my future because I would have this college degree, this college degree that was supposed to guide me to a successful career. I was certain to have it all together, just as soon as I finished college.

The 2 years in my new university went quickly. These 2 years seemed different from the years past though. Now that I had a major that I could focus on, and classes that actually interested me, my perspective on school started to change. I actually enjoyed going to class; I listened to lectures, rarely dosing off; and as for my professors, I actually respected them and found what they had to say insightful and educating. I read what they said to read; I did the homework they assigned and used term papers as an opportunity to expand my knowledge on a topic that interested me. *This whole education process actually became educational!* It changed from being a chore to being my life. As I became more disciplined and my outlook changed, I began to see school in a whole new light. School became my friend and not my enemy. Now this was scary. What was happening to me? *Like* school? How can that be? *I began to experience college as a unique and valuable opportunity, precious, rather than as an extension of high school.* School had always been my enemy, and maybe this is what had held me back for so long. Imagine what an experience this process could have been if only I had taken such pride in my education earlier. Maybe, however, if I hadn't taken such a shift, I wouldn't be able to look back on my past few years with such admiration and excitement. I was so happy to have finally found a way to make sense of all of my years of education. I was excited to celebrate in my realization of what could have been taken from school all along. How exciting—after all this time, I had finally figured it out.

I now wish it hadn't taken me so many years to value this educational system. It is now time to graduate and I am disappointed yet excited at the same time. I wish I could have spent more time enjoying my time and making my education useful. If I had actually spent the time wisely, maybe I wouldn't be so scared of what is ahead. A million thoughts are drifting in my head. Very little of these thoughts are without worry or fright. It is time to exit one door, a huge door, the only door I have ever known, and it is time to find a new door to enter. I am caught in a hallway between two lives. The in-between. Why was I never told about this? Why has graduation been portrayed only as the happiest day in a person's life? Why did everyone leave out the part where I feel scared and confused? I feel trapped, as if I am floating in a constant search for answers. I just keep hoping to wake up one day and a lightbulb will turn on in my head. A lightbulb telling me where to go from here, telling me what it is that will make me happy and successful. Realistically, I know that I am the only one who can turn on this light, and only I can make it happen.

So my question remains, How does one choose the next door to enter? I wonder this daily. How can such a huge accomplishment have turned itself into such a great fear? Hardly a day goes by when, in conversation with another, the topic of my graduation doesn't surface. Once surfaced, the ever-dreaded question is sure to arise: "What's next now that you have finished college?" I cringe when I hear that question, not because I am unsure of what is next or that I feel I am inadequate to survive in this competitive world. I cringe because it is as if the answer that I am supposed to provide should be this great big impressive goal. This goal is something I have been pursuing for years and years and now can't wait to attain. If only it were that easy!

I fear the in-between time—the time in which I am caught between doors, between the label "college graduate" and "person with a career." What if in the process of obtaining future goals I forget what it is that I am after and find myself settling for something that won't be self-satisfying? My biggest fear is the fear of unhappiness, the fear of "settling." There seems to be a hole in my itinerary, a hole that has yet to be filled that I must fill on my own. Please do not allow me to settle. Please do not ever let me wake up forgetting my goals and dreams in search of money or survival. Please allow me the strength to overcome obstacles and speed bumps without losing track of what is ahead.

In a conversation with my best friend, also a recent graduate, we spoke of the times in the past when we relished the idea of being a graduate. We would complain together about the work that we had due and fantasize about the days when we would no longer have this weight on our shoulders. It was always such a great feeling during Christmas break and summer vacation when we would be free from our troubles, free from deadlines; in fact, our only worry was the countdown until school started up again. I look back at these times and these conversations that we had and I now wonder what I was actually thinking. Yes, I knew one day it would all end, but I never imagined that I would look back with admiration for what I had experienced and gained from my time and hard work. My friend and I now speak of our futures and the feeling of entrapment we feel as we make decisions that will alter our lives. My friend just recently described to me how she feels. She said, "I feel as though a ton of bricks is being dropped on my shoulders. I have no clue how to go about figuring out what I want and what is available for me. I am getting sick to my stomach just thinking about it."

Some have chosen graduate school for their next step. For others, it is time to seek employment, to find a career that will provide experience and income for the future. For myself, I feel so excited inside, like a child right before recess. I am impatient—impatient because I am ready to move on with my life. I am ready to be a responsible active adult. I am ready to begin my future, and I feel as though I am driving down a road and it is time to make a turn, but I don't know what corner I should choose. I am impatient because I want to be around that corner now. I cannot wait to begin this new stage in life, if only I could just get there a little faster. If only I could get there without this dead time in the interim.

For everyone, a large choice lies ahead, the first choice in the history of our lives that can solely be made by ourselves. After years of begging for the freedom to be able to make our own choices, here we are, ready to make some of the biggest decisions of our lives. We are overwhelmed with a feeling of excitement, a feeling of fear. We are left pondering, the questions, Am I ready? Can I do this?

Erin Cora

I Am Terrified

Two months until graduation? I am so excited. Am I? Of course I am; don't be ridiculous? Who am I trying to kid? I am terrified. I've never been more scared or questioning of myself in my life. Am I smart? Am I capable? Can I survive out of school? Did I get the right degree? What am I going to do with my life?! On one hand, I am feeling really excited and alive. I am starting a new journey, a new section of my life. Time to be what I want to be and do what I want to do. The main problem is that I have no earthly clue as to what I want to do. I finally know who I am. Or at least I am beginning to understand who I am. I know what kinds of things interest me, but how do I turn that into a career? And what, if anything, does it have to do with what I am earning as my degree (liberal studies)? And did I choose the right course of study in the first place?! Today, I caught myself looking at the class schedule for next semester! I was picking out which classes I'd want to take. OK face it—I don't want to leave school. I love being a student. I love homework (did I just write that?). I love writing papers. College is fun, easy, safe, and good. The job market is scary, tenuous, hard, and boring. I am terrified. And what happens to my brain if it's not being used to think, study, research, and learn? Won't my brain atrophy and turn to mush? But on the other hand, I am getting kind of sick of this school stuff. It does get kind of tedious and causes a tremendous amount of stress. On the other hand, what if the only job I can get hired for is as a receptionist or a grocery checker? What good is a brain full of facts in a mindless boring job? I want to do something intellectually stimulating, but what if "those types of employers" don't want me? And what if I'm not smart enough? I guess it all boils down to the fact that now that I have a "college education" I still feel like I know nothing about what to do about this incredible thing called life. There should be a course in graduating and joining the "real world." Maybe if I'd had that I'd feel more prepared. Probably not!

Lisa Kraft

Graduation and Life After

At a point in my life when I should be filled with joy and a sense of accomplishment, I feel an overwhelming sense of dread. I cannot shake the feeling that my life will soon be over, although I know that it's just beginning.

Maybe I feel this way because, in our society, too many people have ho-hum, dead-end jobs that they have to drag themselves to every day. That is not something that I want. I worry that I won't make enough money to pay off all my loans and get a car, an apartment, and other staples for an independent life. I don't want to have to depend on my parents for years after graduation. Don't I owe it to them to get on with my life after they educated me? Or do I? Maybe I should think about what makes me the happiest and go with that, but I don't even know what that is yet.

Staying in college would make me the happiest at this point in my life. I don't want to graduate so soon. Why can't I take 5 or 6 years like everyone else? Twenty-one years old is still fairly young to be a college graduate these days. Many of my older classmates may have the extra maturity or experience that I lack. These things keep me awake nights.

Then I ponder all of life's big questions, the kind that spring up when you begin to have doubts or question your decisions. Where will I be in 10 years? Am I prepared for rejection? Will I be able to handle it? What about my friends? Will life be too hectic to include them? Are we all going our separate ways? Am I going to have to sacrifice my family for a career? Will I do something that I really enjoy? How do I figure out what that is, and when does the big book of answers fall out of the sky—the one with all the answers to life's important questions, the one that prepares you for entrance into the big bad "real world"?

Sometimes I get a dose of reality; the child inside me is shoved aside, and I hear a voice calmly and rationally saying, "Maryanne don't be ridiculous. You are young, bright, talented and outgoing. All of this negative thought isn't going to do you any good. You will find a job that makes you happy. If you don't then you simply look for another one. Your life is not set in stone with your first job. Take it for what it is—experience, a growing time, a time to place roots—and then feel free to move on. Don't let this change scare you; let it excite you. You are done with school—no more papers, finals, or tests. You can enter our society as a beneficial, contributing member of it. You'll be independent from all that held you back before. This means that you have ceased to be a child! So forge ahead, and don't look back with any regrets."

Well, okay, but I still want my mommy.

Maryanne Wilson

A Graduating Mother

Graduation! I have earned a bachelor's degree. This still seems like a fantasy. I can hardly believe it has come true. How do I feel? Amazed, astounded, flabbergasted—mere words barely sufficient to describe my feelings. I came to college with high hopes and am happy to say they have been more than fulfilled. I achieved the biggest goal of my life, and it feels fabulous.

To reach this day, I had to wade through a lot of muck. I was a single mother on welfare just 11 short years ago, and I had no intention of going back to school. I honestly thought I was too dumb to do it. But my sister talked me into a class at the local community college and the rest is, as they say, history.

The sense of accomplishment and the memories of so many wonderful learning experiences are pure gold to me, certainly worth every ounce of effort and every minute of the 6 years it took me to reach this goal. From a position of impotence, I have been empowered to do whatever I set my mind to. This is heady stuff!

Along the way, I discovered *myself* and the special talents I can bring to bear in this world. I know that I can go on to apply those talents successfully in my chosen field. If I could send a message out to those who feel hopeless about their situation, it would be "Have a goal, find out what you need to do, then work as hard as you can to get there." I know it sounds corny and trite, but I have found that you really can do anything you make up your mind to do, you just have to DO it.

I'm proud to say that I am graduating with honors, and this pleases me because I know how much I sacrificed for those grades. But the grades are not the important thing. What is important is the growth, the experience, and the self-respect I have gained, which have given me a strong foundation for a better second half of my life than the first half.

Having a goal doesn't have to mean school. It is simply what you want enough to make sacrifices for and what you are willing to work hard for. Achieving a goal that requires diligence, hard work, risk taking, and endurance will bring you special rewards that you will carry with you for the rest of your life.

Darra Ross

A Year After Graduating and the Death of My Studentness

I've been thinking about some of the things I have been through in the last year, evaluating whether or not I actually survived the "death" of my studentness or if I haven't really changed at all.

There are times that I catch myself lost in nostalgia, wanting to wrap myself in the warm cocoon of being a student, bereft of responsibility, existing only to learn. I think then that those were such fine times, that everything was perfect, and that I would give anything to go back to those days. It is a very insidious and seductive kind of feeling, this nostalgia. It sneaks up on you and grips you firmly without you knowing it. I think it was Proust who said, "The only paradises are those that one has lost [in the past]."

And it is true. Longing for events of the past is safe and easy because you can blot out the everyday unpleasantries and only remember the sweet flavor of those moments. I don't remember spending a lot of time unhappy because I was unsure of what was happening next, facing the imminent disintegration of my comfortable world. I choose not to remember the times I was angry or bored or upset at someone for some stupid reason that I have long forgotten. So I try to remember that all of my nostalgic moments should be tempered with a certain respect for all the times that weren't perfect. There is no perfect time; yearning to relive the past is foolish. It has taken me a while to figure that one out.

I have also learned that it is easier to be "alternative" in the environment of a college campus (as a student). The forces of socialization seem to be weaker there, if you seek out the right environment. Any of the institutions that I ran into in college seem like small potatoes compared to the institution of "work" and "real life." The urge to conform is quite strong, and I fear that I have succumbed to it. I have sold out as they say. I cut my hair, wear a tie once in a while, act very politely, and let people walk all over me (because it is easier than causing a ruckus).

But is that all on the outside or on the inside as well? Maybe I have just crafted a clever facade, another projection of myself into the everyday life of "my job." Who knows? I can't judge that one accurately.

I have learned one thing, and it may end up being more valuable than anything else I picked up in school. I learned that you can survive the death of who you think you are. I thought I was Matt Maxwell, long-haired semiphilosopher and full-time lazy student. Matt Maxwell is dead—long live Matt Maxwell! I am no longer *the student* (in any official sense). I am a fully functioning, self-supporting member of society, with all the attendant miseries and triumphs that entails. If you are willing to let go of your old models, then you can successfully change. I resisted it for a while, when the answer was really to let go and move on to something else.

I have also picked up a few other things. The surface ultimately does not matter. Yeah, I knew that before, but now I am living it. I may look like a typical larval yuppie, but I still ask questions about how things are. Hell, sometimes I write books about the questions. And I am still capable of great acts of studentness— and sometimes downright stupidity. What you see is not necessarily what you get. And that is damn reassuring at times.

Matt Maxwell

CHAPTER 15

The Career: Friend or Foe?

We live in a society where the object for so many is to do as little work as possible, where the workplace, whether office or home, is looked upon as a place of drudgery and boredom, where work rather than being a creative and fulfilling aspect of one's life is seen as oppressive and unsatisfying. How different is this from Zen! In Zen everything one does becomes a vehicle for self-realization; every act, every movement is done wholehearted, with nothing left over. . . . For what else is there but the pure act—the lifting of the hammer, the washing of the dish, the movement of the hands on the typewriter, the pulling of the weed? Everything else—thoughts of the past, fantasies about the future, judgments and evaluations concerning the work itself—what are these but shadows and ghosts flickering about in our minds, preventing us from entering fully into life itself? To enter into the awareness of Zen, to "wake up," means to cleanse the mind of the habitual disease of uncontrolled thought and to bring it back to its original state of purity and clarity. . . . In Zen all labor is viewed with the eye of equality, for it is nothing but the workings of a dualistically ensnared mind that discriminates between agreeable and disagreeable jobs, between creative and uncreative work. All this does not mean, of course, that attempts at bettering working conditions and making work more meaningful, such as we are witnessing today as a reaction against robotlike mechanization of the workplace, are worthless. But for a worker constantly to resent his work or his superiors, for him to become sloppy and slothful in his working habits, for him to become embittered toward life—these attitudes do most harm to the worker himself and serve little to change his working conditions. When it's time to work one works, nothing held back; when it's time to make changes one makes changes; when it's time to revolt one even revolts. In Zen everything is in the doing, not in the contemplating.

Philip Kapleau (quoted in Thich Nhat Hanh, 1970, pp. 2–4)[1]

From the moment a person starts treating his life as a career, worry is his constant companion.

—Maccoby (1976, p. 202)

One of your major reasons for being in college is to choose for yourself a way of earning your living and to get whatever college can give you by way of preparation for your future job. If you are going to college, you will probably end up in a middle-class occupation. Nowadays, this is almost equally likely for women as for men. In other words, the world expects you to have something called a career. However, *career* is much more than simply a way of earning a living. *Career* is a total life pattern, a distinct way of being in the world. It requires certain character traits and priorities and values. It invades the most intimate spheres of life, from your family life to your digestion to your very dreams.

In this section, I would like to explain this life pattern and compare it with a different, older pattern that is generally dying out in our modern world but that is still available to those who wish to choose it: that of the craftsman. Whether you choose to be a careerist or a craftsman *doesn't depend on the particular field you enter.* You can be a physician-careerist or a physician-craftsman, a teacher-careerist or a teacher-craftsman. *The difference lies in the way you approach your work and integrate it into the rest of your life.*

The most powerful element in the career pattern is competitive ambition. Ambition is a trait so highly valued in our society that it is difficult to even grasp that we have a choice about it. Indeed, we must have a choice about it because, although we begin by choosing careers, careers end up dominating us.

Krishnamurti (1969) has posed the disturbing question "Can an ambitious person really love?" Heavens! We all expect to be ambitious yet successful in love. Can there really be a conflict here? There can and, usually, there is. Ambition is a very intense form of self-involvement that draws much of its power from the strong social approval it is given in our society. It is not the kind of self-involvement I recommend. It is not a self-love, which takes enlightened care of you; rather, it is like a consuming vanity that may lead you to harm yourself and others in all sorts of ways. It is no secret that ambitious people frequently make themselves physically ill through excessive work and constant worry. It is less clearly understood that career is also a psychological pathology.

Within the middle class, careers are one of the major reasons for the failure of marriages. So much time and energy is taken up by the career that there just isn't enough time left for spouses and children. This increases as one moves up the hierarchy. High executives, successful doctors and lawyers, and prominent scientists all work overtime. They travel a lot. Their most powerful emotions revolve around the job, and the job offers plenty of opportunities to form emotional ties that may override the ties of family.

Take, for example, this description, which a top television executive gives of his work life:

My day starts between 4:30 and 5:00 in the morning, at home in Winnetka. I dictate in my library until about 7:30. Then I have breakfast . . . oftentimes

I continue dictating in the car on the way to the office. . . . I will probably have as many as 150 letters dictated by 7:30 in the morning. I have five full-time secretaries, who do nothing but work for Ward Quaal. . . . I get home around 6:30, 7:00 at night. After dinner with the family, I spend a minimum of two and a half hours each night going over the mail and dictating. I dictate on Saturday and Sunday. When I do this on holidays, like Christmas, New Year's and Thanksgiving, I have to sneak a little bit, so the family doesn't know what I'm doing . . .

I've always felt throughout my lifetime that if you have any ability at all, go for first place. That's all I'm interested in . . . I had only one goal in life and that was to be president. (Terkel, 1972, p. 51)[2]

Corporations often demand that the employee's spouse fit their particular bill. They move their employees around whenever it suits them or train employees in various branches of the enterprise. This may mean that the children must change schools every few years or that the wife must sacrifice her job or her community ties. The executive who refuses a promotion because his family doesn't want to move will probably never be offered another one. The joke among IBM executives is that IBM stands for "I've Been Moved."

One of the symptoms of careerism is that people who are deeply involved become incapable of enjoying other people's company unless they can talk constantly about their work. This talk is seldom about the substance of the work but is usually a kind of gossip about who is doing what where. The real question at issue in this social game is placing oneself relative to others in the enterprise or the profession. In the course of these conversations, people score points by being one-up on the latest news or by letting others know about their accomplishments. At a gathering of serious careerists, there is never much hilarity, just a constant buzz of conversations. Frequently, the men separate from the women to pursue the one topic. Recently, at such a gathering of college personnel, I noticed one of the college maids, sitting by herself in a corner. I went over and asked, "What do you think of the party?" She said, "This is sure a peculiar party—no music, no dancing. I think I'll go home." She was the only noncareerist there.

Corporations and other large institutions love careerism because *it guarantees an endless supply of people who will sacrifice everything for the job* and never endanger their chances by questioning those in authority. Maccoby (1976) found that, among the survivors in high positions, most were almost slavishly devoted to the organization in which they worked. (For professions, translate "organization" into "profession.")

The quote with which I began this chapter is from a book I recommend to you. Michael Maccoby's (1976) *The Gamesman* is a study of high-ranking executives. In it, Maccoby shows us how *career* comes to dominate every other aspect of life. Most damning, he found that the longer a man was in a high executive position, the more he hardened his heart. Such men become incapable of ordinary morality. There is no product they will not make if making it would help their career. There is no harm to the community from which they will shrink. Values of personal loyalty, love of family, respect for the world of nature all go down the drain. What is left is an individual who is frequently very effective and brilliant at work but who has lost his or her way in the sense that the only end this person serves is the end of self-glorification.

As old age approaches, such people frequently feel an aching emptiness. They have gotten everything they went after, yet peace of mind, genuine self-respect, and loving relationships with others elude them. At retirement, they are likely to suffer intense feelings of deprivation. Away from their luxurious boardrooms and lecture halls and constantly ringing telephones they feel themselves to be nothing. Because of their very success and power, they have not learned humility. Now, as physical deterioration and death confront them, they are aghast. They cannot accept the inevitable.

Income is of vital importance in most careers, not for what it can buy but because it is society's shorthand for career success. Americans often accuse themselves of being too materialistic, and it is certainly true that we spend enormous amounts of energy acquiring material possessions. In reality, most of these possessions are coveted, not for the physical gratification they give but for the prestige they impart. An expensive house and a Mercedes-Benz are primarily symbols of success. Traditionally, it has been men's success that has been symbolized, while women are used as a sort of Christmas tree on which the men can hang the various baubles signifying their rank.

Far from enjoying these goods directly, we are a culture that really despises the sensual pleasures material goods offer. We are heirs to the Victorian puritans. The executive who has a business meeting in an expensive restaurant is too busy making a deal to really taste the food. It is success that we love, not good sex or beautiful objects or a wonderful scene of nature or a delicious meal. We aren't materialists at all. There is something otherworldly in our disregard of the concrete reality around us. A minister who serves the executives of the automobile industry in Detroit says, "These men are monks—monks who've traded in their prayer books for a production line." We are so lost in symbolism that, in the words of Alan Watts, "We eat the menu and miss the meal." Businessmen, alas, seldom dance by the light of the moon.

But beware the academic conceit that believes that career only attacks industrialists. The academy is full of careerists and so is every other professional field from science to the ministry. Maccoby (1976) says:

> Comparing my own experience in universities, I would say that although academics consider themselves more humane than businessmen, the engineers and managers we interviewed are no more competitive and a lot more cooperative with one another than most professors. If corporate managers engaged in the nitpicking and down-putting common in universities, little would be created and produced. (p. 209)[3]

All this may seem very far away from you and the problems you have at this point. But you have already been bitten by the bug of *career*. School is the beginning of it. If school has made you anxious, this is but a pale forerunner of career competition. You will also have begun feeling the roller-coaster effect of career. This is a phenomenon, which was described in an old but excellent study of upper middle-class people called *Crestwood Heights* (Seeley, Sim, & Loosley, 1967). In it, the author, John Seeley, shows how the course of a career resembles a roller-coaster: Just as you get to the top of one situation, you plunge downhill and start from the bottom of a new situation. Thus, just about the time when high school became manageable and you felt at the top of the system as a senior, you are plunged down to being a freshman in a new, more demanding college environment. Just about the time you get on top of this, it's "whoops" again, and you are in graduate school, where you are a greenhorn and the competition is tougher. From there you careen into your first position. If you fill that one well, you will be pushed higher up to a new position, which will offer new "challenges." This will just go on and on until, just after you reach your highest position, the roller-coaster plunges into the abyss of retirement. You will never be secure. I realized this painfully while I was a young professor, laboring to prepare my doctoral dissertation into a publishable book. One of my friends, who was a few years ahead of me, said to me comfortingly, "You know, it's not really your first book that counts; it's your second book."

You are on the first sharp curve of the roller-coaster now. If you think it is going to let up somewhere ahead, you are kidding yourself. It will never let up until you get off it. Luckily, this isn't the kind of roller-coaster that kills you if you jump off. The jump may be made at any time. It doesn't even necessarily involve abandoning your job, though it could lead to that. Primarily, it is an inward change.

I lost my *career* one day while weeding my garden. I had been a fierce perfectionist. Throughout my schooling, I had worked tremendously hard. It was not just personal ambition, though that was certainly involved. I also had the feeling that to become a scholar was a tremendously high calling, and I stood in great awe of the important men who were my professors. But my first full-time teaching job disillusioned me. Seeing these important people at their own level, I was aghast at the personal rivalries and vanities that seemed to dominate the academic landscape. In these departments, there were people who worked together but had not been on speaking terms for 10 years because of some past rivalry or insult. They admitted to doubts about the Vietnam War but managed to evade anyone who tried to get them to support controversial antiwar action on the campus. Worst of all, they didn't seem to be particularly fascinated by their own research and frequently cared not at all about their teaching. At the first campus, where I only taught for 1 year, I had only one intellectual conversation with a colleague: It was about the style of footnoting in the *American Journal of Sociology* versus the *American Sociological Review*. My second job, at UC-Irvine, was even more disillusioning. Here almost everybody was out for Number One. They sat around discussing their image as a department as if they were advertising executives.

It was about this time that I had a garden for the first time in my life. I had long wanted to garden, and this became my way of comforting myself and assuaging the sense of loneliness I felt around my new colleagues. The hours in the garden sometimes brought me profound peace of mind. A kind of inner silence would settle in on me among the weeds and bulbs and flowers, but the old feeling of having to be a success was still in me. I still had a sinking sensation when I came across a particularly good article I felt I "should have" written. I still felt that I should be anxious to move to a "better" institution. I still felt guilty because I had spoiled my chances at a really first-rate job by letting emotional problems interfere with my graduate work for several years.

So, this one lovely Saturday as I weeded my annual border, the familiar voice inside said to me, "If you spent as much time doing research as you spend in the garden, you would be famous by now." Then a strange new voice came back loud and clear. "Yes, and you wouldn't be in the garden now . . . you'd be off at a conference, reading a paper." At that moment, the heavy mantle of *career* slipped from my shoulders. I knew that I would much rather be in the garden.

I don't mean to imply that it fell away all at once. I also found a slower way of healing myself. Whenever I felt jealousy or disappointment with my career, I just let the discomfort be and let myself feel it, sympathetically, until it vanished. I refused to let these emotions drive me to work harder. As time went on, the feelings became dimmer until, finally, they disappeared altogether. What a freedom it was when I finally knew that I would never have those feelings again. How wonderful to feel nothing but pure pleasure at the success of a colleague. Jealousy is a terrible mistress.

Of course, one alternative to a successful career is to become a sloppy worker, to avoid the work more and more until you turn into a *career* failure. This is the wrong way out. There is real pleasure and genuine self-respect in doing your work beautifully and well. Fortunately, we can reach back a few centuries in our society's history and come upon a quite different way of relating to work, a way that highly values a job well done, but from a different perspective.

Whereas the careerist worships power and gathers up as much of it as he or she can, the craftsman delights in rendering good service. This quality was beautifully expressed by the craftsmen who built the medieval cathedrals of Europe. Their rich, detailed wood and stone carvings decorated even areas on ceilings and behind pillars, which no human worshipper would ever see. For the craftsman, it was enough that God would see it.

The joy of craftsmanship seems to come most easily to people who work directly with aesthetically pleasing materials. This includes crafts that many college students might consider beneath them, such as carpentry or stonemasonry. But there are also many offbeat, middle-class occupations that give aesthetic pleasure. Consider, for example, the words of a binder of rare books and a highly skilled piano tuner:

> You roll out this design and you fill it with egg white. Then you cover it with pure gold leaf. I enjoy restoration very much. . . . You must be very clever with a binding and give it the dignity it deserves. Because the pages are so full of stunning *fantastic* things that say "This is life." So what do you do with a binding like that? I don't know. You just give it a strength. If it's leather or it's cloth or it's paper, you give it strength, an indication of what is inside. . . . Keeping a four-hundred-year-old book together keeps that spirit alive. It's an alluring kind of thing, lovely. Because you know that belongs to us. Because a book is a life. (Terkel, 1972, p. 412)
>
> There is such a thing as piano tuning, piano rebuilding and antique restoration. There's such a thing as scale designing and engineering, to produce the highest sound quality possible. I'm in all of this and I enjoy every second of it. . . . If I'm working on some good Steinway my day goes so fast I don't even know where it's gone. But if I'm working on an uninteresting instrument just the

time to tune it drags miserably. There's something of a stimulus in good sound. . . . I hear great big fat augmented chords that you don't hear in music today. I came home one day and said, "I just heard a diminished chord today!" (Terkel, 1972, p. 419)

Craftsmen are people who love their work for its own sake. Their rewards are intrinsic rather than extrinsic; that is, the process of work is directly rewarding to them. They care very little for higher salaries or more prestigious positions. They may even refuse these if it would change the nature of their work. You can find the parallel in your schoolwork: *The intrinsic reward comes to you when you just plain enjoy an assigned book or find yourself truly fascinated by a research project. The extrinsic reward is the grade.* The two types of rewards compete for your attention. If you care too much about the grade, you may be too tense to ever feel intrinsic pleasure from your studies. If, on the other hand, you love doing a piece of work, it may not matter nearly as much to you how your professor ranks it. Intrinsic rewards are a sort of pay-as-you-go proposition: The fun is in the process. Focusing on extrinsic rewards means focusing only at that point in the very end where you collect your grade or, later, your money or promotion. This empties out the process and concentrates all the meaning at a point outside the process.

As an extreme example of someone who empties out the intrinsic joy of work, consider these feelings expressed by George Allen, a highly successful professional football coach:

Everything we do is based on winning. I don't care how hard you work or how well organized you are, if you don't win, what good is it? It's down the drain. . . . One of the greatest things is to be in a locker room after a win. And be with the players and coaches and realize what's been accomplished, what you've gone through. . . . When you lose it's a morgue. That's the way it should be, because you've failed. . . . Some people can lose and then go out and be the life of the party. I can't. The only time you relax is when you win. If you lose, you don't relax until you win. That's the way I am. It's a state of tension almost continuously. (Terkel, 1972, p. 508)

Anyone whose work brings them in contact with other human beings can render craftsman's service simply by being kind, good-humored, and supportive—replacing the hierarchy's system of subordination and superiority with a simple humaneness. Consider the words of a teacher, an occupational therapist, and a poverty lawyer as they discuss what their human contacts give them by way of work satisfaction:

He is "headmaster" and administrator of the Southern School in Uptown. It's an alternative school. . . : I knew the kids were getting in trouble around here. I simply felt I could teach them and make their troubles less. Someone offered me a store-front church which was used only on Sundays. Someone gave us desks and a couple of tables. . . . We're involved in picking up basic skills that others have neglected to teach the kids. Some of them have feelings of rage, undefined, and they're acting it out in school—dangerously. We try to calm them down. . . . The person who's sixteen realizes he has a lot of catching up to do. . . . They're reaching across and trying to touch something they've never experienced before adulthood. In a specific situation of urban life— poverty. . . . My work is everything to me. (Terkel, 1972, p. 635)

I'm an occupational therapist. For several months I worked with hemiplegics, elderly people who've had a stroke. Half their body is paralyzed. First thing in the morning I'd get to the old men's ward and I'd teach them dressing. They didn't think they could do anything, but they could dress themselves. If people can take care of themselves, they have more self-esteem. . . . Being sick can be like going through early developmental stages all over again. It can have profound growth potential for people. It's like being a child again, to be sick. People who've been seriously ill may come out much stronger, happier. . . . Some kind of learning. (Terkel, 1972, p. 644)

He is a lawyer who quit his job with a corporation to become a poverty lawyer: My clients are Appalachians, Blacks, senior citizens, people in landlord-tenant cases. We're in juvenile court. We represent inmates of the state penitentiary. . . . Every day is different. There's no boredom 'cause there's so much going on. . . . Here you are aware of the suffering of your client. You know the type of landlord he has. You know the pressure he's under. It makes you all the more committed. . . . You get to know them intimately. We're very close. . . . They're my friends. (Terkel, 1972, p. 695)

In Terkel's (1972) book, we find the greatest satisfaction expressed by people who have managed to find jobs outside the official system: the teacher not in the school system, the lawyer not in the corporation. This is hardly surprising because the existing bureaucratic hierarchies are frustrating and dehumanizing. Yet even those who work within the system, in areas where their official position forces them to oppress others, can mitigate the impact for those around them. One of my former students is working now in an employment office. He has to disqualify people from compensation they need, and he fears what this work will do to him as a person. Yet when he told me that the last man he had to disqualify ended up comforting him in his distress at having to break the news, assuring him it wasn't that bad, I knew that my friend was keeping his humanity and spreading a little of it around, even in his bitter position. Most of us are victims of the huge bureaucracies in which we have to work. In this common predicament, it is service for us simply to help each other, to shield each other from the impact of the system.

If you are able to resist the blandishments of *career,* you are a good deal freer to find work outside the system or to make your work within the system creative for yourself and others. I have always enjoyed teaching even though teaching is not much valued in academia. But I followed my heart and spent most of my energy on teaching. I loved designing new courses, inventing all sorts of ways to open my students up to new ideas. That I didn't care about career gave me a wonderful freedom to design my own sphere of work in my own way. My craftsmanship brought me rich rewards all the time in the form of students' responses.

Craftsmanship does not have to be competitive at all. It is just a relationship between you and your work. A real craftsman takes genuine pleasure in the good work of other craftsmen. Being a good craftsman can get you through your work life very nicely.

The role of the craftsman is not entirely without its attendant dangers. The bane of the craftsman is perfectionism. Careerists, too, may be perfectionists, thus exposing them to a dangerous double jeopardy. The craftsman is not immune. Since we were children, adults around us have encouraged us to be perfectionists. The concept "perfect" is certainly a human construct. It never occurs in nature. It implies some sort of perfect cube: straight edges, absolute angles, and absolute control—the world of nature and of our human nature is, by contrast, a totally wiggly world, random in its movements and constantly offering up the unexpected. Do yourself a favor and let the human construct of perfection fade totally from your inner vocabulary. It is as imaginary as nuclear supremacy or the idea that sex is sinful—just a human invention and a particularly troublesome one at that.

The perfectionist is indulging in delusions of grandeur. Perfectionists imagine themselves to be gods, capable of absolute control not only of their own actions but also of the actions of all those others on whom the outcome of the perfectionists' work usually depends. There is a failure of humility here. Let us take our cue from those marvelous Asian painters who always left or created one imperfection in every work of art, just to remind themselves and their audience that nothing is perfect.

I have often been helped by remembering the words of a very successful executive who said to me, "I usually feel that if 50% of my decisions turn out to have been correct, then I am doing well." As a judge of your own work, you should be thorough and competent but never unreasonable. Be a humble craftsman, and you will avoid the pitfalls of perfectionism.

"Okay," you say, "the craftsman's route sounds good to me, but how do I explain this to my parents or my peers who are going to judge me by the money I make or how high I can climb in an official hierarchy?" We have been taught all our lives to be "successful" by the world's standards, so there is a fear that if we don't go for this prize we may be shamed by others or may regret our decision later.

People who are "success" minded will, indeed, have a hard time evaluating the craftsman's role. There is an old saying that when a pickpocket meets a saint, all he sees are pockets. When Coach George Allen looks around him, all he sees is winning or losing. Do you want to go through life with the eyes of a pickpocket? Your *career*-minded friends and parents are suffering from the illusion that there is only one game in town: the rat race. They will even call it that at the same time that they urge you to enter it. They just haven't managed to see beyond the glamorized main event to all the wonderful variety that lies outside. As one who has seen beyond, you must try to educate them.

Doing without some of the extrinsic rewards is not as bad as it sounds. People who are on the extrinsic bandwagon are insatiable. They never get enough. This is because the extrinsic reward is really a substitute: a substitute for the intrinsic satisfactions of craftsmanship—frequently it is also a substitute for the love the careerist missed. That is why it is usually the successful careerist who later regrets. The craftsman has collected his reward all along.

So you don't get to *the top*. The top isn't a terribly comfortable place. It is ceaselessly glamorized in our media. On the screen, it fairly seems to glitter. When you look at it close up, though, you see that the top is full of ferociously ambitious folks who are all afraid of each other. The tensions are sharper here, the rewards of success and failure more dramatic and gripping. The person at the top has to be on his or her guard every moment. When you think about it, only a powerful mythology could make people want to be celebrities—never really free to just move around and live. As one student of mine put it, "All your life you've been looking at these people on TV and thinking, 'Oh Wow!'"

Ambition, so highly valued in our culture, usually arises out of a fierce dissatisfaction with oneself. The lonely man becomes the ambitious man. The cartoonist Jules Pfeiffer said that when he was a kid he was very small and often bullied by bigger kids, so he thought to himself, "Someday I'm going to get big enough to beat everybody up." When he finally realized that he would never be that big, he thought, "Someday I am going to be rich enough to fire everybody." Of course, not everybody who is famous is ambitious. The great operatic tenor Luciano Pavarotti was asked in an interview, "How does it feel to be a superstar?" He said, "My ordinary self doesn't know about it."

Ambition is something that grabs you when you have lost a part of yourself. Schools are brutal to little kids precisely because they mean to take away part of you to offer it back on condition. Sometimes parents begin the process even earlier by offering children only conditional love: "Mother loves you only when you are good." The child who has been trained in this way easily transfers the game to the teacher: "Teacher loves you when you are smart." Pretty soon, children cannot grant themselves approval; they have to get it from the outside, and then they are hooked. This is how society controls us. Once the hook is in, anybody can pull the string and we dance.

The cure for this is self-approval. Our culture is rather suspicious of self-love. The usual misinterpretation of Christianity pits self-love and love of others against each other as if they were two mutually contradictory qualities. Quite the opposite is true. You always take basically the same attitude toward others as you take toward yourself. Merciless perfectionists are hard on themselves and equally hard on others, but the people who take good, sensible care of themselves are also capable of giving good, sensible care to other people. Love is love, whether directed inward or outward. If you can't direct any love inward, you won't really be able to direct genuine love outward. You may have hefty crushes and wrenching "love affairs," but none of these is love.

One final word: If you lose your ambitions—or if reading this section has just made you aware that you aren't really ambitious—don't broadcast this fact around, particularly to your teachers or employers. They think ambition is good, and they would just be affronted. They would probably also dismiss you as not a "serious person."

It is amazing, but inner freedom doesn't show on the outside, except to people who have similar freedom. They recognize it because they are attuned to it. The ambitious ones are too busy projecting their own motives on everybody else to notice people who don't fit their projections. This is very convenient. It means that you can go incognito. If, in addition, you find an area in which you can enjoy being a craftsman, you need not fear for yourself. You will be able to make a good living and have energy left over for living your life.

Is it not possible to live in this world without ambition, just being what you are? If you begin to understand what you are without trying to change it, then what you are undergoes a transformation. I think one can live in this world anonymously, completely unknown, without being famous, ambitious, cruel. One can live very happily when no importance is given to the self; and this also is part of right education.

—Krishnamurti (1970)

Notes

1. From *Zen Keys* by Thich Nhat Hanh. Copyright © 1970 by Doubleday, a division of Bantam Doubleday Dell Publishing Group, Inc. Used by permission.

2. Throughout this chapter, I use excerpts from a marvelous book called *Working*, by Studs Terkel (reprinted by permission of Donadio & Ashworth, Inc. Copyright 1972, 1974 by Studs Terkel). I recommend this book to anyone who is thinking about their future occupation or anyone who is curious about the nature of work in our society. The book contains more than 100 short, revealing interviews with people in every line of work from garbage collector to executive.

3. In the academy, professionalism is often used as a synonym for careerism.

CHAPTER 16

Directing Your Own Development

Making Decisions

In speaking with classes that have been using my book, I have been surprised, but also delighted, to find that students are still asking many of the same questions they were asking when I first began teaching during the 1950s. After all, things do not change as rapidly as the media would have us believe. One question, in particular, struck me because I so clearly remember a group of students who were trying to ask me the same question years ago at UC-Irvine. I say "trying" because I was still teaching conventional sociology then, and it took me a little while to grasp that what they were asking me was urgent and personal: *How do you make decisions?*

This is a very understandable question. Most of you did not have to make major decisions until you got to college, and now, suddenly, you are supposed to decide where to live, what to major in, what career to choose, and whom to love and perhaps even marry. It seems a fitting conclusion to discuss this issue with you.

The first point is that in this domain every decision is revocable and amendable. Indeed, you really cannot know all these answers at this point in your life. You may not yet know which major will delight you or dismay you; you can't yet understand what kind of preparation and work a given career entails; you cannot yet be completely wise about relationships. In all of these areas, you are like a beetle finding its way through the grass. You have a couple of feelers out, so you can tell what is happening a few inches in front of you. If you have ever watched such a beetle, you will know that it constantly redirects its path according to what those feelers encounter. It will bark up many a wrong blade before it finds what it is looking for. But one thing the beetle isn't foolish enough to do is to make an early decision and stick to it, come what may. Only human beings do that. We tend to confuse inflexibility with strength of character. If changing your major costs you an extra semester, so what? It has not been decreed by the Almighty that your education must take 4 years. It is a rather ridiculous idea forced on us by bureaucrats who like to make everything mechanical and schematized.

The spiritual teacher Krishnamurti advises that, as long as there is a "decision" to make, you aren't yet ready to act. At some point you will just know; there will not be any "choice." This suggests that if you still face a difficult choice, you haven't explored the alternatives far enough. For example, if you are torn between two possible college majors, maybe you need to contact some seniors who have majored in each of the two areas and find out how satisfied they were with their choices. You can get the names of seniors from your academic advisor, department secretary, or registrar's office. If you are uncertain about the job possibilities a given course of action will lead to, spend time at your college placement office or contact some personnel departments in the industry involved. If you are wondering whether to transfer to another campus, perhaps you need to make a trip to the proposed institution and spend a few days there. The admissions office there will be glad to see that you meet some students and have the chance to sit in on a few classes.

If you have explored as far as possible and are still facing a difficult choice, it will help if you find a friend and ask him or her to listen first to all the arguments for Decision A and then all the arguments for Decision B. Just in the process of verbalizing the pros and cons you may discover that one side has the better arguments. Or your friend may say, "You certainly don't sound too happy about Decision A." If there is nobody to talk to, try verbalizing the pros and cons out loud (this is important) or try writing them down. You will find it helpful to pull the issue out of the area of thought where it can chase around forever without enlightening you.

Sometimes during these verbalizations a third alternative develops. For example, shortly after I met Ted, I had the opportunity to attend a conference in Hawaii. Because I had never been there, and because my way would be paid, I really wanted to go, but I was torn because I also wanted to spend the time with my newly discovered friend. On my commute from school, I talked out both sides of the question. As I completed the two arguments, a new thought popped into my head, " Why not persuade Ted to come with me?" I did, and we had a wonderful time. Be open to new developments.

In this process of decision making, you will encounter what the world calls "failure" or "mistake." It would be well for you to banish these man-made concepts from your private emotional vocabulary. What the world calls failure or mistake is, for you, an invaluable piece of feedback: "Well, I see that math is just not the right major for me." Finding that out is every bit as valuable as finding out that you like or do well in something. It is all part of a process of elimination to find the most congenial path. It would be better to call these discoveries "negative feedback" and to forget "failure" with its unrealistic assumptions about the process by which people find their way. Remember that in your search for a career, as in love, you only have to succeed once.

In the same vein, keep your mind open to learning what you don't know. This is another piece of negative feedback and is really just as important as knowing that you do know something. For example, I know enough about mushrooms to know that I would need to know a great deal more before I could safely pick them in the forest to eat: absolutely crucial information. Discovering that you don't know something important opens the opportunity for learning and keeps you from making premature decisions.

One day one of my students charged into my office in a panic. She had to decide between spending the next semester in Europe or spending it at a high-toned Ivy League college.

"Well," I said, "it seems to me that you would have a great time whichever alternative you choose." This thought came as a surprise to her. It didn't make her decision for her, but it took off some of the heat. When we are faced with choices we too often think that there is a "right" choice. If we make it, we will be perfectly satisfied, whereas if we make the "wrong" choice, we will be perfectly miserable.[1] This is never the case. There will be good and bad in every alternative. Perhaps this type of thinking is still a reflection of the heaven-hell dichotomy in traditional Christianity. It will help us all to remember that we will always end up with a mixed bag. Of course, we want to choose the better path, but nothing is either perfect or irrevocable.

Making Decisions for Two

Where two people are involved in making a decision, I would recommend to you a process which I call "bidding," because of its similarity to bidding in bridge. In the first round, each person lays on the table exactly what he or she would most like to do. If, on this round, there is a difference of opinion, the second round asks people to indicate how strongly they feel about their choice. At this point, you may find that one person feels much more strongly than the other and you may decide, as we often do, to go the route desired by the person who feels strongest, on the assumption that when things are next the other way around the partner with the weaker desire will give way in turn. It isn't fair always to claim strong feelings just to get your way; there have to be trade-offs here.

Suppose, however, that the partners both feel strongly about their choice. Round 3 then calls for an attempt to find a new solution to the problem. Here, try to be inventive. Perhaps you can compromise by doing a little of each or synergize and come up with a third alternative, which will please you both. For example, when Ted and I were choosing wallpaper for our house, we found that we often disagreed. So our practice was simply to keep looking until we found a pattern that appealed to us both. Try not to make a decision until such a solution presents itself.

The whole trick in this method is for each partner to ask what he or she wants and to lay it clearly on the table. Do not guess what the other person might want and try to go along with it. Only direct statements about one's own position are allowed. It also isn't fair to ask the other partner, "Are you sure you want to go to England?" rather than saying, "I really want to go to France" because this would be an indirect way of stating your own preference.

Some of the techniques discussed under individual decisions can also be applied here. For example, if you are in really deep water, you might go to a neutral third party and lay your case before him or her.

Moving Toward the Periphery

If, in reading this book, you have become aware that you live in a dangerous culture, you have gotten the point. Our culture is dangerous because it is based on false values, values that, if you live by them, can easily destroy your life. As another agent of socialization, college can become a part of this danger, although I hope I have shown you how to move upstream, using whatever currents are available. Here I want to say a few words about your future life and how you can direct your own development.

Because this culture is dangerous, it is well to move to the periphery of it wherever possible. I have already hinted to you that the geographical periphery—that is, the rural areas that exist on the edges of this overwhelmingly urban society—are often much nicer places to live than is the megalopolis.

In the same vein, wilderness—what little remains to us—has a tremendous healing force. Nature, in any of her guises, has this capacity. If you grow your own vegetables, hike in the mountains, take care of animals, or collect rocks, you will be touching the hem of Mother Nature's splendid robes. Whenever I am in the wilderness, I always clean up whatever trash I see (unless it is just too overwhelming). To me, it is like combing the hair of a goddess. She will reward you with a keener appreciation of her wonders. People who have marveled at the complex beauty of a forest floor will never grind their cigarette butts into the duff.

I have spoken to you at length about political radicalism because the radical position is a highly critical one and therefore enables you to see society very sharply and clearly. You should at least expose yourself to some critical viewpoints. The perspectives of minority groups belong in the same category. I have advised minority students to hang on to their subcultures because these are healthier, in many ways, than the dominant culture. Majority students can pick up some of this by taking courses on minorities and by joining groups who work on behalf of oppressed minorities. *The oppressed always see society more clearly than their oppressors.* They have to, to survive.

All of the great religions enjoin charity on us. There are people going hungry and cold in the very city in which you live—down the street from you. The clergy at almost any church or synagogue can tell you which churches are feeding the hungry or serving the poor in other ways. To take part in this work, even by small contributions of money or time, will do great things for your self-esteem. It has this added advantage: In becoming aware of poverty and giving of your own resources, you will ensure that you, yourself, will never feel poor. If, on the other hand, you constantly and enviously look up—toward the richer and more famous—you will always feel poor by comparison.

In America, we have a counterculture that is particularly well represented on college campuses. Although the counterculture reached its greatest influence in recent history during the 1960s, it has always existed in some guise. Ethnically speaking, the counterculture contains an overrepresentation of Jews, non-Whites, Hispanics and people from ethnic groups who came to this country between 1880 and 1920, the years of greatest immigration from southern and eastern Europe. The majority culture, also sometimes called the straight culture, is heavily dominated by the oldest ethnic stocks from England and a few other countries of northern

Europe. In terms of occupation, the majority culture is business oriented, whereas the counterculture is strong in certain professions, including the academic profession and the arts. If you are from a majority culture background, it would pay you to take a peek at the counterculture organizations on your campus, and vice-versa.

If, however, you are already a member of the counterculture, either by upbringing or by your own early choice, I must warn you of this: The counterculture is also another culture. Its belief system is prone to all of the exaggeration and wish fulfillment that distorts any group's belief system. You can become dogmatic and closed-minded in the counterculture almost as easily as in the straight culture. For example, many counterculture folks believe that only holistic medicine should ever be used—that all traditional medicine is utterly wrong. This is taking the useful insights of holistic medicine and running away with them to a place where you might deny yourself important medical help. The individual who values his or her health will be aware of both medical systems and use both.

Another example of counterculture madness was the violent political rhetoric that developed during the radical era from 1959–1974. Although the movement never really did much violence, the rhetoric lost its supporters and was used to justify the violence of police against the movement. It also made possible the work of government agents—provocateurs who pushed some movement groups into violence. At the height of this era, radical students even convinced themselves that they could overthrow the existing elite by violent means. Of course, there was never the tiniest chance of that, but believing it led people into many foolish words and wrong actions.

If you think that you may be a dupe to the counterculture, expose yourself to other points of view. I once did considerable research on right-wing belief systems and organizations. It didn't make a conservative of me, but it opened my eyes to many things, particularly to the realization that right-wingers are also a mixed bag of human beings—some good, some bad, most just people doing their best by their own lights. One of the interesting things I discovered was that the right and left ends of the political spectrum see eye to eye on more matters than the members of either group suspect. This is not surprising, as both oppose the same power structure.

How to Make Changes in Yourself

Sociologists have done much research to show that the individual human being is a very weak reed indeed. People need groups to reinforce their beliefs, to support them in the adoption of new values or ways of life.[2] The phenomenal success of groups like Alcoholics Anonymous and Weight Watchers testifies to the power of the group over the individual. We don't like to hear this because it insults our illusion that we are free agents. But, if we are intelligent about it, this insight can guide us when we want, consciously, to make changes in our lives. *When you want to change yourself, find a group that will support you.* When you join a group, you come in contact with a new set of expectations, and the expectations of others govern our behavior to an amazing and, often, subliminal extent. The strength of this influence increases as your emotional ties with people in the group become deeper and stronger. (By the same token, if you want to rid yourself of influences that pull you in an undesirable direction, you must cut your ties to the people who pull you in that direction.) It is very hard to disappoint people to whom we feel close and on whom we depend for moral support. The interesting thing about this process is that it works even if you are fully conscious of how it works, just as surely as an apple will fall on a physicist's head, even though he knows the law of gravity. If you want to inspire yourself to exercise regularly, take a yoga or physical education course. If you want to meditate regularly, find a group that meets regularly for meditation. If you want to explore the wilderness, join the Sierra Club or the hiking club on your campus. These people will not only encourage you; they will also show you the ropes. If you would like to kick your emotional dependence on grades, it might be an interesting independent study to investigate how Alcoholics Anonymous and Weight Watchers work (go to meetings). Then see if you can organize a "Praise Junkies Anonymous" group on your campus.

Luckily, a large campus offers a tremendous variety of group experiences, although it is also very salutary to get off the campus for some of your group contacts. Just about any change you want to make in yourself will correspond with some group already in existence. If you want to find out what groups are available on your campus, contact the Dean of Students Office. If you need to explore what is available in your city or town, you might begin with the yellow pages under "Associations." From there, you might proceed to the office of the local newspaper. There is nearly always an editor who knows the local group scene. In some cases, you may have to organize a group yourself, a very educational experience. If you are new on campus, by all means join a group. Groups, if they are functioning at all well (not all groups do), usually welcome members and provide you with a place to meet congenial people.

The Search for Enlightenment

In this book, I have talked a good deal about Eastern philosophy and practices like meditation. Reading and practice are valuable, but you should be warned that *if you really wish to pursue enlightenment in the classic Eastern sense, you need to find a teacher and a community of persons who are working together toward this highest of human states.* You need a teacher because you need individual attention. A spiritual teacher can see exactly where you are and which way you have to move. Such a teacher can zero in on the needs of your particular being, something a book can never do. A teacher can also safeguard you against spiritual materialism,[3] making another illusion out of the teachings of liberation.

In working with undergraduates on the practices of Eastern philosophy, I have become aware that very few people of college age are ready for such a commitment. Most of you do not yet feel the need because you have not yet experienced the severest suffering of life. Enlightenment is, above all, a way to end the suffering that accompanies our usual approach to life. I have therefore felt that all I can really do for most of you along this line is to let you know that this path exists. Maybe there will come a time when you wish to take that path, and, at least, you will have some idea where to look.

In the meantime, you must find "teachers" wherever you can. A deep friendship or love relationship can be a very real teacher. The right group can be a teacher. Even a college professor will, at times, be a teacher. Finally, the situations of life with all their positive and negative feedback can also be your teachers. Try to remain open to all these possibilities. Don't be afraid to hear criticism. The saddest sight in life is an old person who has been too stubborn and oversensitive all his or her life to listen to criticism or to take advice. Such a person can never learn. As the weight of the years piles up, their personalities become more dense and impervious and they are, more and more, lost inside a cage of their own making.

There are two opposite kinds of development in people's lives. Some people learn from life and become happier as the years pass; some learn nothing and become ever sadder. Of course, people are complex. They may be growing in some directions, while woefully stuck in others. Be one of the learners. Learners are not afraid of "mistakes." They are humble enough to accept criticism. They approach each day with an empty cup, which may be filled with new experience.

A Meditation and Two Blessings

I think that one reason I always wanted to make learning fun for my students was that I was very lucky in having a father who was a very intelligent and wise man. Schools had not cut him down to size because he was self-educated. He taught me so much about the world and also about life. In his teaching, there was no judgment, no evaluation, no competition, only love. I would like to pass on one piece of his advice, which has been a blessing to me. He said, "Do something which delights you every single day." Do something, however small, even if it is only a 10-minute walk to some lovely spot on your campus or 15 minutes listening to some music you love. I would like to pass on to you my favorite meditation. It is a wonderful one for getting in touch with your body and your feelings.[4]

Sit comfortably, either on the floor, cross-legged, or in a straight-backed chair with your feet on the floor. In either position, make sure the spine is straight from the base of the spine to the top of the head. Remove glasses if you wear them.

Begin by getting in touch with the way the top of your head feels. It may take a few minutes before you get feedback from there. Your feedback may come in the form of a cool or warm feeling, a tension, itching, pricking, whirring, contraction, expansion, or simply feeling your hair on your head. Proceed, bit by bit, to your forehead, eyes, nose, cheeks, ears, chin, and throat. Then go down the back of your head and neck. Now, work down your right arm from the shoulder to the upper arm, elbow, lower arm, and hand. Sometimes what you may feel is the material of your shirt next to your body or the arm of the chair as it touches you. Work down the left arm, then down the front and back of your torso, and down each leg to your feet.

When you have finished, spend what remains of your 20 minutes just watching your breath as it moves in and out of your body. Do not try to change your breathing in any way, just observe it. Be aware of your breath, if it is a long breath or a short breath.

In the course of this meditation, you may, at times, get feedback from an area of your body other than the one you are concentrating on. Just feel that new sensation for a moment, then return to your systematic coverage. You will also find your mind wandering from the exercise. This is inevitable and should not bother you. When you notice that you have drifted off, just bring yourself gently back to the exercise. If you can't remember where you were, start again at the top of the head. Be patient with yourself but persistent. Whatever feelings occur, be a witness or observer, not a critic or judge. Rather, be a scientist in observing whatever is occurring for you at the moment.

Finish your meditation or exercises by repeating this blessing from the Hindu meditation master S. Goenka:

MAY ALL BEINGS BE PEACEFUL

MAY ALL BEINGS BE HARMONIOUS

MAY ALL BEINGS BE HAPPY

Notes

1. In line with our cultural attitudes toward "mistakes" are our attitudes toward "winning" and "losing." When television covers the Olympic games, all it focuses on is who will win. Very often, when announcers ask the athletes to express their feelings, they flatly contradict this emphasis. They are well aware that the difference between a gold medal and a runner-up position is infinitesimal compared with the difference in skill between all the Olympic contestants and the average person. If athletes were actually as hung up on winning as are the television announcers, they would have a hard time performing at all.

2. To convince yourself of the power of groups, see the experiments of Solomon Asch and Muzafer Sherif in Eleanor Maccoby's (1958) *Readings in Social Psychology*.

3. A priceless book on this subject is Chogyam Trungpa's (1973) *Cutting Through Spiritual Materialism*.

4. My thanks to our wonderful yoga teacher, Jane Evans, for this meditation.

Appendix 1

For Teachers and Students Using This Book

I have now had several years' experience in using portions of this book myself, to which I can add the experience of several people who have now used the book and have been in touch with me and sent me student work. Out of this experience come some suggestions for the way teachers and students can evaluate their work on the book.

I have felt unsatisfied with the usual assignment of writing a short paper on the book. Some students did it with enthusiasm, but most seemed to feel the usual lassitude that students bring to required writing.

I would like, instead, to suggest two formats for using the exercises suggested in the book. One format would enjoin all of the students to do one or two exercises and then organize them into groups of five that should meet for a bull session on their results. Evaluation might then simply be made in the form of a report from each group, confirming the presence of the members at this bull session. It has often fascinated me that when students meet without a teacher they are, at first, at a total loss (itself an interesting thing to observe and think about). Eventually, I find that most groups do get off the ground and that they sometimes have much franker discussions than they would with a teacher present.

The other format I would suggest is to have students choose one of the exercises or suggested projects and write a short paper or give a class report on their results. To facilitate this approach, I have compiled an index to exercises and projects and have, in some instances, expanded a bit on the possibilities inherent in these projects. Some are, of course, much shorter than others. This is good because it may serve the wide range of assignment time that different teachers will give to this section of their course.

Index to Exercises

Page

42	Survey students on their memories of grade school. Attention should be paid to the types of schools that respondents attended.
94–95	Students can interview other students about their positive and negative writing or exam-taking rituals, then persuade a few to substitute positive for negative rituals and follow up with interviews. Students should, of course, try substituting positive rituals for their own negative rituals.
112	Substitute *massacre* for *war* whenever you encounter this word in spoken or written work. A month's observations would probably suffice. Other words may be substituted for war.
121	Take a historical incident and research it, either by reviewing media coverage at the time of the incident or by interviewing people who were connected with it, or both.
121	Investigate community institutions (churches, hospitals, parks, schools, etc.) in two neighborhoods with different incomes.
121–122	Involve yourself in the community by doing volunteer work. Read about the area you are working in and write up your experiences. Tutoring other students might also be done.
122–123	Interview combat veterans about war.
122–123	Do an interview survey as preparation for organizing a student group for people of different ethnicities, women, gays, or other groups—or organize a group. These are both fairly long projects.
123	Explore, through interviews and observation, an occupation in which you are interested.
123	Use a leadership position in a campus organization to write a handbook for future leaders.
123	Bring about actual social change (a community garden was suggested).
133	Exercise on self/no-self: Have students organize a group of four or more students and have the group list components of the self and do the ideal-self/real-self exercise. Use the meditation on the self. Have the group discuss the results.
134–136	Have students organize a similar group and do the exercises on the critical voice. They may combine this with the exercise for developing a cool self-judgment. The latter should be done over a period of about six weeks.
136–137	Have students write an essay about their own ancestry, or have them share "roots" information with a small group and write up what they learned from the discussion.
138–140	Do the slowing-down exercises and write up the results.
140–142	Do the exercise for focusing attention on habitual tasks for 1 week, perhaps combined with making notes for 1 day on daydreaming.

146–151	Do the exercise for media versus reality by observing people.
183–184	Prepare for and carry out a rational, mature conversation with your parents on an issue that divides you. Write about the experience.
200	Study a 1960s movement through interviews or media coverage, or both. I find it very useful to have students read foreign press coverage.
205–206	Read the biographies of selfless leaders listed here. Biographies of other people can be substituted if students have other interests.
236–237	Research possible college majors.
237–240	Organize a "Praise Junkies Anonymous" group. Do research into the workings of Alcoholics Anonymous and Weight Watchers as an introduction to the subject. This may take the form of interviews with Alcoholics Anonymous or Weight Watchers members.

Appendix 2

*Buddhist Sociology: Some Thoughts
on the Convergence of Sociology and
the Eastern Paths of Liberation*

For years the overwhelming influence in sociology has been positivism and neo-positivism. In recent years this orientation has come under fire from neo-Marxist radicals and from a school that might be called humanist-existentialist, which is perhaps best represented by the work of Peter Berger. In this essay I would like to suggest yet another alternative tradition from which sociology might draw to its great benefit: the esoteric cores of Hinduism and Buddhism, which have lately come to Western shores in the form of the yoga, Zen Buddhist and Tibetan Buddhist movements, the teachings which Alan Watts has called the Eastern paths of liberation.[2]

In this essay I would like to depart from the more usual practice of looking at these thought systems from a sociological perspective. Instead, I would like to look at the intellectual enterprise and social organization of sociology from within the perspective of the Eastern disciplines. Here is a body of ideas which deal with the human condition and the attainment of wisdom about human life from a standpoint completely different from the science-based enterprise of the West. Just as one who travels to another country learns much about his own, so I hope that a brief trip to this "other country" may yield some useful insights to sociologists.

The Eastern paths may instruct us from several perspectives: their view of man and his relationship to society questions some of the basic theoretical assumptions of our field, while their concept of liberation introduces us to a dimension of human experience which has remained largely hidden from us. Even more important are the potential contributors of the Eastern paths to our basic methodological assumptions. In his commentary on "reflexive sociology," Gouldner (1970) points again to the need to find a way to go beyond the distortions created by self-interest, yet we have nothing in our arsenal more powerful than the incantation of one's possible

---

This essay was written and published by Inge Bell in *Theoretical Perspectives in Sociology*, edited by Scott G. McNall in 1979 (St. Martin's Press).[1] It addresses her thoughts on "Buddhist sociology" in a more traditional scholarly format. We include it in this volume because it speaks directly to so many of the issues raised in this book.

biases in the introductions to our writings. I believe that the disciplines of the Eastern paths speak precisely to this question of overcoming self-interested bias. Finally, and most important, I believe that the insights of Eastern thought provide us with a criticism of our practice as sociologists, professionals, and academicians. In the following pages I would like to speak to the three areas of theory, methodology, and practice as they are illuminated by Eastern philosophy.

Socialization

The process of socialization is a central concern of Western sociology and of the Eastern ways of liberation, but these two approaches to the fundamental human experience see socialization from diametrically opposing viewpoints. Sociology occasionally regards adult socialization as demeaning or damaging—when, for example, people are socialized into prison or the army. Usually, though, the concept refers to the process by which a child is made a member of society, and it is here that the process is seen in a wholly favorable light. Socialization is what makes a child human. Without this process the child would remain an animal. Furthermore, "Socialization helps explain how society is possible at all" (Elkin & Handel, 1960:6). Sociologists have tended to view socialization as a process by which an essentially passive and receptive child, whose main desire is for acceptance by others, is easily imprinted with society's messages. The very term "socialization" implies a process which simply makes the individual fit to live with other human beings. The term "conditioning," for example, immediately suggests quite a different process.

Psychologists have traditionally been far more aware than sociologists of the destructive aspects of socialization. For example, in *Metamorphosis,* Schachtel decries the fact that adults have been so trained by society that they come to experience reality in the very cliches which they will use to tell their friends about it. The myth of a happy childhood reflects the truth that

> there was a time before animalistic innocence was lost, before pleasure-seeking nature and pleasure-forbidding culture clashed in the battle called education, a battle in which the child always is the loser. If they [childhood experiences] were remembered, man would demand that society affirm and accept the total personality with all its potentialities ... (1959:188, 319–20)

Perhaps our inability to see the socialization process as destructive, or at least as conflict-providing, arises out of a general lack of interest in the subjective quality of experience. Very little can be found in sociology, for example, under the rubric of happiness.[3] Sociology seldom addresses itself to the fact which most of us living in this society suspect: that most people are not very happy. Socialization often transforms happy, spontaneous children into tense, emotionally mutilated adults.

In his excellent article "The Oversocialized Conception of Man," Wrong (1967:136) points out that, unlike psychoanalytic theory, which has always seen a tension between society's demands and the pull of instincts, sociology has underemphasized the forces in man which struggle against the acceptance of social discipline. Wrong sees only "drives" or "the body" as sources of nonconformity; he feels they come from totally different sources within the personality. The enlightened man is one who is inwardly free to deviate from societal norms. Yet nothing within compels him to do so. He may choose conformity or nonconformity with equal ease and according to his larger interests.

For the Eastern paths enlightenment[4] is a process of desocialization: the unlearning of everything society has taught us (Watts, 1961:19–21). This is because the Eastern ways see socialization as the weaving of that web of illusion, or *Maya*, which binds the individual to the inventions and distortions, the motives and purposes, of society, which are the causes of his attachment, striving, and suffering. The process of undoing socialization extends even to the most essential conceptualizations, as for example, dividing the world into good and evil or subject and object, to push even beyond this, learning to see the world without human concepts such as comparison and typology—i.e., seeing the world anew even as a child would see it. What is recognized here is that not only do society's codes turn into "hang-ups" for the individual, but the very freshness of experience is dulled and grayed by the conceptual web which societies weave.

The question naturally arises: Is all socialization deleterious? Can or should it be avoided altogether? Obviously, socialization into some culture is an inevitable part of the human condition. Parts of the process are wholly valuable: when we learn a language, we can communicate; when we learn technology, we can manipulate the environment; when we learn the social rules, we can maneuver in society. The dangerous component of socialization is illusion which arises out of an unwillingness to accept reality. For example, we have many illusions of life after death, and, in our own society, we have the illusion that we can become immortal or emotionally secure through fame and celebrity. Then there are the myths of legitimation by which we are taught to fear or worship or lust after power. And above all is the master illusion of a self separate from its environment, an object separate from its ground, a free will by virtue of which society can hold us responsible for breaking rules.

The distinction between useful and harmful or illusion-forming socialization parallels Krishnamurti's distinction between technological and psychological thought. The former is obviously useful to man, while the latter is tied to and generated by concern for the fate of the "self." It is from this type of thought that the Eastern paths seek to free us (Linssen 1958:119).

The process of desocialization envisaged by the Eastern paths implies no resocialization. If the Westerner has merely exchanged Western culture for Japanese or Indian culture, the process has gone wrong. In *Invitation to Sociology* Berger (1963) refers to the Eastern concept of *Satori* as being just like any conversion to a new belief system, but this is a fundamental misunderstanding. *Satori* is a consciousness beyond culture and beliefs. One piece of evidence on this score is the practice common in most Eastern disciplines of providing the student with a lengthy period of isolation from all human contact. Resocialization, on the other hand, always involves immersion in a new social setting. The attainment of *Satori*, while often accompanied by immersion into a new group, hinges strongly on an individual's experience of himself, by himself. It involves an implicit assumption that the human being can regain contact with an "original" or "authentic" self which lies behind the overlay of culture.

That the core of the teachings is separate from accompanying Oriental cultural practices is brought out clearly by Trungpa (1966) as he describes the process of adapting Tibetan Buddhism to the Western setting. He says of his Tibetan teachers: "they taught about a basic sanity that has nothing to do with time and place. They taught about the neurotic aspects of the mind and the confusion in political, social, and other structures of life, which are universal" (1966: 249). After an auto accident Trungpa shed the last trappings of Tibetan culture: "This led to my taking off the robe. The purpose of this was to gain for me personally the strength to continue teaching by unmasking, and also to do away with the exotic externals which were too fascinating to students in the West" (1966: 252).

The student is not learning a new thought system in the usual sense, but is assimilating a thought system which denies the validity of all thought systems. Negation, rather than assertion, is the hallmark of this enterprise. "the spiritual life represents a process of disengagement from the tyrannical thought symbols which dominate our life and actions. This disengagement is not, however, the giving up of one enclaving thought habit and its substitution by another" (Powell 1967:134). As Krishnamurti (1978) has said: "thought must put an end to itself." The possibility of desocialization without resocialization is nowhere recognized in sociology, but it is precisely this which constitutes enlightenment or liberation in the Eastern sense.

The liberated person, by attaining a higher consciousness, has regained the qualities of childhood. "To such, his every deed expresses originality, creativity, his living personality. There is in it no conventionality, no conformity, no inhibitory motivation. He moves just as he pleases. His behavior is like the wind which bloweth as it listeth. He has no self encased in his fragmentary, limited, restrained, egocentric existence. He is gone out of this prison . . . " (Fromm, Suzuki, and De Martino 1960:16).

The Self

One of the most heavily stressed ideas of the Eastern paths is the necessity of dropping the ego, or the concept of no-self. This easily leads to confusion because the term "ego" is not used here to designate the integrative, controlling, and reality-testing aspects of self which social scientists usually mean by that term. Rather "ego" or "self" refers to the conflict between an "ideal self"—who I ought to be—and a "real self"—who I think I really am—both of which are obviously acquired from society. As we pit these two illusory images against each other, we generate tension, emotional imbalance and a constant concern with the self.

Sociologists recognize that socialization normally results in the creation of an ideal self. Although they see that anxiety may be caused if the ideal and real selves are too divergent, this is considered an abnormal or unusual outcome, and the ideal self is viewed as necessary in enabling the individual to develop self-disciplined, goal-directed action (Broom and Selznick 1955:92). For the Eastern ways, on the other hand, the ideal self is merely another refusal to accept reality fully, while the whole syndrome of self is an invention of society which creates constant and fruitless concern.

Sometimes sociologists do explicitly recognize the fact that anxiety is a prevalent condition. Broom and Selznick (1955:89) believe that the long period of dependency during which socialization takes place makes man the "anxious animal." What is implied here is that such anxiety is an inevitable part of being human. Watts (1961:71) notes more precisely what society does to make the individual anxious: "Social conditioning as we know it depends entirely on persuading people not to accept themselves." But there is a way out. The liberated person is as human as anyone else, but "his liberation lies in the fact that he is not in conflict with himself for being so."

Put in terms of role theory, sociology holds that certain roles are central to the integration of one's personality; the individual stakes his self-respect on the successful carrying out of such roles. The role thus creates a burden of anxiety, while at the same time limiting the person's outlook to the perspective on the world he gets from his particular role. This is seen as normal and inevitable. But the liberated individual is precisely one who "no longer confuses his identity with his social role . . . He plays his role instead of taking it seriously." Watts points out that at the moment when we cease to take the role seriously, "it is possible to go on behaving as rationally as ever—but with a remarkable sense of lightness" (Watts 1961:49).

Of course, sociologists see that a particular role may be false. The con man who "cools out the mark" (Goffman 1967) does not believe a word he is saying, but he is motivated by a serious need to be successful in another role, namely, that of a con man. What sociology seems to miss is that an enlightened person may have at his disposal a collection of roles, none of which he takes seriously and none of which he uses to confer identity on himself.

The Eastern ways regard as fictitious and misleading the notion that there is a person whose actions we can control, an entity which exists over time. There is only a series of occurrences or experiences. This difficult notion may perhaps be glimpsed in the experience of anyone over forty who looks back on himself at thirty or twenty or fifteen and says to himself, "That was really somebody else; how I felt about life then bears almost no resemblance to how I feel now." It is only social structure which imposes on the individual the definition of a continuously existing person who is the same at twenty, forty, and eighty. After discussing the way an individual rewrites his own life history with every new perspective he attains, Berger (1963:106) sees that "the self is no longer a solid, given entity that moves from one situation to another. It is rather a process, continuously created and re-created in each social situation that one enters, held together by the slender thread of memory. . . . " Although the clarity of Berger's insight is rare, most sociologists do see that the self is a social construction, but they assume it is a necessary construction, one without which the individual could not function. Symbolic interactionists such as G. H. Mead (1934) and Herbert Blumer (1934/1962) emphasize that the self is a process rather than a fixed entity. Still they see the self as a real identity and structure that underlies the growth process—that is, the concept of self for the symbolic interactionists presupposes a structure from which growth can be evaluated.

The Eastern paths tell us that in our normal socialized state we are victims of ignorance or forgetfulness (*Avidya*) of our true nature (often described as our true God-like nature). During our formative years, we adopt certain personality traits as ways of dealing with our environment. For example, a child with a bullying parent learns to play depressed to get that parent's sympathy or buy his or her neutrality. Eventually, the depressive role becomes habitual. The individual now feels trapped inside the role. It looms before him as if it were an alien power, and it buffets him about. He has forgotten that he invented the response—that once he "was God," i.e., he was and is the shaper of his own soul.

Berger (1963:140–45, 147 and 148) comes very close to the Eastern view when he uses the model of society as drama. He writes that "deception and self-deception are at the very heart of social reality. . . . " Then he introduces the strictly Western notion of existential despair to explain why everyone cooperates in the deception. It is because society hides from us "the naked terrors of our condition." These terrors seem to consist of a mixture of the fear of death and the fear of discovering ourselves alone in a vast, impersonal universe. "In the end we must return to that nightmare moment when we feel ourselves stripped of all names and all identities." What Berger does not seem to see is that the fear of death and of the cosmos, a psychological fear, is also a social invention which has been particularly strong in Western civilization. Many societies do not share our horror of death, and the Eastern paths of liberation regard as the most precious *Satori* that moment when we "find ourselves stripped of all names and all identities."

The Western view generally ignores the enlightenment dimension just as it often ignores the quality of experience. In terms of role theory, this means that nowhere in our analysis do we have the tools which might enable us to tell the difference between the role-playing of Watts or Suzuki's enlightened man and the performance of one who is so attached to the illusion of his role that he suffers a heart attack or an ulcer. We touch upon this hidden dimension frequently in indirect ways: when, in the sociology of knowledge, we study the way thought is shaped by society, we are looking at the creation of *Maya*, of illusion. When we study the causes and treatment of mental illness, we are involved in trying to move people toward enlightenment; when we study Maslow's (1962) work on self-actualizing people we are looking at some of the characteristics of higher consciousness. Yet the underlying dimension is seldom explicitly recognized. It is, of course, a dimension that cannot be summarized in a few words. Indeed, since the enlightened state is a state beyond language, it is impossible to pinpoint through language alone. Becoming enlightened is not primarily an intellectual process, and, although the intellect may help, it may also hinder. Keeping one's emotional balance in life or becoming adept in the use of "skillful means" of living resembles the process of learning to ride a bicycle or play a musical instrument. You cannot learn this by reading books about it. You can learn only by practice. In order to recognize what enlightenment is, we must ourselves be enlightened. We can judge enlightenment only to the point where we have ourselves arrived.

With Eastern views of socialization and self, we have moved beyond the intellect. But might not sociology be the discipline which is willing to ask the question:

In understanding human life, just how far can pure intellect take us? And if it can take us only so far, what else is there? Eastern philosophy suggests that there is something more valuable than the conceptualizing, knowledge-accumulating intellect. This is sometimes called "basic intelligence": our ability to perceive and deal with reality without reference to accumulated idea systems. Basic intelligence is what gets us out of a burning building. The question for us is whether sociology can incorporate into its framework the development of such an intelligence.

Methodology

The Eastern paths also speak to us on the most basic questions of our methodology. Having accepted the positivist approach, Western social science has also accepted the idea that the scientist qua scientist has little to do with the scientist as a person. The separation supposedly goes in two directions: who I am is not supposed to influence my study of human behavior, and my study is not expected to reflect back on who I am. We lack a tradition, a system, which would enable us to develop a meaningful perspective on this problem.

Unfortunately, sociologists have made the mistake of putting mechanical methodologies in the center of their objectivity training rather than developing a far more fruitful line of thought initiated by Mannheim's sociology of knowledge,[5] and furthered by C. Wright Mills's insistence that the sociologist must understand his own position in history and how this shapes his perception, or the more recent ideas of Gouldner's reflexive sociology (1970:511–12): a sociology of sociology.

Gouldner points out that most sociological theorizing is an effort to cope with the feeling of being threatened by one's world, and that objectivity is possible only when the theorist rises above these personal feelings. But how can he do this? Neither Mannheim nor Mills nor Gouldner tells us. They imply that we must develop an intellectual understanding of our self-interest and the processes by which this shapes our ideas. But is intellectual understanding enough to neutralize the powerful emotions of self-preservation? I think not. Mannheim (1936) is the perfect case in point. In *Ideology and Utopia* he develops a brilliant analysis of how social position forms ideology and then falls into the same trap himself by arguing that the "floating intelligentsia" is somehow not rooted in society in the same way as social classes and is thus, alone, able to see objectively. He has rescued the transcendent role of the scholar from the suspicion he cast upon it and enshrined his own group as the only one capable of this saving grace. All his intellect did not avail against the pull of his personal commitments.

Because self-interest is rooted in emotion, it cannot be overcome by intellect alone. The Eastern paths offer an ancient and highly developed discipline which can liberate us from the pull of self-interest and develop an attitude which accepts the often threatening world and its inevitable flow of change. Self-interest will lose its hold over our minds only as we disengage ourselves from self.

Because "men's highest values, no less than their basest impulses, may make liars of them" (Gouldner, 1970:499), we must liberate ourselves from our noblest as well as from our basest desires. Eastern mysticism sets out to do this, to free us from *all* opinions, values, and preconceptions. What I am asserting is that clear insight into society begins with detachment from one's own emotions. The self cannot be, as in the positivist model, sealed off from the material it studies; it can only be made fully open to every aspect of that material. Only then can we attain the kind of awareness which Gouldner (1970:494) refers to as "an openness to bad news."[6]

Toward an Enlightened Sociology

Just as enlightenment does not come through intellect alone, so its fruits cannot be purely theoretical. To be real, enlightenment must revolutionize the practice of sociology. One conclusion which is implied by enlightened self-appraisal is that teaching must be restored as a central value of our profession. The furtherance of enlightenment requires personal contact between teacher and student, and it is in this relationship that we can offer the greatest contribution to society.

As a teacher, I have for years been frustrated by how little study of sociology tells students about living a satisfying life. As critics of the social structure, we can stimulate students to generate ideas about changing society in order to make life better for larger numbers of people. And, indeed, this is an invaluable contribution; perhaps it is the major contribution to be expected from a science which sees how irrevocably the individual's life is tied to the whole fabric of society. But what do we say to students who have to live their lives right now and in the future in a world they never made and perhaps cannot affect very much? Shouldn't the field which claims to study people in their totality—as citizens, producers, consumers, parents, lovers, friends—have something to say about how to raise the quality of life for the individual? Students who have not yet been schooled in what the field consists of continue to have expectations of gaining insight and wisdom for their own lives. For the most part they continue to be disappointed.[7]

The Eastern ways of liberation speak precisely to the question of how to live a satisfying life in given circumstances. For contrary to popular Western opinion, these schools of thought do believe in changing what can be changed, and they also concentrate on how to live with what cannot be changed.[8] This involves developing a gut-level understanding and acceptance of what the universe is about and what our place in it is. Because we are self-centered, we believe that there is a right and wrong to everything, right being whatever makes us comfortable, safe, and happy, and wrong being whatever threatens our safety, pleasure, or desire for control. The Eastern ways tell us that we cannot control the universe to suit our egotistical fantasy. Change is constant and is the way of the universe. To accept this is also to accept our losses and our eventual demise with equanimity. Fortunately, sociology does in some ways contribute to the development of this type of enlightenment.

The development of objectivity in the student can be a discipline at least somewhat similar to the disciplines of the Eastern paths. It involves a systematic attempt to expand self-centered awareness beyond the parochial situation in which everything in society is judged according to whether it fulfills or frustrates our desires. The wealthy student must learn to see the society through the eyes of the poor (Mills 1959); the young must understand how the world looks to the old. This is not a purely intellectual process, but it involves learning how the other feels by becoming, if only momentarily, the other.[9]

Another important contribution of social science to objectivity is cultural relativism, the insight that no social codes or systems are intrinsically right or wrong. Rather, they are all divergent manifestations of humans' culture-building capacity.[10] This is certainly an excellent foundation for the difficult process of learning to see through the absolutes of one's own culture.

We must design the learning experience to educate the heart as well as the head. I would suggest, as just one example, that we require of every sociology major a year living in some part of society never before experienced by that student. I would discourage any reading before this field placement. Let the student experience without prejudgment: Afterward, there will be no need to urge them to read what others have said about their field environment. On a lower level sociodrama can simulate the experience of taking other social roles; so can meetings with young workers, welfare mothers, millionaires, and others.

Toward a Practicing Sociology

For the Eastern paths, "Physician, heal thyself" is a primary dictum. This is learning what must be judged by the practice to which it leads. In sociology, though, our practice fails to reflect our expertise in human relations and group behavior. Although sociologists have studied academic institutions and the workings of many academic disciplines, we appear to have drawn few lessons which we can apply to ourselves. Human relationships in sociology are not markedly better than those in other disciplines.

We are full of ideas for reforming society but make little connection between these ideas and our day-to-day actions. We deplore the effects of careerism in big business, at the same time that we groan under the strain of careerism ourselves.[11] We theorize about "community" while our junior colleagues live in fear of losing their jobs. We argue for greater equality in America while despising our own students as unworthy of our attention. We believe that we want to improve society, but our immediate personal motive is career advancement. We acquiesce in a viciously competitive system of publish-or-perish which floods our field with an indigestible and actually obstructive body of material, most of which, produced under competitive duress, only demeans those who write it while wasting the time of those who read it. We seem unconcerned with the possibility that the emphasis on academic research is designed by the power structure to neutralize us as an influence on the young or within the wider community. Our research is funded by the Ford Foundation, Rockefeller, and the Department of Defense, as if the sociology of knowledge did not clearly tell us what sources of funding do to the bias of the recipients. We learn sociology, but we do not learn *from* sociology.

These contradictions reflect on our professional practice and on ourselves. Consciousness of institutional oppression begins with an awareness of one's own situation. Where this awareness is radically enhanced, opposition to oppressive institutions must follow. Far from being a recipe for privatization or inaction, the Eastern paths provide insights and suggestions for effective social change, beginning precisely in that arena which we are best able to influence—ourselves and our immediate environment.

Sociologists are good at questioning the values of mainstream America, but we generally remain blind to the myths of our own academic subculture. To the extent that we demythologize American culture for the student, we lift the veil, but we quickly follow this act of desocialization with an act of resocialization. In place of the myths and values of the dominant culture, we put the myths and values of the academy. We create a new illusion, *academaya*. We cannot see through the role of the professional, with all its striving, competition, and deadly seriousness. We do not see that a career is a highly developed form of concern with the ego, nor do we show how easy it is to control a person who is intent on career success. To the extent that we take ourselves seriously as sociologists and academicians, we continue to propagate the illusion, the goal attachment, and the suffering. Like our popular and high culture, which features almost exclusively the activities of obsessively goal-oriented heroes, American sociology accepts and practices goal-orientation as the only possible mode of human conduct.

Put in terms of power and authority, the ways of enlightenment seek to liberate the individual from the authority of society and those who rule it, from scriptures and even from religious tradition. We enlighten our students to the edge of liberation only to ensnare them again in the authority structure of the academy and the related professions. Insofar as these structures are ultimately tied by a thousand threads to the power structure of the larger society, we make them and even their very vision of reality subservient to those who rule.

Notes

1. Copyright 1979 by St. Martin's Press. From *Theoretical Perspectives in Sociology* by Scott McNall. Reprinted with permission of St. Martin's Press, Inc.

2. This article purposely does not begin with the traditional review of the literature. The standard review is a rigid and largely empty formula which keeps us from communicating with each other directly with fresh and new ideas. It discourages breadth, rewards overspecialization, and constantly ties our thought to the past. I would prefer to strive for that state of lucid awareness which Krishnamurti (1969) refers to as "Freedom from the Known."

Since I urge sociologists to look into Eastern thought, I would also like to recommend some books which I have found valuable in beginning my explorations into their subject. First, I suggest any of the works of Alan Watts. Although some purists consider him a hedonist, he speaks to us as a Westerner and is fairly easy to understand. Second, any works of Krishnamurti. In both these cases I say "any work" by these authors, because all their books are segments in the same running commentary. Also: D. T. Suzuki, *An Introduction to Zen Buddhism;* Fromm et al., *Zen Buddhism and Psychoanalysis;* Chogyam Trungpa, *Meditation in Action, Cutting Through Spiritual Materialism,* and *The Myth of Freedom and the Way of Meditation;* Tarthang Tulku, *Gesture of Balance;* Eugene Herrigel, *Zen in the Art of Archery;* and Robert Powell, *Zen and Reality.*

Since this is not a discipline which can be mastered purely by intellectual means, those serious about pursuing it should become conversant with the practice of meditation, as it is explained in these books or taught by one of the many applied schools of Eastern thought in this country.

3. Although, of course, the issue of happiness is implicit in much sociological writing, the only book-length work explicitly related to the subject is Bradburn and Caplowtiz, *Reports on Happiness.*

4. Some readers of this article have indicated that the terms "enlightenment" or "liberation" (I use the term here interchangeably) are not fully defined. This is difficult because the term "enlightenment" is much like the term "sociology"; if you could fully define it, you would be a fully trained sociologist; if you could fully understand enlightenment, you would be fully enlightened. I try throughout this article to indicate what enlightenment is by tying it into the theory and practice of sociology. For those who like short definitions, however, I offer the following: enlightenment or liberation is the freedom from desire, total acceptance of reality, including the reality of self; it is freedom from all egotistical concern, what Krishnamuri calls "psychological thinking" as opposed to "technical thinking" (i.e., I think technically about the substance of my field, but have no thoughts as to how I rank in relation to others). Ultimately, it is a seeing beyond the concepts and categories of one's culture. The following quotations may also be helpful: "a certain silence of the mind, an inner transparence, a mental relaxation" (Linssen 1958); "Understanding the nature of bondage results in liberation (Suzuki 1964) ("Understanding" here means something broader than the action of intellect alone). "Satori may be defined as intuitive looking into, in contradistinction to intellectual and logical understanding. Whatever the definition, satori means the unfolding of a new world hitherto unperceived in the confusion of dualistic mind . . . " (Suzuki 1964).

5. One reader of this essay criticized it for not subjecting the Eastern teachings to the analysis of the sociology of knowledge, but this would be seeing the teachings through our own social science thought system. This is precisely what I avoid in speaking from within the assumptions of Eastern thought. From these assumptions the sociology of knowledge does not hold because Eastern thought differs from other philosophies in that it is a negation of all philosophy. In that sense it takes the implication of knowledge that all thought has irrational roots more seriously than we do.

6. In terms of Krishnamurti's distinction between technical and psychological thought, sociology is a mixed case. Our information processing becomes entangled with the personal needs which we project onto our material.

7. Once I was asked by a class of young prison inmates what sociology had to tell them about how to save their lives. After much thought I finally came up with the following contribution: Since upward mobility involves, above all, learning to take on another class-culture, those desiring mobility should make informal, friendship contracts with middle-class people. This was probably a truthful suggestion, but the setting only brings out the usual irony: people are stuck in existing social situations. How can they survive them?

8. The Western stereotype of the yogi sitting in his Himalayan cave only applies to some Western practitioners. From others we have a very different example. Gandhi and his present Indian followers are probably the most dramatic instances of social action. But we have innumerable other examples of yoga and Buddhist teachers who have founded schools, mental hospitals, and similar institutions and of those many who have generally spent their lives teaching. Nor have their teachings always ignored social ills. Krishnamurti's speeches and writings are filled with critical comments on the functioning of modern society.

9. This is, of course, not the kind of learning envisaged by those who regard sociology as parallel to natural science. I am reminded of a class in race relations I taught in the 1960s. The students had read Baldwin and other very angry black intellectuals without comment. Then I invited a black radical to class who was so angry he almost failed to communicate altogether on a verbal level. Afterward all sorts of students came up to me and said, "You know, they're really mad!" and "For the first time I think I grasp what Baldwin was all about." When sociology functions at this level, it is fully in tune with the way of the Eastern paths (Fromm et al. 1960:118). It should be emphasized that I am not arguing for a totally subjectivist position, but only that the kind of knowledge necessary for the study of people must be both intellectual and emotional.

10.   For those who fear that cultural relativism will leave us without any standard of judgment, and hence paralyzed, the Eastern paths offer an answer. The truly enlightened can see through the myriad cultural forms to a more ultimate, underlying reality.

11.   In his excellent book on careerism in corporations, Michael Maccoby follows his description of corporate careerism with this observation: "Comparing my own experience in universities, I would say that although academics consider themselves more 'humane' than businessmen, the engineers and managers we interviewed were no more competitive and a lot more cooperative with one another than most professors. If corporate managers engaged in the nitpicking and down-putting common in universities, little would be created and produced. If managers treated their subordinates with the neglect and contempt common in the attitude of professors to graduate students, no one would work for them" (Maccoby 1976:209).

References

Babbie, E. (1998). *Plagiarism*. Retrieved September 1, 2004, from www.csubak.edu/ssric/Modules/Other/plagiarism.htm

Beattie, M. (1987). *Codependent no more*. San Francisco: HarperHazelden.

Becker, E. (1973). *The denial of death*. Boston: Freepress Paperbacks.

Bell, I. (1972). *Involvement in society today*. Del Mar, CA: CRM.

Bell, I. (1979). Buddhist sociology. In S. G. McNall (Ed.), *Theoretical perspectives in sociology* (pp. 53-68). New York: St. Martin's.

Berger, P. L. (1963). *Invitation to sociology: A humanistic perspective*. Garden City, NJ: Doubleday-Anchor.

Blumer, H. (1962). Society as symbolic interaction. In A. Rose (Ed.), *Human behavior and social processes* (pp. 84-98). Boston: Houghton Mifflin. (Original work published 1934)

Bradburn, N. M., & Caplowitz, D. (1965). *Reports on happiness*. Chicago: Aldine.

Broom, L., & Selznick, P. (1955). *Sociology* (4th ed.). New York: Harper & Row.

Carroll, L. (1960). *Alice's adventures in wonderland*. New York: Signet. (Original work published 1865)

Cohen, S., & Taylor, L. (1976). *Escape attempts*. Middlesex, UK: Penguin.

Cuber, J. F., & Harroff, P. B. (1966). *Sex and the significant Americans*. Baltimore: Penguin.

Delpit, L. (1995) *Other people's children: Cultural conflict in the classroom*. New York: The New Press.

Derber, C. (1983). *The pursuit of attention: Power and individualism in everyday life*. London: Oxford University Press.

De Rougement, D. (1941). *Love in the western world*. New York: Harcourt Brace.

Dickens, C. (1982). *Great expectations*. New York: Penguin.

Domhoff, W. G. (1975). *The Bohemian grove and other retreats: A study in ruling-class cohesiveness*. New York: Harper & Row.

Elkin, F., & Handel, G. (1960). *The child and society: The process of socialization*. New York: Random House.

Ellis, A., & Bernard, M. (Eds.). (1983). *Rational-emotive approaches to the problems of childhood*. New York: Plenum.

Ellis, D. (1984). *Becoming a master student* (4th ed.). New York: College Survival.

Evans-Pritchard, E. E. (1940). *The Nuer*. London: Oxford University Press.

Fischer, L. (1963). *The essential Gandhi*. New York: Random House.

Freire, P. (1970). *Pedagogy of the oppressed*. New York: Continuum.

Fried, R. (1995). *The passionate teacher*. Boston: Beacon Press.

Fried, R. (2001). *The passionate learner*. Boston: Beacon Press.

Friday, N. (1977). *My mother, my self*. New York: Delacorte.

Fromm, E., Suzuki, D. T., & De Martino, R. (1960). *Zen Buddhism and psychoanalysis*. New York: Harper & Row.

Gardner, J., & Jewler, J. (1992). *College is only the beginning*. Belmont, CA: Wadsworth/ITP.

Goffman, E. (1967). Cooling out the mark. In P. I. Rose (Ed.), *The study of society: An integrated anthology* (pp. 89-105). New York: Random House.

Goldberg, N. (1986). *Writing down the bones: Freeing the writer within*. Boston: Shambhala.

Gouldner, A. W. (1970). *The coming crisis of western sociology*. New York: Basic Books.

Herrigel, E. (1971). *Zen in the art of archery*. New York: Vintage, Random House.

Holt, J. (1982). *How children fail*. New York: Delacorte.

Kastenbaum, R. (1998). *Death, society and human experience*. Needham Heights, MA: Allyn & Bacon.

Kensington Ladies' Erotica Society. (1984). *Ladies' home erotica.* Berkeley, CA: Ten Speed Press.

King, M. L. (1958). *Stride toward freedom.* New York: Harper & Row.

Kohn, A. (1986, September). How to succeed without even trying. *Psychology Today,* 22-28.

Kohn, A. (1993). *Punished by rewards: The trouble with gold stars, incentive plans, A's, praise, and other bribes.* New York: Houghton Mifflin.

Krishnamurti, J. (1969). *Freedom from the known.* New York: Harper & Row.

Krishnamurti, J. (1970). *Think on these things.* New York: Harper & Row.

Krishnamurti, J. (1974). *On education.* Bramdean, UK: Krishnamurti Foundation Trust.

Levy, J. (1966). *Cesar Chavez.* New York: W. W. Norton.

Linssen, R. (1958). *Living Zen.* New York: Grove.

Loewen, J. (1996). *Lies my teacher told me.* New York: Touchstone.

Maccoby, E. (1958). *Readings in social psychology* (3rd ed.). New York: Holt, Rinehart & Winston.

Maccoby, M. (1976). *The gamesman.* New York: Simon & Schuster.

Malcolm X. (1977). *The autobiography of Malcolm X.* New York: Ballantine.

Malinowski, B. (1985). *Sex and repression in savage society.* Chicago: University of Chicago Press. (Original work published 1927)

Mannheim, K. (1936). *Ideology and utopia: An introduction to the sociology of knowledge.* New York: Harcourt Brace.

Maslow, A. (1962). *Toward a psychology of being.* Princeton, NJ: Van Nostrand.

Matthiesen, P. (1978). *The snow leopard.* New York: Bantam.

Mead, G. H. (1934). *Mind, self and society.* Chicago: University of Chicago Press.

Mills, C. W. (1959). *The sociological imagination.* Oxford, UK: Oxford University Press.

Nhat Hanh, T. (1970). *Zen keys.* New York: Doubleday.

Nhat Hanh, T. (1985). *A guide to walking meditation.* Nyack, NY: Fellowship.

Parsons, T. (1951). *The social system.* Glencoe, IL: Free Press.

Peck, M. S. (1978). *The road less traveled.* New York: Simon & Schuster.

Piven, F. F., & Cloward, R. A. (1979). *Poor people's movements.* New York: Vintage.

Powell, R. (1961). *Zen and reality.* Middlesex, UK: Penguin.

Powell, R. (1967). *Crisis in consciousness.* Greenwood, SC: Attic.

Putney, S., & Putney, G. (1964). *The adjusted American: Normal neuroses in the individual and society.* New York: Harper & Row.

Rico, G. L. (1983). *Writing the natural way.* Los Angeles, CA: Jeremy P. Tarcher.

Salzman, J. (1993). *If you can talk, you can write.* New York: Warner.

Schachtel, E. (1959). *Metamorphosis.* New York: BasicBooks.

Schiller, D. (1994). *The little Zen companion.* New York: Workman.

Sedaris, D. (2000). *Me talk pretty one day.* New York: Little, Brown and Company.

Seeley, J. R., Sim, R. A., & Loosley, E. W. (1967). *Crestwood Heights.* New York: Wiley.

Sennett, R., & Cobb, J. (1971). *The hidden injuries of class.* New York: Vintage.

Smith, D. N. (1974). *Who rules the universities?* New York: Monthly Review Press.

Stevens, B. (1970). *Don't push the river.* Moab, UT: Real People.

Suzuki, D. T. (1964). *An introduction to Zen Buddhism.* New York: Random House.

Suzuki, S. (1970). *Zen mind, beginner's mind.* New York: Weatherhill.

Sykes, C. J. (1989). *PROFSCAM: Professors and the demise of higher education.* Washington, DC: Regnery Gateway.

Terkel, S. (1972). *Working.* New York: Random House.

Trungpa, C. (1966). *Born in Tibet.* Baltimore: Penguin.

Trungpa, C. (1969). *Meditation in action.* Berkeley, CA: Shambhala.

Trungpa, C. (1973). *Cutting through spiritual materialism.* Berkeley, CA: Shambhala.

Trungpa, C. (1976). *The myth of freedom and the way of meditation.* Berkeley, CA: Shambhala.

Tulku, T. (1977). *Gesture of balance.* Emeryville, CA: Sharma.

Watts, A. W. (1961). *Psychotherapy East and West.* New York: Ballantine.

Watts, A. W. (1996). *The Book: On the taboo against knowing who you are.* New York: Pantheon.

Wrong, D. (1967). The oversocialized conception of man in modern sociology. In P. I. Rose (Ed.), *The study of society: An integrated anthology* (pp. 136-146). New York: Random House.

Zinn, H. (1964). *SNCC: The new abolitionists.* Boston: Beacon.

Zinn, H. (1980). *A people's history of the United States.* New York: Harper Colophon.

Index

Academia
and censorship of new ideas, 80
and class system, 77
and financial issues, 77
and freedom of information, 80
history of, 105–6
and information, dissemination of, 148
and jobs, 78
and scholarly objectivity, 76–77
secret language of, 73–74, 75
and sociology, enlightened, 256
and specialization, 76, 79, 106
See also professors; universities and
access to powerful upper class
Accommodations, living, 30–31, 49
Activities
and balance, finding, 51
cities, exploration of nearby, 31
and counterculture groups, 238–39
and heterogeneity of students, 115–16
and independent study, 123
juggling, 13–14
sports, 32, 119, 229, 231, 242n1
Adjusted American, The (Putney and
Putney), 161
Affirmative action, 206–9
AIDS, 169, 176–77
Allen, George, 229, 231
Ambition, and careers, 224, 232–33
Animal House, 13
Apartment accommodations, 31
Applied arts, 119
Area studies, 118
Asian students, 28
Assertiveness training, 187
Augustine, St., 153
Australia, 45–48
Autobiography of Malcolm X, The
(Malcolm X), 205

Balance, finding
and classes, choices of, 17–18
and entertainment, 14–16
and juggling activities, 13–14
and maximizing/minimizing style
of culture, 140–41
and sexual relations, 169
and study schedules, 50–51
and time, conception of, 16–17
and time management, 14–16, 30
Baldwin, James, 77, 104
Becker, E., 156
*Becoming a Master
Student* (Ellis), 52
Berger, P. L., 249, 252
Bernard, M., 187
Birth control, 169–70, 176, 177
Bluebooks, and exams, 101–2
Blumer, H., 251
Boards, university and college, 78
*Book: On the Taboo Against Knowing
Who You Are, The* (Watts), 48
Broom, L., 251
Brown vs. the Board of Education, 208–9
Buddhism. *See also* Buddhist sociology
classes, 120
and enlightenment, 240, 249, 257n4
and maya, 252
and practice, 111
and present moment,
attention to, 141
and satori, 249–50, 257n4
and self, 130, 131–33, 133, 250–53
and self-realization, 223
and wisdom, 109
Buddhist sociology
about, 247–48, 256n2
and enlightened sociology, 254–55,
257nn7, 9, 258n10

and methodology, 253–54, 257n6,
257nn5, 6
and self, 250–53
and social action, 254, 257n8
and socialization, 248–50
and sociology, practicing, 255–56
Budgets, 33, 34

California Proposition 209,
206, 208
Campus tours, 31
Careers
and ambition, 224, 232–33
and careerism, 224–29, 233n3,
255, 258n11
vs. craftsmanship, 56, 228–29, 230–31
and families, 224–25
and grades, 51–52
and graduation issues,
210–12, 218
and independent study, 123
and job satisfaction, 228–33
and moving, 225
and multiple careers, 224
and parents, 188–89
and professors, 60–61, 62
vs. rural lifestyle, 56–57
and self-realization, 223
and time management, 224–25
and travel abroad, 127
Carnegie, Andrew, 78, 79
Carroll, L., 73
Catholic Church, 109, 167–68. *See also*
Christianity
Cesar Chavez (Levy), 206
Cheating, 88–89. *See also* plagiarism
Chinese opera, and oral reports, 99–101
Christianity, 107–8, 109, 112,
130, 167–68
Classes. *See also* grades
and balance, finding, 17–18
Buddhism, 120
choices of, 17–18, 120
and Eastern thought, 120
economics, 118
English, 96
fiction, 119
history, 118–19
interdisciplinary, 120
language/linguistics, 119
literature, 119
meditation, 120
minorities, 118
natural science, 119

pass/fail classes, 52–53
philosophy, 119
political science, 118–19
and questions, asking, 2
religion, 119–20
social science, 128n3
sociology, 118, 119
stake in, 37–38
student actions during, 63–64
and study schedules, 50–51
and travel abroad, 126, 127–28
ungraded classes, 52–53
and wisdom, 118–20
and writing skills, 96–97
yoga, 120
Class system. *See also* minorities;
upper mobility
and academia, 77
and model upper middle-class
personality, 205, 206
and professors, 61–62
in societies, 75
and upper class, 77, 78–79, 103–4
College education, 7–10, 78–79,
103–4, 116
College is Only the Beginning (Gardner
and Jewler), 52
Community colleges, 29, 30
Competitiveness, vs. sexual
attraction, 155
Condoms, 169–70, 176, 177
Confessions (Augustine), 153
Connelly, Ward, 206, 208, 209
Contraception, 169–70, 176, 177
Control issues, and romantic love,
162–63
Counseling, psychological, 117
Counterculture groups, 238–39
Courses, college. *See* classes
Craftsmanship, 56, 228–29, 230–31
Crestwood Heights (Seeley, Sim &
Loosley), 226–27
Critical thinking, 54–55
Cuber, J. F., 173
Culture
and counterculture groups, 238–39
and Krishnamurti, 257n8
and mass media, 147
maximizing/minimizing style of,
140–41
and media culture, 148–49
and minorities, 198
and romantic love, 154–55
and sociology, practicing, 255–56

travel abroad and adjustments to
differences in, 126
and upward mobility, 198
Curriculum. *See* classes

Davis, Angela, 78
Daydreams, 141–44
Death, Society and Human Experience
(Kastenbaum), 177
Decision making
about, 235–37
and changes in self, 239–40, 241
and counterculture groups, 238–39
individualized, 4–5
and mistakes, 237, 242n1
and partners, 237
and periphery of
society, 238–39
De Martino, R., 144, 250
Depression, 171, 172n4
Derber, C., 116
De Rougement, D., 158
Desocialization, 129, 140, 144,
249–50, 257n4
Destiny's Child, 160
Direct experience, 121–24
Dormitory accommodations, 30–31, 49

Eastern thought. *See* Buddhism;
Buddhist sociology
Ebert and Roeper, 15
Economics classes, 118
Education, college, 78–79, 103–4, 116
Educational institutions. *See* academia
Elkin, F., 248
Ellis, D. B., 52, 187
Employment, 33–38, 52, 56, 78
English classes, 97
Enlightenment, 240, 249, 257n4
Entertainment, 14–16
Essential Gandhi (Fischer), 206
Evans-Pritchard, E. E., 138
Exams, and bluebooks, 101–2
Existentialism, 119–20

Families. *See also* parents
and assertiveness training, 187
and careers, 224–25
and home living situation, 49
immigrant, 182, 184–85
travel abroad, and independence
from, 127
Fiction classes, 119
Fieldwork projects, 121–24

Financial issues, 77, 126, 189–90,
212–13
Fischer, L., 144, 206
Fraternities, 3, 22–23, 31
Freedom, 126–27, 150
Freedom from the Known
(Krishnamurti), 112
Freedom of information, 80
Freire, P., 53–54
Freshmen issues, 2
Fried, R., 39–40
Friendships
and heterogeneity of students,
115–16
and networking, 3–4, 31
and orientation, 3
and romantic love, 164–67, 177n1
and self, 2–3
Fromm, E., 144, 250, 257n9
the future
and grades, 47–48
and graduation issues, 212,
213–18, 219
preparations for, 47–48, 122–23
and travel abroad, 127

Gamesman, The (Maccoby), 225
Gandhi, 110, 257n8
Gardner, J., 52
Gibson, J. W., 61–62
Goffman, E., 251
Good Samaritan story, 157
Gouldner, A. W., 247–48, 253, 254
Grades
and Australia, 45–46
and careers, 51–52
and the future, 47–48
and internalization of grading system,
39–40, 44–46, 49–53, 58n1
vs. learning, 40–45
and parents, 188
pressure of achieving good, 40–45
rules about, 39, 49–52, 58n1
and self-confidence, 43
and study skills, 51
and thinking, critical, 54–55
vs. ungraded classes, 52–53
Graduation issues
careers, 210–12, 218
and financial issues, 212–13
and the future, 212, 213–18, 219
and single mother students, 219–20
and socialization, 221
and studentness, death of, 220–21

Guidance issues, 1–2
Guide to Walking Meditation
    (Nhat Hanh), 140

Handel, G., 248
Harroff, P. B., 173
Hasidic sect, 109
High Anxiety, 155
High school experiences, 4–6, 10, 56, 97
Hinduism, 111
History classes, 118–19
HIV virus. *See* AIDS
Holiday, Billie, 153
Holt, J., 48
Home living situation, 49
Homosexuality issues, 155–58
How Children Fail (Holt), 48
Humanities. *See* social sciences

Idealism, about college experience, 10
Ideology and Utopia (Mannheim),
    110–11, 253
Independent study, 122–24
Independent Woman (song), 160
Integrity, academic, 83–87
Interdisciplinary classes, 120
Internalization of grading system, 39–40,
    44–46, 49–53, 58n1
International students, 27–28
Internet information, and plagiarism,
    83–84, 85
Introspection, 3
Invitation to Sociology (Berger), 249

Jewler, J., 52
Jobs, 33–38, 52, 56, 78
Joint major course of study, 124
Judaism, 109

Kapleau, P., 223
Kastenbaum, R., 177
King, M. L., Jr., 205–6
Knowledge, 103–4, 110, 111, 112
Kohn, A., 42, 48
Krishnamurti, J.
    and ambition, 224, 233
    and Buddhist sociology, 256n2
    and culture, 257n8
    and decision making, 236
    and desocialization, 132,
        144, 249, 250
    and Enlightenment, 257n4
    and knowledge, 112
    and thought, 257n6

Landmark Education, 37
Language/linguistics classes, 119
Laziness, 50, 134
Learning, 40–45, 69, 72n3, 241
Levy, J., 206
Life issues, 5–7
Life Skills for Women course, 28
Linseen, R., 249, 257n4
Listener/listening, practice of, 116–17
Literature classes, 119
Little Zen Companion (Schiller), 64–65
Living accommodations, 30–31, 49
Loosley, E. W., 226
Love. *See* real love; romantic love
Love in the Western World
    (De Rougement), 158

Maccoby, M., 224, 225, 226, 258n11
Major course of study, 124, 128n3
Malcolm X, 205
Malinowski, B., 135
Mannheim, K., 110–11, 253
Married-with-children students, 25–27
Marx, K., 110
Maslow, A., 144, 252
Mass media, 145–48, 150–51
Matrix, The, 70
McGrane, B., 61–62
Mead, G. H., 251
Media, mass, 145–48, 150–51
Meditation, 120, 241–42
Me Talk Pretty One Day (Sedaris), 156
Mills, C. Wright, 74, 253, 254
Minimizing/maximizing style of
    culture, 140–41
Minorities. *See also* upward mobility
    and academic issues, 203
    and affirmative action, 206–9
    and bicultural, becoming, 204–6
    classes about, 118
    and culture, 198
    and enrollment issues, 200, 201
    and individualism, 205–6
    and model of upwardly mobile,
        198–99, 210n3
    and model upper middle-class
        personality, 205, 206
    and morale, 201, 209–10
    and painful path, 197–98
    and parents, conflicts with, 190
    and power, majority, 204
    and pride, 203–4
    and socialization, 202–3
    and unity issues, 197, 200–201, 205, 209

and universities, minority, 209
and Whites, 197, 198, 210n1
Molestation/rape, 23–25
Mystics/mysticism, 108–9,
110–12, 120

Natural science classes, 119
Neighborhoods, exploration of, 31
Networking, 3–4, 31
Neurotic relationships, 171, 172,
174, 186–87
Nhat Hanh, T., 140, 223
Nontraditional experiences
Asian students, 28
international students, 27–28
married-with-children students,
25–27
single mother students, 219–20
transfer students, 29–32
Nuer people, 135

Off campus accommodations, 31
Olympic games, 242n1
Oral reports, 99–101
Orientation, benefits of, 3–4
"Oversocialized Conception of Man,
The" (Wrong), 248

Parents. *See also* families
and acceptance, 193
and adult-children, relationships with,
190, 191, 192, 193
and careers, 188–89
and college experiences, positive,
190, 191
and communication, incapacity for,
194–95
and conflicts with children, 187,
190, 193–94
and culturally patterned conflicts,
182, 183–85
and cutting off children, 179
and estrangement from children,
182–83
and financial issues, 189–90
and grades, 188
and love, 185–86, 194–95
and marriage, restructuring, 193
and minorities, 190
and negotiations with children,
193, 194
and relationship with children,
180–81
and responsibilities to children, 191

and separating from children, 193
and upward mobility of children, 190
Parsons, T., 74–75, 80n3
Participation coordinator (PC) programs,
68–71, 72n3
Partying, 19–20, 22–25
Pass/fail classes, 52–53
Passionate Teacher, The (Fried), 39–40
Peck, M. S., 172
Pedagogy of the Oppressed (Freire), 53–54
Philosophy, 105, 106, 119
Plagiarism, 83–87
Political science classes, 118–19
Polynesian people, 135
Powell, R., 144, 250
Procrastination, 50, 134
Professors. *See also* academia
about, 59–60
careers of, 62
choosing, 62–63, 67
and class systems, 61 62
and community colleges/small
colleges, 59, 60
and independent study, 123–24
and popularization of subjects,
61, 79, 80
and publication of books, 60,
71n1, 79
role of, 53–54
and students, 61, 63–64, 65–66
and teaching, 60–65, 69, 72n3
and temporary contracts, 61
and universities, 59, 60, 61–62
Proposition 209, California, 206, 208
Protestantism, 109
Psychology, 106, 107–8, 118
*Punished by Rewards, The Trouble with
Gold Stars, Incentive Plans, A's, Praise,
and Other Bribes* (Kohn), 48
Pursuit of Attention, The (Derber), 116
Putney, G., 144, 161
Putney, S., 144, 161

Quakers, 109, 110
Queer Eye for the Straight Guy, 157

Rape/molestation, 23–25
Real love, 172–76, 185–86
Reeves, G. H., 57
Rejection from colleges, 7–10
Relationships. *See also* real love;
romantic love
and assertiveness training, 187
and idealism about college, 10

vs. introspection, time of, 3
long distance, 12–13
neurotic relationships, 171, 172,
    174, 186–87
with professors, 66
with self, 2–3
and single life, 10–11
Religion classes, 119–20
Religious beliefs. *See specific religions;
    specific sects*
Research issues, 106–7
Riles, W., 78
Road Less Traveled, The (Peck), 172
Rockefeller, John D., 78, 79
Romantic love. *See also* relationships;
    sexuality issues
    vs. anxiety, 155
    and bad relationships, 165, 177n1
    and being/walking in love, 163–64
    and condoms, 176, 177
    and control issues, 162–63
    and culture, 154–55
    and depression, 171, 172n4
    and falling in/out of love, 61–163
    and family relationships, 167, 177n2
    and friendships, 164–67, 177n1
    and hate/hostile relationships, 167
    history of, 158–59
    and homosexuality, 155–58
    and mass media, 159, 167
    and men, independent, 170–71
    and music, popular, 153–54, 159
    myth of, 159
    and negativity, effects of, 160
    and reality, 159
    vs. real love, 172–76
    and self, 161–62, 170–72
    and sexual relations, 167–70
    and socialization, 161
    and woman, independent, 160, 170
    and women, independent, 160, 170–71
Rural lifestyle, vs. careers, 56–57
Russia, and class systems, 75

Samaritan story, Good, 157
Satori, 249–50, 257n4
Schiller, D., 64–65
Science, 106, 119
Sedaris, D., 156
Seeley, J. R., 226
Self
    and bicultural, becoming, 205
    and Buddhism, 130, 131–33
    and Buddhist sociology, 250–53

changes in self, 239–40, 241
and Christianity, 130
and critical voice, 134–36
and culture, 130–31, 140–41, 141
and daydreams, 141–44
and depression, 171, 172n4
and feelings, 134
forgetting, 117
and ideal self, 133
and introspection, 130
knowledge of, 2–3
and mass media, 148–49
mass media, and identity of, 147
and men, independent, 170–71
and romantic love, 161–62
and roots/heritage, 136–38
and self-acceptance, 170–72, 232
and self-confidence, 43
and self-knowledge, 104, 105, 111,
    112, 117
self/no-self exercises, 133
and self-realization, 223
and time, concept of, 138–40, 144n2
and woman, independent, 160, 170
Self, 130–31
Self-Expression and Leadership (SELP)
    course, 37
Selznick, P., 251
Senior's advice, 2–3
Sex and the Significant Americans (Cuber
    and Harroff), 173
Sexuality issues, 66, 155–58, 167–70,
    176–77
Sexually transmitted diseases (STDs),
    169, 170
Shakespeare, W., 15
Shakespeare in Love, 15
Silence, practice of, 110, 112
Sim, R. A., 226
Single life, 10–11
Single mother students, 219–20
Socialization
    and Buddhist sociology, 248–50
    and desocialization, 129, 140
    and graduation issues, 221
    and homosexuality issues, 157
    and mass media, 145
    and minorities, 202–3
    and romantic love, 161
    and upward mobility, 201–3
    and wisdom, 112–13
Social sciences, 73–74, 75, 95–96, 106–7,
    128n3
Sociological Imagination, The (Mills), 74

Sociology
    Buddhist sociology, 254–55, 257n7
    classes, 118, 119
    of knowledge, 110
Sororities, 31. *See also* fraternities
Specialization, 76, 79, 104, 106
Spiritual discipline, 116, 120, 128n1,
    240, 241–42
Sports, 32, 119, 229, 231, 242n1
STDs (sexually transmitted diseases),
    169, 170
Stride Toward Freedom (King), 205–6
Students. *See also* parents
    Asian students, 28
    and classes, actions during, 63–64
    and communication with
        professors, 61
    and freshmen issues, 2
    heterogeneity of, 115–16
    international students, 27–28
    married-with-children students,
        25–27
    and parents, acceptance of, 193
    and professors, 63–64
    and relationships with professors,
        65–66
    single mother students, 219–20
    and studentness, death of, 220–21
    transfer students, 29–32
    *Who's Who Among American High
        School Students*, 88
Study schedules, 50–51
Suzuki, D. T., 144, 250, 252
Suzuki, S., 112, 144, 257n4

Teachers. *See* professors
Teaching, 60–65, 69, 72n3
Teaching assistants (TAs), 67–68, 71
Terkel, S., 225, 229, 230
Theology, 105, 106, 107–8. *See also*
    specific religions; specific sects
Therapy, psychological, 117
Thinking, critical, 54–55
Thomas, W. I., 160
Tibetan Buddhism, 250
Time, concept of, 16–17, 30,
    138–40, 144n2
Time management
    and balance, finding, 14–16, 30
    and careers, 224–25
    and grades, rules about, 49–50
    and jobs, 33–34
    and laziness, 50, 134
    and study schedules, 50

Time-off breaks, 56
Tours, campus, 31
Transfer students, 29–32
Travel abroad, 32, 46–47, 56, 120, 125–28
Trungpa, C., 144, 250
Twelfth Night (Shakespeare), 15, 16

Ungraded classes, 52–53
Universities. *See also* academia
    and boards, 78
    vs. community colleges, 29, 30
    and minority universities, 209
    and professors, 59, 60, 61–62
    and rejection from, 7–10
    and transfer students, 29–30
Universities
    and college education, 7–10, 78–79,
        103–4, 116
Upper class, 77, 78–79, 103–4
Upward mobility. *See also* class system
    and academic issues, 203
    and affirmative action, 206–9
    and bicultural, becoming, 204–6
    and culture, 198
    and enrollment issues, 200, 201
    and individualism, 205–6
    and model upper middle-class
        personality, 205, 206
    and morale issues, 209–10
    painful path of, 197–98
    and parents, conflicts with, 190
    and power, majority, 204
    and pride, 203–4
    and self, effects on, 205, 206
    and socialization, 201–3
    and unity issues, 197, 200–201, 209
    and Whites, 197, 198, 210n1
U.S. Department of Defense, 79

Watts, A. W., 48, 144, 226, 251, 252
Weltanschauung, and exams, 102
*Who's Who Among American High School
    Students*, 88
Will and Grace, 157
Wisdom
    and Buddhism, 109
    and Christianity, 107–8, 112
    and classes, 118–20
    and college education, 116
    and direct experience, 121–25
    and experience, 104–5
    and Hasidic sect, 109
    and mystics/mysticism, 108–9, 110–12
    and Quakers, 109, 110

and self-knowledge, 104, 105
and socialization, 112–13
and theology, 107–8
Work, 33–38, 52, 56, 78
Writing skills
and clarity, 93
creativity in term papers, 91–92
and English classes, 97
and high school, 97
and mentors, 97
and padding papers, 94
positive feedback to improve, 92
and positive thinking, 94–95
and research, 95

and revisions, 92–93
and rituals, 94
and secret language of academia, 94
and social science papers, 95–96
and strategies for assignments, 98–99
and topics, 93
and writing classes, 96–97
Wrong, D., 248–49

Yoga classes, 120

Zen Buddhism. *See* Buddhism
*Zen Mind, Beginner's
    Mind* (Suzuki), 112

About the Author and Contributors

Inge Bell, emeritus professor of sociology at Pitzer College, close friend and colleague, died April 29, 1996. Born in 1930 in Austria, Inge and her family escaped from the Nazis, emigrating to this country in the 1940s. She grew up in Claremont, California, just blocks from Pitzer's campus, which in 1968 was to become her academic home, within which she would shape the bulk of her distinguished academic career.

Inge earned her PhD at the University of California at Berkeley during the 1960s, a decade that expressed and clarified the values and sensibilities that would subsequently inform her lifelong perspective on teaching and scholarship. At Berkeley, Inge was heavily involved in the civil rights movement, contributing especially to the organization and functioning of the first Berkeley/Oakland chapter of the Congress of Racial Equality (C.O.R.E.). Her work with C.O.R.E. soon became a central research interest, resulting eventually in the publication of her first book, *C.O.R.E: The Strategy of Non-Violence.*

Inge's capacity to join her personal and civic commitments to her professional activities was in evidence early in her academic career. She refused to compartmentalize her life. For example, following Inge's personal explorations into the meditations of Zen Buddhism, she fleshed out the humanism embedded in its practice and theory, themes she went on to weave into her 1979 classic essay "Buddhist Sociology."

Inge took early retirement from Pitzer College in 1982 in order, as she put it, "to think, to write and, most importantly, to tend to my garden." And she did all three with much zeal and enthusiasm. She continued her conversations with colleagues, exchanging ideas, information, and insights. Inge also wrote and published the enormously influential *This Book Is Not Required* (1985) during her retirement. The book gained widespread circulation and adoption, winning praise and admiration from colleagues in all academic disciplines. Written as an undergraduate "survival manual," *This Book Is Not Required* is a humane repository of wise sociologically informed observations; it has taught and will continue to teach countless students how to flourish during their college years. And, we would add, Inge's garden became the envy of many in and around Ft. Bragg, California, where she retired with her husband, Ted Hoffman.

Inge lived her life as a warm, loving, and wise human being. She was an incredible *listener,* capable of transcending her own concerns and making herself available to those in need of a sympathetic ear. Scores of colleagues and friends and a multitude of students benefited from Inge's understanding and wisdom over the years. Inge Bell enriched the lives of everyone she touched, and she enriched our discipline of sociology with her humanistic voice and vision. Although we are thankful that her voice and vision will continue in print and memory, Inge herself will be sorely missed.

Glenn A. Goodwin

Al Schwartz

Professors Emeritus, Pitzer College

Team Bell

The student team came together to approach the task of revising Inge Bell's book, *This Book Is Not Required,* in the wake of her death.

The team was a dynamic collection of individual perspectives, a gathering of strengths. Each person responded to a different facet of the book. One person commented this it is a book about diversity. Another remembered that Dr. Bell spoke of minorities leaving their families behind. A few members of the group were in transition: graduating, getting married, moving, applying to graduate schools. They heard Bell addressing the emancipation quandary. Fittingly, Bell wrote in metaphors, extending in different directions. What emerged was a multifaceted whole.

The team as a group shared a common task: to preserve Bell's message and make it more accessible to others. All agreed that a first step could be to modernize the language. We are entering a new millennium—how does this impact the readership? Several members of the team had something new to contribute, an expansion of Bell's philosophy. Each could bring a new segment, to be distilled through the group as a whole.

Regarding the process of revision, the team agreed to first work together to distill Bell's original text and then to contribute individual voices to the whole. It was important to first step into the domain of Bell's world. As with an historic building, the job was to preserve and to renovate.

The question at issue was how to maintain the integrity of Bell's voice—its intensity and impact—while updating language and references. The team agreed that the function of updating was to enhance the field of relevance and reader responsiveness.

In the end, the voice that speaks would be that of the new entity, the collective voice of Bell, her readers, those who want to continue her legacy. The team spoke of making the book an organic event, an open conversation, by allowing for ongoing enhancements. Several spoke of having a moral obligation to find the language to continue giving Bell's message to contemporary student readers.

Patricia Harriman

Jasleen Ahuja is an undergrad at the University of California, Los Angeles (UCLA), is 20 years old, and is still figuring out what decisions she needs to make to have the "perfect life" she's always dreamed about. Those decisions are tough but have resulted in an English major, political science minor, and, ideally, law school in the near future. Choosing an educational route may be a tough decision, but it is one of the most rewarding.

Lynette Albovias graduated from University of California at Irvine (UCI) with a bachelor's in economics and a minor in management. Future plans include obtaining work experience in marketing and, ultimately, a master's degree in business administration. Lynette believes that the dynamic ideas of Bell's book are powerful because they reveal a truth specific to each reader. Contrary to Bell's title, Lynette believes that Bell's book should be required in a student education course to allow the truth to come through. It was both an honor and a privilege to be part of a team working to update Bell's ideas so that they can continue to speak their truth to students.

Ann Amigable is a work in progress: continually learning and growing because her hunger for life is never satisfied. God continually blesses her, which is evident when you look at her family, friends, and life. She is eternally grateful and indebted to all the people who have touched her life and who have opened her eyes a little wider, so she can truly see the world and herself.

Sheyda Bogosyan was born in Istanbul, Turkey, to two Armenian parents. At the age of 7, she was told that her family was moving to Los Angeles, so she packed her bags and stepped foot into the land of opportunity. She attended a private Armenian school from 1st through 12th grade, so naturally it had a big influence on her personality. She attended UCI and graduated with a degree in psychology. She currently works as a behavioral therapist for autistic children and plans on pursuing a career in special education. She is extremely grateful to be given the opportunity to contribute to the editing of this book because it made such a big impact on her life when she first read it. She hopes her contribution to this book will help make a few students' college lives just a bit easier, or at least seem a bit more normal.

Lauren Bragg, from Lake Tahoe, California, believes in saving the earth, protecting wonderful creatures from extinction, and achieving peace and harmony for all. She has her beliefs, which nobody can take away—ever. She believes that one day, one moment, one person can change your life forever. Carpe diem and no regrets!

Mariae Bui. Perfect.

Jeff Chen was born in Taiwan to parents who believed opportunity and education were more abundant in the United States. Due to his multicultural background, Jeff found his scholastic calling in the field of sociology, where he could further his understanding of people, groups, cultures, and social interaction. Jeff learned early that to succeed, as both a person and a scholar, one needs to take advantage when opportunities present themselves. His involvement in the sociology major, and his ambition to immerse himself in diverse activities, led him to participate in Team Bell. Jeff is now pursuing a postcollegiate career that will incorporate the social and academic tools he learned at ULCA, while allowing him to maintain and expand his multicultural heritage.

Kenneth Chow grew up in the small town of Caruthers, where he could stand on his rooftop staring into the horizon and seeing nothing but grapevines. He is in his fourth year at UCLA and sees nothing but pollution in the sky, with the occasional star here and there. He found this book enticing because everyone can relate to it, and the issues involved are important for a well-balanced life. Kenneth plans on becoming a business consultant to help those who want to simplify their lives and fulfill their dreams. He dedicates this book to everyone in search of the truth and, most of all, to his lovely parents for providing him the opportunity to be who he is today.

Michelle Chung is a graduate of UCI and finds herself at the intersection of the many avenues that life has led her on. Her belief in the strength of knowledge and the power that it possesses inspires her to pass on the wisdom of her predecessors to those who desire to cultivate curiosity about the past and imagination of the future.

Erin Cora was born and raised in Southern California and has survived a school system that she spent years rejecting. In the end, she found relief and, more important, blessings and appreciation for her journey. A Chapman University graduate, she is now pondering the next journey in her life. Presently, she is searching for a career that can incorporate the knowledge and wisdom she has gained and also provide her with the opportunity for personal growth. She is pursuing a life of completeness, blending a self-fulfilling career, love, fun, and happiness.

Andrea Crane is a Chapman University sociology student who has studied in both the United States and Australia. She plans to attend graduate school in California to further her studies in the field of sociology, particularly gender studies. Apart from sociological endeavors, Andrea is also a published poet and art student.

Veronica Fematt has walked many different paths throughout life, some very rocky, others serene. Her life story could be summarized by the following equation: immigrant parents + the American dream = upper middle-class life + divorce = poverty—basically your average hardship novel. Veronica came to UCLA as a transfer student, even though all bets were against her. She is most thankful for having so many different and challenging life experiences, allowing her to see the world through multiple lenses—what she believes is key to actually making a real difference in the world. Her ultimate goals are to do social research, publish a few books, and become a professor at a university. She thanks her mom, Rosaura Lavenant—her inspiration to succeed—for always challenging her and her sisters to set high aspirations. Watching her mom jump all the hurdles and triumph makes it impossible for Veronica to call anything difficult. Gracias.

Tatian Greenleaf grew up in Berkeley, California, and graduated from UCI in 1997 with a bachelor's degree in sociology and a minor in computer science. As a member of the orientation staff there, he helped prepare incoming students for university life. As an undergraduate, Tatian worked as a teaching assistant, leading discussion sections in "Sociology of the Media" and "The Social Psychology of Higher Education." Tatian also served as the editor-in-chief of the UCI yearbook, an award-winning publication. He now works for a test-prep company, coordinating and teaching courses for high school and college students, and plans to pursue a master's degree in education and continue to teach.

Sharon Greg, having journeyed through several phases of life, has chosen and achieved many goals. She likes being helpful to others. She has a wonderful family, a degree in social work, and usually tells people that she is the "Mom" of the social sciences division at Chapman University. For the time being, she is content to remain where she is and explore some options for the next phase of her life.

John Gunderson received his PhD from Claremont Graduate University. He has taught at the secondary and university level for many years. He currently teaches at Dana Hills High School in South Orange County and at Chapman University. His work is grounded in the belief that passionate teaching and learning can transform education and the lives of individuals. He is happily married and the proud new father of twin boys.

Patricia Harriman—administrator, poet, mother, student—enjoys the many facets of life and her role within them. She has experienced life in the ministry, has published numerous poems, has worked in administration for 20 years, is raising the last of three children, and is pursuing a degree in comparative literature and mythology.

Rick Hartman, 24 years old and currently a salesman and student-in-waiting, is on a 7-year degree program with a major in philosophy. Major area of interest and driving passion is an exploration of the space where language, identity, and the world somehow come together and, at the same time, generate each other in some strange form of dependent origination. Committed to transforming the boundaries of what is possible for human beings to think through a change in their relationship to language. More important, the proud new companion of a German Shepherd puppy.

Christine Hebling is an English and peace studies graduate from the small, liberal arts–oriented Chapman University, where she fumbled her way through many of the mistakes Bell discusses. This is also where she found much comfort in Bell's (and students') prose. She wishes to pursue the elusive craft of writing.

Katherine Ho attended UCI, majoring in music performance and sociology. Coming from a very culturally diverse background and family, she finds that culture and the complex ways we all carry ourselves within our close relationships continue to be the creative drive in one's educational career and life. A man named Michael Bartel once said, "Happiness is a conscious choice, not an automatic response." She hopes that this book will help people to see that in this world you have a choice, in your education and any other aspect in life.

Jordon Kagan was born in Ghana and spent the first 10 years of his life in Africa and the rest in the United States, all the while maintaining a close connection to his family's home in Israel. Jordon's career and education goals have ranged from computers to philosophy to psychology to sociology, which is where he stands now. He plans on getting into consulting after graduation, and his dream is to one day become a futurist. His passion is technology, and he would love to study it and predict its future. Jordon has enjoyed working on this project immensely and truly appreciates the value of this book and the wisdom contained within it.

Sara Kalawi was born in Montreal, Canada, and is the product of a Lebanese father and a French-Canadian mother. For this reason, she has always felt that she relates well to the lives of a diversity of people. When she first read this book, Sara was intrigued by the diversity of topics covered and touched by the number of students who shared their words. She has found the book to be a useful tool in terms of college emotional survival and only wishes she could have found it earlier in her adolescent life. She takes pleasure and honor in contributing to this book and hopes her thoughts are appreciated and useful.

Daniel Kauahi, born and raised in Hawai'i, meandered some 27 years and finally ended up as an undergraduate at Chapman University. He is forever proud of his Hawai'ian heritage and strives to keep the Hawai'ian culture alive. *E ola mau ka olelo Hawai'i.*

Stavros Kavoulakis. Dare disturb the universe. Dare to eat a peach. Fight the intractable tide and sail the irresistible wind during the storm. Squeeze the universe into a ball and roll it toward anything you set your sights on. Live your life with a bang and not a whimper.

Christopher Patrick King. We are students in the Class of Life. We are individual, walking experiments. The power of our humanity is that we can teach each other, while still learning what life is all about for ourselves. May all the students hear the love with which we write and know they are not alone. May they see the world as one endless chance to grow and mature. And may the students, empowered with a heart-filled passion, then become teachers in love and in life. Thanks to all of you for teaching me.

Arelene Lozano, a Chicana from the San Fernando Valley, attended UCI, double majoring in sociology and international studies and being actively involved in campus, community, and political social movements. Armed with natural charisma and a passion for public service, she is going to change the world! Live to make a difference every day, and before you know it you have a revolution.

Lawrence Lu is someone who simply wishes to be a kid again and forever. He longs to look at the world with the wide-eyed optimism that plagues the youthful and feel the comfort of being part of a loving, genuine family. "Getting real" and "growing up" are not among his chosen hobbies. As a graduate of UCLA with a degree in psychology, he believes that everyone, at some point in life, is truly happy and that there is not a thing in the world more important than trying to find your way back, even for just a moment, even if it takes a lifetime.

Bernard McGrane received a PhD from New York University. He has taught at a wide variety of universities—Vermont College, Colby College in Maine, Cuesta Community College, UCLA, and Pitzer College. He currently teaches at Chapman University and UCI. He has studied Tibetan Buddhism under Chögyam Trungpa Rinpoche and transformative education with Landmark Education. He is the author of *Beyond Anthropology, Society and the Other,* and *The Un-TV and the 10 MPH Car—Experiments and Personal Freedom and Everyday Life.* He is also featured in two educational videos: *The Ad and the Id: Sex, Death, and Subliminal Advertising* and *The Ad and the Ego: Advertising and Identity.*

Lisa Miyake was born in Tokyo and was raised in Orange County, California. Lisa is a second year mass communications and Japanese double major at UCLA. She enjoys making the most of her years as an undergraduate by being involved with on-campus organizations, and she plans to work as a coordinator for international relations with the Japan Exchange and Teaching Programme after graduation. Future plans include going to law school, working in the field of international relations, and making the world a better place.

David Edward Mushegain (1975–), a native of California with family roots stemming from the nation of Armenia, as of NOW, is in the process of surrendering to the nomadic nature of this, a universe. His curiosity lies within the transfer from knowledge to wisdom to nothingness and our willingness to free ourselves enough to become aware of this. David has been a student of a system and, throughout, a student of our environment. He hopes we will, through the time that does not exist, realize we are all part of a tribe and our mother earth and externally celebrate this community.

MyPha Ninh, whose name is two musical notes (mi and fa), always defines herself by her differences, such as her cultural difference: She emigrated from Vietnam at the end of June 1990. MyPha plays the violin, loves to read, writes poems, draws, and moves to music. She recommends students read and reread *This Book* as often as they need to—with an open heart full of wounds to be healed. MyPha further recommends *Mind over Mood,* by David Greenberger.

Nkemdilim Nwosu is a graduate of UCLA, where she obtained a bachelor of arts in sociology, with a specialization in communication studies. As an undergraduate, she worked as the editor-in-chief for UCLA's *Nommo* newsmagazine during the 2002–2003 school year. Her talent is writing, and she is currently working toward becoming a major TV script- and screenwriter.

Melissa Reggiardo graduates from UCLA in 2005. After graduation, she plans to take a year off from academics to pursue a few of life's other pleasures: rest, work, and travel. Graduate school is in the future, but the specifics are currently undecided; such details will undoubtedly fall into place when the time is right.

Kristin Rydberg is an overworked and underpaid college student who, upon first reading of Inge Bell's book, discovered that she was an unassuming victim of a stagnant educational system. Now she aspires to become an educator who is willing to move beyond the institution of education and challenge students to pursue true knowledge and wisdom. She hopes that her contribution to this book will inspire you to do the same.

Gagendeep Sandhu graduated from UCI with a bachelor of arts in psychology and sociology. Gagendeep has worked as a rape crisis counselor with a nonprofit organization and just received a master's in psychology.

Artin Sodaify was born in Los Angeles, California, and was raised in a modestly priced area of Beverly Hills. Artin attended elementary and high school in Beverly Hills and graduated from UCLA with a degree in sociology in 2003. UCLA instigated Artin's profound interest for education. As a sociology major, he learned about the working and elitist classes and the discrepancies between the two. Interest and study of the media taught Artin its pervasive and habitual control on people's perceptions, behaviors, and emotions. The social stratification of our society, coupled with the potent influence of the media, is difficult to ignore and resist. However, if we determine and acknowledge our true wants, needs, and ambitions, and become better aware of the inhibiting guidance of the media, we will live our ideal lives. Knowledge, not money, is the ultimate power.

Gary Tomlinson is a person who is uncomfortable talking about himself in the third person. He claims to be an empirically synoptical existentialist with mystical overtones, believes in process over Prozac, and regularly practices generic self-improvement. Tomlinson says that the secret of a good life is to give love—receive love—be safe—be happy—and be creative.

Ann Tsueng is a third-year undergraduate at UCLA. Someday her biography will be filled with exciting details that make people wish they knew her. For now this is all there is.

Christie Vong was born in Thailand and was raised in Southern California. She pursued her bachelor's in sociology and social science at UCI. As cliché as it sounds, she hopes that in the future she can make a difference in the world, if not touch one person's life.

Andy Wang, barely over 21 years old, is a Los Angeles native and the son of immigrants from Taiwan. Andy is a typical college student, reaching the brink of his education, that edge where we fall off into the much-vaunted real world. But having learned his way off the road, overworn with unwilling travelers, he has confidence that he can navigate the wild world on his own terms. If he has learned anything in college, it's that we are to prepare ourselves to take on the world, not to mold ourselves into what the world expects us to be. He's ready—send him off!

Rhonda Wofford was born in California's Los Angeles County and resides in Santa Clara County. She is a graduate of Chapman University with a bachelor's degree, the first in her family to have graduated from college. She is currently employed at Intel and is applying to master's degree programs. She has crossed the boundaries and thrived in an atmosphere of racism and sexism. A Black woman with the desire for success, she has confronted and amended her substandard primary education. A Black woman who desires to just be recognized as an outstanding citizen, she knows that the word *black* will always come before the word *citizen*.

Shawna Wood is a second-year English major at UCLA who hopes to pursue a career in writing. Through this book, she strives to help those like her who never felt that getting straight A's was more important than learning to achieve real success in college, not just the kind that shines on transcripts. She also wants to thank all the people who have given her the ability to recognize what is worth fighting for in life.